Counterfeit Justice

Conflicting Worlds
New Dimensions of the American Civil War
T. Michael Parrish, Series Editor

Mrs Dass Ibernet

Counterfeit Justice

THE JUDICIAL ODYSSEY OF TEXAS FREEDWOMAN AZELINE HEARNE

DALE BAUM

LOUISIANA STATE UNIVERSITY PRESS
BATON ROUGE

Published by Louisiana State University Press

Manufactured in the United States of America
First printing

Frontispiece: Signature of "Mrs Press [Puss?] Hearne"

Designer: Tammi L. deGeneres
Typeface: Goudy Old Style, Sabon
Typesetter: J. Jarrett Engineering, Inc.
Printer and binder: Thomson-Shore, Inc.

Library of Congress Cataloging-in-Publication Data
Baum, Dale, 1943-
Counterfeit justice : the judicial odyssey of Texas freedwoman Azeline Hearne / Dale Baum.
p. cm. — (Conflicting worlds : new dimensions of the American Civil War)
Includes bibliographical references and index.
ISBN 978-0-8071-3405-4 (cloth : alk. paper) 1. Hearne, Azeline. 2. African American women—Texas—Robertson County—Biography. 3. Freedmen—Texas—Robertson County—Biography. 4. African Americans—Texas—Robertson County—Biography. 5. African Americans—Legal status, laws, etc.—Texas—Robertson County—History—19th century. 6. African Americans—Land tenure—Texas—Robertson County—History—19th century. 7. Land grants—Texas—Robertson County—History—19th century. 8. Robertson County (Tex.)—Race relations—History—19th century. 9. Robertson County (Tex.)—Biography. I. Title.
F392.R63B38 2009
305.48'8960730764239092—dc22
[B]
2008041290

The paper in this book meets the guidelines for permanence and durability of the Committee on Production Guidelines for Book Longevity of the Council on Library Resources. ♾

To Regina Kelly,
the lead plaintiff in the ACLU's
2002 lawsuit against drug task force sweeps
targeting African Americans in Hearne, Texas.

Contents

Maps

Acknowledgments

THIS BOOK WOULD NOT have been possible without the encouragement and help of many people. My colleague Bob Calvert convinced me that the story of what happened to a forgotten Texas freedwoman named Azeline Hearne could be written without a run of extant local newspapers—a situation that I constantly lamented. Librarian and genealogist Bill Page showed me that Azeline's story and the history of Robertson County, in which she resided, could be reconstructed not just from materials buried in the files of the county courthouse but also with the aid of other sources that I never considered or knew existed. When I had no confidence in my ability to reassemble the chaotically filed pleadings in the major court cases in which Azeline was involved, attorney Joe Bax assembled them in order and wrote detailed outlines of what had transpired. The discussion in chapter 7 dealing with the lawsuit filed by her against her attorney draws heavily upon his summary of this extraordinary case.

I am thankful to many members of the black community in Hearne, Texas, especially Leola Malone, Glenn Arthur Mack, John H. Miles Jr., and his daughter Sherina Miles, who generously shared their recollections of countless burdens shouldered through the years by African Americans in Robertson County. I was, and will remain, haunted by their desire to know about Azeline. Their heartfelt hope for my "success" in writing about a Robertson County freedwoman, about whom they unnecessarily apologized for not being able to recall, became the passion that drove me to complete this book.

I wish to thank the members of the following institutions for their assistance: the Old Military Records Division of the National Archives, the Center for American History at the University of Texas at Austin, South Texas College of Law, the Fondren Library at Rice University, and the Archives Division of the Texas State Library. Special appreciation goes to the staff at the interlibrary loan desk at Evans Library at Texas A&M University. Among the many to whom I owe a supreme debt of gratefulness for their assistance are: Andrew Torget, who tracked down materials not yet microfilmed in the National Archives and provided constant encouragement and helpful criticisms; Cornelia A. Starkey, the district clerk of Robertson County, whose helpfulness and friendliness made my research trips to the courthouse in Franklin, Texas, such pleasurable experiences; and J. Morgan Kousser and Barry A. Crouch, whose scholarship and advice shaped my interpretations of the politics of the Reconstruction era and the work of the Freedmen's Bureau, respectively. I wish to acknowledge the grant for this book that I received from the Women's Studies Program at Texas A&M University.

A debt of gratitude is also owed to the following: Deborah B. Hicks of Love Abstract Company in Franklin, Texas, and Amy Price of Lawyers Title Company in Bryan, Texas, for helping me find old cadastral maps for specific areas of Robertson and Brazos Counties; my neighbors, Cindy and Dan Quinn, and members of their church, for assisting me with researching the genealogies of the Hearne and Lewis families; Kenneth W. Howell of Prairie View A&M University, for believing in this project from the beginning and giving me helpful comments on drafts of the manuscript; and Donaly E. Brice, for helping me at every stage of my research at the Texas State Archives.

I would be remiss if I did not thank the following: Christopher Tomlins of the American Bar Foundation for his insightful suggestions for improving the manuscript, Ann Todd Baum, Cyndy Brown, and Michael Baker for their meticulous editing of every page, and my colleagues at Yonsei University in Seoul, Korea, for providing me, as a visiting professor, with accommodations wonderfully conducive to my writing of this book. The many individuals, including friends, family members, and former students, who expected me to do my best job in writing about the life and times of Azeline Hearne know who they are. I thank them all, and I hope that I have met their expectations.

I acknowledge ownership of all the errors of fact contained in this book, and far more importantly I claim all the mistakes in interpretation that are presented here.

Abbreviations Used in Notes

BRFAL	Bureau of Refugees, Freedmen, and Abandoned Lands
CAH-UT	Center for American History, The University of Texas at Austin
COCADT	Correspondence of the Office of Civil Affairs of the District of Texas, and the Fifth Military District, and the Department of Texas, 1867–1870
CCM	Commissioners Court Minutes
CCM-PM	Commissioners Court Minutes–Police Minutes
CCO	County Clerk's Office
DTH	Department of Texas Headquarters
GO	General Orders
HFMD	Headquarters, Fifth Military District
MDC	Minutes of the District Court
NA	National Archives, Washington, D.C.
ODC	Office of the District Clerk, Civil Cases Disposed Of
PF	Probate Files

PM	Probate Minutes
RCC	Records of the County Court
RD	Record of Deeds
RG	Record Group
SO	Special Orders
THC-TAMU	Texas History Collection, Texas A&M University Archives
TNHT	*The New Handbook of Texas*
TSL-AD	Archives Division, Texas State Library, Austin, Texas
WRC-RU	Woodson Research Center, Fondren Library, Rice University

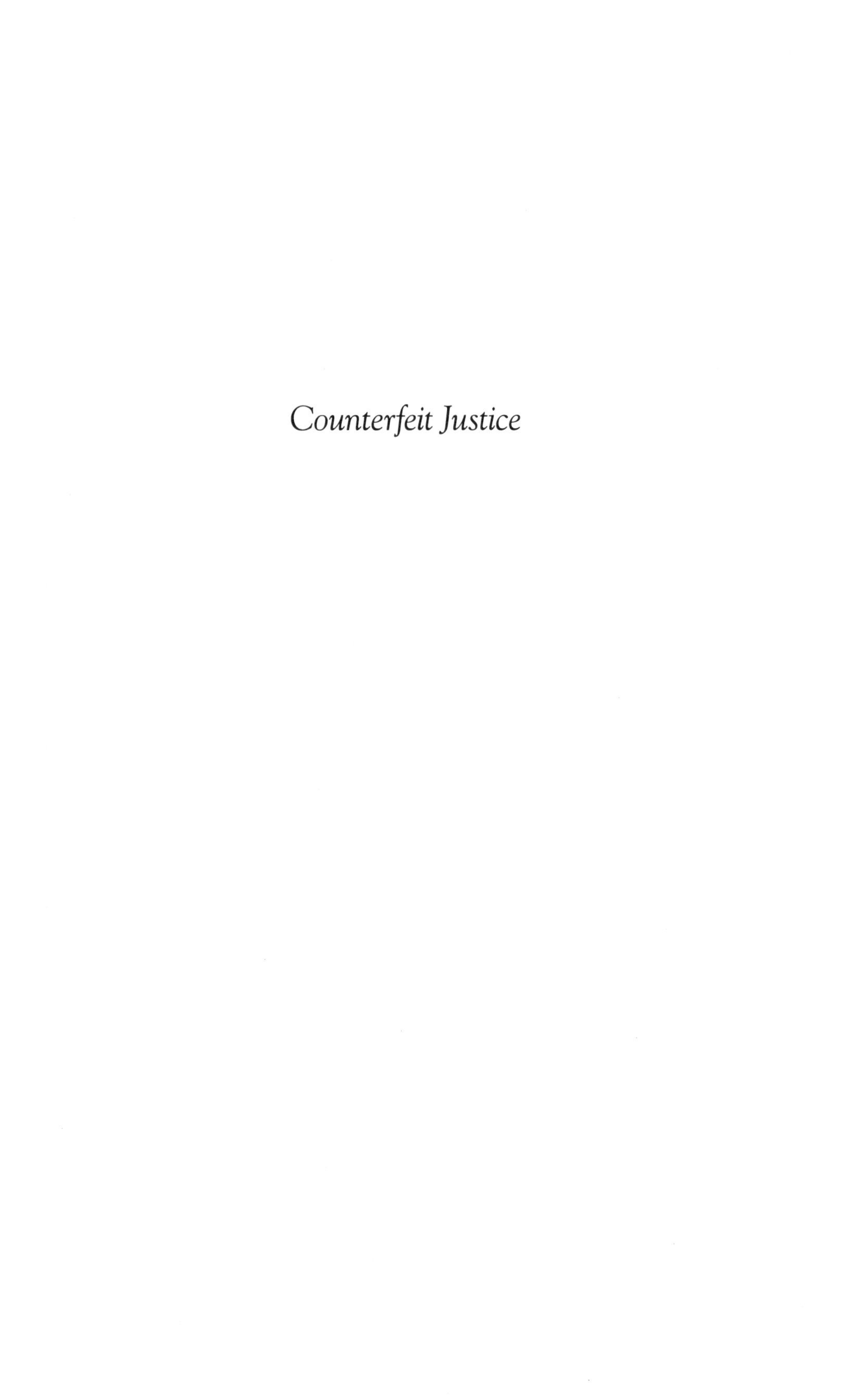

Counterfeit Justice

Introduction

> It must be remembered that Assaline Hearne is an ignorant freedwoman and from her status in society is deprived of that physical protection which others possess.
>
> —HARVEY D. PRENDERGAST, ATTORNEY FOR AZELINE HEARNE, TO CHARLES E. MORSE, N.D.

BY THE END OF the twentieth century all recollection of Azeline Hearne had vanished in the slow eddies of time. When her name appears in surviving documents, it is usually spelled "Assaline" or "Asaline" or, less frequently, "Azalene," and incorrectly most often as "Adaline." Because she was born into slavery in probably a French-speaking area of Louisiana, the various spellings of her slave name are corruptions of the uncommon name "Azéline," a surname that by the turn of the twenty-first century still remained on France's official list of legally acceptable feminine *prénoms*. While the accent would have normally been placed on the second syllable, the recurrent appearance of her name written as "Assaline" indicates that Anglo Texans mimicked the pronunciations of former slaves, who placed the accent on the first syllable. Her name was not limited exclusively to black women. The name "Azeline" or "Asaline" was frequently used as a middle name of southern white women in the nineteenth century.[1]

1. For information about the French *prénom* "Azéline," see: www.prenoms.com/echerche/prenom.php/fiche/azeline (accessed Jan. 21, 2003). Azeline was the contemporary of a white woman whose name appears in the county courthouse records as "Assaline Dechard" (see *P. C.*

Except for a glimpse into her legal battles and difficulties immediately after her emancipation from slavery, most of Azeline's story is and will remain unknown. The antebellum "Slave Schedules" of the federal manuscript censuses do not contain her name, or for that matter the name of any slave. Nor can she be located in any census taken after the Civil War. However, the federal census enumerators who visited the Hearne family plantations in Louisiana and Texas in 1850 and 1860, respectively, listed what, by a process of elimination, had to have been her respective ages, making calculation of her year of birth possible. Enough other pieces of information can be recovered from obscurity to construct an outline of her story—a narrative that neither she nor the major players in her legal disputes could ever have assembled by themselves.[2]

Azeline survived forty years as an enslaved female only to become in her old age a reclusive, sickly, and impoverished woman wandering from place to place in the Brazos River "bottomlands" in Robertson County, Texas. She was never acknowledged by society to have in any way influenced the course of historical events. Yet her life revealed as much about the period of Reconstruction after the American Civil War as the lives of many who attained distinction through their fame or extraordinary achievements. Although U.S. congressional control of the course of Reconstruction allowed freedom's first generation of African Americans to play a central role in the postwar adjustments that radically changed the world the slaveholders had made, what happened to Azeline demonstrated the limits to what could have been achieved in the way of securing legal equality and fair treatment for the former slaves throughout the postwar South.

During slavery Azeline had cohabitated with her unmarried and wealthy master, Samuel ("Sam") R. Hearne. She bore him four children, only one of whom survived early childhood. When Sam Hearne died in 1866, his will acknowledged, to the dismay of his brothers and cousins, his years

---

Dechard vs. Assaline Dechard, Case No. 2027, [February Term, 1875], Book "M," p. 416, MDC, Robertson County, Texas).

2. On Samuel R. Hearne's plantations in Louisiana and Texas, the only female slaves with matching ages are a twenty-five-year-old listed in 1850 and another one recorded as thirty-five years of age in 1860. See: Bureau of the Census, *Population Schedules of the Seventh Census of the United States, 1850,* Microfilm Roll #242, Louisiana [Slave Schedules] "Bienville—Concordia," p. 887, M432, NA (1963); and Bureau of the Census, *Population Schedules of the Eighth Census of the United States, 1860,* Microfilm Roll #1312, Texas [Slave Schedules] vol. 2 (307–628), "Robertson County," p. 25 [printed p. 316], M653, NA (1967).

of miscegenation by its bequeathal of his entire estate to his twenty-year-old mulatto son with a provision that he take care of his mother, Azeline. When her son died in early 1868, she, as her son's sole legatee under Sam's will, became the owner of Sam's estate, which included one of the most profitable cotton plantations in East Texas—a circumstance making her briefly one of the wealthiest former slaves in the South. As a consequence, from the late 1860s to the early 1880s, she became a familiar figure at the Robertson County District Court, where she was sued numerous times by dozens of litigants, including on one occasion by her own lawyer. Facing throughout this period the vulnerabilities of a southern black woman in an unashamedly white racist patriarchal society, Azeline was an obvious target for predatory whites. Her experience with the law, lawyers, and the courts occurred in an environment of volatile postwar and worsening post-Reconstruction race relations, in which the large majority of whites determinedly sought to dilute and demolish black civil rights, including not only voting rights but also—and just as importantly—basic property rights.

Azeline was the first freedwoman to be a party to three separate civil lawsuits appealed all the way to the Texas Supreme Court, and the first former slave in Robertson County indicted on criminal charges of perjury. Her life intersected the careers of a host of both notable and notorious people. She was briefly the landlord of ex-slave Israel S. Campbell, later memorialized as the "Father of Negro Baptists in Texas" because he was the first to ordain black Baptist preachers. The bevy of attorneys who represented her, sued her, and took advantage of her included William Pitt Ballinger, a prominent Galveston lawyer who twice declined appointments to the Texas Supreme Court; William H. Hamman, the state's first oil prospector, who accepted on two successive occasions the gubernatorial nomination of the Greenback Party; and Harvey D. Prendergast, a prominent corporate lawyer and special judge in Robertson and Travis Counties in the 1870s and 1880s. For a brief period after the war, anti-secessionist and ex-slaveholder Benjamin ("Ben") Brown protected her from attacks by white terrorist groups and the Ku Klux Klan. Brown, who briefly served as a Freedmen's Bureau agent for the federal government, was one of the most notorious gang leaders in the annals of east-central Texas criminal history.

The manner in which agents of the Freedmen's Bureau, Republican officeholders, local attorneys, and wealthy white members of the extended Hearne and Lewis families dealt with Azeline largely determined the nature of her legal problems. The motives of these and other individuals with whom she interacted are difficult to evaluate due to gaps in the available historical record as well as the unreliability of secondary historical accounts based on local Reconstruction folklore about "Negro supremacy" and "carpetbagger misrule." Therefore, much of her story must be couched in the language of conjecture and probability. Speculation, however, about why the major performers in her story acted as they did is grounded in the most recent scholarship on the Reconstruction era and placed in the context of the history of Robertson County, where most of the drama of her life unfolded.[3]

Too little is known about Azeline prior to her master's death to reveal the nature of her personal life under slavery. Nor does her story cast additional light on any of the major antebellum political events caused by recurrent disagreements over slavery between the northern and southern states. Yet the first half of her life as an enslaved woman illustrated how a system of permanent racial and chattel slavery put people, both white and black, in circumstances that compelled them to grapple with deep-seated moral predicaments. As a light-skinned slave mistress, described as "a yellow woman, almost white," she embodied one of the major ethical dilemmas that a southern slaveholding society was continuously forced to confront. Her master's fornication and miscegenation were potentially destructive to slave discipline and, if recklessly flaunted, were condemned as scandalous by white society. Even if one assumes that Azeline was thankful for her owner's special treatment toward her, the precarious position of being her master's concubine conflicted with all major principles of basic morality.[4]

Azeline's story reveals a great deal about the tumultuous period of readjustment immediately following the Civil War. No other period of Texas history has been as mythologized as Reconstruction. About a fifth of the

3. Histories of Robertson County depicting blacks during Reconstruction as either misguided victims of carpetbagger and scalawag manipulation or as an incapacitated race menacing the stability of civilized society include Norman L. McCarver and Norman L. McCarver Jr., *Hearne on the Brazos* (San Antonio: Century Press of Texas, 1958), p. 25; J. W. Baker, *A History of Robertson County, Texas* (Waco, Tex.: Printed by Texian Press, 1970), pp. 160–65; and Richard Denny Parker, *Historical Recollections of Robertson County, Texas, with Biographical & Genealogical Notes on the Pioneers & Their Families* (Salado, Tex.: Anson Jones Press, 1955), pp. 46–47. For a discussion of the evolution of scholarly interpretations of Reconstruction, see Eric Foner, *Reconstruction: America's Unfinished Revolution, 1863–1877* (New York: Harper & Row, 1988), pp. xix–xxvii.

4. Joshua L. Randall to Joel T. Kirkman, June 8, 1867 (quotation), "Subassistant Commissioner Records filed under 'Sterling, Texas,'" Letters Sent: Entry #3769, account pp. 36–37, BRFAL, [unmicrofilmed], RG 105, NA; and Harriet A. Jacobs, *Incidents in the Life of a Slave Girl,* ed. Nellie Y. McKay and Frances Smith Foster (New York: Norton, 2001), p. 47.

adult white male population of Robertson County died fighting for the Confederate cause, and a couple hundred more were maimed or injured. Not only did a cult of mourning arise but the myth of a "Lost Cause" soon developed in response to the profound disruptions faced by white society in the postwar era. More importantly, after years of regarding slavery as a natural and beneficial labor system and believing that the descendants of black Africans were an inherently inferior species, the large majority of whites refused to agree to changes that mandated, at least in theory, equal justice for the former slaves. Pervasive racism provided a powerful obstacle to the willingness of whites to view the legal rights of former slaves as matters guaranteed by law.

Although the experience of Reconstruction at the grassroots level in Texas varied greatly from one county to the next, Robertson County was in many ways typical of other counties containing large concentrations of ex-slaves. Black and white populations were of roughly equal proportions, and black voters, who made up the overwhelming majority of the Republican constituency, remained a force to be reckoned with in local politics until the late 1890s. From 1876 to 1900, Robertson County was in the Republican column in the balloting for presidential electors. The freedpeople, including Azeline, were unquestionably actors in shaping their own fate, and neither they nor their white political allies, northern "carpetbaggers" and local "scalawags," were all ignorant, corrupt, or opportunistic, as propagandistic southern journalists characterized them. Most Republican leaders, white and black, were courageous men who formed the cutting edge of an innovative attempt to build a truly biracial democracy on the ashes of slavery. All in all, the achievements of Reconstruction were rather remarkable, and even though most were eventually undone, they at least created a memory of another, more favorable time when blacks briefly received at least a semblance of fair treatment. More importantly, the accomplishments of the Republican governments, not just in Robertson County but throughout the South, set the agenda a century later during the civil rights movement of the 1960s for attaining a more equalitarian vision for America's future.[5]

Azeline's story, nevertheless, lays bare many depressing details of post–Civil War interrelationships of race, gender, and power. Because it is impossible to sever her story from an assessment of the white men who wielded the vast majority of economic and social influence in Robertson

5. W. Dean Burnham, *Presidential Ballots: 1836–1892* (Baltimore: The Johns Hopkins Press, 1955), p. 803; and Edgar Eugene Robinson, *The Presidential Vote, 1896–1932* (Stanford, Calif.: Stanford University Press, 1934), p. 346.

County after the war, the political world of Reconstruction at the local level is explored here in detail. As a consequence, Azeline, in the absence of evidence of how she felt or acted, remains often at the edges of the unfolding drama. As a freedwoman with no training to prepare her to make the transition from a former slave concubine to a courtroom protagonist, she found herself forced to make decisions in difficult circumstances not of her own choosing. The odds of her getting her way were overwhelmingly stacked against her. Although she admittedly never controlled events as much as events controlled her, and she often found herself ill advised and disheartened once drawn into the shadow of the law, she evolved over the years from a puzzled and legally ransacked defendant to a feisty and courageous plaintiff who came tantalizingly close not only to setting a precedent in the virtually underdeveloped Texas case law dealing with attorney malpractice but also to achieving a modicum of revenge against those who had defrauded her for over a decade.

The betrayal of Azeline by many individuals, especially military authorities and Republican Party officials, who in hindsight one would have expected to help her the most, thwarted her attempts to receive fair and impartial treatment. Moreover, the same influential whites who controlled public affairs before the war dominated her life after slavery with their deceit and greed. Their manipulation of a judicial system insensitive to providing justice to those denied it under the application of the common law and devoid of any meaningful oversight of the professional obligations of attorneys or executors to their clients or beneficiaries all but precluded any chance she had of receiving something other than counterfeit justice. Even admitting, in the words of one former Texas slave, that emancipation "in poverty and trials and tribulations," and "even amidst the most cruel prejudices," was "sweeter than the best fed or the best clothed slavery in the world," would not change the fact that Azeline survived years of enslavement only to be beset by the burden of freedom.[6]

What follows is an attempt to bring back to life the heretofore untold story of how calculating and devious attorneys and the wealthy collateral kin of Azeline's former master cheated her out of her considerable lawful inheritance. The sequence of events begins in the early 1850s, when her master, Sam Hearne, brought her with him from Caddo Parish, Louisiana, to the banks of the Brazos River in the rich alluvial bottomlands of Robertson County, Texas.

6. Former slave H. C. Smith, quoted in Alwyn Barr, *Black Texans: A History of Negroes in Texas, 1528–1971* (Austin, Tex.: Jenkins Publishing Company, 1973), p. 37 (quotations).

Chapter 1

No Place for a White Man to Live

> There is quite a large portion of the county bottom land, and on the Brazos [River] those lands are in width from three to five miles, and in quality, I presume, to any in the world.
>
> —William H. Hamman, quoted in Smith, "The Life and Times of William Harrison Hamman"

The history of the Brazos River is deeply entwined with the story of Anglo American settlement in Texas. Eighteenth-century Spanish explorers christened it "el Rio de los Brazos de Dios," or "the Arms of God." Originating in the West Texas rolling plains and flowing over eight hundred miles to the Gulf of Mexico, its meanderings through its lower stretch define the western boundary of Robertson County, separating it from Milam and Burleson Counties. Here, the much smaller but equally muddy and silt-tinged Little Brazos River runs parallel three to five miles to the east of the Big Brazos. Between these two rivers lies the richest farmland in Robertson County, if not the entire state, known as the "Brazos Bottoms." From time immemorial to the present day, floods have deposited in the bottomlands topsoil originally carried away by erosion of the dark black earth from miles upstream.[1]

1. Norman L. McCarver and Norman L. McCarver Jr., *Hearne on the Brazos* (San Antonio: Century Press of Texas, 1958), p. 1 (quotations); and "Brazos River," in Ron Tyler, Douglas E.

In 1850 the population of Robertson County numbered only 934, of whom nearly 30 percent were slaves. During the remainder of the decade, with the arrival of many new settlers desiring to grow cotton in the fertile bottomlands, the county's population grew more than fivefold, climbing by 1860 to 4,997, of whom nearly half were slaves. Although some cotton had been planted as early as 1840, livestock raising and subsistence agriculture had remained predominant until the early 1850s. Between 1850 and 1860 the number of cotton bales produced increased fifteenfold, and Robertson County became typical of the other counties in the central Brazos River Valley of East Texas, where white men of every political party affiliation were interested in land, cotton, and slaves. Under the leadership of such men, Robertson County gravitated toward the political catastrophe of secession and resulting civil war.[2]

Arrival of the Legendary Pioneering Hearne and Lewis Families

Sometime during the summer or fall of 1853, Sam Hearne, a thirty-seven-year-old Georgia-born slaveholder, left his plantation near Shreveport in Caddo Parish, Louisiana, and moved to Robertson County. Just two years earlier he had purchased a large tract of unimproved land in the Brazos River bottomlands—a place considered "no place for a white man to live" because of its abundance of poisonous snakes, poor drainage, and reputation for outbreaks of yellow fever and cholera. Here, Sam made his home for the rest of his life. In many ways, he was representative of the thousands of planters from the older states of the lower South who migrated in the 1850s into Texas to grow cotton with slave labor. However, beginning with his first documented appearance at the county seat in 1851, Sam was something other than what he seemed.[3]

A lifelong bachelor, Sam died in the fall of 1866. His decision to bequeath his entire estate to his illicit mulatto son outraged and embarrassed his brothers and cousins. At the turn of the century, Sam's surviving female cousins—Rhoda Lee (Hearne) Cox, or "Aunt Rhoda," who was known as "the cyclopædia of the family," and Adeline Missouri (Hearne)

Barnett, Roy R. Barkley, Penelope C. Anderson, and Mark F. Odintz, eds., *The New Handbook of Texas* (hereafter cited as *TNHT*), 6 vols. (Austin: The Texas State Historical Association, 1996), 1: 716–17.

2. "Robertson County," *TNHT*, 5: 621-23.

3. McCarver and McCarver, *Hearne on the Brazos*, p. 7 (quotation).

Lewis, the widow of Charles Lewis—figuratively took a hatchet to the Hearne family tree and removed Sam's name from the genealogical record. While genealogists commonly list the names of family members who committed terrible transgressions with no additional information beyond their birth and death dates, no such consideration was extended to Sam. His cohabitation with his son's mother during slavery, and the problems it caused his wealthy relatives for decades after his death, apparently rivaled murder and treason.[4]

Sam was a member of the pioneering Hearnes, for whom cotton growing was an extended family enterprise. From their previous home sites on adjoining farms not far from the Texas state line in Caddo Parish, most of the family clan arrived in Robertson County in 1852. Under the leadership of Sam's older brother, Christopher Columbus, or "Lum" as he was commonly called, they came with their ox wagons loaded with household goods, farm tools, rifles with ammunition, and lockboxes containing money and valuables, along with the supplies necessary for establishing a general merchandise store. Eighty to one hundred slaves walked the entire two-hundred-mile trip in front of the wagons while herding numerous mules, cattle, oxen, pigs, and horses ahead of them. Because the bottomlands were thickly covered with cedars, cottonwoods, winged elms, hackberries, pecans, and hickory trees, the Hearnes probably carried as many as three axes for each male slave.[5]

The route they took from northwestern Louisiana into Texas led them across the Sabine River into Panola County, and then on to the old Spanish colonial town of Nacogdoches. From there they turned westward on the San Antonio Road, or the legendary El Camino Real, over which "history stalked into Texas." They passed through the heart of the East Texas "Piney Woods" region when traveling through Cherokee and Houston Counties, then forded the Trinity River and traveled along the boundary lines between Madison and Leon Counties and finally between Brazos and Robertson Counties. Their destination was the small but well-known town of Wheelock, the county seat of Robertson County and a

4. William T. Hearne, *Brief History and Genealogy of the Hearne Family: From A.D. 1066, when they went from Normandy with William the Conqueror over to England, down to 1680. [sic] when William Hearne the London Merchant came to America, and on down to A.D. 1907* (Independence, Mo.: Press of Examiner Printing Company, 1907), p. 640 (quotations).

5. McCarver and McCarver, *Hearne on the Brazos*, pp. 6–7; Dallas *Morning News*, December 28, 1930, sec. A&F, p. 1; and John Henry Brown, *Indian Wars and Pioneers of Texas* (Austin, Tex.: n.p., n.d., reprint ed., 1988), p. 264.

major stagecoach stop on the post oak grasslands, or high prairie, on the "Houston & Waco Road."[6]

Sam had previously scouted the area, along with his cousin, Horatio ("Rasche") Reardon Hearne, and Rasche's brother-in-law Charles Lewis. They were the first three members of the extended Hearne family to buy tracts of land in the southern part of the Brazos Bottoms, where, because of conflicting claims of ownership, clearing land for growing cotton lagged far behind the northern part. Pending lawsuits over land titles caused Sam, Rasche, and Charles to protect their land purchases by contracts and bonds rather than by deeds. In case of successful challenges to their titles, they thus stood to avoid paying a large part of the original purchase price and receive compensation for losses sustained in having made improvements on another person's land. Subsequent purchases of land by the Hearnes and Lewises often followed similar legally intricate patterns of acquisition. Sam's brother Lum, who had also made prior trips into the area to purchase land in the Bottoms, bought "a beautiful site" in Wheelock for his homestead that served as an initial base of operations for those who arrived with him in 1852. With their overseers and slaves, the Hearnes began clearing their Brazos Bottom lands sixteen miles to the west in the southwestern part of the county.[7]

All the Hearnes were related by blood or marriage. Cousins had married cousins, brothers had married sisters from another family (Armstrong), and sisters had likewise married brothers from other families (Lewis and Powell). Keeping the main family lines straight was a challenging undertaking. Sam's side of the family was originally from Alabama by way of Georgia. His mother's maiden name was Elizabeth Ransom, and therefore

6. "El Camino Real" (first quotation), [Official Texas State Historical Marker, 1972; one mile east of Hwy 6 at Benchley on the Old San Antonio Road], Robertson County, Texas; and "Petition of Samuel R. Hearne," [November Term, 1861], p. 352 (second quotation), CCM, Robertson County, Texas.

7. "Contract for Deed" and "Agreement and Bond," Britton Dawson to Samuel R. Hearne, November 20, 1851, and Britton Dawson to Horatio R. Hearne and Charles Lewis, November 20, 1851, "Deeds-Transcribed 1849–1851," Book "P," pp. 323–32, Microfilm Reel #963280, RD, CCO, Robertson County, Texas; McCarver and McCarver, *Hearne on the Brazos,* pp. 6–7; "Horatio Reardon Hearne," in *Transcript Synopsis of A–P Records Relating to Robertson County "Families" 1838–[?],* Microfilm Reel #964224, CCO, Robertson County, Texas; Richard Denny Parker, *Historical Recollections of Robertson County, Texas, with Biographical & Genealogical Notes on the Pioneers & Their Families* (Salado, Tex.: Anson Jones Press, 1955), p. 75; Lawrence Ward St. Clair, "History of Robertson County, Texas" (M.A. thesis, University of Texas, 1931), pp. 95 (quotation), 96; and Ivory Freeman Carson, "Early Development of Robertson County" (M.A. thesis, North Texas State College, 1954), p. 5.

he and his brothers and sisters were known as the "Ransom Hearnes." The other side of the family clan was known as the "Miles Hearnes." Before marrying Sam's uncle, Nancy Miles had "inherited quite a fortune" and had a distinguished pedigree traceable to Revolutionary War General Nathanael Greene.[8]

The Hearnes believed in big families; like most planters they counted children as material assets. But why they ran the risk of inbreeding is a mystery. Even the slaves, the human chattels that the Hearnes owned, considered a marriage between first cousins to be taboo. Yet without fear of endogamy, Sam's sister, Priscilla Hearne, had married her cousin Rasche, and Sam's brother George Washington ("Wash") Hearne, had married his cousin Frances Calloway Hearne. To complicate matters, not only did Rasche and Priscilla and Wash and Frances, share a common set of grandparents, but their grandparents were also first cousins. Such circumstances increased, albeit slightly, the statistical chances of Sam's nephews and nieces, in this case the children of his brother Wash and his sister Priscilla, being born with recessive genes—a biological calamity that could not possibly have gone unnoticed. Nevertheless, "the marriage of cousins," according to one contemporary observer of southern slaveholders, was "almost the rule rather than the exception."[9]

No evidence suggests that slaveholders believed they had the right to demand the marriage of their father's brother's daughters to safeguard their bloodlines from becoming polluted or moribund. To the contrary, their endogamous preferences were primarily a way to create or preserve wealth, power, and status. Endogamy cemented ties of cooperation and loyalty and consolidated land and property within a generational age group. The success that the Louisiana generation of Hearnes and Lewises

8. Hearne, *Brief History and Genealogy of the Hearne Family,* pp. 623–24 (quotation). Elizabeth Ransom gave birth to eight children who survived childhood. From oldest to youngest were Lum, Sam himself, followed by Tabitha, Priscilla, Mary, twin brothers Alfred ("Alley") L. and Selby W., and finally, George Washington ("Wash"). The children of Nancy Miles who lived to adulthood, in the order of their births, were Ebenezer ("Ebb"), Horatio ("Rasche") Reardon, Rhoda Lee, Asa Hoxey, Adeline Missouri, and Frances Calloway. See ibid., pp. 623–24, 631, 636–39, 651–54.

9. Allen Weinstein, Frank Otto Gatell, and David Sarasohn, eds., *American Negro Slavery: A Modern Reader,* 3rd ed. (New York : Oxford University Press, 1979), p. 280 (quotations). The first-mentioned common set of grandparents was William and Tabitha Hearne, who died in Alabama in the 1830s; the second set was Thomas and Sally Hearne, who had died in Maryland in the 1760s. See: "Pedigree Chart Download GEDCOM," [Thomas and Sally Hearne], www.FamilySearch.com/af/pedigree_chart.asp?recid=43811593 (last updated March 22, 1999, Intellectual Reserve, Inc., 1999; accessed Oct. 26, 2002).

subsequently achieved in antebellum Robertson County was largely due to their management of their plantations, slave labor forces, and mercantile stores as one large family business.[10]

Not all the Ransom Hearnes and Miles Hearnes migrated to Texas. And not all those who settled in Robertson County during the antebellum period arrived in Wheelock in 1852. Known to be among the large group that camped on Lum's Wheelock property in 1852 were Rasche and Priscilla, along with Sam's brother Alfred L. Hearne, or "Alley," who came with his wife Charlotte (Armstrong) Hearne. Apparently Alley's twin brother, Selby W. Hearne, died on the way into Texas or in Wheelock soon after his arrival, because in early 1853 his wife, Nancy K. (Armstrong) Hearne, was appointed the guardian of his estate and of their three minor children. Accompanying Charlotte and Nancy were their younger sisters and their widowed mother, Harriett Armstrong. Sam's cousin Adeline came with her Connecticut-born husband, Charles, and their three children, of whom the oldest was a six-year-old son named Henry Lee.[11]

Subsequently, in 1854 Sam's cousin Ebenezer ("Ebb") Hearne arrived with his wife Minerva and their sons William and Lorenzo. And in 1859, Sam's youngest brother Wash arrived with his wife Frances. If the sworn testimony of Rasche, Sam's cousin and brother-in-law, is reliable, then Sam himself did not make the 1852 trip but permanently returned to Robertson County some time during the following year. Circumstantial reasons support Rasche's claims that Sam arrived afterward and took immediate possession of the 903 acres of land that he had purchased two years earlier in the Brazos Bottoms.[12]

Sam's mother died in 1853 in Louisiana, and perhaps he stayed behind long enough to be with her during a prolonged illness that caused her death. As a bachelor living adjacent to his married siblings, he had most likely lived with his mother since his father's death in 1844. In 1850 the census enumerator for Caddo Parish recorded Sam as a "planter" at

10. McCarver and McCarver, *Hearne on the Brazos,* pp. 6–7.

11. Book "G," [February (?), 1854], p. 82, and Book "H," [January 1856], pp. 112–13, Microfilm Reel #964208, PM, CCO, Robertson County, Texas; McCarver and McCarver, *Hearne on the Brazos,* p. 6; and Mary Collie-Cooper, comp., *Robertson County Texas 1860 Census,* [typescript, July 4, 1985], pp. 8 and 66, Evans Library, Texas A&M University, College Station, Texas.

12. "An Agreement," made by the attorneys and filed in folder 3, [June Term, 1873], in *Eliza Cornelia Willett (Reynolds) vs. Charles Lewis, et al.,* Case No. 662, ODC, Robertson County, Texas; and "E. Hearne" and "G. W. Hearne," Registration No. 234 and No. 947, pp. 211 and 229, *Voter Registration Lists, 1867–1869,* Microfilm Reel #VR-10, Robertson County, Texas, TSL-AD.

the head of a household consisting of only three individuals: his widowed "mother"; a slave "overseer"; and an eighty-two-year-old man with no occupation or relationship listed. Sam was not among the group of his kinfolks who appeared together in 1853 at the Robertson County courthouse to pay their county and state taxes, but the following year the tax assessor listed him among them on the tax rolls. Sam and his brothers had often purchased land in Louisiana in joint ownership, and Rasche and Charles Lewis bought the first family land in Robertson County as common owners. But Sam's acquisition of land in his own name suggests his determination from the start to live in relative social isolation on the land that he had purchased on the banks of the Brazos River.[13]

The bulk of the slaves that Sam owned in 1850 most likely made the 1852 trip. Whether some of them stayed behind in Louisiana with him cannot be known. But what is known is that in 1853 Azeline, a twenty-eight-year-old, light-skinned female with an unusual French name, and Doctor ("Dock") Samuel Jones Hearne, her seven-year-old son with an equally curious name, were with Sam when he arrived in Robertson County, and that they and Sam did not initially live in Wheelock. After a brief stay on the Samuel R. Moss farm, on Spring Creek close to the edge of the Brazos Bottoms, Sam completed building his log cabin manor house on the southeastern corner of his land. Here, on his Brazos River plantation, Sam lived for the remainder of his life with Azeline and Dock.[14]

Azeline had caught Sam's eye sometime during the 1840s. She was twenty-one years old in 1846, when Dock was born. She had at least one sister, about whom virtually nothing is known except she, as most likely the slave of either Sam or his extended family, also made the trip to Robertson County. On some level Sam had to have realized that unless he sold Azeline and her young son to a buyer who would take them away, it would be impossible to hide his paternity of her child. Moreover, Dock

13. United States, Bureau of the Census, *Population Schedules of the Seventh Census of the United States, 1850,* Microfilm Reel #230, Louisiana, Caddo Parish, Schedule 1 (Free Inhabitants), p. 695 (quotations), [printed p. 348], M432, NA (1963); Robertson County Tax Rolls, 1838–1882, Tax Rolls for 1853 and 1854, Microfilm Reel #1198–01, CCO, Robertson County, Texas; and *John Bell vs. C.C. Hearne, et al.,* Louisiana Supreme Court, 10 Louisiana Ann. 515 (1855), La. LEXIS 277, Decided 1855.

14. Bureau of the Census, *Population Schedules of the Seventh Census of the United States, 1850,* Microfilm Reel #242, Louisiana [Slave Schedules] "Bienville—Concordia," p. 887, M432, NA (1963); Agreements and Bonds dated November 20, 1851, "Deeds-Transcribed 1849–1851," Book "P," pp. 323–32, Microfilm Reel #963280, RD, CCO, Robertson County, Texas; and "An Agreement," made by the attorneys and filed in folder 3, [June Term, 1873], in *Eliza Cornelia Willett (Reynolds) vs. Charles Lewis, et al.,* Case No. 662, ODC, Robertson County, Texas.

had one brother and two sisters, who presumably had died at childbirth, because in the 1850 and 1860 slave schedules they are neither identified as mulattoes nor matched by their ages. Sam's extended family and the entire slave community in the southern half of the Brazos Bottoms undoubtedly knew that Sam was the father of Azeline's children. Most of the slaves on the nearby plantations of his brothers and his cousins had resided in Caddo Parish when Dock was born. Sam's "consanguineous amalgamation," or "miscegenation"—a pejorative word not yet in the American vocabulary—was common knowledge.[15]

Direct evidence of how Sam and Azeline's white neighbors in the Brazos Bottoms viewed their cross-racial relationship does not exist, although in a sworn deposition taken in 1860 to establish Sam's continual residence on his 903 acres after he arrived in Robertson County, wealthy landowner Jesse Mumford, who operated a ferry on the Brazos River to the south of Sam's plantation, made a reference to "Samuel and his wife"—a rather generous concession to Sam's slave concubine. But Jesse, like Sam, was something of a sexual renegade himself, having been indicted in 1838 for adultery, and at the time he signed his affidavit he was cohabiting, while still unmarried, with another woman half his age. Far more revealing is the level of disdain for Sam on the part of Robertson County public officials, as gauged by a perusal of the courthouse records, which yield a glimpse of the Hearne and Lewis families' activities during the antebellum and Civil War years.[16]

15. "Interrogatories and Cross Interrogatories to Assaline Hearne," August 16, 1882, and Henry Lee Lewis to Harvey D. Prendergast, January 29, 1885, [Special File], *Assaline Hearne vs. H.D. Prendergast,* Case No. 3069, ODC, Robertson County, Texas; Henry Hughes quoted in Eugene D. Genovese, *Roll, Jordan, Roll: The World the Slaves Made* (New York: Pantheon Books, 1974), p. 418 (quotations); Bureau of the Census, *Population Schedules of the Seventh Census of the United States, 1850,* Microfilm Reel #242, Louisiana [Slave Schedules] "Bienville—Concordia," p. 887, M432, NA (1963); and Bureau of the Census, *Population Schedules of the Eighth Census of the United States, 1860,* Microfilm Reel #1312, Texas [Slave Schedules] vol. 2 (307–628) "Robertson County," p. 25 [printed p. 316], M653, NA (1967). Northern Democrats during the Civil War invented the term "miscegenation" by combining the Latin *miscere,* "to mix," with *genus,* "race." See Martha Hodes, "The Mercurial Nature and Abiding Power of Race: A Transitional Family Story," *American Historical Review* 108, no. 1 (February 2003): 107.

16. "Answers to Interrogatories by Jesse Mumford," September 24, 1860 (quotation), in folder #2, in *Eliza Cornelia Willett (Reynolds) vs. Charles Lewis, et al.,* Case No. 662, ODC, Robertson County, Texas; and "Jesse Mumford," in *Transcript Synopsis of A–P Records Relating to Robertson County "Families" 1838–[?],* Microfilm Reel #964224, CCO, Robertson County, Texas.

The court of county commissioners summoned Lum and his cousin Rasche for jury duty in 1853, and it appointed them, along with Alley, Nancy, and her mother Harriett, to employ their slaves as workers on county roads. The following year it appointed Rasche to the county's slave patrol for the precinct that included most of the family's plantation lands. Lum, Rasche, Alley, and Charles Lewis also served as slave patrollers, road overseers, and jurors throughout the remainder of the 1850s and during the war years. After Sam's cousin Ebb and brother Wash arrived, they also served on a regular basis in these capacities. A few minor lapses in the family's otherwise excellent record of civic service occurred when Lum pleaded guilty for refusing to accept a certain appointment as a public road supervisor, and during the war when he failed to appear as a witness in a criminal case. During the last years of the war, Ebb paid a fine for his failure to appear as a member of a grand jury, and Rasche, Wash, and Alley were each fined for being defaulting jurors. However, the most baffling contradiction regarding the Hearne family's public service was the absence of Sam's name among the lists of men in Robertson County called for jury duty or appointed to the slave patrols.[17]

Because Sam owned a plantation acknowledged as one of the finest in the bottomlands, it beggars belief why he was never selected as a juror or patroller. Although the county commissioners required Sam to put his slaves to work every year on the public roads, such obligations were perfunctory and entailed few decisions or judgments on his part. When Sam filed a petition detailing plans for a new public road starting on his plantation at the Brazos River and then running east out of the bottomlands to the Houston & Waco Road, the commissioners studiously failed to name him among those they selected in his neighborhood to write a report on the road's feasibility. Although the probate records list Sam at the same frequency as his other family members as either a creditor or debtor for assorted amounts of money in the accounts of various deceased individuals, he never received a court appointment as an executor, appraiser,

17. Book "I," pp. 175, 213, 220, 223, and 336, and Book "J [1–451]," pp. 55, 135, 156, 196, 244, 246, 247, 330, 362, 364, 398, 428, 435, 436, and Book "J [452–922]," 463, 474, 487, 499, and 501, MDC, Robertson County, Texas; and "Volume C [1842–1856]," p. 228, 231, 239, 253, 263, 276, 308, 329, and passim, CCM, Robertson County, Texas; "February 1856–August 1863," pp. 1, 7, 259, 293, 315, 361, 368–69, 377, and passim, CCM, Robertson County, Texas; *The State of Texas vs. Columbus [sic] C. Hearne,* Case No. 236, Book "J [1–451]," p. 42, MDC, Robertson County, Texas; "Volume H [1853–1858]," pp. 17–18, 65, and 617–18, Microfilm Reel #964208, PM, CCO, Robertson County, Texas; "February Term, 1864," p. 21, and "January Term, 1865," pp. 59–60, CCM-PM, Robertson County, Texas.

or partitioner of property or lands. Sam, in sharp contrast to others in his extended family, did not enjoy the confidence or respect of Robertson County's public officials.[18]

Piecing together other bits of information in the courthouse files reveals that Sam bought whiskey and brandy many times on credit at Greenwood ("Green") Brown's store, where he also purchased small amounts of ferrous sulfate to make ink. Sam had a penchant for attending estate sales, where he bought many sundry household items as well as horses, especially "bay, jack, and jennett [*sic*] colts." Sam's transactions with a saddle maker and with another man from whom he rented a racehorse, wound up in the only civil lawsuits, other than those over land titles, to which he was a party. The latter suit resulted in an embarrassing grand jury indictment late in 1864 against him for horse stealing, but he was never arrested, arraigned, or tried for this offense. Although Sam never received any court appointment as a guardian, he continued his family's tradition of taking an interest in indigent children. He signed a petition to have an orphaned boy "bound out" to a certain Jehue and Elizabeth Stokes, although no similar petition was filed for an eleven-year-old boy named Napoleon McCandless, who at the same time was unexplainably living in Sam's household. The only other person enumerated as residing with Sam was his slave overseer. Finally, Sam was the only member of his extended family who was not a member of the Masonic Order, a "paying patron" of any of the county's public schools, or a member of any church.[19]

Sam lived in the shadow of his prominent family members. His brother

18. "Volume C [1842–1856]," [February Term, 1854], p. 268, [February Term, 1855], pp. 183 and 314, and vol. labeled "February 1856–August 1863," [February Term, 1856], p. 6, [May Term, 1856], p. 112, [March Term, 1863], p. 407, and "Petition of Samuel R. Hearne," [November Term, 1861], p. 352, CCM, Robertson County, Texas; "Volume I [1858–1861]," Microfilm Reel #964208, [July Term, 1860], passim; and "Volume J [1861–1863]," Microfilm Reel #964209, PM, CCO, Robertson County, Texas.

19. "[Account of] Mr. S.R. Hearne Bo[ught]t of Greenwood Brown," Re: Estate of Samuel R. Hearne, Docket #134, PF, CCO, Robertson County, Texas; Estate Sale of Elizabeth Black, "Volume H [1853–1858]," January 17, 1857, p. 342, Microfilm Reel #964208, PM, CCO, Robertson County, Texas; Estate Sale of Milton Rose, "Volume J [1861–1863]," March 22, 1862, pp. 173–74 (second quotation), Microfilm Reel #964209, PM, CCO, Robertson County, Texas; *Jonathan Smith vs. J. W. Griffin & S. R. Hearne,* Case No. 854, Book "J [1–451]," p. 509, and *The State of Texas vs. Samuel R. Hearne,* Case No. 443, [Fall Term, 1864], Book "J [452–922]," pp. 507 and 540, MDC, Robertson County, Texas; Collie-Cooper, comp., *Robertson County Texas 1860 Census,* pp. 2, 41, and 65; Bureau of the Census, *Population Schedules of the Seventh Census of the United States, 1850,* Microfilm Reel #230, Louisiana, Caddo Parish, Schedule 1 (Free Inhabitants), p. 648, M432, NA (1963); "In the Matter of Andrew Cook, A Minor," "Volume I [1858–1861]," [February Term, 1860], pp. 326–28 (second quotation), Microfilm Reel #964208, PM, CCO, Robertson County, Texas; and Patrons of "David

Lum established the mercantile firm of Hearne & Spence, a partnership with Isaac C. Spence, who was a well-known local merchant before the Hearnes had arrived. Lum's slaves baked bricks of the highest quality for his retail business, and they built, in the typical style of southern plantation houses, his landmark two-story brick house in Wheelock. Desiring to be closer to their plantation lands, Rasche and Ebb established permanent residences on small tracts of land on the eastern side of the Little Brazos River. They were neighbors on opposite sides of an old Spanish trail (present-day Old Hearne Road) that wandered through the hillsides rising up out of the nearby mosquito-infested bottomlands. On the eve of the Civil War, the bustling activities at their home sites constituted "the largest plantation system in the county." Looking westward about three miles in the distance from just below the slave quarters on the cliffs of the hills on Ebb's homestead, was Sam's plantation edging up against the Big Brazos. Farther to the northwest were located the residences and plantation lands of Alley and Charles Lewis, and just to the north of them, in turn, were the plantation lands of Wash and Lum.[20]

Sam's cousin Adeline Lewis and her New England–born husband Charles rapidly rose to the pinnacle of Robertson County society. As a devoted Christian routinely welcoming traveling ministers into the family's home, Adeline took the lead in establishing the county's first Presbyterian church. Charles was a charter member of the Masonic Order, an ardent patron of the common schools, and a court appointee assigned to supervise the surveying of the new county seat in Owensville. In 1859, at the age of thirty-nine, he was elected to represent Robertson and Milam Counties for a two-year term in the Texas legislature.[21]

The Hearnes and Lewises in the 1840s had been Louisiana Whigs. In Texas they shared the strong loyalty of Robertson County voters to the so-called Opposition to the Democrats: early on as Whigs; during the mid-

---

Ellwood's School" and "James Wilson's School," [February 1856–August 1859], [November Term, 1859], pp. 225–26 (third quotation), CCM, Robertson County, Texas.

20. St. Clair, "History of Robertson County," pp. 95–96; Collie-Cooper, comp., *Robertson County Texas 1860 Census,* p. 4; "Volume C [1842–1856]," [August Term, 1853], p. 248, CCM, Robertson County, Texas; Book "I," [Spring and Fall Terms, 1851], pp. 31 and 62, MDC, Robertson County, Texas; and J. W. Baker, *A History of Robertson County, Texas* (Waco, Tex.: Printed by Texian Press, 1970), p. 130 (quotation).

21. St. Clair, "History of Robertson County," pp. 93 and 163; Parker, *Historical Recollections of Robertson County,* p. 169; "Walter S. South Journal," entry for May 1, 1864, in Ruth M. Hull Papers, THC-TAMU, College Station, Texas; and Rhea Hughston Williams, "History of Education in Robertson County" (M.A. thesis, Southern Methodist University, 1937), p. 41.

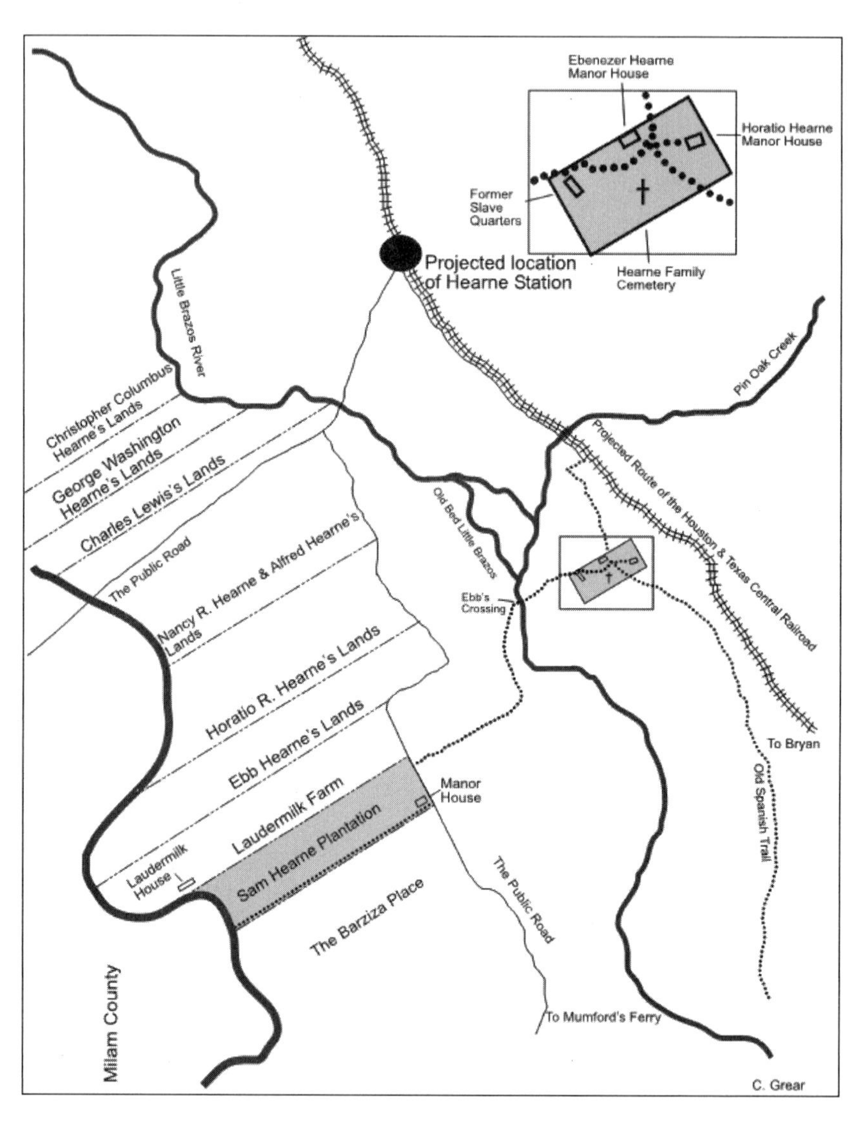

Azeline Hearne's Neighborhood in the Brazos Bottoms at the End of the Civil War

1850s as Know-Nothings; and later as "Union Democrats," or followers of Sam Houston, the old hero of the Texas Revolution. The county was in the anti-Democratic column in the gubernatorial elections of 1855, 1857, and 1859 and was represented in the state legislature throughout the late 1850s by opponents of the Democrats. Yet the county's voters chose Democrats Franklin Pierce and James Buchanan over Winfield Scott and Millard Fillmore, respectively, in the presidential elections of 1852 and

1856—results that revealed most of the county's voters shared a core of the same basic political beliefs. Steadfast Whigs such as the Hearnes and Lewises sympathized with the doctrine of "states' rights" as a means of defending southern interests, mainly the rights of slaveholders. And zealous proslavery Texas Democrats supported the notion that the South enjoyed certain *national* rights beyond a guarantee that slavery was sacrosanct where it already existed, namely, constitutional rights to take slaves into any territory that was part of the United States and have them returned should they run away into the northern states. Voters of whatever political persuasion detested self-righteous northern abolitionists and believed that the election of a president pledged to limit the expansion of slavery would constitute a sufficient reason to break up the Union. Any man disagreeing in public with these views risked being targeted as an opponent of slavery and a traitor to the South.[22]

Although the Hearne and Lewis families shared many of the same concerns as the Texas Democrats, they tended whenever possible to sidestep the slavery issue for fear of threatening the existence of the American Union. In Robertson County, as elsewhere in slaveholding East Texas, there existed plenty of room for public debates over the most persistently discussed issue in antebellum southern politics, namely, how best to ensure the expansion and future of slavery. Along with many other slaveholders in the Brazos Bottoms, the Hearnes and Lewises believed, at least before Abraham Lincoln's election in 1860, that slavery would be safer within the Union than outside it. They worried that unnecessarily agitating the slavery issue, a tendency associated with the ultraproslavery wing of the Democratic Party, would trigger disunion and probable civil war. Houston, who was not only "the giant of Texas politics" but also an unwavering unionist with presidential ambitions, repeatedly articulated this view. Sam and his brothers and cousins followed the lead of Charles Lewis and were among Houston's staunchest supporters.[23]

When Houston, while still in the U.S. Senate, ran for the Texas gover-

22. Randolph B. Campbell, *A Southern Community in Crisis: Harrison County, Texas, 1850–1880* (Austin: Texas State Historical Association, 1983), pp. 155–56; and Paul R. Scott, "The Democrats and Their Opposition: A Statistical Analysis of Texas Elections, 1852–1861," [typescript], THC-TAMU, College Station, Texas. In 1856 Lum Hearne and his wife Mary Ellen christened their son Millard Filmore, albeit with their distinctive spelling, in honor of the ex-Whig president and a presidential contender running on the American Party or Know-Nothing ticket. See: Hearne, *Brief History and Genealogy of the Hearne Family,* p. 794.

23. Dale Baum, *The Shattering of Texas Unionism: Politics in the Lone Star State during the Civil War Era* (Baton Rouge: Louisiana State University Press, 1998), pp. 18–19; and Campbell, *A Southern Community in Crisis,* pp.147–79, quotation on p. 157.

norship in 1857, he carried Robertson County. He also ran extremely well in many other old Opposition strongholds in the interior river valley counties of East Texas, but his defeat, his first ever at the polls, at the hands of Democratic candidate Hardin R. Runnels was less remarkable than the narrow margin by which he lost. Two years later, in 1859, Houston staged a dramatic political comeback by defeating Runnels's bid for reelection. Joining Houston on the triumphant Opposition, or "Union Democratic," ticket in Robertson County was Charles Lewis, but the election that brought him to the state senate also returned Democratic majorities to the legislature. Before the legislature convened, John Brown made his raid on the federal arsenal at Harper's Ferry. In the midst of the ensuing ferocity of antiabolitionist sentiment, Charles's course of action reflected the political ideals of intransigent Houston supporters. In an unsuccessful attempt to block the selection of the zealous proslavery Louis T. Wigfall as U.S. senator, Charles joined a bloc of dogged unionists and voted for Albert H. Latimer, a wealthy North Texas planter who, after the war, became a member of the Republican Party. Charles's commitment to the American Union was eventually destroyed by Lincoln's election, but up until then, Charles and his brothers-in-law and their cousins, including Rasche, Ebb, Lum, Sam, Alley, and newly arrived Wash, had hoped that secession could be avoided.[24]

Throughout the momentous national political events of the 1850s, the Hearnes acquired additional Brazos bottomland. By the outbreak of the Civil War, the total acreage, including Sam's 903-acre tract, owned by the combined Hearne, Lewis, and Armstrong families, exceeded 12,000 acres. At least 2,500 of these were under cultivation and in 1860 produced over 1,190 bales of cotton—an amount accounting for almost one-fifth of the total number of bales produced in the entire county. If sold at the market price of about ten cents a pound, the cotton bales (at 450 pounds per bale) would have represented a market value close to $53,550. The Hearnes, following accepted guidelines of statewide behavior, underevaluated, for both the tax assessor and census taker, the "cash values" of their farms at close to $150,000—a figure that did not include the much higher value of their slaves, mercantile stores, and other personal property. Not only were their antebellum plantations worth twice this reported

24. Baum, *The Shattering of Texas Unionism*, pp. 19–25; Dallas *Herald*, August 10, 1859, p.1; Llerena B. Friend, *Sam Houston: The Great Designer* (Austin: University of Texas Press, 1954), pp. 326–27; and State of Texas, Legislature, *Journal of the House of Representatives, Eighth Legislature* (Austin: Printed by John Marshall & Co., State Printers, 1860), p. 175.

amount, but also no single family ever had occupied and owned, or for that matter subsequently would control, more land in the Robertson County Brazos Bottoms. A sizable area of the Brazos Bottoms was called "the Hearne Bottoms" throughout the second half of the nineteenth century and into the early twentieth century, regardless of actual ownership.[25]

Every single acre of bottomland controlled by Sam and his extended family fell under continuous litigation throughout the entire antebellum period, the ensuing Civil War years, and the immediate postwar era. After the war, when Ebb faced additional compromising settlements over the title to his land, he lamented that he had already "paid for his plantation four times." Not until 1870 were the Hearne and Lewis families' titles to their bottomland plantations more or less cleared of all significant title conflicts. One exception would be the title to the "old Sam Hearne place." Ownership of the 903-acre Brazos River plantation remained embroiled in litigation for another decade and was not resolved until 1884.[26]

Litigation in the Bottomlands over Conflicting Mexican Land Grants

Sam had purchased his plantation in the fall of 1851 from Britton Dawson for $903 in cash and a promissory note for $1,128.75, equaling a common price of $2.25 per acre for unimproved bottomland. With the use of slave labor to clear the land, Sam knew that his first cotton crop would easily pay for his entire investment. Knowing also that there were specific claims not yet adjudicated, he gave Dawson a note for the balance due, which would become payable only when Dawson furnished him with a valid warranty deed. If Dawson failed subsequently to deliver such a deed, then Sam's promissory note would become void. In addition, Dawson signed an

25. Robertson County Tax Rolls, 1838–1882, Tax Rolls for 1860, Microfilm Reel #1198–01, TSL-AD; Bureau of the Census, *Eighth Census of the United States, 1860,* Agricultural Census, Production of Agriculture, Robertson County, Texas, "Schedule 4," Microfilm Reel #6, pp. 3 and 17–18, M653, NA (1967); Galveston *Weekly News,* August 14, 1860, p. 2; and Richard G. Lowe and Randolph B. Campbell, *Planters and Plain Folk: Agriculture in Antebellum Texas* (Dallas: Southern Methodist University Press, 1987), p. 103.

26. Ebenezer Hearne quoted in Joshua L. Randall to Joel T. Kirkman, May [27], 1867 (first quotation), "Subassistant Commissioner Records filed under 'Sterling, Texas,'" BRFAL, [unmicrofilmed], 1865–1869, RG 105, NA; "Road overseer for Precinct 28," [Special Term, 1876], p. 94 (second quotation), CCM [March 1876–September 1879], Robertson County, Texas; *John R. Hearne vs. Solomon L. Gillett,* Case No. 4898, Supreme Court of Texas, 62 Tex. 23 [1884 Tex. LEXIS 182], June 10, 1884; and *Asaline Hearne vs. H. D. Prendergast,* Case No. 5219, Supreme Court of Texas, 61 Tex. 627; 1884 Tex. LEXIS 161, May 22, 1884.

obligation stating that upon his inability to furnish the deed, he would pay $4,000 to Sam. In brief, if someone with better title subsequently evicted Sam from the land, then Dawson would be, in effect, offsetting some of the losses that Sam would suffer in having made improvements on somebody else's land. To the north of Sam's land, and also located on the east bank of the Big Brazos, Rasche Hearne and Charles Lewis purchased 1,476 acres with a similar agreement.[27]

Throughout the antebellum years, Sam had kept pace with his family in acquiring more land. He bought, for reasons that are unclear, 320 acres located in neighboring Limestone County and a land certificate from the Fort Bend County Board of Land Commissioners for 1,156 acres of land located in Young County far away on the western frontier, near Fort Belknap. Sam also purchased an additional 106 acres in the Brazos Bottoms near his original 903-acre tract at a price that reflected a fair market value of about $20.30 an acre for cleared or improved bottomland. The seller requested the county probate court make out a proper deed to Sam, but the deed itself, if conveyed or delivered, was never recorded. Nor did Sam subsequently pay taxes on the nearby 106-acre tract, suggesting that by the end of the Civil War years he no longer claimed ownership of it.[28]

On the eve of the war, Sam's Brazos River plantation produced on 280 acres of cleared bottomland 175 ginned cotton bales of 450 pounds each—an output exceeded by only eleven other planters or farm managers in the county, including his brothers Lum and Alley and cousin Rasche. At ten cents per pound for ginned cotton, Sam's 1860 crop sold for at least $7,500—an amount slightly exceeding the value he declared his plantation to be worth to the tax assessor-collector in that same year. His plantation also produced 2,700 bushels of Indian corn and 180 bushels of sweet potatoes. In addition, he owned 200 pigs, 180 cattle, 19 horses, and 24 oxen, donkeys, and mules. As was customary, Sam understated to the federal census enumerator the "cash value" of his plantation to be $19,176. Its real market value was acknowledged at the time to be closer to $50,000. By accounting merely for price inflation, this amount would

27. Agreements and Bonds dated November 20, 1851, "Deeds-Transcribed 1849–1851," Book "P," pp. 323–332, Microfilm Reel #963280, RD, CCO, Robertson County, Texas.

28. Request of Dred Dawson as legal guardian of the children of Emily Galloway, Book "I," [July Term, 1860], pp. 452–53, Microfilm Reel #964208, PM, CCO, Robertson County, Texas; Robertson County Tax Rolls, Tax Rolls for 1854–1866, Microfilm Reel #1198–01, TSL-AD; and "In the Estate of S.R. Hearne dec'd H.D. Prendergast adm'r," Book "W," [May 22, 1882], pp. 376–77, PM, CCO, Robertson County, Texas.

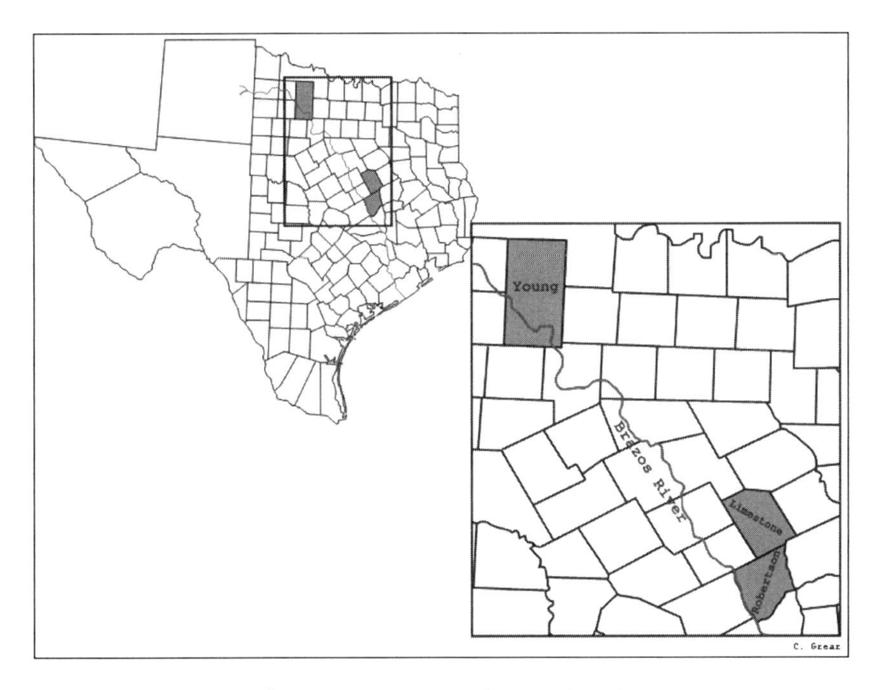

Robertson, Limestone, and Young Counties

have been equivalent to $925,000 at the turn of the twenty-first century. By any economic measure, Sam was a wealthy planter.[29]

The litigation over land titles in the southern half of the Robertson County bottomlands cannot be understood without reference to three grants issued by the Republic of Mexico before Texas became an independent republic. In 1825, when the Mexican government relegated to the states, including Coahuila and Texas, the administration of public lands, the law included a provision for giving grants to those who had served as government officials or army officers. Such grants could be used for the purposes of speculation rather than settlement. In 1833 José Francisco Ruiz, who was one of only two native-born Texans to sign the Texas Declaration of Independence, received four leagues of land on the eastern side

29. Bureau of the Census, *Eighth Census of the United States, 1860,* Agricultural Census, Production of Agriculture, Robertson County, Texas, "Schedule 4," Microfilm Reel #6, pp. 17–18 and passim, M653, NA (1967); Lowe and Campbell, *Planters and Plain Folk,* p. 103; Robertson County, Tax Rolls 1838–1882, Tax Rolls for 1860, Microfilm Reel #1198–01, TSL-AD; Joshua L. Randall to Joel T. Kirkman, June 8, 1867, account pages 36–37, "Subassistant Commissioner Records filed under 'Sterling, Texas,'" BRFAL, [unmicrofilmed], RG 105, NA; and *The Inflation Calculator,* www.westegg.com/inflation (accessed Feb. 15, 2003).

of the Brazos River. Directly below the Ruiz grant, José Antonio Manchaca received a title to six leagues. Manchaca, not to be confused with the pro-Texas revolutionary of the same name, was a member of the militia of the Texas Republic in 1839, when he was tried for treason and sentenced to death, only to be pardoned by President Mirabeau B. Lamar a few days before his scheduled execution. Finally, on the eve of the Texas Revolution in 1835—in an action that defied common sense but not the Mexican colonization laws—George Antonio Nixon, an Irish Mexican land commissioner for the empresario grants managed by the Galveston Bay and Texas Land Company, received a grant of 11 leagues that overlapped the Ruiz and Manchaca grants. The Nixon grant consisted of a huge 48,708 acres and ran 16 miles along the Brazos River. Numerous known and unknown individuals claimed ownership of the Robertson County bottomlands by virtue of being able to trace their titles directly back to Ruiz, Manchaca, and Nixon.[30]

Once Texas became a separate republic, the Robertson County Board of Land Commissioners began issuing headright certificates for tracts of land, the purpose of which was, like the former generous Mexican land grant policies, to attract genuine permanent settlers. Grantees could sell away all rights attached to these land entitlements, but if their headrights were located within a Mexican land grant, they could guarantee their title only to the headright certificate itself. In addition, they would have to make a quitclaim deed, which passed on to the buyer all interest or rights in the land but did not profess that such a deed constituted a valid title. When Sam purchased his plantation in 1851, there was never any doubt that he had purchased it from the lawful heir of the original headright issued to Dred Dawson in 1838 during the existence of the Lone Star Republic. Yet Sam knew that his bottomland acres fell within both the Manchaca and Nixon grants and was aware that the title to his 903 acres was under litigation.[31]

30. St. Clair, "History of Robertson County," pp. 40–45, 47, 102–3, and 116–19; "Interrogatories to Jacob Kuechler," November 23, 1872, in folder #2, in *Eliza Cornelia Willett (Reynolds) vs. Charles Lewis, et al.,* Case No. 662, ODC, Robertson County, Texas; "Description of the Henry Gillum Papers," George Antonio Nixon Collection, 1799–1917, Special Collections Division, The University of Texas at Arlington Libraries, Arlington, Texas, http://libraries.uta.edu/SpecColl/findaids/guideHist3.htm; "Ruiz, José Francisco," and "Menchaca, José Antonio [1795–?]," *TNHT,* 5: 711–712, and 4: 617.

31. *Cannon's Administrator vs. Vaughan,* Supreme Court of Texas, 12 Tex. 399 [1854 Tex. LEXIS], Decided 1854; Robert A. Calvert, Arnoldo De León, and Gregg Cantrell, *The History of Texas,* 3rd ed. (Wheeling, Ill.: Harlan Davidson, Inc., 2002), pp. 89–91; and Parker, *Historical Recollections of Robertson County,* pp. 142–145.

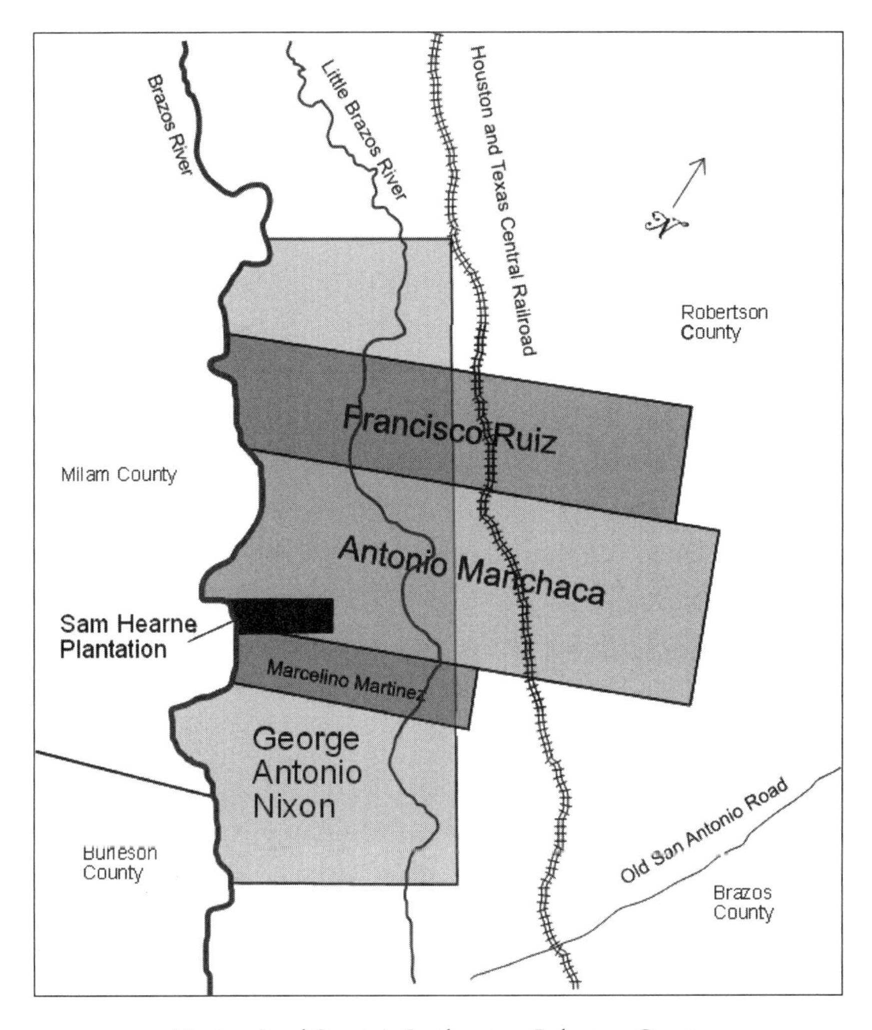

Mexican Land Grants in Southwestern Robertson County

Dating from 1844, the "heirs of Allen Reynolds" claimed a large portion of the Dawson headright by virtue of inheriting it from someone who could trace ownership directly back to Manchaca. Reynolds was an early settler who had helped Stephen F. Austin with legal matters regarding immigration to the Mexican province of Texas. At his death in 1837 he left behind a very valuable estate, and much time had been spent over the years trying to determine via deaths, births, and marriages precisely who had an interest in it. The case drifted to two other counties before returning to Robertson County, where it was on the district court docket in 1851, when Sam had purchased the 903 acres. In addition, Britton Dawson, who sold part of his father's headright to Sam, had a lawsuit pending against "the heirs of George Antonio Nixon." Others joined Dawson's complaint, requesting that the county surveyor be ordered to determine what all parties already knew, namely, where exactly the Nixon grant fronted the Brazos River. On the one hand, these inexorable, protracted, and numerous lawsuits were annoyances to genuine settlers like Sam who enjoyed excellent legal positions by having apparent titles to lands that they continuously occupied in opposition to all others. On the other hand, the littering of the court dockets with lawsuits to disentangle the ownership of the bottomlands proved a lucrative source of steady income for lawyers hired by litigating parties.[32]

Any cloud cast over Sam's title by Nixon heirs disappeared in 1857, when Priscilla A. Duffield, the sole heir at law of Nixon, appointed an agent to settle all her business in Texas. Rather than risking outcomes of jury trials, her agent was determined to settle as many cases as possible against those whom he argued held false claims to lands belonging to his client. Because Duffield had no strategy to defeat the overlapping claims of Ruiz or Manchaca claimants, her agent busily negotiated with a host of residents in the southwestern Brazos Bottoms, including Sam Hearne. In consideration for the sum of $1,126, Sam bought all of Duffield's rights to his land, which fell within in the eleven leagues granted to Nixon. Sam must have been quite pleased. His title was forevermore free of the claims of any of the legal heirs of George Antonio Nixon.[33]

Wriggling free of the Manchaca plaintiffs, however, proved more difficult. Yet a colossal advantage had accrued to Sam in the spring of 1854, when the lawsuit initiated by the Reynolds heirs was dismissed. The plaintiffs and defendants, after being ordered by the court, had failed to gather additional new participants to the litigation following the deaths of most of the original parties. By 1858, when the Reynolds heirs regrouped, Sam enjoyed a superior legal position over most of his summoned codefen-

32. *The Heirs of Allen Reynolds vs. Britton Dawson,* Case No. 180, Book "I," [Fall Term, 1851], pp. 43 (first quotation)–44, MDC, Robertson County, Texas; *Britton Dawson vs. William C. Duffield & Wife,* Case No. 346, Book "I," [Fall Term, 1851], p. 54 (second quotation), MDC, Robertson County, Texas; and "Statement of Facts," in *Eliza Cornelia Willett (Reynolds) vs. Charles Lewis, et al.,* Case No. 662, ODC, Robertson County, Texas.

33. Power of Attorney from Priscilla A. Duffield to George W. Shelton, February 18, 1857, Book "M," pp. 558–59, and Warranty Deed, July 13, 1857, and filed for record in August of 1859, Book "M," pp. 667–68, Microfilm Reel #963278, RD, CCO, Robertson County, Texas. On the same day, July 13th, Shelton settled with Rasche Hearne and Charles Lewis. See ibid., pp. 671–72.

dants, including members of his own extended family. He had no difficulty proving adverse and continual possession of his plantation for the prior four years. In addition, by 1861 Britton Dawson had also freed himself from claims of the Reynolds heirs and thus agreed to defend the title that he had conveyed ten years earlier to Sam against anyone who might try to claim the 903 acres. At this point Sam and his lawyers knew that his title to the Brazos River plantation was, in effect, virtually unassailable. He had no reason to enter into compromise settlements with any or all of the Reynolds heirs or, for that matter, with any other person who might attempt to lawfully claim ownership of his plantation.[34]

Slave Mistresses and Antebellum Miscegenation

Sam did not live long enough to see, during the administration of his estate after the Civil War, the continuance of the litigation stemming from the resurfacing of the Manchaca claimants. He died at fifty years of age in the fall of 1866 during the period of Presidential, or "Johnsonian," Reconstruction. But then again, if he had lived through the tumultuous years of the Reconstruction era, he would have faced an infinitely greater set of potential difficulties because, as he certainly knew, white southern society considered as scandalous an acknowledged cohabitation and mating across racial lines.

Texas, under Mexican rule and empresario regulations, had imposed no legal prohibitions on marriages between whites and blacks, and unions and marriages between Tejanos and Anglos had made many regions into a considerable ethnic melting pot. However, during the years of the Texas Republic and early statehood, Robertson County remained a small frontier community dominated by pioneers from Tennessee. By 1850 the county contained relatively few slaves and was devoid of both Mexican-born settlers and the offspring of unions between Tejanas and Anglo men. The subsequent dramatic influx of newcomers with their slaves shifted the origins of the majority of the population to those born in the lower South. Although the Texas state legislature customarily approved petitions to emancipate the mulatto children born of casual unions originating in the colonial era and the courts routinely maintained the rights of interracial children and their mothers, dating back to the less restrictive period, as

34. Summons, "Samuel R. Hearne & others," September 20, 1858, in *Eliza Cornelia Willett (Reynolds) vs. Charles Lewis, et al.*, Case No. 662, ODC, Robertson County, Texas; Warranty Deed, September 10, 1861, and filed for record on September 12, 1861, Book "N," pp. 299–300, Microfilm Reel #963279, RD, CCO, Robertson County, Texas.

beneficiaries to property under valid wills, Sam Hearne had good reason never to publicly acknowledge his relationship with Azeline or his paternity of Dock.[35]

In the late antebellum period, white society in Robertson County held that sexual intercourse outside marriage and the mixture of the black and white races were immoral and deplorable. Whites could never have been expected to recognize Azeline or Dock, even if both were beloved by Sam, as anything other than a mongrelized "species of property" or "just other niggers" who were "as marketable as the pigs" on his plantation. As a single slaveholder living with a slave concubine, Sam was governed by a set of obligatory social rules. In the mixed company of whites, he could neither flaunt his illicit affair with a slave woman nor boast about having a slave mistress. If he had, his relatives would have accused him of insanity or alcoholism—allegations that they did make after his death.[36]

Even if Sam indiscreetly admitted among other men to having a slave concubine, then the relationship had to be in the context of "wenching," or having casual, not serious, sexual intercourse as a purely private affair licensed by slaveholder promiscuity. Corollaries to these social mores were: the offspring of any union between a white man and an enslaved woman would never inherit a higher status than the mother; the chastity of white women must be reverentially upheld; and the adulterer or fornicator must not commit other immoral acts suggesting his entire behavior was recklessly depraved. Whatever concerns might have weighed on Sam's mind, the bottom line was that he knew he could never marry the mother of his children, and he had to admit that his own flesh and blood were born into slavery.[37]

Although Sam knew that having sexual relations with enslaved females and siring mulatto children was not against the law, he had to have been aware that his fornication, miscegenation, and concubinage were poten-

35. Randolph B. Campbell, *An Empire for Slavery: The Peculiar Institution in Texas, 1821–1865* (Baton Rouge and London: Louisiana State University Press, 1989), pp. 10–34, 45–48, and 201–208; and Ancestry.com, *1850 and 1860 United States Federal Census* [online database] (Provo, Utah: The Generations Network, Inc., 2005 and 2004).

36. James Madison Hall, "A Journal of the Civil War Period by James Madison Hall, 1860–1866," entry for May 29,1865 (first quotation), James Madison Hall Papers, CAH-UT, Austin, Texas; Genovese, *Roll, Jordan, Roll,* p. 429 (second quotation); Harriet A. Jacobs, *Incidents in the Life of a Slave Girl,* ed. Nellie Y. McKay and Frances Smith Foster (New York: Norton, 2001), p. 32 (third quotation).

37. Bertram Wyatt-Brown, *Southern Honor: Ethics and Behavior in the Old South* (New York: Oxford University Press, 1982), p. 309 (quotation).

tially detrimental to slave discipline. When white men, whether masters, overseers, or neighboring nonslaveholders, had sexual intercourse with female slaves, their behavior could cause more trouble on a plantation than, in the words of one contemporary of the period, "all else put together." As one prominent historian of American slavery has pointed out, behavior ranging from seduction to rape of mostly young and single slave girls was common enough on most southern plantations to make life wretched for a marked minority of black women and their men. It was thus most likely not an accident that among the slaves owned by Sam in 1850 in Louisiana, only one-third of them remained with him on his plantation in 1860 in the Texas Brazos Bottoms. He most likely sold away slaves with whom he could not work out uneasy accords regarding his cohabitation with Azeline—a situation of which his other slaves were without doubt aware.[38]

Sam's own prosperity, along with the influence and wealth of his extended family, made him far less vulnerable to gossip and attack than he otherwise would have been. But even if Sam followed the understood social rules and benefited from deference to his high social status, it is unlikely that his miscegenation presented him with, in the words of one historian, "almost no ethical problem." Chances were that Sam's sisters and female cousins singled him out for resentment because they would have considered his behavior a threat to their families. In addition, Sam's conduct served as an agonizing reminder of one of the abolitionists' most lurid critiques of slavery, that the slave system permitted white men to sexually exploit black women. Sam must have listened nervously to the repeated blistering attack on the abolitionists by proslavery southerners—their claim that the abolitionists, if successful in destroying slavery, would sink the United States to the infernal depths of a racially amalgamated nation.[39]

38. Genovese, *Roll, Jordan, Roll,* pp. 421 (Haller Nutt quoted on) and 415; Bureau of the Census, *Population Schedules of the Seventh Census of the United States, 1850,* Microfilm Reel #242, Louisiana [Slave Schedules] "Bienville—Concordia," p. 887, M432, NA (1963); and Bureau of the Census, *Population Schedules of the Eighth Census of the United States, 1860,* Microfilm Roll #1312, Texas [Slave Schedules] vol. 2 (307–628) "Robertson County," p. 25 [printed p. 316], M653, NA (1967).

39. Wyatt-Brown, *Southern Honor,* p. 309 (quotation). Because attitudes toward race in the antebellum South were complex, generalizations about miscegenation and slavery are difficult to make. See: Wilbur J. Cash, *The Mind of the South* (New York: Alfred A. Knopf, 1941), passim; Earle E. Thorpe, *Eros and Freedom in Southern Life and Thought* (Durham, N.C.: Printed by Seeman Printery, 1967), passim; and Genovese, *Roll, Jordan, Roll,* esp. pp. 413–31.

Because the details of Azeline's relationship with Sam can never be recovered, many questions about the nature of their relationship remain. Had Sam deliberately chosen to mate with her rather than bow to family pressure to marry one of his cousins or a sister of one of his brothers' or cousins' wives? Or was Azeline the half-sister of one of the wives of his cousins or brothers? If she had been the half-sister of Adeline Lewis, the interest shown by the Lewis family during the late 1870s in acquiring "the old Sam Hearne place" would make considerable sense. Or had Azeline given up a slave spouse of her choice, and perhaps even children, to become Sam's mistress? In this regard, had Sam initiated his relationship with her as an act of sexual exploitation? The disparity in power in the antebellum South between white men and female slaves strongly suggests that most liaisons that produced racially mixed children were forced upon black women. Most interracial affairs began, continued, and ended in acts of inexcusable mistreatment of enslaved females.

Ex-slave Harriet Jacobs described the insidious "atmosphere of licentiousness and fear" in which a slave girl was reared and had to endure throughout her life: "When she is fourteen or fifteen, her owner, or his sons, or the overseer, or perhaps all of them, begin to bribe her with presents. If these fail to accomplish their purpose, she is whipped or starved into submission to their will. . . . [R]esistance is hopeless." Sexual assaults committed most frequently upon single black women tended to be more stark and vicious when they occurred in rural plantation areas, where violence against slaves helped whites perpetuate racial dominance. Without knowing how Sam began his relationship with Azeline, and assuming even the best possible scenario—that she at some point was appreciative of his attentions—the position in which they found themselves did more than, as Jacobs reflected, "[confuse] all principles of morality"; it made "the practice of them impossible."[40]

Feelings of love and affection were never straightforward matters in the tormented circumstances of slavery. Problems, like hidden traps just below the surface, constantly surrounded Sam and Azeline and threatened to ensnare them at any moment. The unbridgeable chasm between them might have seemed less formidable, given the fact that, as a bachelor, he was not betraying a wife, but his control over Azeline always extended beyond what he won from her merely through his acts of kindness. Putting

40. Jacobs, *Incidents in the Life of a Slave Girl,* pp. 44 and 47 (quotations); Genovese, *Roll, Jordan, Roll,* pp. 415, 422–423, 426–428, and 461; and Campbell, *An Empire for Slavery,* pp. 201–203.

aside how their relationship might have started and also ignoring how its continuance for many years might have emotionally scarred them and perhaps others, their liaison undeniably ended with affectionate devotion to one another. During the last years of his life, Sam cherished Azeline and he loved Dock, the sole surviving child that she bore him. Sam Hearne was not supposed to love his own child. Nor was he expected to fall in love with the mother of his child. But he did.

Chapter 2

Thar Am No Parties on Marster's Plantation

> Him [Ebenezer Hearne] says "taint fo' parties he have de plantation, but 'tis fo' wo'k." De only time weuns have any fun am on Christmas Day. Ise don't know what parties an' dancin' am 'till aftah surrendah.
>
> —HATTIE (HEARNE) COLE IN GEORGE P. RAWICK, *The American Slave: A Composite Autobiography*

THE ECONOMY OF ROBERTSON County flourished on the eve of the Civil War because of slavery. Speculation in slaves and cotton lands might have hindered the growth of local industries, but investment in slave agriculture in no way deflected capital away from more productive alternative business ventures. Money invested in prime field hands, available through the Houston and Galveston slave markets, and the purchase of cotton lands in the rich alluvial bottomlands of the nearby Brazos, Colorado, and Trinity Rivers yielded unrivaled returns for East Texas planters. By 1860 the prices of slaves and cotton land were at all-time highs. While slave property provided a key source of tax revenues, the use of slave labor also had added benefits for local communities, such as work that slaveholders and their "hands" performed on the public roads in their neighborhoods. Never doubting that slavery was profitable and advantageous, the Hearne and Lewis families joined the overwhelming majority of the county's leaders in their confidence about the institution's future development. Such optimism was not misplaced: the American slaveholding South dominated the supply of raw cotton used by a growing textile industry that ranked among the world's largest industries.[1]

Slave ownership was impracticable without the belief that blacks were inferior to whites in every way except in performing hard physical labor. Slaveholders found justification for the use of slave labor in the supposed characteristics of the human beings they enslaved. One of Robertson County's most illustrious residents, Alexander W. Terrell, later appointed minister to Turkey by President Grover Cleveland, summed up the conventional portrayal of the Old South's "estimate of the Negro." According to Terrell, many brave Confederate soldiers "willingly died" in their convictions that they were "right" about the Negro's inherent inferiority and suitability for enslavement. Their beliefs included the notions that black Africans had been created separately from white Caucasians, and heredity "through unknown centuries of barbarianism" had inculcated in the African "the supremacy of his animal nature." As a consequence, without the discipline of slavery blacks would revert to uncivilized behavior: they inevitably would become treacherous, unmanageable, and wretched wards of the state. In Terrell's words, with skulls "as thick as a buffalo's" and bodies imparting "a repulsive odor," blacks had no mental capacity for any of the higher sentiments, abilities, or emotions. Such racial stereotypes allowed Terrell and other whites to conclude that blacks could not experience the horrible oppression of slavery the way white people would.[2]

Not only did slavery foster unashamed racist assumptions, it also led to more than a few bizarre, yet widely accepted, sociological conclusions. For example, Terrell believed that white southern society had found in slavery "the black key stone in the arch" that upheld the social structure. As he saw it, slavery exempted "our own race from field labor" and thus allowed "the white master's ample leisure for study and progress." Every great civilization, according to Terrell, had recognized the necessity for

1. Randolph B. Campbell, *An Empire for Slavery: The Peculiar Institution in Texas* (Baton Rouge: Louisiana State University Press, 1989), pp. 67–95.

2. Alexander W. Terrell, "The Negro," [undated manuscript (1908?)], pp. 1–24 (quotations on pp. 2 and 10), CAH-UT, Austin, Texas. Terrell is perhaps best known for his authorship of the state's Terrell Election Law, which created the direct primary system for political party nominations. See Lewis L. Gould, *Alexander Watkins Terrell: Civil War Soldier, Texas Lawmaker, American Diplomat* (Austin: University of Texas Press, 2004), pp. xi and 154–55.

advanced people to exploit the labor of their inferiors. Because members of the superior race, including nonslaveholding whites, enjoyed a common dominance over blacks, slavery had provided the foundation for liberty and equality among all white men. Terrell nostalgically recalled that divisions between "rich and poor" whites had not existed prior to emancipation, because "the poorest man . . . felt the full measure with his rich neighbor the pride of caste which separated him from the slave."[3]

According to Terrell's logic, mulattoes such as Azeline and her son Dock, with whom Terrell was well acquainted, had a "delicate constitution" and thus were "less capable of breeding than the full blood Negro." Mulattoes were infertile, more subject to illness, and less able to withstand working in the hot sun—circumstances that were due to nature's abhorrence of efforts "to establish a hybrid species permanently in the animal kingdom." Because mulattoes were "bad breeders" when they mated among themselves, they frequently propagated "with an individual of the pure blood of either parent." Additional observations had taught Terrell that fertility among mulattoes was "in proportion to the nearness of the first crop" and that, in general, their capacity to have children disappeared over time no matter with whom or at what time of the year they mated. Terrell's views regarding interracial progenies underscored the conventional wisdom among the slaveholding classes that black Africans were a separate and inferior species that would defile mainstream society if allowed to mate freely in the absence of restrictions.[4]

The need for elaborate controls over slaves caused Robertson County whites to experience anxieties characteristic of what the foremost scholar of Texas slavery has called "a society under siege." These fears in turn reinforced justifications for the status quo, stifled the free exchange of ideas, created a heightened degree of defensiveness, and prompted an ideological counterattack on northern society. After John Brown was, as Terrell put it, "canonized as a saint by New England preachers for organizing Negro slaves to assassinate the white people of Virginia," traumatized southerners became outraged beyond reconciliation. Brown's raid fulfilled the

3. Terrell, "The Negro," pp. 8 (fourth and fifth quotations) and 18 (first, second, and third quotations). Many nonslaveholding whites living in areas containing few slaves did not share Terrell's idea about the absence of class conflict during slavery. See Hinton Rowan Helper, *The Impending Crisis of the South: How to Meet It* (New York: A. B. Burdick, 1859).

4. Terrell, "The Negro," p. 16 (quotations); and Frederick Law Olmsted, *The Cotton Kingdom: A Traveller's Observations on Cotton and Slavery in the American Slave States,* ed. Arthur M. Schlesinger Sr. (New York: Modern Library College Editions, 1984), pp. 459–60.

prophecies of the extreme proslavery Texas Democrats, who had repeatedly warned that an abolitionist-led slave insurrection might someday try to create a free-soil republic on the ruins of the plantation South.[5]

Into the Vortex of Secession and Civil War

Up until Brown's raid, the Hearne and Lewis families had criticized zealous proslavery Democrats for unnecessarily raising the specter of secession in order to evade imaginary threats to slavery. The family's political stance had been a viable one because the passage of the Kansas-Nebraska Act in 1854 had placed the North, rather than the South, on the defensive. Moreover, the Opposition had benefited from the South appearing throughout the late 1850s to be in firm control of the national political system. Extreme states' rights Democrats had emerged as the most influential advisors of President James Buchanan, a proslavery Pennsylvanian who detested abolitionists. Southern slaveholders and proslavery northerners also controlled the U.S. Supreme Court, which in the Dred Scott decision embraced the extreme proslavery interpretation of the constitutional debate over slavery in the western territories. In the wake of Brown's raid, which was easily snuffed out, state senator Charles Lewis continued to believe that slavery would be safer within rather than out of the American Union, but few of his constituents in Robertson County shared his steadfast and unconditional unionism. If the 1859 state elections had been held after Harper's Ferry, Lewis, along with most other successful Opposition candidates, including Sam Houston, would have been defeated.[6]

The reaction of the Hearnes and Lewises to the breakup in early 1860 of the national Democratic Party is unknown, but they probably sympathized with the refusal of Texas Democrats to accept Senator Stephen A. Douglas of Illinois as their party's nominee. The South could not be expected to trust Douglas to dispatch federal troops to the rescue the next time another John Brown arose. Douglas had claimed in the wake of the Dred Scott ruling that slavery could still be excluded from the territories, where it had, according to the highest court of the land, a lawful right to be. Once the movement to run Governor Houston on an independent electoral ticket collapsed, the Hearne and Lewis families turned to ex-Whig John Bell of Tennessee, who at the very least shared Houston's vision of

5. Campbell, *An Empire for Slavery,* p. 256 (first quotation); Terrell, "The Negro," p. 6 (second quotation); and Dale Baum, *The Shattering of Texas Unionism: Politics in the Lone Star State during the Civil War Era* (Baton Rouge: Louisiana State University Press, 1998), p. 8.

6. Baum, *The Shattering of Texas Unionism,* pp. 7, 37–38.

triumphing over the narrow sectional appeals of John C. Breckinridge, the candidate of the splinter "Southern Rights" Democrats, and Abraham Lincoln, the unacceptable candidate of the purely northern "Black Republican" Party.[7]

Four candidates—Lincoln, Douglas, Bell, and Breckinridge—were in the race for the presidency in the summer of 1860, when federal census enumerator G. H. Love rode into the southern Brazos bottomlands of Robertson County. Love visited the plantation lands of brothers Rasche and Ebb and their cousins Sam, Alley, and Wash at the peak of what became known throughout the lower South, during the presidential campaign, as the "Texas Troubles." News of fires of suspicious origin in a few North Texas towns had spread rumors that slave arsonists led by northern abolitionists were at work plotting insurrections and destruction of property. After subsequent conflagrations during the extraordinarily hot days of July and August seemed to reenact the scenario of Harper's Ferry, Robertson County generated its share of rumors, hysteria, and vigilance committees. The local frenzy culminated in early September with the extralegal lynching of two men for "tampering with slaves."[8]

To get to the entrance of Sam's plantation, Love crossed the Little Brazos River at "Ebb's Crossing" on the private road twisting down to the Bottoms from Rasche and Ebb's homesteads in the nearby uplands (see map 1). After continuing southwest about three more miles, Love traveled another two-fifths of a mile on the public road between the Little and Big Brazos Rivers. Part of Love's routine as a census taker requested slaveholders or their overseers to call the slaves to the plantation house in order to have them lined up by age for counting. Enumerators recorded their sex, age, and color (whether a "mulatto" or "black"), along with whether they were fugitives from the state, deaf and dumb, blind, or insane. The actual names of the slaves were irrelevant and thus not recorded.[9]

7. Walter L. Buenger, *Secession and the Union in Texas* (Austin: University of Texas Press, 1984), pp. 45–55; and Baum, *The Shattering of Texas Unionism,* pp. 38–40.

8. Mary Collie-Cooper, comp., *Robertson County Texas 1860 Census,* [typescript: July 4, 1985], pp. i and 1; *Northern Standard* (Clarksville), September 22, 1860, p.1; Buenger, *Secession and the Union,* pp. 55–56, 75; and William W. White, "The Texas Slave Insurrection of 1860," *Southwestern Historical Quarterly* 52, no. 3 (January 1949): 259–85 (quotations on p. 276).

9. J. W. Baker, *A History of Robertson County, Texas* (Waco, Tex.: Printed by Texian Press, 1970), p. 258; Bureau of the Census, *Population Schedules of the Eighth Census of the United States,* 1860, Microfilm Roll #1312, Texas [Slave Schedules] vol. 2 (307–628) "Robertson County," p. 25, [printed p. 316], M653, NA (1967).

Love listed Sam as the owner of twenty-four slaves, but it is doubtful that Sam or his overseer assembled all of them for Love to view personally. In the column for "color," Love neglected to list any slave as a "mulatto," though Azeline and Dock were both unmistakably light-skinned. Based on Love's enumeration, only six of Sam's slaves could have been among the human chattels listed as his possessions in the previous federal census taken in Louisiana. The only slave corresponding to the lone four-year-old mulatto male enumerated in 1850 was one of two fourteen-year-old males listed by Love, making 1846 Dock's year of birth and also establishing him to have been, at his death in 1868, of legal age at over twenty-one years. In addition, and by a similar process of elimination, Azeline had to have been the twenty-five-year-old female slave in 1850 who appeared as one of two thirty-five-year-old females in 1860, making 1825 her year of birth. No other enslaved female, with the exception of a ninety-year-old woman, was older than Azeline, and the next youngest was eighteen years of age. Azeline could not have been as old as ninety or as young as eighteen—ages incompatible with having a fourteen-year-old son.[10]

Love presumably enumerated all of Sam's slaves. If Azeline or Dock had been temporarily on the plantations of Sam's relatives, it would have been unlikely for Love to list them as belonging to someone other than Sam. Although Sam mixed his slaves with those belonging to his brothers and cousins on shared work assignments and freely traded ownership in slaves to facilitate slave sexual unions, it is doubtful, given the high values placed on slaves, that ownership itself was shared or commingled. No runaways were listed among his slaves. Nor were any indicated to be physically or mentally disabled. Altogether, Sam owned eleven females and thirteen males. On his plantation stood four slave cabins, which most likely housed the extended families of four male heads of households.[11]

10. Bureau of the Census, *Population Schedules of the Seventh Census of the United States, 1850*, Microfilm Roll #242, Louisiana [Slave Schedules] "Bienville—Concordia," p. 887, M432, NA (1963); and Bureau of the Census, *Population Schedules of the Eighth Census of the United States, 1860*, Microfilm Roll #1312, Texas [Slave Schedules] vol. 2 (307–628) "Robertson County," p. 25, [printed p. 316], M653, NA (1967).

11. Bureau of the Census, *Population Schedules of the Eighth Census of the United States, 1860*, Microfilm Roll #1312, Texas [Slave Schedules] vol. 2 (307–628) "Robertson County," p. 25, printed p. 316, M653, NA (1967); Elmer Grady Marshall, "The History of Brazos County, Texas" (M.A. thesis, University of Texas at Austin, 1937), pp.125–51; and Statement of Hattie (Hearne) Cole in George P. Rawick, ed., *The American Slave: A Composite Autobiography*, supp., ser. 2, vol. 3: "Texas Narratives," pt. 2 (Westport, Conn.: Greenwood Press, 1979), p. 776.

In the antebellum South every slave had an owner and a price. On the eve of the Civil War, prime field hands sold for around $1,800 in the Galveston slave market. Particularly attractive or "fancy" light-skinned females, most probably such as Azeline, could fetch as high as $5,000 and were often purchased for urban prostitution. On the other hand, disabled, sickly, or even dying slaves could be obtained at huge discounts. Between 1852, when the bulk of the Hearne clan first arrived in Robertson County, and 1860 on the eve of the Civil War, the average value of a slave in the county appreciated from $470 to $626. By way of comparison, in 1860 the average value of a slave owned by the extended Hearne family was $716, or $90 higher than the average value of a Robertson County slave. In 1860 the Hearne, Lewis, and Armstrong families paid taxes on 250 slaves at a declared value of $178,939. The value of their slaves exceeded the "cash values" of their plantations. At the turn of the twenty-first century, the value of their property in slaves would have exceeded 3.3 million dollars.[12]

Declared values to local tax assessors and collectors were always less than market values. Moreover, the number of slaves the extended Hearne family reported to county tax assessors was invariably less than reported to federal census takers. The latter discrepancy reflected the tendency to excuse planters from paying capitation taxes on incapacitated, elderly, and newborn slaves. In 1860 Sam paid taxes on only eighteen of his twenty-four slaves. According to enumerator Love's schedules, the entire Hearne, Lewis, and Armstrong clan owned 283 slaves, or 33 more than they declared to the local tax assessor. Of additional interest was Love's undercount of mulatto slaves on the Hearne family plantations by a number far exceeding the omissions of Azeline and Dock.[13]

On the combined Hearne, Lewis, and Armstrong plantations, Love should have found about thirty more mulatto slaves, assuming their prevalence should have mirrored the national ratio of just over thirteen out

12. Eugene D. Genovese, *Roll, Jordan, Roll: The World the Slaves Made* (New York: Pantheon Books, 1974), p. 416; Robertson County Tax Rolls, 1838–1882, Tax Rolls for 1860, Microfilm Reel #1198–01, TSL-AD; Campbell, *An Empire for Slavery,* pp. 67–95: Rupert N. Richardson, Ernest Wallace, and Adrian Anderson, *Texas: The Lone Star State,* 5th ed. (Englewood Cliffs, N.J.: Prentice Hall, 1988), p. 182; and *The Inflation Calculator* www.westegg.com/inflation (accessed Feb. 15, 2003).

13. Bureau of the Census, *Population Schedules of the Eighth Census of the United States,* 1860, Microfilm Roll #1312, Texas [Slave Schedules] vol. 2 (307–628) "Robertson County," pp. 1–3, 25–27, [printed pp. 307–8, 316–17], M653, NA (1967); Robertson County Tax Rolls, 1838–1882, Tax Rolls for 1860, Microfilm Reel #1198–01, TSL-AD.

of one hundred—a ratio that represented an increase of about two percentage points over the 1850 proportion. The accuracy of the census statistics is, of course, questionable, along with the frequent postwar claim that for every hundred blacks in Texas there were probably at least sixteen mulattoes. Although all figures underrepresented the actual mulatto population, the percentage of mulattoes among enslaved individuals of African descent indisputably increased during the last fifteen years of slavery. More importantly, while a significant rise in the number of sexual relationships between white men and black women arose, the racial attitudes of southern white society toughened against miscegenation.[14]

While the Hearne, Lewis, and Armstrong families continued to obtain more slaves and acquire additional lands throughout the 1850s, they also reassessed during major sectional political crises the value of the American Union to their welfare. Brown's raid and Lincoln's election constituted a double shock from which most slaveholders never recovered. The latter highlighted a radical change in the basic premises of American governance—the rejection by the overwhelming majority of the free states of the venerable national commitment to slavery. Although Charles Lewis had endorsed the Bell and Douglas anti-Lincoln "Fusion" ticket, there is no evidence that he or his extended family subsequently sided with the overwhelming majority of Robertson County voters favoring secession in the February 1861 statewide popular referendum. The Hearnes and Lewises, along with most of their slaveholding counterparts, might have believed that Lincoln's election represented a "declaration of war on the South," but newspaper accounts of the large secessionist rally held in the county seat of Owensville made no mention of their presence. Their absence was consistent with their anti-Breckinridge stance in the presidential election. On the other hand, it is even more unlikely that they joined at the polls the 16 percent of Robertson County voters, most of them foreign-born or nonslaveholders, who cast ballots against secession in the February referendum.[15]

14. Lynn Anne McCallum Freeman, "Miscegenation and Slavery: A Problem in American Historiography" (M.A. thesis, Queen's University, 1991), pp. 2 and 71; Galveston *Daily News,* February 10, 1867, p. 2; and Joel Williamson, *New People: Miscegenation and Mulattoes in the United States* (New York: Free Press, 1980), p. 58.

15. *The Southern Intelligencer* (Austin), October 10, 1860, p. 1 (quotation), and March 27, 1861, p. 2; Manuscript Election Returns for 1861, Folder for Robertson County, Secretary of State Records, RG 307, TSL-AD; Marshall, "The History of Brazos County," p. 78; and Ada Margaret Smith, "The Life and Times of William Harrison Hamman" (M.A. thesis, University of Texas, 1952), pp. 45–51.

The Hearnes and Lewises most likely agreed with the position taken by their prominent slaveholding neighbor Josephus Cavitt, who also had been a Houston supporter and unwavering unionist before Lincoln's election. Cavitt decided against voting in the secession referendum. In his words, the "numbers in favor" were so considerable that expressing a divergent view was likely to result in "unpleasant and frequently dangerous altercations." At this moment in Texas history, an abstention in the secession referendum election, or for that matter even a no-vote, was not yet considered a declaration of disloyalty to the newly formed Confederacy. The decisive moment came when the outcome of the statewide balloting was known. The Cavitt, Hearne, and Lewis families, and many other former Houston men, followed their state into the Confederacy. At a special session of the state legislature, Charles Lewis stepped forward, in contrast to the dramatic refusal of Governor Houston, to take the new prescribed oath of allegiance to the Confederate States of America.[16]

Life in "the Hearne Bottoms" during the Civil War Years

Unyielding unionists were rare in Robertson County, but not nonexistent. An antebellum Houston supporter with the unusual name Telemachus ("Telephus") Johnson, a neighbor of Sam and Azeline, not only fought secession with all his ability but also remained "an out and out Union Man" throughout the entire ensuing Civil War. As a consequence, the "Ultra Secessionist Men" allegedly subjected him to "more abuse and persecution" than any other person in the county. Only his "extraordinary shrewdness and unflinching nerve," combined with his status as a large slaveholder, saved him from extralegal retaliation. Being on good terms with his immediate neighbors Sam, Ebb, and Rasche, and their overseers, also shielded him. They refused to appear as witnesses against him when he was charged with the criminal wartime offense of putting his bondsmen in charge of lands detached from his home residence.[17]

16. Josephus Cavitt to Andrew Johnson, September 7, 1865 (quotations), in James Marten, *Texas Divided: Loyalty and Dissent in the Lone Star State, 1856–1874* (Lexington: University of Kentucky Press, 1990), p. 44; and State of Texas, *Journal of the House of Representatives of the State of Texas: Extra Session of the Eighth Legislature* [Journal of Adjourned Secession] (Austin: Published by John Marshall, State Printers, 1861), p. 126.

17. Harvey Mitchell to Andrew J. Hamilton (quotations), August 21, 1865, folder 14, box 49, Governors' Papers: Hamilton, RG 301, TSL-AD; Collie-Cooper, comp., *Robertson County Texas 1860 Census,* p. 65; Bureau of the Census, *Population Schedules of the Eighth Census of the United States,* 1860, Microfilm Roll #1312, Texas [Slave Schedules] vol. 2 (307–628) "Robertson County," pp. 22 and 25, M653, NA (1967); *The State of Texas vs. Telephus A.*

The Charles Lewis generation of the extended Hearne family felt no need to distinguish itself on the battlefields of the Civil War. Charles became subject to the draft in the fall of 1862 but served only in the Texas Home Guards as a private, and yet he earned the title "Colonel" for reasons that are unknown. According to local histories, he provided the Confederate cause "very substantial aid of a kind it stood most in need of." When the age limits for the draft were expanded to forty-five in the fall of 1862, Rasche, Alley, and Ebb purchased substitutes, and Wash obtained an occupational exemption when, in the following year, he was sworn into Confederate military service as a "beef driver." By February of 1864 only Lum and Sam were liable to the draft, but they too avoided conscription. Among the Hearne and Lewis family members, only Sam's name is missing from the secondary source materials listing rosters of Confederate soldiers and members of the Texas Home Guards—a circumstance congruent with his disappearance from his family's genealogical record. Yet Sam is clearly listed on the original manuscript rosters of the Robertson County men in "Killough's Company" of Texas State Troops. Sam and his brothers and cousins, if they had so desired, could have easily procured exemptions from the Confederate draft laws under the notorious "twenty-nigger" exclusion, but there is no evidence that they did. Of the second generation of Hearnes and Lewises, only Ebb's sons, William and Lorenzo, served in the Confederate army.[18]

Sam's cousin Rasche earned his postwar title of "Captain" by accepting wartime command of one of the county's precincts, or "patrol beats." As a precaution against slave uprisings, the beats were patrolled by men appointed by the court of county commissioners—the forum responsible for county governance and consisting of all justices of the peace and the county judge. The commissioners' court also required that public supplies of gunpowder, lead, and gun caps be distributed equally throughout the

---

Johnson, Case No. 401, [Spring Term, 1864], Book "J [452–922]," p. 491, MDC, Robertson County, Texas; Hans Peter Nielson Gammel, comp., *The Laws of Texas, 1822–1897,* 10 vols. (Austin, Tex.: The Gammel Book Company, 1898), 5: 484.

18. Norman L. McCarver and Norman L. McCarver Jr., *Hearne on the Brazos* (San Antonio: Century Press of Texas, 1958), p. 118 (first and second quotations); *Texas Confederate Military Service Records,* [microform], compiled from muster rolls in the Texas State Archives, 1999, Microfilm Reels #4, #7, and #8, TSL-AD; Janet B. Hewett, ed., *The Roster of Confederate Soldiers, 1861–1865* (Wilmington, N.C.: Broadfoot Publishing Co., 1995), 7: 396; "Muster Roll of State Troops of Beat No. 2, 3, & 6 of Robertson County, Tex. for July 1863" (third quotation), box 3S167, and "A List of names liable to the Draft Beats No. 2, 3, & 6," [undated], box 2J98, Josephus Cavitt Papers, CAH-UT, Austin, Texas.

county's beats and that captains serve as trustees for indigent families whose breadwinners were away from their homes in military service. In January 1862 state law required local slave patrols to visit at least once a week "anywhere that Negroes might unlawfully assemble." Such additional policing responsibilities became more difficult when thousands of "refugeed" (a variant of the word "refuge" coined by contemporaries of the period) slaves arrived in Robertson County.[19]

Slaves transported by their masters during the war into Texas for protection from advancing Union forces enlarged the so-called black belts of the Brazos River bottomlands from Waco to Navasota—or from McClellan County to Grimes County, with Falls, Robertson, and Brazos Counties located in between. Although the exact number of slaves brought into the central Brazos River Valley region for safekeeping cannot be determined, between 1860 and 1864 the number of bondsmen rendered in Robertson County for taxation more than doubled, and in adjacent Brazos County it nearly tripled. One eyewitness's remembrances many decades later overestimated the number of refugeed slaves at the beginning of 1865 on just the "Sam Hearne place" at more than seven hundred.[20]

The presence of hundreds of refugeed slaves accounted for a few otherwise perplexing statements made by Hattie (Hearne) Cole about her life under slavery on Ebb Hearne's plantation. Born in 1854 and interviewed in her old age, Hattie described herself as a "non-knowledge nigger" due to having been born "in slavetime." She recollected that in "de qua'tahs" on Ebb's plantation lived over "200 cullud fo'ks"—a conjecture equal to more than three times the number of slaves claimed by Ebb on tax rolls during the war years. Presumably, Ebb either rented land to refugee masters or hired refugeed slaves. Because the plantation bottomlands of the extended Hearne family were congregated close together, it is not surprising that Hattie incorrectly believed that Ebb "owned all de land far back to the Brazos River . . . as far as you could see."[21]

19. Lawrence Ward St. Clair, "History of Robertson County, Texas" (M.A thesis, University of Texas, 1931), pp. 127–28; [February 1856 to August 1863], May 20, 1863, CCM, pp. 381–84, and *Orders of the County Court of Robertson County,* [1863–1871], [January Term, 1865], p. 53nn., CCM-PM, Robertson County, Texas; Gammel, comp., *The Laws of Texas, 1822–1897,* 5: 498 (quotation).

20. Campbell, *An Empire for Slavery,* pp. 243–46; Robertson County Tax Rolls, 1838–1882, Tax Rolls for 1860 and 1864, Microfilm Reel #1198–01, TSL-AD; Recollection of W. A. Adair in "Early Days in Brazos Bottom" in the Bryan *Daily Eagle,* March 29, 1926, p. 4 (quotation); and Baum, *The Shattering of Texas Unionism,* appendix, note "a" on p. 244.

21. Statements of Hattie (Hearne) Cole in Rawick, ed., *The American Slave,* supp., ser. 2,

During Hattie's remembrances of slavery, recounted during the Great Depression of the 1930s, she waxed nostalgic when discussing food rations provided on Ebb's plantation: "Most ob de cullud fo'ks am happy 'cause deys am fed good." Every Sunday morning at nine o'clock "cullud couples" lined up first at the smoke house and then at the shed containing brown sugar and honey. Cornmeal, bacon, and lard were plentiful, and every day of the week an elderly slave distributed milk, butter, and sometimes eggs, to the heads of households. Ebb apparently allowed his slaves all the food they wanted, but he worked all of them according to a set of rigid rules that most likely reflected routines observed on the plantations of his relatives.[22]

A bell rang in the mornings and slaves poured out of their cabins. Overseers shouted out orders, and "ever'thing" was in a "hustle." Slaves went to their assigned places to begin work: most started walking down to the fields; others set out to milk cows and tend farm animals; and others entered into nearby structures, including weaving, tanning, barber, and laundry rooms and blacksmith, shoe, and carpenter shops. Ebb required his slaves to work steadily but never to "over rush" through their assigned tasks. If slaves became ill, they merely had to inform Ebb or an overseer to get permission to lie down in their cabins. Ebb hired doctors to administer to sick slaves whose miseries could not be cured by traditional herbal remedies, such as spice and pepper teas. Hattie believed that the Hearnes were sensible about caring for the general physical health of their slaves, but her recollections and other available evidence suggest that life under slavery on the Hearne family plantations was psychologically dreadful.[23]

When asked about entertainment or merrymaking on Ebb's plantation, Hattie responded: "No Sar! Thar am no parties on Marster's plantation," and she recalled Ebb's words to the effect that it "'taint fo' parties he have de plantation, but 'tis fo' wo'k." The only time anyone had "any fun" was on Christmas Day, when everyone had "cake an' pie" to eat. Otherwise, she asserted: "Ise don't know what parties an' dancin' am 'till aftah surrendah." More than any other facet of the behavior of Ebb's bondsmen, control over their every movement was the main goal of his rules and regu-

vol. 3: "Texas Narratives," pt. 2, p. 776 (quotations); and Robertson County Tax Rolls, 1838–1882, Tax Rolls for 1861, 1862, 1863, and 1864, Microfilm Reel #1198–01, TSL-AD.

22. Statements of Hattie (Hearne) Cole, in Rawick, ed., *The American Slave,* supp., ser. 2, vol. 3: "Texas Narratives," pt. 2, pp. 776–77 (quotations).

23. Ibid., pp. 777–78 (quotations).

lations. Ebb was "pa'ticular 'bout de young fo'ks gwine off de place." Not surprisingly, such confinement was often tested: "'Cause de Marster am so tight 'bout lettin' de cullud fo'ks go off to 'joy dem se'ves once on awhile, de young fo'ks breaks de rule." Upon returning before dawn, they could "sneak in, but aftah daylight, someone can see dem" and punishment in the form of a whipping was certain, including its precise manner of implementation: "Dey jus' puts dey face down on de ground, den dey am lashed wid a rawhide. De Marster don't 'lows fo' to draw blood. Co'se thar am wales on thar body."[24]

Hattie's description summons up the story of Matthew Gaines, a self-taught slave preacher on Lum Hearne's plantation. Lum repeatedly whipped Gaines for his penchant to slip away to preach to slaves on neighboring plantations. When Gaines later became an "outstanding leader" in the Republican-dominated Twelfth Texas Legislature, he was uncommonly quiet about the particulars of his life during slavery, but the few words that he did speak revealed his resentment toward Lum: "I can remember when old master gave me 500 lashes and said he only raised the ashes on me, and next time he would reach the clean dirt." Gaines ran away in 1863 to West Texas, and, although eventually caught, he avoided being returned to Robertson County.[25]

The rules on the antebellum Hearne family plantations had been most likely similar, if not completely uniform. But the recollections of W. A. Adair, who lived as a youngster on Sam's plantation for three years during the war, reveal that by 1864 a serious rift had developed between Sam and his relatives. Adair's stepfather John T. Mills, who had unsuccessfully run in 1849 for the Texas governorship, moved his family away from its home in East Texas near the Louisiana border soon after the war's outbreak. Over fifty slaves to be protected from liberation by federal troops came with the Mills family. Adair's description of slave managers and slave musicians provide a rare glimpse into an extraordinary breakdown of slave discipline on Sam's plantation during the last days of slavery.[26]

The Mills family in 1864 was either renting all or a large section of

24. Ibid., p. 779 (quotations); and Winthrop D. Jordan, *White Over Black: American Attitudes Toward the Negro, 1550–1812* (Chapel Hill: University of North Carolina Press, 1968), pp. 55–56.

25. Merline Pitre, *Through Many Dangers, Toils, and Snares: The Black Leadership of Texas, 1868–1900* (Austin, Tex.: Eakin Press, 1985), p. 157 (first quotation); Matthew Gaines quoted in the Brenham *Banner,* August 15, 1871; and "Gaines, Matthew," *TNHT,* 3: 43.

26. Adair, "Early Days in Brazos Bottom," p. 4; "Mills, John T.," *TNHT,* 4: 750; and Robertson County Tax Rolls, 1838–1882, Tax Rolls for 1864, Microfilm Reel #1198–01, TSL-AD.

Sam's plantation and had agreed to pay its county and state taxes. When Judge Mills returned to the Confederate army, he left in charge Garret King, one of the county's appointed slave patrollers. A disagreement soon arose between King and Mrs. Mills over management of the bondsmen. After talking with the older slaves, she informed King that his services were no longer needed and appointed dependable slaves to assist her in looking out for the family's well-being. Subsequently, "a trusted [N]egro slept on the front gallery of [the Mills family's] house every night." As the landowner, Sam had to uphold Mrs. Mills's decision, which was a violation of wartime measures criminalizing actions by slaveholders who permitted any slave to pretend to be in charge of other slaves. There is no reason to believe that slave managers or "nigger overseers," as one former Robertson County slave called them, were in charge of any parts of the extended family's lands or slaves other than on Sam's plantation.[27]

Life on Sam and Azeline's plantation became considerably more exciting after the Worthington family from South Carolina arrived in late 1864. The Worthingtons brought with them hundreds of slaves, including a slave band with sixteen brass instruments accompanied by a drum and a few other creatively self-made musical devices. The slave musicians played before white and black audiences every evening, but neither Sam's relatives nor their slaves were among those who enjoyed these nightly festivities. Such revelry would have been at odds with the stern routines recalled by Hattie Cole. Yet slaveholding neighbors joining Sam and Azeline in attendance included the Moss, Dial, and Westbrook families, along with newcomers to the Brazos Bottoms, the Laudermilks and Wilsons. If Azeline's long-standing friendships, dating from the years in Louisiana, with Sam's relatives' slaves were now severed, she at least had opportunities to mingle with the new refugeed slaves and those owned by the Moss, Dial, and Westbrook families.[28]

During the last years of the war, there were other corroborating signs that Sam had parted ways with his relatives. In 1864 he reported ownership to the county tax assessor of a mere eleven slaves—ten fewer than he

27. Adair, "Early Days in Brazos Bottom," p. 4 (first quotation); Robertson County Tax Rolls, 1838–1882, Tax Rolls for 1864, Microfilm Reel #1198–01, TSL-AD; Commissioners Court Minutes [February 1856 to August 1863; February Term, 1861], pp. 302–3, CCM, Robertson County, Texas; and Gammel, comp., *The Laws of Texas, 1822–1897,* 5: 484, 601–3, 608–10, and 762–63; and Statements of Henry Freeman in Rawick, ed., *The American Slave,* supp., ser. 2, vol. 4: "Texas Narratives," pt. 3, p. 1434 (second quotation).

28. Adair, "Early Days in Brazos Bottom," p. 4.

had claimed in 1862. Sam's slave property, in sharp contrast to his brothers' and cousins', had shrunk to less than half of what it had been during the late antebellum period. After the fall of Vicksburg had cut off Texas from the rest of the Confederacy, Sam pondered the consequences of what he and many others believed would be an impending southern defeat. During this period he angered his relatives by drafting a last will and testament recognizing his paternity of Dock and his relationship with Azeline. At the same time, Sam's friendship with a small farmer and horse trader named John S. Deveraux devolved into a serious disagreement.[29]

Sometime during the war Deveraux and Sam had entered into an oral contract, whereby Deveraux apparently lent Sam a horse in exchange for the right to farm a section of Sam's land. But their involvement with one another exceeded their interest in horse trading, breeding, or racing. Both had fathered children with enslaved women. And, as later developments would establish, both were on the verge of writing wills benefiting their illicit offspring along with their mothers. How to lawfully accomplish such goals, however, proved complex. Deveraux was the first to try. Since 1859 he had been cohabitating with his former slave Mary Catharine ("Cate") Dial. In the spring of 1864, he wrote a will stating that he wanted his property at his death to be used to procure "the freedom of a certain [N]egro woman named Cate aged about twenty years" and her children. When Deveraux proclaimed his desire to emancipate "any other child or children that Said woman Cate now a Slave may have by me," he admitted not only paternity of her children but confessed his continuation of fornication, miscegenation, and interracial cohabitation. Nor were these declarations the end of Deveraux's self-incriminating statements.[30]

Cate and her children were not the personal property of Deveraux at the time he wrote his will. They belonged to Dr. William H. Dial, one of the frequenters to the nightly festivities on Sam's plantation, who owned the farm upon which Deveraux was cohabitating with Cate. Under the terms of his will, Deveraux appointed an executor as his agent and trustee

29. Robertson County Tax Rolls, 1838–1882, Tax Rolls for 1858, 1862, and 1864, Microfilm Reel #1198–01, TSL-AD; and Joshua L. Randall to Joel T. Kirkman, June 8, 1867, account pp. 36–37, "Subassistant Commissioner Records filed under 'Sterling, Tex.,'" BRFAL, [unmicrofilmed], RG 105, NA.

30. Joshua L. Randall to Joel T. Kirkman, June 8, 1867, account pp. 36–37, and William H. Farner to Charles Griffin, July 9, 1867, "Subassistant Commissioner Records filed under 'Sterling, Texas,'" BRFAL, [unmicrofilmed], RG 105, NA; and "Will of John S. Deveraux," dated May 28, 1864, and filed on January 3, 1868 (quotations), "In the Matter of the Estate of John S. Deveraux," Docket #50, PF, CCO, Robertson County, Texas.

to act for Cate and "to use all proper diligence to procure the freedom" of Cate and her children. He wrote in his will a caveat that if the "limits of the law" would not allow the accomplishment of his goal, then he wanted his executor to take Cate and her children out of the state to some "suitable place" where they would be free—a course of action that was clearly illegal under Texas law, although at this time freedom or slavery for Cate and her children was caught up in all the uncertainties of Lincoln's Emancipation Proclamation. Deveraux's will, signed and witnessed in May 1864, was not filed for probate until the first days of 1868, or a full six months after he was shot and killed by John R. Harlan, a prominent Robertson County resident. By then the issue of procuring the emancipation of his children and their birth-mother was beside the point, but whether they would benefit financially from his estate proved another matter altogether.[31]

By the fall of 1864, Deveraux and Sam had a falling out. Sam apparently did not return Deveraux's horse, prompting a Robertson County grand jury to hand down a criminal indictment against Sam for "horse stealing." For over two years the district court repeatedly ordered Sam to appear as a defendant in the case, in which conviction carried a normal punishment of five years in the state penitentiary. Why the many writs issued for Sam's arrest proved completely ineffectual remains a mystery. The case against him was routinely continued and dropped from the docket only after his death in the fall of 1866. Local authorities made no effort to prosecute him. Were they merely content to have humiliated him on the testimony of a fellow miscegenationist for whom they also had little or no respect? Perhaps so, because when the winter of 1864–65 approached, they had, like most Confederate Texans, far more on their minds.[32]

After the fall of Atlanta in 1864, only the most stalwart of heart in

31. "Will of John S. Deveraux," dated May 28, 1864, and filed on January 3, 1868 (quotations), "In the Matter of the Estate of John S. Deveraux," Docket #50, PF, CCO, Robertson County, Texas; Gammel, comp., *The Laws of Texas, 1822–1897,* 5: 22–23; William H. Farner to Charles Griffin, July 9, 1867, "Subassistant Commissioner Records filed under 'Sterling, Texas,'" BRFAL, [unmicrofilmed], RG 105, NA; and *The State of Texas vs. John R. Harlan,* Case No. 494, [Fall Term 1868], Book "J [452–922]," pp. 754–55, MDC, Robertson County, Texas.

32. *The State of Texas vs. Samuel R. Hearne,* Case No. 443, [Fall Term, 1864], Book "J [452–922]," pp. 507 and 540, and [Spring Term, 1867], Book "J [452–922]," p. 575, MDC, Robertson County, Texas. On the penalty for a conviction for "horse stealing," see: *The State of Texas vs. James G. Halloway,* Case No. 521, and *The State of Texas vs. Hiram Nixon,* Case No. 470, Book "J [452–922]," pp. 521 and 608, MDC, Robertson County, Texas.

Robertson County sustained any hope for the Confederate cause. News of the South's inevitable "surrender," the most dreaded word in the vocabulary of ardent Confederates, was just a matter of time. Yet Texans did not feel defeated. Their state had avoided being a major arena of military operations; its economy, in contrast to other southern states, had not been as disrupted by the war; and the refugeed slaves had helped to increase the amount of land under cultivation for growing cotton. Proximity to Mexico had allowed planters, including Sam and his relatives, to market their cotton throughout the war years via San Antonio to Matamoros, where ships could come and go without fear of the Union blockade. Not even the ominous decline of the South's military fortunes by spring of 1865 could obliterate all confidence in the institution of slavery. Not, that is, until occupation of the state by U.S. soldiers, who finally arrived in Galveston on June 19, 1865—a date forever celebrated as "Juneteenth" by former Texas slaves—when the buying, selling, and hiring of slaves legally ended.[33]

Postwar Lawlessness and Violence

Robertson County's ex-Confederates and officeholders worried about how their economy would function without a coerced system of dependable labor at harvest time, to say nothing of their fear of widespread disorder produced by the absence of slave codes restricting black behavior. Yet the lawlessness that plagued the county at the immediate end of the war began with the return of disbanded Confederate soldiers traveling home on the roads to San Antonio or Waco. At the crossroads in Wheelock, they helped themselves, as one resident recalled, to whatever they wanted, "such as groceries, meat, hogs, or chickens or cattle." Gangs of thieves soon harassed anyone traveling the roads. On five separate occasions highwaymen robbed a stagecoach arriving from Houston. Nobody was prepared for such "a lawless state without purpose or direction." A decade later a county officeholder recalled "the days of 1865 and 1866" as constituting "a sort of dog-eat-dog life" when everyone had "to carry six shooters."[34]

33. Robert Delaney, "Matamoros, Port for Texas during the Civil War," *Southwestern Historical Quarterly* 58 (April 1955): 473–87; Ernest Wallace, *Texas in Turmoil, 1849–1875* (Austin, Tex.: Steck-Vaughn Co.,1965), pp. 125–27, 301; and Ralph A. Wooster, *Texas and Texans in the Civil War* (Austin, Tex.: Eakin Press, 1995), pp. 106–7.

34. Interview with Mrs. Phoebe Arnett [interviewed by Miss Effie Cowan], in *American Life Histories: Manuscripts from the Federal Writers' Project, 1936–1940, http://memory.loc.gov/ammem/wpaintro/wpahome.html* (accessed July 6, 2008), File No. 240, p. 2 (first quo-

At some point in the summer of 1865, a contingent of federal soldiers stationed in the neighboring Brazos County town of Millican rode into the southern half of the Brazos Bottoms in Robertson County. The presence of the "bluecoats" in the midst of the finest cotton plantation lands in the state drove home to local residents the daunting realization that the Confederacy had lost the Civil War. The soldiers stopped methodically at each plantation and ordered the freedpeople to be assembled. Groups of former slaves dressed in gunnysacks faced mounted soldiers, one of whom moved to the forefront with a piece of paper from which he read loudly and clearly. Many of the slaves on Ebb's plantation did not immediately comprehend the words. Nor had Ebb considered it necessary to prepare his slaves for this moment. As his former slave Hattie Cole recalled, "Ise don't know what it am in de papah, but w'en de sojer am through readin,' him says, 'Yous am free, an' citizens ob de United States. Dat means yous can go whar yous lak.'"[35]

The soldier's words, or perhaps Hattie's recollections of them, were misleading, but not solely because the 1857 U.S. Supreme Court decision in the Dred Scott case, which barred black Africans from holding U.S. citizenship, was still the law of the land. Other forces were at work. As Hattie subsequently explained, "[D]e sojers am mistaken. . . . Weuns am not 'lowed to do as weuns please. Weuns am in'fered wid by de Ku Klux Klan, white caps weuns calls dem." Military authorities quickly found themselves powerless to protect the ex-slaves from violence or guarantee them basic justice and fair play. Under President Andrew Johnson's undemanding Reconstruction policies, the former secessionists and ex-Confederates were in the process of being restored to power without any federal commitment to prevent a restoration of slavery in all but name. Hattie's recollections, along with those of other Robertson County ex-slaves, contradict the enduring myth that organized white terrorist groups, such as the white brotherhoods, White Caps, or Ku Klux Klan–type organizations, "became active in 1867" only in retaliation against the commencement of Congressional Reconstruction.[36]

---

tation); Baker, *A History of Robertson County,* p. 160 (second quotation), and Thomas J. McHugh quoted in ibid., p. 518 (third, fourth, and fifth quotations).

35. Statements of Hattie (Hearne) Cole in Rawick, ed., *The American Slave,* supp., ser. 2, vol. 3: "Texas Narratives," pt. 2, p. 779 (quotations).

36. Ibid., p. 779 (first quotation); Winship Allen quoted in Baker, *A History of Robertson County,* p. 467 (second quotation); and statements of Louis Young in Rawick, ed., *The Ameri-*

In the Brazos bottomlands an appalling degree of brutality against the ex-slaves occurred in 1865 and 1866. It began, in one instance, right after the first appearance of the same contingent of federal troops that had visited the Hearne and Lewis plantations. Ex-slave Ella Washington recalled digging up potatoes when the Union troops arrived on the plantation of her master, Conway Oldham Barton. After the soldiers summoned Ella out of the field and read aloud the June 19th proclamation, Barton told her and his other former slaves that they could stay on his land for a few days until they made up their minds where to go. Immediately, in Ella's words, "somethin' funny happen dare." When the newly freed slaves drank water out of the plantation well, they got cramps and by nighttime they started to die: "They dies like flies, so fast dey couldn't make de coffins for dem." Survivors claimed that Barton had poisoned the well. With his world turned upside down, Barton, who in the words of his contemporaries had "difficulty adjusting to Reconstruction," died within three years, amidst plans to migrate to Mexico.[37]

For the ex-slaves who immediately tested their new freedom by leaving their plantations and often walking into towns occupied by federal troops, the situation could be similarly appalling. As a young former slave, Annie Day remembered a story repeatedly told to her about the fate of those who flocked into Millican, then the northern terminus of the Houston and Texas Central (H&TC) Railroad. In her words, "Dey wuz awful hungry and de storekeepers dere give 'em barrels of apples to eat and de apples had been poisoned, ad dey killed a lot of de colored people." Such alleged evil acts, described by witnesses before the Congressional Joint Committee on Reconstruction or filed in reports by Freedmen's Bureau agents, went unpunished, along with hundreds of reported atrocities like it throughout East Texas. On this dark side of the spectrum of white behavior, there often existed a desire to destroy what one could no longer control. In late

---

can Slave, vol. 5, pt. 4, pp. 232–34. There is no practical way to distinguish between the Ku Klux Klan established in the wake of the First Reconstruction Act and its earlier imitators. See Barry A. Crouch, "A Spirit of Lawlessness: White Violence, Texas Blacks, 1865–1868," *Journal of Social History* 18 (Winter 1984): 217–32.

37. Statement of Ella Washington in Rawick, ed., *The American Slave,* vol. 5, pt. 4, p. 133 (first and second quotations); Joshua L. Randall to J. P. Richardson, December 24, 1867, Microfilm Reel #14, BRFAL, RG 105, M821, NA (1973); and Richard Denney Parker, *Historical Recollections of Robertson County, Texas, with Biographical & Genealogical Notes on the Pioneers & Their Families* (Salado, Tex.: Anson Jones Press, 1955), pp. 128–29 (third quotation).

1865, in areas where the army or the Freedmen's Bureau proved unable to establish order beyond the limits of the county seats, one bureau official claimed that "blacks are frequently beaten unmercifully, and shot down like wild beasts, without any provocation, followed by hounds, and maltreated in every way."[38]

The general sentiment among the large majority of Texas whites was that, in the immediate wake of their emancipation, the ex-slaves constituted a permanent and subordinate class of paid, albeit coerced and thus dependable, laborers who possessed "no rights which the white man was bound to respect"—a notion that in 1865 was, at least in theory, in harmony with the laws of the United States. Few disagreed with the well-regarded Austin *Weekly State Gazette* when it pronounced that the freedmen were "an inferior and degraded race, upon whom has long rested and still rests the curse of Heaven."[39]

Presidential Reconstruction and the Arrival of the Freedmen's Bureau

Against a backdrop of violence against blacks, which reached staggering proportions in the immediate postwar period, Sam Hearne's calculations on how best to navigate the new and uncertain times must have preoccupied him and dominated many of his conversations with Azeline. At the time of her emancipation, Azeline was forty years old. Although slavery was abolished, the antebellum Texas criminal law against miscegenation was incontrovertibly in force. Any last wills and testaments that Sam might have drawn up before emancipation he now destroyed, but his intention remained as strong as ever to provide for Azeline and their son Dock in case of his death.[40]

By the summer of 1865 Robertson County had a full component of newly appointed officeholders selected by provisional governor Andrew J. Hamilton. Because Hamilton wanted to reconstruct the coalition of voters

38. Statements of Annie Day in Rawick, ed., *The American Slave,* supp., ser. 2, vol. 4: "Texas Narratives," pt. 3, p. 1160 (first quotation); and Inspector General William E. Strong quoted in Gregg Cantrell, "Racial Violence and Reconstruction Politics in Texas, 1867–1868," *Southwestern Historical Quarterly* 93, no. 3 (1990): 333–34 (second quotation).

39. *Dred Scott, Plaintiff in Error, vs. John F. A. Sandford* quoted in "Dred Scott Case: The Supreme Court Decision" (first quotation), www.pbs.org/wgbh/aia/part4/4h2933.html (accessed June 10, 2003); and *Weekly State Gazette* (Austin), June 9, 1866 (second quotation).

40. Joshua L. Randall to Joel T. Kirkman, June 8, 1867, "Subassistant Commissioner Records filed under 'Sterling, Texas,'" Letters Sent: Entry #3769, account pp. 36–37, BFRAL, [unmicrofilmed], RG 105, NA.

who had opposed the "Southern Rights" Democrats on the eve of Texas secession, he took seriously who should be allowed to participate in elections to choose delegates to a state constitutional convention that, in turn, would organize an acceptable state government. In the case of Robertson County, he restored to power, with one exception, the same set of men who had been in office at the time of the surrender. The fact that most of them were old antebellum pro-Houston men meant little to the outspoken and persecuted unionist Telephus Johnson. He soon was complaining that the "same set of sycophants" was still after him. In terms of opening up the way to the labyrinth of freedom for the county's former slaves, including Azeline and Dock, the importance of the provisional county government was eclipsed by the Freedmen's Bureau.[41]

Established by the Union army during the war to assist both white and black refugees, its full name was the Bureau of Refugees, Freedmen, and Abandoned Lands. At the end of the war, it faced the unprecedented task of supervising the transition of millions of ex-slaves from the cruel work patterns of slave days to a system of wage labor determined by fair and reasonable contractual agreements. Although understaffed, the Freedmen's Bureau was, nevertheless, committed to the independence of the freedmen "in a way that the former masters and most white southerners were not." Continuously hampered by white resentment and hostility, the bureau accomplished no more than what was at all possible, and thus the degree of equitable treatment experienced by the freedpeople invariably fell short in many instances from their expectations and hopes. In few places in the ex-Confederate states did the Freedmen's Bureau get off to a more dismal start than in Robertson County.[42]

Sam's name was missing from a list of Robertson County planters, including Rasche, Ebb, and Lum Hearne and Charles Lewis, who solicited military authorities to appoint wounded Confederate war veteran John C. Roberts as the first bureau agent for their county. A teetotaling former Know-Nothing who had once worked as a bookkeeper for one

41. Carl H. Moneyhon, *Texas after the Civil War: The Struggle of Reconstruction* (College Station: Texas A&M University Press, 2004), p. 30; Harvey Mitchell to Andrew J. Hamilton, August 21, 1865 (quotation), box 49, Governors' Papers: Hamilton, RG 301, TSL-AD; and "Appointment to Office Under Provisional Government," September 1865–July 1866, and "Robertson County Officeholders," in *Registers of Elected and Appointed State and County Officials,* Microfilm Reel #4, pp. 74–75, 143–46, and Microfilm Reel #3, pp. 667–70, TSL-AD, Austin, Texas.

42. Herman Beltz quoted in Barry A. Crouch, *The Freedmen's Bureau and Black Texans* (Austin: University of Texas Press, 1992), p. 131 (quotation).

of the Hearne and Lewis merchandising stores, Roberts was passed over by headquarters in the late months of 1865 for another Confederate war veteran, Dr. William H. Farner. As the first bureau agent for the Brazos River counties clustered near the railroad terminus of Millican, Dr. Farner proved to be enthusiastic about his unpaid job, but he left a host of problems in his wake for others to clean up. In May of 1866 military authorities issued orders for his arrest for mistreating the freedmen.[43]

The Kentucky-born Farner, who claimed to have attended both medical and law schools in Philadelphia, lived in Iowa on the eve of the war with his wife and eight children. His antebellum career had spanned work as a physician, druggist, newspaper editor, civic leader, noted lecturer, and a U.S. Army surgeon. After the outbreak of the war, he became a surgeon in a Confederate regiment. Federal troops captured him around the time of their brief occupation of Galveston during the last months of 1862. After being paroled he worked in a military hospital in the Shreveport area. Sometime in 1863 he refugeed twenty Louisiana slaves, whom he valued for tax purposes at $14,000, for safekeeping to Brazos County. Visiting Galveston in late 1865, Farner ingratiated himself with Brevet Brigadier General Edgar M. Gregory, Texas's first assistant commissioner of the Freedmen's Bureau, who, although sympathetic to the plight of the ex-slaves, was easily impressed by loyal Texas citizens or northern men "who talked a good line." After filling Gregory's ears with considerable nonsense and half-truths, Farner asked to be appointed as a bureau agent.[44]

Farner claimed to have canvassed Iowa in 1856 for his old "schoolfellow" John C. Frémont—an action that had given Farner, in his words, "a power and influence among the masses that revolutionized the state." He also boasted that he published in Des Moines the first Republican Party

43. Petition from Robertson County citizens to Edgar M. Gregory, undated [1865], Microfilm Reel #18, BRFAL, RG 105, M821, NA (1973); Baker, *A History of Robertson County,* pp. 394–95; William H. Sinclair to Captain Byron Porter, May 30, 1866, Records of the Assistant Commissioner for the State of Texas, Microfilm Reel #1, vol. 1, p. 235, BRFAL, RG 105, NA; and William L. Richter, *Overreached on All Sides: The Freedmen's Bureau Administrators in Texas, 1865–1868* (College Station: Texas A&M University Press, 1991), p.137.

44. William H. Farner to Joshua L. Randall, August 14, 1867, box 56, folder 6, Governors' Papers: Pease, RG 301, TSL-AD; Libbie Nolan, "The Great Civil War: Opposite Sides," *Landmark* [The Waukesha County (Wisconsin) Historical Society] 26 (Spring 1983): 24; Leona Postell, "Father and Son, Confederate and Federal Soldiers," *Landmark* 13 (Summer 1970): 4; "W. H. Foriner [*sic*] by E. C. Knox (Agent)," 1864 Taxable Year, p. 73, in Ruth J. Hary and Janis J. Hunt, comp., *Abstract Book 1863–1866 Brazos County Tax Assessor-Collector, Brazos County, Texas,* [typescript: undated], The Carnegie Center of Brazos Valley History, Bryan, Texas; and Richter, *Overreached on All Sides,* pp. 51–52, and p. 289 (quotation).

newspaper ever printed in Iowa *at the same time* that he was the chairman of the Democratic State Executive Committee! Only his involvement for six months in 1857 with the relatively unimportant pro-Republican *Iowa Citizen,* followed by his temporary editorship of a pro-Democratic newspaper in Council Bluffs, can be readily documented. Putting aside Farner's convoluted political allegiances and immodest statements, his actions as a Freedmen's Bureau agent were more consistent with being a northern Confederate sympathizer and an eleventh-hour slaveowner than with ever having been, in his words, an "out-and-out" prewar Iowa Free Soiler and Republican.[45]

Local authorities and prominent planters in Robertson County claimed that the freedmen worked well in the remainder of 1865 and during 1866, although doing only about two-thirds of the work that they had been forced to perform while enslaved. Some worked for wages ranging from eight to ten dollars a month, depending on the terms of their contracts, while others worked for a third of the crop. Because the freedmen highly valued their right at the beginning of each year to move about to negotiate new contracts, planters with good reputations as employers held an advantage in the hiring process. But many planters disliked the contractual system and complained about other planters tampering with or enticing away "their freedmen." Anxious to recapture the world market for cotton, planters in postwar Texas often viewed bureau agents as labor brokers who, for a fee, would prevent annoyances inherent in a free labor market. In Robertson County far too many freedmen, whether working for wages or shares, labored with only the mere hope that they might be fairly treated or even paid. When a few freedmen left their places of employment after their employers took unwarranted disciplinary actions against them, Dr. Farner was not among their advocates or defenders.[46]

45. William H. Farner to Charles Griffin, July 9, 1867 (first and second quotations), "Subassistant Commissioner Records filed under 'Sterling, Texas,'" BFRAL, [unmicrofilmed], RG 105, NA; William H. Farner to Joshua L. Randall, August 14, 1867 (third quotation), box 56, folder 6, Governors' Papers: Pease, RG 301, TSL-AD; Nolan, "The Great Civil War: Opposite Sides," p. 24; Galveston *Daily News,* August 8, 1869, p. 8; *Iowa State Daily Register,* May 2, 1866, p. 1; and Katherine Young Macy, "Notes on the History of Iowa Newspapers, 1836–1870," *University of Iowa Extension Bulletin,* July 1, 1927, Bulletin No. 175, pp. 85–89. Farner should not be confused with his son, William H. Farner Jr., who was appointed in 1869 by military authorities as the clerk of the district court in Freestone County. Cf.: Richter, *Overreached on All Sides,* p. 323, n. 50.

46. William H. Wheelock's description of Robertson County in the *Texas Almanac for 1867* (Galveston, Tex.: Richardson & Co., 1867), p. 150; Richter, *Overreached on All Sides,* p. 52; and Joseph B. Kiddoo to Champe Carter Jr., June 2, 1866 (quotation), Mircofilm Reel #4, BRFAL, RG 105, M821, NA (1973).

Farner was too sympathetic to the planters and often too quick to administer cruel physical punishment to the ex-slaves. Complaints of his neglecting his duties toward the freedmen, punishing them by stringing them up by their thumbs, appointing additional bureau agents without authorization, and his alleged addiction to whiskey triggered his removal from duty. The next bureau agent to have a disheartening impact on the morale of the freedmen was a local Robertson County merchant and wounded Confederate veteran named Champe Carter Jr. Although he had been one of the agents illegally appointed by Farner, Carter obtained his appointment through his connections with the managers of Ranger & Company, a Galveston firm that operated several plantations near the town of Sterling, located on the edge of the county's northern Brazos bottomlands.[47]

In the spring and summer of 1866, Carter, as the Freedmen's Bureau agent stationed in Sterling, followed in the footsteps of the discredited Farner. Carter even lamented the decree from headquarters prohibiting stringing up the freedmen "in military style" by their thumbs. Such discipline, according to Carter, had resulted in "a fine, *very fine,* influence in this section." Carter soon faced accusations of charging planters for his services. He also exasperated headquarters by his constant inquiries into when he would obtain a salary, be reimbursed for office supplies, be able to hire assistants with powers similar to "a sheriff," and have troops stationed at Sterling to assist him in coercing the freedmen to uphold their contracts. Carter also wanted answers to a myriad of questions about the freedmen, such as how to start schools, take care of the indigent, and punish them for crimes against their own race. This last situation, he claimed, comprised the majority of cases brought before him.[48]

Carter informed headquarters that "confusion strife and *disaster*" would result if the freedmen disregarded their contractual obligations during harvest time, when their labor was in great demand. Only "physical punishment—or the fear of it," he proclaimed, would resonate enough within their "fickle nature" to make them respect the rights of their employers. In general, Carter found the freedmen in Texas "far below . . . in

47. Charles E. Morse to William H. Farner, January 22, 1866, Microfilm Reel #1, and Charles Harrison to William H. Sinclair, May 3, 1866, Microfilm Reel #6, and Charles E. Morse to Champe Carter Jr., January 25, 1866, Microfilm Reel #29, and Citizens of Sterling, Texas, to Edgar M. Gregory, February 12, 1866, Microfilm Reel #29, and "Report of Changes among Officers and Agents . . ." [signed by Edgar M. Gregory], March 31, 1866, Microfilm Reel #29, BRFAL, RG 105, M821, NA (1973).

48. Richter, *Overreached on All Sides,* p. 65 (first and third quotations); and Champe Carter Jr., to William H. Sinclair, June 2, 1866 (second quotation), "Subassistant Commissioner Records filed under 'Sterling, Texas,'" BRFAL, [unmicrofilmed], RG 105, NA.

intelligence & moral feeling" the ones he recalled in his home state of Kentucky. As he explained to headquarters, unless one had been "thrown in personal contact with them," as he had been in his capacity as a bureau agent, one could "form no idea how stupid, ignorant & deprave[d] *some* of them are."[49]

By the end of August, military authorities had relieved Carter of his duties, ostensibly because of his inability, due to his Confederate army service, to take the oath required for continuance as a bureau agent. Yet among themselves they used the example of his tenure, as well as that of Dr. Farner, to argue that only regular army officers, rather than civilians, could be trusted with the interests of the freedmen. Although Farner and Carter had favored the planters to the injury of the freedmen in the matter of labor and contracts, any fair evaluation of their tenures as bureau agents must be placed in the larger political context of the immediate postwar period. From the outset of emancipation, white "Secret Committees," or "brotherhoods," had threatened and beaten blacks who either signed or considered signing labor contracts—symbols of their newly acquired freedom believed wrongly bestowed upon them by Yankee troops. More importantly, Farner and Carter, as agents of the unloved federal government, fell under intense criticism from the new Texas regime brought into power by Presidential Reconstruction. Because of Democratic Party vilification directed at Robertson County's Republican officeholders, Carter subsequently maintained supportive ties with them in the early 1870s, and Farner was a fervent radical Republican before leaving the state in the mid-1870s. Both of them also had extensive interactions with Azeline and Dock and played roles in the Freedmen's Bureau administration of Sam Hearne's estate.[50]

In 1866 the overwhelming majority of white men in Robertson County approved of the work of the state constitutional convention, which had been dominated by ex-Confederates and a small group of conservative prewar unionists. By stating that military defeat determined its only options, the convention grudgingly accepted the repeal of the ordinance of

49. Champe Carter Jr., to Joseph B. Kiddoo, June 19, 1866 (first, third, fourth, and fifth quotations) and June 6, 1866 (second quotation), Microfilm Reel #4, BRFAL, RG 105, M821, NA (1973).

50. Champe Carter Jr., to Joseph B. Kiddoo, June 19, 1866, Microfilm Reel #4, and SO No. 105, HFMD: Galveston, August 29, 1866, Microfilm Reel #19, BRFAL, RG 105, M821, NA (1973); Baker, *A History of Robertson County,* p. 161 (first quotation); James M. Smallwood, "When the Klan Rode: White Terror in Reconstruction Texas," *Journal of the West* 25 (October 1986): 4 (second quotation); Galveston *Daily News,* November 18, 1867, p. 3; and San Antonio *Express,* August 10, 1869, p. 2.

secession, negation of the Confederate debt, and abolition of slavery but did not ratify the Thirteenth Amendment. The convention went no further than to protect blacks in their right to own property and allow them to enter into contracts, to sue and be sued, and testify in cases involving only themselves or other blacks. It excluded them altogether from politics, denying them the right to vote, hold office, and serve on juries. In addition, and ominously for the future, the convention empowered the state legislature to establish a coercive and oppressive labor system aimed at the freedmen. Convention president James W. Throckmorton, a prewar unionist and reluctant Confederate who sided with former secessionists against provisional governor Hamilton, privately summed up the convention's attitude toward President Johnson's Reconstruction requirements as having been opposed to any changes "except those required of a degraded and fallen people."[51]

In the following June election, the convention's proposed constitutional amendments were not partisan issues, but the simultaneous balloting to choose a governor, legislature, and county officials reflected political divisions that had first emerged at the convention. The small minority of discontented pro-Hamilton supporters, or "Union Republicans," was hopelessly pitted against the ex-Confederates, or "Secession Party" men, and "Conservative Unionists." After failing to get Hamilton to accept their nomination, the Union Republicans chose Elisha M. Pease, a former governor and steadfast unionist, who doomed his candidacy from the outset by endorsing a program of justice toward the ex-slaves. Pease's position on the issue of voting rights for blacks proved far too controversial: if Congress were to demand black suffrage, he would acquiesce on the condition that literacy tests qualified the new voters. Pease's opponent was Throckmorton, who ran at the head of the "Conservative Unionist," or Democratic, ticket. Throckmorton opposed extension of any civil or political rights to blacks and pledged to fight to rid Texas of the Freedmen's Bureau. Convinced that a vote for Pease was a vote in favor of congressional Republicans who "openly proclaimed social and political equality with the [N]egro," Texans voted statewide four to one for Thockmorton.[52]

51. Baum, *The Shattering of Texas Unionism*, pp. 131–32; and James W. Throckmorton quoted in Ben Procter and Archie P. McDonald, *The Texas Heritage* (St. Louis, Mo.: Forum Press, 1980), p. 97.

52. Baum, *The Shattering of Texas Unionism*, pp. 145–46 (quotations); Procter and McDonald, *The Texas Heritage*, p. 97; and James M. Smallwood, *Time of Hope, Time of Despair: Black Texans during Reconstruction* (Port Washington, N.Y.: Kennikat Press, 1981), pp. 130–31.

Robertson County favored Throckmorton over Pease by a lopsided vote of 493 to 8. A vote for Pease did not necessarily translate into a concern with guaranteeing basic justice to the ex-slaves. At least one or two of the county's Pease voters were pragmatic prewar or wartime officeholders who believed that Congress would be so infuriated by a Throckmorton victory that it would retaliate by singling out certain groups of ex-Confederates, *namely, themselves,* for political castigation, such as possible disfranchisement and prohibition from holding office. Their thinking paralleled the argument made by former postmaster of the Confederacy John H. Reagan who prophesied from his Massachusetts jail cell that a limited form of black suffrage (as had been endorsed by Pease) was the only way to avoid further undesirable changes, such as passage of a revolutionary Civil Rights Act guaranteeing citizenship and fundamental civil rights to the former slaves. Robertson County conservatives scorned Reagan's advice. Instead they placed their trust in President Johnson and Governor Throckmorton to protect them from "the hell hounds of radicalism," who embodied nothing less than "miscegenation filth seized from the [Charles] Sumner sewer."[53]

There is no evidence that Sam and his brothers or cousins bothered to vote in the June election. None of the Hearnes or Lewises, as owners of prewar taxable property valued at more than $20,000, filed for individual or special presidential pardons, which were, at least in theory, additional requirements for their being placed on the county's list of qualified voters. Sam's extended family clan grumbled about postwar labor shortage problems and spoke gloomily "more or less of going to Brazil." Other than charges brought in the fall of 1865 by federal treasury agents against Sam's younger brother Wash for unlawfully "concealing" seventy-three bales of cotton belonging to the former Confederate government, little is known about the activities of the Hearne and Lewis families until Sam's death in November of 1866.[54]

53. Manuscript Election Returns for 1866, Folder for Robertson County, Secretary of State Records, RG 307, TSL-AD; Baum, *The Shattering of Texas Unionism,* pp. 151–54; John H. Reagan, *Memoirs, with Special Reference to Secession and the Civil War,* ed. Walter Flavius McCaleb (New York: Neale Pub. Co., 1906), pp. 286–95; James W. Throckmorton to Benjamin H. Epperson, January 21, 1866, [copy] (first quotation), in "Throckmorton Papers and Letter Book," CAH-UT, Austin, Texas; and *Weekly State Gazette* (Austin), June 16, 1866 (second quotation).

54. Joshua L. Randall to Joel T. Kirkman, May 29, 1867 (first quotation), "Subassistant Commissioner Records filed under 'Sterling, Texas,'" BFRAL, [unmicrofilmed], RG 105, NA; *Records of the Adjutant General's Office, 1780's–1917,* Case Files of Applications from Former

In the larger framework of political affairs, most complaints former slaveholders lodged against federal policies during 1865 and 1866 were unwarranted. Texas was reconstructed with as few changes as possible. The same group of men, often the same antebellum officeholders, was restored to political power and leadership. The terms upon which the state was reconstructed had been remarkably undemanding. There were no treason trials, no significant disfranchisement or punishment of former secessionists or Confederates, and no major confiscation of property. Whites found themselves more united behind President Johnson than they had ever been on any issue since Texas statehood, including even secession in 1861. By way of comparison with other ex-Confederate states, Texas's landscape and infrastructure, as well as its antebellum social structure and landownership patterns, had been left virtually untouched by the war. The failure of radical Reconstruction was arguably all but guaranteed before it even began: a solid and enduring social and economic system based on the principle of white supremacy provided valuable resources for former rebels determined to tenaciously resist and eventually destroy the many radical changes that Texas Republicans subsequently tried to impose.[55]

At the time of Sam's prolonged illness in the fall of 1866, the exclusion of the freedpeople from all political affairs and their inability to play any role whatsoever in the governmental process of Presidential Reconstruction must have weighed heavily on his mind. The fate of Azeline and Dock could not be detached from the dominant reality that they were ex-slaves. For Texas blacks, what had been in 1865 a time of optimism had devolved, by 1866, into a time of anguish. They had no illusions of being accorded justice by the state and local administrations dominated by the newly elected Conservative Democrats. Governor Throckmorton believed that, unless coerced, the "nigs," whom he described as the "most inferior of God's creatures that wear the forms of men," would never work productively or take care of themselves in their new freedom. Following Throckmorton's recommendations, the Texas legislature, in repealing the antebellum slave codes, wrote a series of labor, vagrancy, and apprentice laws

Confederates for Presidential Pardons ("Amnesty Papers") 1865–1867, Group 1: Pardon Applications Submitted by Persons From the South, RG 94, M1003, NA (1977); and William H. Wheelock to Andrew J. Hamilton, September 29, 1865 (second quotation), folder 24, box 50, Governors' Papers: Hamilton, RG 301, TSL-AD.

55. Carl H. Moneyhon, *Texas after the Civil War: The Struggle of Reconstruction* (College Station: Texas A&M University Press, 2004), pp. 3–5 and 188–205.

designed to reenslave the freedmen. The detailed laws, collectively known as the "Black Codes" and cunningly worded in nondiscriminatory language to evade a challenge to their legality posed by the Civil Rights Act of 1866 and later the Fourteenth Amendment, were as severe as those passed earlier by any other ex-Confederate state. In addition, and undoubtedly known to Sam, the legislature reaffirmed the criminal prohibition on intermarriage between blacks and whites.[56]

Most Robertson County whites refused to acknowledge the changed status of the ex-slaves, and the more mean-spirited among them tried to counteract the presence of federal troops and Freedmen's Bureau agents, who tended to "excite" in the minds of the freedmen "ideas about the great blessings of being free." When white terrorists endorsed Throckmorton's demand to dismantle the Freedmen's Bureau and took it upon themselves to enforce the iniquitous Black Codes, which violated many terms in the standard labor contracts routinely approved by the bureau, they not only placed Farner and Carter squarely on the defensive but made plantation areas of East Texas extremely dangerous places for all bureau agents. Consequently, at one time or another both Farner and Carter welcomed the support of Benjamin ("Ben") Brown, an Alabama-born former slaveholder and prewar unionist.[57]

Immediately after emancipation in the summer of 1865, the fifty-four-year-old Brown, to the abhorrence of many whites, armed some ex-slaves to assist him in quelling the widespread lawlessness plaguing Robertson and other nearby counties. He quickly won a reputation as "a terror" to lawbreakers of whatever race or political persuasion. More significantly, Brown and his armed posse, or "his Men with his Dogs," protected freedmen employed by his planter allies in the Brazos Bottoms from harassment by clandestine white brotherhoods, who, in retaliation in the winter of 1865–66, "set on fire" Brown's house near Sterling. His farm had served as a sanctuary for ex-slaves seeking fair employment opportunities as well as protection from criminal attacks carried out with inexcusable impunity by armed bands of whites.[58]

56. Smallwood, *Time of Hope, Time of Despair,* pp. 130–31; Baum, *The Shattering of Texas Unionism,* pp. 146–61; James W. Throckmorton to Louis T. Wigfall, December 30, 1867 (first quotation), and James W. Throckmorton to Benjamin H. Epperson, December 10, 1866 (second quotation), in "Throckmorton Papers and Letter Book," CAH-UT, Austin, Texas; and Barry A. Crouch, "'All the Vile Passions': The Texas Black Codes of 1866," *Southwestern Historical Quarterly* 97, no. 1 (1993): 13–34.

57. Galveston *Daily News,* February 3, 1867, p. 2 (quotations).

58. Joseph Allen Myers, "Life of Joseph Allen Myers: Written in the Month of November

Brown, described by contemporaries of the era as "constantly hunting the lawless element in central Texas," was a principled man, albeit in the most antisocial and perverse way, because he believed that what was right and wrong were completely extralegal private concerns. Former antisecessionists, consistent wartime Union men, such as Telephus Johnson, and a handful of freedmen comprised the core group that either rode with him or supported him immediately after the war. His brothers, Earle ("Early") Brown and Greenwood ("Green") Brown, helped handle his feared bloodhounds. Ben's posse, a motley group of vigilantes fiercely loyal to him and his brothers, won widespread support from many wealthy planters in the bottomlands, including the Hearnes and Lewises, who resented White Cap and Klan interference with their black employees.[59]

Up until his illness, Sam regularly patronized Green Brown's merchandise and liquor store on the edge of the bottomlands, but there is no evidence, at least prior to 1868, that he or his brothers and cousins rode with Brown's posse. At a later date, in a notorious act of vigilante justice, Rasche Hearne helped Brown track down and summarily lynch a freedman who had assaulted a white woman. Nevertheless, Sam might have sought out Brown, who routinely had served as an administrator of decedent estates, for advice and assistance. Brown and his brothers, however, most likely held Sam at arm's length, being loath to risk alienating Sam's well-respected white heirs and kinfolks—his brothers Lum, Alley, and Wash, and his cousins, Ebb and Rasche, as well as his cousin's husband Charles Lewis, and Ebb's sons, Lorenzo and William—who were known to be on "bad terms" with Sam. Thus Sam chose a relatively unknown individual, Dr. Jeremiah Collins, for help in preparing and executing his

---

1927" [typescript, taken from a ledger with the handwritten text of Joseph Allen Myers, by William Allen Myers, November 20, 2001], pp. 13–14 (first and second quotations), Bryan Public Library, Bryan, Texas; Collie-Cooper, comp., *Robertson County Texas 1860 Census,* p. 23; Statements of Hattie (Hearne) Cole in Rawick, ed., *The American Slave,* supp., ser. 2, vol. 3: "Texas Narratives," pt. 2, p. 780 (third quotation); and statements of Louis Young in Rawick, ed., *The American Slave,* vol. 5, [pt. 3 & 4], pt. 4, pp. 232–34.

59. Collie-Cooper, comp., *Robertson County Texas 1860 Census,* pp. 23, 28, and 59; Myers, "Life of Joseph Allen Myers," p. 13 (quotation); "Brown's Store, Robertson County, Texas," [Credit account of S. R. Hearne, 1863–1864], Re: Estate of Samuel R. Hearne, Docket #134, PF, CCO, Robertson County, Texas; Book "J [1–253]," [Fall Term, 1855], p. 9, MDC, Robertson County, Texas; Joshua L. Randall to J. P. Richardson, December 24, 1867, Microfilm Reel #14, and Charles Garretson to Joshua L. Randall, October 12, 1867, Microfilm Reel #1, BRFAL, RG 105, M821, NA (1973); Thomas H. Norton to HFMD, July 12, 1869, Register #2, p. 55, Microfilm Reel #3, COCADT, RG 393, M1188, NA (1981); and Galveston *Daily News,* July 22, 1870, p. 3.

will. Collins was the physician in whose care Sam increasingly found himself during his illness.[60]

Dr. Collins had arrived in Texas in the late 1850s and, since 1864, had been living in Robertson County. Under President Johnson's procedures for Reconstruction, the Irish-born Collins had registered to vote by taking the amnesty oath. Although he owned no real estate or taxable personal property, under some agreement he was farming or managing part of Telephus Johnson's lands near Sam's plantation. Collins was well regarded by a wide range of individuals. Both Conservative Democrats and the tiny white group of Union Republicans subsequently recommended him for local political appointments when Congress took control of Reconstruction. The freedmen also had confidence in him because he treated their illnesses in return for their promises to pay him in the future. Collins also protected from ostracism and violence an elderly peripatetic northern missionary, the Reverend Richard Sloan.[61]

Reverend Sloan arrived in Texas sometime during the second half of 1865. He made the acquaintance of hundreds of Robertson County former slaves by his travels "up and down the Brazos River" in late 1866. The Freedmen's Bureau hired him to teach a school for the freedmen at Port Sullivan in neighboring Milam County. In optimistic reports, Sloan took credit for having established numerous black churches and schools. Because of his habit of residing for periods of time with ex-slaves in their cabins and his enthusiastic loyalty to the Republican Party, Sloan's life had been threatened many times. Planters, as a rule, did not favor any influx of northern preachers or teachers informing blacks of their rights under the Civil Rights Act of 1866, but because blacks were now able to negotiate their services for higher wages, planters soon learned that unfair treat-

60. Statements of Sam Eaves in the Bryan *Daily Eagle,* July 22, 1926, p. 4; Joshua L. Randall to Joel T. Kirkman, June 8, 1867 (quotation), Sterling, Texas, "Subassistant Commissioner Records filed under 'Sterling, Texas,'" Letters Sent: Entry #3769, account pp. 36–37, BFRAL, [unmicrofilmed], RG 105, NA; and [Original Last Will and Testament of Sam'l R. Hearne], Re: Estate of Samuel R. Hearne, Docket #134, PF, CCO, Robertson County, Texas.

61. "J. Collins," Registration No. 984, *Voter Registration Lists, 1867–1869,* Microfilm Reel VR-10, Robertson County, Texas, TSL-AD; Robertson County Tax Rolls, 1838–1882, Tax Rolls for 1866, Microfilm Reel #1198–01, TSL-AD; A. L. Brigance to James W. Throckmorton, June 9, 1867, [copy], box 55, folder 24, Governors' Papers: Throckmorton, RG 301, TSL-AD, Austin, Texas; William H. Farner to Joshua L. Randall, August 14, 1867, box 56, folder 6, and Joshua L. Randall to Joel T. Kirkman, August 26, 1867, box 56, folder 9, Governors' Papers: Pease, RG 301, TSL-AD; "Invoice of the property of Dr. J. Collins Dec'd," filed January 21, 1868, and "Petition filed by W. H. Hamman counsel for petitioner [T. A. Johnson]," filed March 16, 1868, "In the Matter of Jeremiah Collins Dec'd," File #A18, Case No. 0437, PF, CCO, Robertson County, Texas.

ment of employees during the previous year led to difficulties in hiring an adequate labor force for the coming season. As a consequence, many plantation managers in Azeline's neighborhood, such as Dr. Collins and W. W. ("Buck") Watts, encouraged the construction of black churches and schools in order to entice the freedmen to stay after their contracts had expired.[62]

The Last Will and Testament of Samuel R. Hearne

On September 17, 1866, during his illness, Sam wrote out his last will and testament in his own handwriting. His will was most likely prepared by counsel, but because it followed the typical format of the era he might have written it himself without paying for the services of an attorney. Just as his white relatives feared and anticipated, he bequeathed his entire estate to his son Dock with a contingency provision for the care of Dock's mother Azeline. Sam included a detailed legal description of his 903-acre plantation, complete with metes and bounds that, while not legally required to describe a parcel of land, indicated his determination to err on the side of caution if his will wound up contested by his collateral white relatives. He named Dr. Collins as his executor and also appointed him Dock's guardian. Then as now, to name a guardian of a minor child when the natural mother is alive was unusual, and the selection of Collins was not made contingent upon the prior death of Azeline. Again, Sam erred on the side of caution. In spite of the recent passage of the Civil Rights Act, Dock and Azeline could expect no substantive concern for their newly acquired legal rights at the hands of local authorities. Nor would common sense have allowed Sam to identify Azeline as his wife, because such a claim prior to the adoption of the Fourteenth Amendment and Republican Party control of the Texas Supreme Court would have jeopardized the bequeathal of his estate to Dock. The selection of Collins was not just prudent; under the extraordinary circumstances, it was imperative.[63]

Conveyed to the courthouse in Owensville in his own "ambulance,"

62. Joel T. Kirkman to Joshua L. Randall, August 1, 1867, and endorsement of Joel T. Kirkman on letter from Edward Miller to Charles Garretson, April 30, 1867, "Subassistant Commissioner Records filed under 'Sterling, Texas,'" BRFAL, [unmicrofilmed], RG 105, NA; Richard Sloan to Edmund J. Davis, December 3, 1870, folder 143, box 69, Governors' Papers: Davis, RG 301, TSL-AD; Richard Sloan to Joel T. Kirkman, June 1, 1867 (quotation), and Richard Sloan to Edwin M. Wheelock, April 20, 1867, Records of the Superintendent of Education for the State of Texas, 1865–1870, Microfilm Reel #4, BRFAL, RG 105, M822, NA (1973).

63. [Original Last Will and Testament of Sam'l R. Hearne], Re: Estate of Samuel R. Hearne, Docket #134, PF, CCO, Robertson County, Texas.

a carriage adapted to carry him during his illness, Sam signed his will in the presence of two subscribing witnesses: Alfred L. Brigance, an ex-secessionist who had been recently elected chief justice, or county judge, on the Conservative Democratic ticket; and J. L. Conoly, a notary public who before the war had been a merchant in neighboring Falls County. Perhaps the selection of Conoly as a witness was unplanned, but the selection of County Judge Brigance was deliberate, especially given Sam's concerns that his brothers and cousins would almost certainly contest his will.[64]

Sam died two months later. The exact date in November is unknown, but Azeline later recalled that he died in the original log-framed manor house that he had built when he first occupied his Brazos River plantation in the fall of 1853. He passed away in the company of Azeline and Dock, a few of his former slaves, and many former refugeed freedmen who remained on his land after their emancipation. They most likely buried Sam somewhere on the southeast corner of his plantation near the manor house, just off the public road running between the Big and Little Brazos Rivers. Sam was not accorded any burial plot in the Hearne family cemetery, which was located more appropriately out of the floodplain in the uplands, on what came to be called the "estate place plantation" of his cousin Ebb's landholdings. In sharp contrast to the resting places of his generation of white relatives, the location of Sam's gravesite remains unknown.[65]

At the time of Sam's death, Freedmen's Bureau officials had assigned new agents, both U.S. Army veterans, to Millican and Sterling to deal with the problems caused by civilian agents Farner and Carter. Second Lieutenant Lemuel K. Morton, who received the Sterling appointment, soon realized that "the very friendly way" the planters had received him would be of "short duration" once they realized that he would not approve of their tying up the freedmen by their thumbs as punishment. He discov-

64. [Original Last Will and Testament of Sam'l R. Hearne], Re: Estate of Samuel R. Hearne, Docket #134, PF, CCO, Robertson County, Texas; Bureau of the Census, *Population Schedules of the Eighth Census of the United States, 1860,* Microfilm Roll #1293, Schedule 1, "Falls County, Texas," p. 7, [printed p. 146], M653, NA (1967); W. W. Watts to Oscar F. Hunsaker, August 25, 1867 (quotation), Microfilm Reel #9, BRFAL, RG 105, M821, NA (1973); and Joshua L. Randall to Joel T. Kirkman, August 26, 1867, box 56, folder 9, Governors' Papers: Pease, RG 301, TSL-AD.

65. "Interrogatories and Cross Interrogatories to Assaline Hearne," August 16, 1882, *Asaline Hearne vs. H. D. Prendergast,* Case No. 3069, ODC, Robertson County, Texas; *Transcript Synopsis of A–P Records Relating to Robertson County "Families," 1838–[?],* [The old Hearne family cemetery] (quotation), Microfilm #964224, CCO, Robertson County, Texas.

ered that many of the labor contracts he examined were "regular frauds and swindles" that had placed the freedmen "too much in the hands of the employer." Morton also recognized that he would be powerless to stop the violence routinely committed by whites upon blacks. Like his counterpart in Millican, Morton would only be able to report the crimes to civil authorities, who, in turn, would do nothing. Even crimes committed by blacks on other blacks would be ignored, because imprisoning freedmen entailed the loss of their productive labor in the fields.[66]

After fewer than three months into his assignment Lieutenant Morton had had enough. In December he requested to be mustered out of the army. During his brief tenure as bureau agent, Sam died. Morton's reports document that Sam's death occurred during the height of a major cholera epidemic in the Brazos Bottoms. Yet it is doubtful that Sam himself succumbed to what was referred to by contemporaries of the period as "the cholery," which caused in many places a "regular stampede" of freedmen out of their homes. Sam's illness predated the outbreak of cholera by at least four or five months, and no reference to it as a cause of his death has survived. To the contrary, Sam's wealthy collateral kin attributed his death to prolonged alcoholism and dissipation, which rendered him "non compos mentis" when he wrote his will. Their opinions, however, were tainted by their self-interest in discrediting Sam's last will and testament.[67]

It will never be known whether Sam heard the news before he died of the resounding Republican Party victory in the November 1866 "off-year" congressional elections. Even assuming that Sam had, there would never have been any expectation on his part that Dock or Azeline would go to the courthouse to deposit his will in the probate court. The filing of Sam's will depended completely on the action of Dr. Collins. Although Sam would have been disappointed with his physician's refusal to be the

66. SO No. 113, September 19, 1866, cited in "Report of Changes among Officers and Agents of the Bureau of Refugees, Freedmen, and Abandoned Lands on duty in the State of Texas for the month ending September 30th 1866," [signed by Joseph B. Kiddoo], Microfilm Reel #29, and Lemuel K. Morton to Joseph B. Kiddoo, September 30 (quotations), Microfilm Reel #7, and BRFAL, RG 105, M821, NA (1973).

67. Lemuel K. Morton to Joseph B. Kiddoo, September 30, 1866, Microfilm Reel #7, and November 6, 1866 (first and second quotations), Microfilm Reel #7, and "Register of Letters Received," vol. 1, December 5, 1866, Microfilm Reel #3, p. 314, BRFAL, RG 105, M821, NA (1973); and George Washington Hearne and Horatio R. Hearne answer to petition of James W. Cunningham, December 31, 1866 (third quotation), Re: Estate of Samuel R. Hearne, Docket #134, PF, CCO, Robertson County, Texas.

administrator of his estate and the guardian of his son, Collins nevertheless performed a courageous act of tremendous importance: he filed Sam's will for record. Had he failed to do so, Sam's brothers and cousins would never have been compelled to begin maneuvering through legal channels in order to get possession of their deceased relative's plantation.[68]

Immediately after Sam's death, his relatives took control of his Brazos River plantation and initiated legal proceedings in the probate court designed to demolish any inheritance by Dock. Confident that they would eventually get Sam's will set aside in the district court, they could not have predicted that an ensuing legal struggle for control of Sam's estate would result in his twenty-year-old mulatto son being confirmed in his complete ownership of it by the U.S. government. Nor could they possibly have foreseen that Dock's death two years later in early 1868 would make Azeline, as Dock's sole surviving heir under Sam's will, the owner of the Brazos River plantation and thus, in turn, one of the wealthiest former slaves in the entire South.[69]

68. Will of Samuel R. Hearne, September 17, 1866, and filed for record on November 28, 1866, vol. "O," pp. 302–4, PM, CCO, Robertson County, Texas, and [Original Last Will and Testament of Sam'l R. Hearne], Re: Estate of Samuel R. Hearne, Docket #134, PF, CCO, Robertson County, Texas.

69. "Petition of G. W. Hearne and Horatio R. Hearne," [Application for Administration *Pro Tem* Upon the Estate of Sam'l R. Hearne dec'd], November 30, 1866, vol. "O," pp. 294–95, PM, CCO, Robertson County, Texas.

Chapter 3

A Supposed or Pretended Will

> My said son shall furnish his mother with a comfortable and liberal support during her natural lifetime . . .
>
> —[ORIGINAL WILL OF SAMUEL R. HEARNE], SEPTEMBER 17, 1866

AT THE TIME OF the passage of the Civil Rights Act of 1866, there existed thousands of children of former slaveholders who, during slavery, had considered concubinage as their right. Legitimizing children born of former slave parents was on track to becoming an easy reform, but subjecting the white population to the same rule was considerably more difficult. If Samuel Hearne had not written a last will and testament making his son, Doctor Samuel Jones Hearne, the primary inheritor of his estate and his son's mother, Azeline Hearne, a principal legatee, then they would have had no status whatsoever under the law as possible heirs to his property. But Sam wrote a will, and under a strict interpretation of the current Texas law his will controlled the line of inheritance. His bequest, which included the Brazos River plantation, tracts of land in Limestone and Young Counties, and shares of H&TC Railroad stock, contained one stipulation: Dock would be obligated to take care of his mother for the remainder of her life. Should he fail to do so, she could petition to have one hundred acres of the Brazos River plantation set aside for her exclusive benefit. In addition, she would receive one-third of Sam's personal property that had been on hand at his death, and upon her own death the one hundred acres would revert to Dock.[1]

Azeline might have shared her thoughts with Sam about his will or the contingency provision in it for her, but as someone whose existence had been dependent upon the whims of others, she most likely understood the importance of keeping her own counsel, if not masking many of her true feelings. One thing is certain: Sam never prepared either Azeline or Dock for making complex legal or financial decisions. A wide range of individuals consistently referred to them as "unsophisticated & ignorant" of the workings of the law. Sam had unquestionably pinned all his hopes for their future welfare on his friend and physician, Dr. Jeremiah Collins.[2]

Deeply concerned about the administration of his estate, Sam arranged for a financial incentive for Dr. Collins if he were to become its executor. Collins would be permitted to pay himself seven hundred dollars "as compensation for his trouble" once the administration was closed. For accepting the guardianship of Sam's minor son Dock, Collins would be allowed to take an additional 5 percent of all cash receipts and payments, with the exception of the money given over to Dock upon settlement. The will was unclear, however, regarding whether Collins would be simultaneously guardian of Dock and of Dock's inherited estate. Guardianship of the estate would still have been necessary for Dock's benefit even while Azeline was still alive. This issue was never addressed because Collins refused to be the executor of Sam's estate or the guardian of his son.[3]

The Probating of Samuel R. Hearne's Will

At the time of Sam's death, Dr. Collins had found himself caught between his obligations to Sam, on the one hand, and deference to Sam's relatives, on the other. He was unwilling to jeopardize his relationship with Sam's brothers and cousins by putting himself in the middle of what he knew would devolve into drawn-out legal battles over the validity of Sam's will and the administration of his estate. Collins enjoyed particularly strong ties with former state senator Charles Lewis and his wife, Adeline, who

1. [Original Last Will and Testament of Sam'l R. Hearne], Re: Estate of Samuel R. Hearne, Docket #134, PF, CCO, Robertson County, Texas.

2. [Unsigned Letter to Brevet Major General Joseph J. Reynolds], February 11, 1868 (quotation), frames 0715–0721, Microfilm Reel #39, COCADT, RG 393, M1188, NA (1981).

3. Joe G. Bax, "A Summation of the Proceedings of the Probate and District Courts of Robertson County Relative to Asaline Hearne," [typescript manuscript in possession of the author, June 5, 2000], p. 54; and [Original Last Will and Testament of Sam'l R. Hearne] (quotation), Re: Estate of Samuel R. Hearne, Docket #134, PF, CCO, Robertson County, Texas.

was Sam's cousin. When Collins died in 1867, Charles became the most important surety for the administrators of his estate and also voluntarily collected many debts owed to the deceased doctor for the benefit of his widowed wife.[4]

Within three days after Collins filed Sam's will for record, two of Sam's relatives, his brother Wash and his brother-in-law and cousin Rasche, petitioned the probate court to be temporarily appointed coadministrators of his estate. More pointedly, Wash and Rasche claimed they were the actual "next of kin to S. R. Hearne" and, although "a supposed or pretended will" had been filed, his property remained neglected and unprotected due to the absence of an administrator. The court appointed them administrators for one month rather than for an indefinite period and required them to file a $10,000 bond. Knowing full well the determination of the Hearne and Lewis families to have Sam's will annulled, the court opted to keep Wash and Rasche on a relatively short tether. Meanwhile, Sam's brother Alley seized control of Sam's plantation. Wash, Rasche, and Alley, along with the entire extended Hearne family, knew that members of the local bar, like sharks circling in the water, were watching with tremendous fascination the unfolding events surrounding Sam's estate. If the Hearnes and Lewises believed that merely preventing Dr. Collins from accepting its executorship had cleared the way for their getting hold of it, or that their temporary administration would go unchallenged, they were mistaken.[5]

The gossip sparked by the embarrassment to the Hearne family by the public disclosure of the content of Sam's will rapidly spread to surrounding counties. At some point during the first half of December 1866, Falls County attorney Thomas P. Aycock, a former state representative, avid secessionist, and Confederate army veteran, offered Azeline and Dock his legal services. Aycock advised them that, up against the overwhelming odds favoring Sam's wealthy white relatives in a district court trial, their only hope to sustain Sam's will and keep his Brazos River plantation was to convey to him one-half of their interest *in the entire estate.* Wit-

4. "Admt's Bond," filed October 29, 1867, and "Administrator's Bond," filed June 29, 1868, and "Inventory," [and statements by Harvey D. Prendergast], filed September 30, 1868, "In the Matter of Jeremiah Collins Dec'd," Docket #A18, Case No. 0439, PF, CCO, Robertson County, Texas.

5. "Petition of G. W. Hearne and Horatio R. Hearne," [Application for Administration *Pro Tem* Upon the Estate of Sam'l R. Hearne dec'd], November 30, 1866 (quotations), vol. "O," pp. 294–95, PM, CCO, Robertson County, Texas; "S. W. [*sic*] Hearne dec'd: Bond," filed November 30, 1866, Re: Estate of Samuel R. Hearne, Docket #134, PF, CCO, Robertson County, Texas.

nesses falsely attested to Dock and Azeline having fully understood the terms of the contingency-fee agreement that they signed. The contract lay bare their helplessness in protecting what, by any fair standard of justice, should have belonged to them with no need to sacrifice half to keep the other half.[6]

Aycock hastily cobbled together an agreement with a few men residing near Sam's plantation to assist in probating Sam's will. The group included James W. Cunningham, an Arkansas-born newcomer whose name surfaced the following year as possible local political appointee, and Dred Dawson Jr., a well-respected landowner and longtime neighbor and friend of Sam and Azeline. Cunningham filed an application written by Aycock for the administration of Sam's estate "with the will annexed," meaning that Cunningham accepted the validity of Sam's will and, as administrator, he would implement its terms. Cunningham further alleged that, in the wake of Dr. Collins's refusal to take any action regarding the will, "some of the collateral kindred . . . well knowing of the existence of [the will], and wholly disregarding [it]," obtained a temporary administration and, in effect, now controlled Sam's estate.[7]

To make sure that the probate court understood the situation, Cunningham further declared, "The persons who have taken out [the temporary administration] are adverse to the will, and would not apply for its probate." Because Dock and Azeline were "not capable of properly claiming and protecting their rights," they had appealed to him for assistance. The court then appointed Cunningham as administrator with the will annexed and required him to post a bond for $20,000—an amount presumably equal to the current market value of the Brazos River plantation. At the same time, Dock requested that Cunningham be appointed as his legal guardian. The court, without stating the grounds for disqualifying Azeline, who was, after all, the young man's living mother, appointed Cunningham as the guardian of both Dock and the estate held by him

6. Dallas *Herald,* April 18, 1860, p. 1; *Thomas P. Aycock vs. Asaline Hearne,* Case No. 1113, Book "K," pp. 57–58, MDC, Robertson County, Texas; and [Unsigned Letter to Brevet Major General Joseph J. Reynolds], February 11, 1868, frames 0715–0721, Microfilm Reel #39, COCADT, RG 393, M1188, NA (1981).

7. Petition of James W. Cunningham, "Applicant for Administration with the Will Annexed of S. R. Hearne, dec'd," [filed December 18, 1866], vol. "O," pp. 300–304 (quotations), PM, CCO, Robertson County, Texas; William H. Farner to Joshua L. Randall, August 14, 1867, Governors' Papers: Pease, box 56, folder 6, RG 301, TSL-AD; "J. W. Cunningham," Registration No. 458, August 5, 1867, p. 217, *Voter Registration Lists, 1867–1869,* Robertson County, Texas, Microfilm Reel VR-10, TSL-AD.

as a minor child—an appointment that required an additional bond. The clerk of the county court then tacked a notice on the courthouse door informing the public that a petition to have Sam Hearne's will probated had been filed and anyone wishing to contest it must appear at the courthouse within ten days.[8]

Wash and Rasche, as expected, contested the probate court's decision recognizing Sam's will as valid. They now conceded that Sam authored the will, which they initially had labeled as bogus, but they claimed that Sam, due to excessive and continued intoxication impairing his judgment prior to his death, had not been of sound mind when he wrote it. In a separate follow-up petition, Rasche requested that he, as Sam's next of kin, be appointed as administrator with the will annexed after the court removed Cunningham. After filing a motion claiming Sam was not mentally capable of handling his affairs when he wrote his will, Rasche was now willing to accept the will's validity and be legally bound to execute its terms. The lawyers who routinely gathered at the courthouse viewed Rasche's petition with varying degrees of sarcastic amusement. Among the citizens of Robertson County, the contest over Sam's will had become a popular social drama—a source of entertainment for those speculating on not only who would eventually win or lose, for most bets at the beginning of 1867 heavily favored the Hearne and Lewis families, but also who would be among the first to perjure themselves when questioned about Sam's state of mind when he wrote his will.[9]

After Dr. Collins had deposited the will in the probate court, Chief Justice Alfred L. Brigance, who had witnessed Sam sign and seal it, made comments supportive of the Hearne family. Even though Brigance knew that Sam intended that his estate should go to Dock and Azeline, he recognized that Sam's brothers and cousins, who had been at odds with Sam over matters of inheritance since the last years of the war, would hold a trump card in any contest over the will in the district court. No jury comprised exclusively of white men would allow one of the most profit-

8. "Petition to Probate the Will of Samuel R. Hearne dec'd," [December Term, 1866], vol. "O," pp. 300–304 (quotations), PM, CCO, Robertson County, Texas; and "Notice" December 18, 1866, Re: Estate of Samuel R. Hearne, Docket #134, PF, CCO, Robertson County, Texas.

9. Joshua L. Randall to Joel T. Kirkman, June 8, 1867, account pp. 36–37, "Subassistant Commissioner Records filed under 'Sterling, Texas,'" BRFAL, [unmicrofilmed], RG 105, NA; "G. W. Hearne and Horatio R. Hearne: Answer to petition of James W. Cunningham," December 31, 1866, and "Petition of H. R. Hearne for Letters Testamentary," filed December 31, 1866, withdrawn by counsel on January 14, 1867, Re: Estate of Samuel R. Hearne, Docket #134, PF, CCO, Robertson County, Texas.

able antebellum plantations in the county to fall into the hands of former slaves. But before drafting a lawsuit designed to destroy any inheritance by Dock, the Hearne and Lewis families waited to see if Cunningham, who owned no real estate or taxable personal property, would be able to post sufficient secured bonds within the requisite twenty days. The total amount required for the executorship and guardianship was $25,000, which at the turn of the twenty-first century would have been comparable to having to post bonds calling for collateral valued at over a quarter of a million dollars.[10]

Just after Congress began its investigation of President Johnson's Reconstruction policy in early January 1867, Cunningham filed his required bonds. The court issued him letters of administration, appointed individuals to appraise Sam's estate, and ordered them to file a complete inventory. Cunningham's main surety was Dred Dawson, whose considerable landholdings in the bottomlands constituted more than ample security. Others signing Cunningham's bonds were Enoch T. Aiken, Martin V. Garner, and James M. Crook—farm managers whose personal assets were, like Cunningham's, of little or no consequence. Cunningham's administration was now seemingly on track. Aycock, in accordance with his agreement with Azeline and Dock, stood to become the owner of half of Sam's total estate, which would have included half of the 903-acre Brazos River plantation. However, as anticipated, the Hearnes and Lewises swiftly filed a lawsuit against Cunningham in the Robertson County District Court.[11]

Rasche withdrew his motion to be appointed administrator of Sam's estate with the will annexed, and then joined his cousins Wash, Alley, and Lum as plaintiffs against Cunningham's administration in contesting the validity of Sam's will. One of Sam's second cousins, Lorenzo D. Hearne, then filed an application in the probate court to have himself named in place of Cunningham as administrator of Sam's estate *with the will annexed*. Finally, a host of Hearne "family members," including Sam's sister Priscilla (Rasche's wife) and Sam's widowed sister-in-law Nancy K. Hearne, signed a letter to the court supporting Lorenzo's application for

10. Robertson County Tax Rolls, 1838–1882, Tax Rolls for 1865 and 1866, Microfilm Reel #1198–01, TSL-AD. What cost $25,000 in 1866 would have cost $271,518.59 in 2000. See the "Inflation Calculator," www.westegg.com/inflation (accessed July 22, 2003).

11. "J. W. Cunningham adm'r with the will annexed of S. R. Hearne dec'd," and "J. W. Cunningham Guardian of the Doctor Samuel Jones Hearne minor heir of S. R. Hearne, dec'd," vol. "O," pp. 312–14, PM, CCO, Robertson County, Texas; and *Thomas P. Aycock vs. Asaline Hearne,* Case No. 1113, June 18, 1875, Book "O," p. 5, MDC, Robertson County, Texas.

Cunningham's removal. In an action constituting a small degree of fraud, Sam's younger brother Selby W. Hearne also signed, *even though he had died fourteen years earlier.* The petitioners preferred that "some proper person," namely, Lorenzo, be appointed administrator pending outcome of the lawsuit in the district court to set aside Sam's will.[12]

Twenty-one-year-old Lorenzo, who was Ebenezer Hearne's son, was only one year older than Dock, but Lorenzo, along with his older brother William, enjoyed well-regarded reputations in postwar Robertson County. They had been the only members of their family to enlist or serve in the Confederate army—actions that absolved them from their relatives' prewar unionism and subsequent draft dodging during the war. Lorenzo asserted that he, not Cunningham, was Sam's next of kin and that Cunningham had posted a bond with insufficient security. The latter assertion was a jibe at Cunningham's landless status. Lorenzo stated that he would accept full, or even limited, powers, depending on whatever the court decided, as administrator with the obligation to carry out the terms of Sam's will and to do so under the supervision of the court.[13]

The attorneys for Sam's relatives were, in effect, offering the probate court a compromise solution. Lorenzo's petition, in which he accepted the validity of Sam's will and pledged himself to implement its terms, represented a position between two extremes: the lawsuit filed by Wash, Rasche, Alley, and Lum to set aside Sam's will, which would deny any semblance of fair play to Dock and Azeline, on the one hand, and the opportunistic Aycock and Cunningham scheme that excluded Sam's brothers, cousins, nephews, and other relatives from acquiring management of Sam's plantation, on the other. Lorenzo's gambit would at the very least contain within his family the untidy consequences of Sam's now publicly acknowledged disreputable and embarrassing behavior. More importantly, the Hearnes and Lewises realized that they, like Aycock and his collaborators, could easily find enough latitude within the boundaries of Sam's will to manipu-

12. "Petition of H. R. Hearne for Letters Testamentary," filed December 31, 1866, withdrawn by counsel on January 14, 1867, and "Lorenzo D. Hearne Applicant for administration with the will annexed of the Estate of Samuel R. Hearne dec'd," filed January 14, 1867, and "Pet[itio]n," filed January 28, 1867 (quotations), Re: Estate of Samuel R. Hearne, Docket #134, PF, CCO, Robertson County, Texas; and *A. L. Hearne, et al. vs. J. W. Cunningham, Administrator,* Case No. 978, MDC, Robertson County, Texas.

13. Janet B. Hewett, ed., *The Roster of Confederate Soldiers, 1861–1865,* 16 vols. (Wilmington, N.C.: Broadfoot Publishing Co., 1995), 7: 396; and "Lorenzo D. Hearne Applicant for administration with the will annexed of the Estate of Samuel R. Hearne dec'd," filed January 14, 1867, vol. "O," pp. 325–27, PM, CCO, Robertson County, Texas.

late Dock's inheritance to their own advantage. Mandated court supervision would pose no problem because they knew that Dock and Azeline would be powerless to enforce the privileges and rights legally owed them by an administrator.

Aycock's claim to compensation in the form of ownership of half the estate's value would evaporate unless he was able to demonstrate the necessity of his legal services on behalf of securing Dock and Azeline's rights. With much at stake and the odds now heavily against him, Aycock filed an objection to Lorenzo's petition. He charged Lorenzo with being hypocritical in his willingness to take an oath to carry out the terms of a will written by a person whom Lorenzo had publicly judged to be mentally impaired. Lorenzo, argued Aycock, was in league with his relatives, who had attacked the will and who were now plaintiffs in a lawsuit to have it annulled. But in point of fact neither Lorenzo nor his father Ebb was a party to the district court lawsuit—a situation that had not been left to chance. Aycock also claimed that Lorenzo, as Sam's second cousin, was not Sam's next of kin and thus not a proper person to be administrator. But sufficiently worried about Lorenzo's factual claim that Cunningham was completely unrelated to Sam, Aycock filed another petition. In an act of pure desperation, Aycock brought Azeline into the court proceedings as a litigant.[14]

In January 1867, at a time when the notion still prevailed that a white woman, much less a "freedwoman of color," was unable to act effectively in the courts by herself or be granted any official position of responsibility, Azeline made her first of many appearances as a litigant and petitioner. She requested the probate court allow her to apply for letters of administration of Sam's estate in the event of Cunningham's removal—a demand that, if granted, would have made her the first ex-slave ever in Texas to achieve such rights and duties. Aycock, who wrote this petition on her behalf, would have been shocked had the probate court approved her request. Her inability to read and write, which rendered her powerless to carry out her functions by herself, all but disqualified her, but otherwise, logic and common sense were on her side. Unlike Sam's brothers and cousins, she was a principal legatee of his will and, moreover, she was the mother of the will's most important beneficiary. Further still, all

14. "Petition of J. W. Cunningham in Opposition to L. D. Hearne's petition for the removal of the Said Cunningham as administrator," filed January 28, 1867, vol. "O," p. 326, PM, CCO, Robertson County, Texas; and *A. L. Hearne, et al. vs. J. W. Cunningham, Administrator,* Case No. 978, MDC, Robertson County, Texas.

the Hearne family next of kin were plotting to destroy her son's inheritance, and thereby trying to recover for themselves the Brazos River plantation contrary to Sam's wishes. At this point focus was riveted on the administration of Sam's estate and Azeline's unprecedented, albeit hopeless, petition—matters that quite understandably eclipsed the issue of the guardianship of Dock.[15]

Azeline had taken her first step into the unknown realm of the law the moment she and Dock had signed the contingency-fee agreement with Aycock for his legal services, but she had no idea where the agreement would take her or what would be its consequences. She had little, if any, concept of herself as a legal protagonist. Nor did she know how deeply she would become enmeshed in the components of a mysterious legal system. Years later Azeline would evolve into one knowing far more about the workings of the law than almost anyone else in the county, but now when the probate court handed down its rulings on the petitions before it, she could not have understood Aycock's explanation why the court decided to select Lorenzo as the administrator of Sam's estate.

The probate court ordered that Lorenzo be appointed administrator pending a resolution of the case in the district court to contest Sam's will. Lorenzo's father Ebb and his uncle Rasche, knowing that the progress of the suit could linger on the court docket for a long time, signed as sureties on Lorenzo's bond. Although the court did not appoint Lorenzo administrator with the will annexed, he nevertheless had the power to take possession of all Sam's property. Moreover, the court suspended Cunningham's administration during the will contest—an action that proceeded with the acquiescence of Aycock, who recognized the futility of any request to reopen it. Demonstrating that a calculated business venture had overshadowed any enduring concern for his clients, Aycock now turned his back on Dock's welfare and never again discussed with Azeline the pending litigation over Sam's will in the district court—a venue that he knew would heavily favor the Hearnes and Lewises.[16]

15. "Petition of Asaline Hearne," filed January 28, 1867, vol. "O," pp. 325–27, PM, CCO, Robertson County, Texas.

16. "Co[urt] Letters to Lorenzo D. Hearne," February 23, 1867, and "Bond, as Adm'r Pendente Lite," filed February 25, 1867, and "Citation. To J. W. Cunningham, Doctor Samuel Jones Hearne, Minor Heir of S. R. Hearne Guardian," March 4, 1868, Re: Estate of S. R. Hearne, Docket #134, PF, CCO, Robertson County, Texas; vol. "O," pp. 326–27, PM, CCO, Robertson County, Texas; and *General Index to Probate Minutes, 1838–1928* (2 vols.), vol. 1: "Doctor Samuel Jones Hearne (minor), Heir of S. R. Hearne, J. W. Cunningham Administrator [no papers exist]," CCO, Robertson County, Texas.

In short, within three months of Sam's death the probate court, in regard to his estate, had opened a temporary administration and then closed it; had begun an administration with the will annexed and then suspended it; and had opened an administration, albeit without the will annexed, pending the outcome of the litigation over the will's validity. By the end of February 1867, when Lorenzo had managed to become administrator, the Hearne and Lewis families held the upper hand in determining the future of Sam's estate. And equally as important, until the case contesting Sam's will was resolved, the ownership of Sam's plantation was up in the air and its title could be considered as "encumbered," or subject to the liability of pending litigation. Had Sam known that Dock and Azeline would find themselves in such a disadvantaged situation after his death, he would no doubt have been disconsolate. Perhaps Dr. Collins had been courageous to file Sam's will for probate, but his refusal to do anything further proved a staggering blow to Dock and Azeline's chances to achieve simple justice.[17]

What occurred in the winter of 1866–67 in the Robertson County Probate Court was, nevertheless, unprecedented. Although Congress had passed the revolutionary Civil Rights Act in April 1866, local authorities and the overwhelming majority of the white population viewed Dock and Azeline's emerging privileges under the law as formless and imprecise at best. They were persons who, as Aycock expressed it, were "not capable" of claiming their legal rights. His admission was revealing, because he, as their attorney, stood to gain considerable compensation for merely securing for them the same basic rights that any white individuals in comparable circumstances would have enjoyed without much expense or difficulty. At a time when blacks possessed, at least in theory, the same "full and equal benefit of the laws and proceedings" that whites enjoyed, Robertson County denied freedom's first generation of African American citizens their right to file marriage certificates, while collecting from them as new citizens the yearly $1.50 capitation, or poll, tax.[18]

17. Bax, "A Summation," pp. 57–58.

18. "Petition for Probate of Will," filed December 18, 1866, Re: Estate of Samuel R. Hearne, Docket #134, PF, CCO, Robertson County, Texas; "Petition to Probate the Will of Samuel R. Hearne dec'd," vol. "O," pp. 300–304 (first quotation), PM, CCO, Robertson County, Texas; "The Civil Rights Act, 1866," in *United States Statutes at Large: Compiled, Edited, and Indexed by Authority of Congress under the Direction of the Secretary of State* (Washington, D.C.: U.S. G.P.O., 1937), 14: 27 (second quotation); and Robertson County Tax Rolls, 1838–1882, Tax Rolls for 1866, Microfilm Reel #1198–01, TSL-AD.

The issue of the guardianship of Dock and the security of his estate had vanished in the legal maneuverings. Cunningham subsequently ignored his legal managerial responsibilities. He filed no reports, paid no court costs, and answered no citations to attend to these matters. In point of fact, the probate court's notation that Dock was "over fourteen years of age" pinpointed him on Sam's Louisiana plantation in 1850 as the four-year-old mulatto male slave who subsequently appeared as the fourteen-year-old male slave on Sam's Brazos River plantation in 1860. The date of the latter census enumeration revealed that Dock was twenty years of age when he had requested Cunningham be appointed as his legal guardian. When U.S. military authorities dramatically dismissed the will contest pending on the docket of the district court in July 1867, Dock was at most a mere five days short of twenty-one years of age—the legal age of majority in the state of Texas.[19]

Congressional Control of Reconstruction

U.S. government intervention into the matter of Sam Hearne's estate occurred in the wake of extraordinary political developments. By the summer of 1867, Congress had enacted its own Reconstruction plans and altered the entire course of southern history. Passed over President Johnson's veto in March 1867, the First Reconstruction Act divided all the ex-Confederate states, except Tennessee, into five military districts and declared their existing civil governments to be provisional and subject to martial law. Texas became part of the Fifth Military District—a jurisdiction that was superior to civil institutions and could rule alone or could allow existing civil institutions to function. Readmission to the Union re-

19. "Petition to Probate the Will of Samuel R. Hearne dec'd," vol. "O," pp. 300–304 (quotation), PM, CCO, Robertson County, Texas; "Citation. To J. W. Cunningham, Doctor Samuel Jones Hearne, Minor Heir of S.R.H. Guardian," March 4, 1868, Re: Estate of Samuel R. Hearne, Docket #134, PF, CCO, Robertson County, Texas; *General Index to Probate Minutes, 1838–1928* (2 vols.), vol. 1: "Doctor Samuel Jones Hearne (minor), Heir of S. R. Hearne, J. W. Cunningham Administrator (no papers exist)," CCO, Robertson County, Texas; "Exhibit A," *A. L. Hearne, et al. vs. J. W. Cunningham, Adm'r, et al.*, Case No. 978, [Spring Term, 1868], Book "J," p. 668, MDC, Robertson County, Texas; Bureau of the Census, *Population Schedules of the Seventh Census of the United States, 1850*, Microfilm Reel #242, Louisiana [Slave Schedules] "Bienville—Concordia ," p. 887, M432, NA (1963); and Bureau of the Census, *Population Schedules of the Eighth Census of the United States, 1860*, Microfilm Roll #1312, Texas [Slave Schedules] vol. 2, (307–628) "Robertson County," p. 25 [printed p. 316], M653, NA, (1967).

quired that Texans reconvene a state constitutional convention by universal adult male suffrage. Former slaves, most of them illiterate and many of them still dressed in gunnysacks, would thus participate as voters with full civic and civil rights in the process of Reconstruction. The new state constitution would have to include a provision for black suffrage, and the new legislature would have to adopt the Fourteenth Amendment. Only then would the U.S. Congress vote on whether to readmit the state's senators and representatives. These congressional acts theoretically offered the possibility for blacks to become active agents, rather than simply pawns, in southern politics.[20]

A supplementary congressional act tried to exclude former secessionist leaders from participating in the Reconstruction process. It provided that an eligible voter must swear that before the war he had never held a state office or had taken an oath to uphold the U.S. Constitution and afterward engaged in rebellion against the Union or given aid to its enemies. If enforced, this act would disfranchise most of Robertson County's established political leaders, including Charles Lewis. The same act required the army to register eligible voters and set the process in motion for the election of delegates to the constitutional convention. Congress subsequently granted district military commanders the extraordinary power to remove and appoint civil officials.[21]

The start of Congressional Reconstruction in March shocked the white residents of Robertson County, who were already angry over the Freedmen's Bureau January ruling that it would no longer permit enforcement of some of the worst features of the state's Black Codes. Few whites could fathom changes that threatened to eliminate labor laws regulating the freedmen, not to mention to allow them to vote, serve on juries, and hold political office. Democratic Party leaders charged northern Republicans with unleashing a "stupendous revolutionary scheme" with "fanatical malignity" that would artificially elevate the degraded African race to full civic and legal equality with the superior Caucasian race. They claimed the radical Republicans sought to impose on the defeated and powerless

20. Dale Baum, *The Shattering of Texas Unionism: Politics in the Lone Star State during the Civil War Era* (Baton Rouge: Louisiana State University Press, 1998), pp. 161–62; Carl H. Moneyhon, *Republicanism in Reconstruction Texas* (Austin: University of Texas Press, 1980), pp. 58–59; and James M. Smallwood, *Time of Hope, Time of Despair: Black Texans during Reconstruction* (Port Washington, N.Y.: Kennikat Press, 1981), pp. 132–33.

21. Moneyhon, *Republicanism in Reconstruction Texas,* pp. 58–59.

South a vindictive Reconstruction program that had as its ultimate goal the racial amalgamation of the white and black races.[22]

By the summer of 1867, Democrats derisively called southern-born whites or southerners by long-term residence who embraced the Republican Party "scalawags," newly arrived northerners joining them "carpetbaggers," and emerging African Texan political leaders "nigs," "nigras," or "niggers"—terms already widely used by most whites to refer to all African Americans. The lines were sharply drawn: an overwhelming number of the white population fell squarely in the anti-Republican camp. Moreover, no common ideological ground existed upon which ex-secessionists and ex-Confederates on one side could make compromises with scalawags, carpetbaggers, or blacks on the other. Although passage of the so-called Military Bill, or First Reconstruction Act, prompted a temporary decline in violent crimes committed against blacks in Texas and Robertson County, bureau agents everywhere continued to document the fearful state of affairs in their respective districts along with the many heartbreaking grievances of the freedpeople.[23]

Into this beginning of the most extraordinary political revolution ever in Texas history appeared a new Freedmen's Bureau agent for Robertson and Milam Counties. Headquarters in Galveston appointed Joshua L. Randall, a young civilian law student from Maine to be the bureau agent stationed in Sterling. Randall differed from his predecessors, Champe Carter Jr. and Dr. William Farner, who had been far too subservient to the planters. Nor was Randall comparable to Lieutenant Lemuel Morton, who had good intentions but proved not up to the job of assisting the freedmen to achieve fair treatment at the hands of their employers. Although Randall found his assignment difficult and daunting, he nevertheless was the first agent to win the genuine trust of the ex-slaves. Admittedly, Randall's influence at headquarters far exceeded that of his predecessors because his recommendations, in the wake of Congressional Reconstruction, could result in the removal from office of any Robertson County official. As his

22. William L. Richter, *Overreached on All Sides: The Freedmen's Bureau Administrators in Texas, 1865–1868* (College Station: Texas A&M University Press, 1991), p. 99; Oran M. Roberts, quoted in Lelia Bailey, "The Life and Public Career of O. M. Roberts, 1815–1883" (Ph.D. diss., University of Texas, 1932), pp. 199–200 (quotations); and Randolph B. Campbell, *A Southern Community in Crisis: Harrison County, Texas, 1850–1880* (Austin: Texas State Historical Association, 1983), p. 275.

23. Baum, *The Shattering of Texas Unionism,* p. 162 (first, second, and third quotations); and Moneyhon, *Republicanism in Reconstruction Texas,* p. 58 (fourth quotation).

popularity grew among blacks, the hatred toward him by whites accelerated. Not only was his life threatened by outlaw gangs, white brotherhoods, and Klan klaverns, no less than Alexander Terrell's mother-in-law, Elizabeth Mitchell, was among the first to advocate Captain Randall's assassination.[24]

Upon speaking to the freedmen on his arrival in April 1867, Randall learned that many planters had cheated their employees out of the wages promised them for the previous year. Determined to end this widespread practice, he confronted one of the worst offenders: a "Mrs. Mitchell" who, if complaints lodged against her were "any where near correct," owed back wages ranging from $2,000 to $3,000 to the freedmen on her cotton plantation. Her cordiality toward Randall vanished when he pointed out that, even according to the falsified entries in her ledger, she owed money to most of her employees and would have to settle fairly with them. Calling him the tool of "some great abolition nigger-worshipper," she informed him that she would never pay her freedmen "because it would set a bad precedent." She then appealed to military authorities in Galveston to "protect" her from Randall, who had insulted and threatened her in her own house. She circulated a petition alleging that he had tried to foment a race riot, and she spread the word that she was placing a one-thousand-dollar price on his head.[25]

Mrs. Mitchell's ploy worked. Headquarters ordered Randall to desist in the entire matter and defend his actions. In spite of detailed reports describing her outrageous behavior, including her participation in the stringing up of her employees by their thumbs and refusal to pay them for their labor, all hope disappeared for setting her trial date and collecting employee back pay. Randall thereafter sent in his reports and letters to headquarters "only at the risk of his life." During his ongoing difficulties with Mrs. Mitchell, and amidst his many duties, concerns, and fears for his safety in the spring of 1867, Randall received a letter from Azeline Hearne.[26]

24. Andrew J. Torget, "Carpetbagger on the Brazos: The Texas Freedmen's Bureau in Robertson County," *Agora: An Online Undergraduate Journal of the Humanities* 1, no. 2 (Winter 2000): 1–14; James M. Smallwood, Barry A. Crouch, and Larry Peacock, *Murder and Mayhem: The War of Reconstruction in Texas* (College Station: Texas A&M University Press, 2003), p. 49; and Richter, *Overreached on All Sides,* pp. 256–57.

25. Torget, "Carpetbagger on the Brazos," pp. 5–6 (quotations on p. 6); and Richter, *Overreached on All Sides,* p. 257.

26. Torget, "Carpetbagger on the Brazos," p. 6–7; and Richter, *Overreached on All Sides,* p. 257 (quotation).

Azeline's letter to Randall, like so many other documents, has dissolved with the passage of time. It is thus impossible to determine its exact date and who served as her amanuensis. Based on other surviving documents that refer to it, she most likely wrote letters to both Randall in Sterling and military authorities in Galveston. She straightforwardly detailed the circumstances surrounding the Hearne family's seizure of Sam's plantation and the extent to which Lorenzo's actions had violated the intentions of Sam's will. The individual who helped her seek assistance from the Freedmen's Bureau was not Aycock. He later claimed under oath to have had no knowledge of Azeline's dealings with the bureau. Nor was it likely Dr. Collins, who had made his decision to file the will and do nothing further. The person who most probably assisted Azeline was Dr. Farner, the discredited former bureau agent who now embraced the Republican Party and its policy of Congressional Reconstruction. Yet another likely Samaritan, the Reverend Richard ("Rich") Sloan, an elderly missionary of the U.S. Christian Commission, cannot be ruled out.[27]

Reverend Sloan was teaching in neighboring Milam County at the Port Sullivan freedmen's school. He was on good terms with Dr. Collins, Buck Watts, and a few other plantation managers in Azeline's neighborhood. Around the same time Azeline wrote her letter, the Freedmen's Bureau opened a school for sixty pupils on Rasche's plantation, and other nearby plantation owners and operators, including Collins and Watts, contributed land and money to build a black church. Sloan, who worked tirelessly to organize black churches and schools, was unquestionably aware of the circumstances surrounding Azeline and Dock. And they, in turn, most likely had attended one of the black churches that he had established, had often heard him preach, and had become personally acquainted with him.[28]

In the ensuing flurry of bureau correspondence provoked by Azeline's complaint, Randall acknowledged that he had been aware of her case for some time. From talking with many "who had some knowledge of the facts," he reported that Sam had unquestionably intended that all his property go to Dock with a provision that Azeline, whom Randall de-

27. Joshua L. Randall to Joel T. Kirkman, June 8, 1867, account pages 36–37 (quotation), "Subassistant Commissioner Records filed under 'Sterling, Texas,'" BRFAL, [unmicrofilmed], RG 105, NA; and *Thomas P. Aycock vs. Asaline Hearne,* Case No. 1113, February 20, 1871, Book "K," pp 57–58, MDC, Robertson County, Texas.

28. Richard Sloan to Edwin M. Wheelock, April 11, 1867, Records of the Superintendent of Education for the State of Texas, 1865–1870, Microfilm Reel #4, BRFAL, RG 105, M822, NA (1973).

scribed as "almost white," should have a suitable subsistence income from the property during her lifetime. Yet without explaining further, Randall added that, by most accounts, Sam had been "somewhat dissipated for some time previous to his death." In regard to Sam's Brazos River plantation, Randall placed its value conservatively at "upwards of $20,000.00" but admitted that its prewar value would have been easily over twice this amount. He enclosed Azeline's letter, which he asserted "will explain itself," and asked headquarters for advice and instructions.[29]

Headquarters ordered Randall to gather information about the Hearnes. He replied that they all enjoyed good reputations as "honest, reliable, responsible, and wealthy men" but limited his discussion to plantations owned by Lum, Wash, Rasche, and Ebb. Randall interviewed Lorenzo's father, Ebb, at length. Ebb had about 450 acres in cultivation, with 250 acres in cotton and 200 acres in corn. All his crops were "in the very highest state of cultivation." Due to "labor concerns," the price of bottomland was currently "uncertain," but Ebb's 1,085-acre plantation had to be worth, according to Randall, at least $20,000. According to Ebb, if the plantation could be run "favorably in regard to labor" (what this meant precisely Randall did not say), it would easily fetch over twice that amount. Freedmen worked the plantation on shares, supposedly getting one-third of the entire crop and having free use of all farm implements and work animals. Ebb had a small store on his plantation and sold, generally on a cash basis, largely to the freedmen on the neighboring plantations rather than to his own sharecroppers.[30]

Ebb's cousin Wash owned a plantation said by some to be "the finest in the county." Of some 800 acres cleared, Wash had 600 acres in cultivation. He allegedly paid wages of fifteen dollars a month to his hands. His small plantation store sold principally to his own employees. Randall reported with considerable skepticism that all the Hearnes complained "of being poor," of having to worry about ongoing litigation over their land titles, and being so discouraged with the new order of things that they

29. Joshua L. Randall to Joel T. Kirkman, June 8, 1867, account pp. 36–37 (quotations), "Subassistant Commissioner Records filed under 'Sterling, Texas,'" BRFAL, [unmicrofilmed], RG 105, NA; and Oscar F. Hunsaker to Joel T. Kirkman, July 31, 1867, Microfilm Reel #14, BRFAL, RG 105, M821, NA (1973).

30. Joel T. Kirkman to Joshua L. Randall, May 18, 1867, and Joshua L. Randall to Joel T. Kirkman, May 27, 1867 (quotations), Miscellaneous Records Entry #3767, "Subassistant Commissioner Records filed under 'Sterling, Texas,'" BRFAL, [unmicrofilmed], RG 105, NA.

talked "more or less of going to Brazil." Randall might have generalized a few of his impressions of the Hearnes from his acquaintance with Ebb, who immediately after emancipation had faced a labor shortage caused by freedmen unwilling to work in gangs for wages on his plantation. Ebb shared his cousin Lum's discouragement with postwar plantation agriculture. In 1866 Lum rented out his plantation and moved to Houston to manage one of the family's mercantile stores.[31]

Major Oscar F. Hunsaker's July 15th Interdict

The information on the Hearnes supplied by Captain Randall resulted in headquarters ordering Major Oscar F. Hunsaker, a Freedmen's Bureau field agent for the state-at-large, to go to Robertson County and investigate matters regarding Sam's estate. Hunsaker, a Galveston attorney who had served as a legal advisor to the bureau, held an extraordinary commission directly from Brevet Major General Charles Griffin, who was then commanding the Military District of Texas and earning a reputation among his critics as a man "as mean as the meanest radical in Texas." Hunsaker had been the first appointment under General Griffin's reversal of a hiring ban against using civilian Texans, such as Farner and Carter, to fill local bureau positions. As a special agent of the bureau, Hunsaker could do virtually whatever he determined "proper and right to promote and secure the interest of the beneficiaries" of Sam's estate. Headquarters ordered Captain Randall to "render Major Hunsaker every aid" in carrying out his investigation and implementing his decisions.[32]

Hunsaker had an additional function: he was a scalawag political consultant who recommended appointments of bureau agents whom he believed could help the Texas Republican Party to secure delegates in the upcoming elections to the state constitutional convention. Although Hunsaker had been born in Illinois, he was a Texan by his long-term residence in the state and a southerner by his service in the Confederate army. While

31. Joshua L. Randall to Joel T. Kirkman, May 27, 1867 (quotations), Miscellaneous Records Entry #3767, "Subassistant Commissioner Records filed under 'Sterling, Texas,'" BRFAL, [unmicrofilmed], RG 105, NA.

32. James W. Throckmorton to Benjamin H. Epperson, September 5, 1867 (first quotation), Benjamin H. Epperson Papers, CAH-UT, Austin, Texas; Joel T. Kirkman to Oscar F. Hunsaker, June 26, 1867 (second and third quotations), Microfilm Reel #1, and Joshua L. Randall to J. P. Richardson, November 4, 1867, Microfilm Reel #14, BRFAL, RG 105, M821, NA (1973); and Richter, *Overreached on All Sides,* p. 184.

serving as president of the newly formed National Republican Association of Galveston, he had demonstrated genuine enthusiasm for achieving justice for the city's former slaves. After local officials ignored his writs of habeas corpus, he had recommended to headquarters the release from jail of black prisoners who endured, under intolerable conditions, more time behind bars awaiting trial than they would have received if they had been found guilty. One former Texas antisecessionist newspaper editor expressed fears that Hunsaker was a radical demagogue who sought to exploit the aspirations of the freedmen for his own advancement.[33]

Hunsaker's actions regarding the handling of Sam Hearne's estate proved to be among the most controversial of his career. According to handed-down legends of Yankee perfidy during Reconstruction, Hunsaker was responsible in Robertson County for "a most villainous swindle & extortion together with malfeasance in [the Freedmen's Bureau] office." However, precisely what he did and how and where he had gone wrong were full of twists and turns and mitigating circumstances and, with the passage of time, were misunderstood and eventually forgotten.[34]

After his arrival in Sterling in early July 1867, Hunsaker reported to headquarters that the condition of the freedpeople was "as abject now as when slaves." Of all the sections of Texas that he had visited, he found the Robertson County Brazos Bottoms "the most disloyal." The freedmen were constantly being killed, beaten, and abused at alarming rates, and in every instance when they had tried to hold "meetings of a political character" they had been so intimidated that they became "afraid to speak in oposition [*sic*] to the white race." If this climate of repression continued, Hunsaker predicted, the registration process and the election would be "humbug." To make matters worse, the "Civil Law and officers" in the county were "a farce," because instead of punishing criminals and wrongdoers "they sheild [*sic*] the offenders." Although Hunsaker found Randall to be a "very honorable, efficient and trusty gentleman," his decisions were "disregarded and abrogated with impunity." Against this background of wretched circumstances, Hunsaker sent out messen-

33. Richter, *Overreached on All Sides,* p. 185; Dallas *Herald,* May 11, 1867, p. 1; Moneyhon, *Republicanism in Reconstruction Texas,* p. 65; *Index to Compiled Service Records of Confederate Soldiers Who Served in Organizations from the State of Texas,* Microfilm Reel #18, Microcopy #227, TSL-AD; and "O. F. Hunsaker," Registration No. 201, p. 221, *Voter Registration Lists, 1867–1869,* Microfilm Reel VR-5, Galveston County, Texas, TSL-AD.

34. [Unsigned Letter to Brevet Major General Joseph J. Reynolds], February 11, 1868 (quotation), Microfilm Reel #39, frames 0715–0721, COCADT, RG 393, M1188, NA (1981).

gers to summon Lorenzo Hearne and his sureties—the parties whom he wished to bring to trial in what he referred to as "the will case."[35]

On the day before Hunsaker was scheduled to sit in judgment of the administration of Sam's will, the freedpeople in the northern section of the Brazos Bottoms asked his permission to hold religious services. They explained that, since the passage in March of the Military Bill, they "had not been permitted to do so." Hunsaker and Randall told them to hold their Sunday church meeting at the usual time, but when both traveled the two miles from Sterling to check up on matters, the freedmen ran up to them from everywhere claiming that "four *desperados* went to their church & told them to leave the building or be killed—that 'the *d——d Yankees* and *Negroes couldn't rule this county,* that the *d——d Negroes* should not hold church.'" The outlaws had "*shot down*" two freedmen "*in cold blood.*"[36]

Randall mounted a posse comprised of himself and Hunsaker, two soldiers, and around one hundred armed freedmen to track down the criminals, who, when overtaken by surprise, resisted arrest. In the ensuing exchange of gunfire, two of the perpetrators were taken prisoner. According to Hunsaker's report, Randall "displayed great courage and ability in the whole affair." Hunsaker, however, was dismayed. Since his arrival in Robertson County, the number of murdered blacks had reached a total of eight—an average of one killed every two days during his stay. Civilian authorities had taken no action. Nor would turning over the two apprehended men to the civil authorities assure that justice would prevail. Even if they were prevented from breaking out of jail, their subsequent trials would be mockeries of justice. When headquarters demanded names of persons who could replace the current set of officeholders, Randall replied that among the whites in the county there were only three or four truly loyal men. They all, according to Randall, were "in constant *danger of their lives.*"[37]

35. Oscar F. Hunsaker to Joel T. Kirkman, July 9, 1867 (quotations), Microfilm Reel #6, BRFAL, RG 105, M821, NA (1973).

36. Oscar F. Hunsaker to Joel T. Kirkman, July 16, 1867 (quotations), Microfilm Reel #6, BRFAL, RG 105, M821, NA (1973).

37. Oscar F. Hunsaker to Joel T. Kirkman, July 16, 1867 (first quotation), Microfilm Reel #6, and Joshua L. Randall to Joel T. Kirkman, July 15, 1867 (second quotation), Microfilm Reel #7, and Joshua L. Randall to DTH, "Register of Letters Received," vol. 2, p. 301, Microfilm Reel #3, BRFAL, RG 105, M821, NA (1973); and Endorsement of A.H.M. Taylor, July 18, 1867, on letter of Joshua L. Randall to Joel T. Kirkman, June 18, 1867, "Subassistant Commissioner Records filed under 'Sterling, Texas,'" BRFAL, [unmicrofilmed], RG 105, NA; and

The next day, following his exhilarating, although perilous, posse ride, Hunsaker conducted his formal military investigation into the legality of Sam's will. Before him appeared Lorenzo, Rasche, and Wash. After ruling that the will was valid, Hunsaker ordered them to rectify their administrating the estate to the detriment of Dock, the rightful heir. The version of an account book presented by the Hearnes showed that they had collected some $5,700 for the sale of cotton and other payments to the estate, of which all but $1,560 had been paid out to cover expenses or debts. Other evidence, however, indicated that several accounts presented as having been settled in full were in reality settled at a discount. Caught lying about their handling of Sam's estate, the Hearnes meekly watched Hunsaker adjust their figures to reflect the markdowns in the estate's liabilities, resulting in a settlement to Dock of $2,206.41. Rasche paid this amount to the Freedmen's Bureau and received a receipt stating that the amount represented full settlement of the accounts of both his and Wash's administration and Lorenzo's subsequent administration. In his report to headquarters, Hunsaker stated that "a great deal of fraud and injustice" had been committed by the Hearnes and, as a consequence, he recommended that they "be made to pay in addition to said amount at least from one to two thousand dollars more."[38]

Hunsaker then exercised his powers bestowed upon him under authority of the Fifth Military District to prohibit any further action in the civil courts in regard to issues involved in settling Sam's estate. On July 15, 1867, under the overall command of the U.S. Army, the Freedmen's Bureau took over its administration. Hunsaker sustained Sam's will, terminated Lorenzo's administration of Sam's estate, and withdrew all lawsuits and matters involving it from the local courts. His orders were duly written into the records of both the county and district courts:

> Hon'r. Judge of the County Court Robertson Co. Texas
> Sir.
>
> I am directed by Major Gen. Griffin [Agt?] Bureau R.F.& A.L. State of Texas to notify you to suspend all further control

---

C. A. Thompson to Joel T. Kirkman, August 14, 1867, folder 6, box 56, Governors' Papers: Pease, RG 301, TSL-AD.

38. Oscar F. Hunsaker to Joel T. Kirkman, July 31, 1867 (quotations), Microfilm Reel #14, and Joshua L. Randall to J. P. Richardson, November 4, 1867, Microfilm Reel #14, BRFAL, RG 105, M821, NA (1973); and Oscar F. Hunsaker, "1st receipt," July 15, 1867, [copy], Microfilm Reel #29, COCADT, RG 393, M1188, NA (1981).

> in the matters appertaining to the Estate of Samuel R. Hearne, dec'd—To call the adm'r thereof to a settlement of his adminis-tration immediately—the Bureau of R.F.& A.L. having assumed the supervision of the same—That your Court take no further action in said cause. That this order be spread upon the records of said Court—You will report your action in conformity with this order to the undersigned at Galveston Texas.
>
> Very respectfully your obt. servant
> Oscar F. Hunsaker
> Agt. Bu. R.F. & A.L.

As required, local officials expeditiously wrote to Hunsaker to authenticate that they had properly executed his orders.[39]

What measures Lorenzo had taken in early 1867 for planting cotton and other crops on what was still called "the Sam Hearne place" remain unknown. Presumably the bureau allowed Lorenzo's sharecropping or hiring arrangements with freedmen to continue for the remainder of the year. Unfortunately, huge gaps regarding the bureau's management of the Brazos River plantation for the period 1867–68 exist in the Freedmen's Bureau papers and the correspondence of the military district's Office of Civil Affairs. Letters and documents pulled from files to review controversies over Sam's estate were either lost or misplaced. After the bureau terminated Lorenzo's administration and took control of the Brazos River plantation, even the names of those in charge of running the plantation remain a mystery.

It is known, however, that Hunsaker immediately paid Rasche's $2,206.41 settlement over to Dock—an amount of money roughly equivalent to over two years wages as could be earned by skilled carpenters in Houston or Galveston. The receipt signed "Docter J. Hearn" is the only signature of Dock's known to have survived. At the same time, and in accordance with the powers vested in him, Hunsaker appointed a new acquaintance, the notorious Ben Brown, as a Freedmen's Bureau agent. Hunsaker counted on Brown to assist Randall in quelling white violence against the ex-slaves and guaranteeing the physical safety of the freedpeople living and working on the Sam Hearne place, once a magnificent antebellum plantation

39. Alfred L. Brigance to Charles Griffin, August 30, 1867 (quotation), Microfilm Reel #10, Joshua L. Randall to J. P. Richardson, November 4, 1867, Microfilm Reel #14, BRFAL, RG 105, M821, NA (1973).

but now decreed provisionally by the federal government to be owned by Dock, a former slave, all in accordance with his father's will.[40]

Brown, it will be recalled, enjoyed a postwar reputation as a gang leader who imposed his personal brand of law and order upon criminals of both races. Captain Randall might have had reservations about Brown's behavior, but no extant written disapproval of Brown by Randall can be located. One contemporary of the era years later recalled Brown as a "famous Negro runner" who minimized "race riots and Negro criminality" during Reconstruction. Although he tracked down and administered impromptu punishment to freedmen wrongdoers, "Massa Bud Brown" was nevertheless extremely popular among the former slaves. He dealt honorably with them as a labor contractor by matching them to jobs they might otherwise not have found. He protected the personal safety of freedmen under contract with his planter friends and neighbors, such as former large slaveholder and prominent ex-secessionist Dr. Benjamin F. Hammond. Given the levels of violence against the freedmen, Brown was a logical choice as a bureau agent. With the authority of the U.S. Army behind him and supported by his posse of white and black gunmen and his bloodhounds, he brought enthusiasm and efficiency to his new job. But his behavior soon placed him in disfavor with federal authorities.[41]

Brown's report, written in late August, of his arrest and killing of a prisoner in his custody cost him his job as a bureau agent. Instead of sending his report to the acting adjutant attorney general of the Freedmen's Bureau, he wrote directly to General Griffin. His jumping up the chain of command and the content of his report raised more than a few eyebrows at headquarters. After Bob Leach, a known persistent lawbreaker, had shot a freedman to death merely because "he was a damned nigger," the civil authorities, as usual, took no action. Randall ordered Brown to arrest and, in Brown's words, "dispose" of Leach. Brown and his men and dogs tracked down and arrested Leach, but while conveying him back to Sterling he "attempted to make his escape whereupon a guard fired upon him

40. "Receipt of D. S. J. Hearne" (quotation), enclosed in Oscar F. Hunsaker to Joel T. Kirkman, July 31, 1867, Microfilm Reel #14, and A. P. Ketchman to Charles Griffin, September 2, 1867, Microfilm Reel #16, and Charles Griffin to O. O. Howard, August 17, 1867, Microfilm Reel #1, BRFAL, RG 105, M821, NA (1973).

41. Sam Eaves quoted in the Bryan *Daily Eagle,* July 22, 1926, p. 4 (first and second quotations); Statement of Louis Young in George P. Rawick, ed., *The American Slave: A Composite Autobiography,* vol. 5, [pt. 3 & 4], pt. 4 (Westport, Conn.: Greenwood Press, 1979), p. 233; Statement of Hattie (Hearne) Cole in Rawick, ed., *The American Slave,* supp., ser. 2, vol. 3: "Texas Narratives," pt. 2, p. 780 (third quotation).

killing him almost instantly." Brown and his posse effectively preempted any chance for the all-too-common outcomes, a jailbreak or jury nullification. Although Leach was a proverbial dead man as soon as Brown captured him, additional incriminating words in Brown's report sealed the end of his brief career as hired gunman for the Freedmen's Bureau.[42]

Brown had pledged himself to stopping the routine disarming of blacks by white terrorist groups. After one Robert Savile killed a freedman who refused to give up his shotgun, Brown gave his men orders to take Savile "dead or alive." When Savile "showed a disposition" to resist arrest, Brown's men "fired upon him killing him instantly." Claiming that a few persons were "complaining terribly" of his handling of Leach and Savile, Brown requested authority to deal harshly with his critics. He asked for "authority to arrest and put a moderate fine upon [the complainers]," adding that "it would have a good effect," by allowing him to carry out his duties "without expense to the Government." He bragged that within little over a month he had made Robertson County "entirely free of lawlessness" and pledged to keep it "in that desirable condition." He then reported that "the best citizens of Freestone County" had implored him to rid their county "of assassins, murderers, and thieves." If General Griffin approved, Brown proclaimed, he was ready and able to extend his peacekeeping operations on behalf of the federal government beyond the limits of Robertson County.[43]

Brown's appointment as a bureau agent had occurred at the same time the army removed James W. Throckmorton as an "impediment to Reconstruction" and appointed in his place former governor and unwavering unionist Elisha M. Pease. Floods of requests to remove local officeholders followed the ensuing removal of most other Conservative or Democratic state officeholders. Newly formed grassroots Republican organizations believed that appropriate removals and appointments would further help secure the election of Republican delegates to the state constitutional convention. Once Griffin received authorization to dismiss any county official who held office in violation of the Congressional Reconstruction Acts, the way was paved for extensive local removals. The purge of Robertson

42. Joshua L. Randall to Joel T. Kirkman, August 31, 1867 (first quotation), Microfilm Reel #21, and Benjamin Brown to Charles Griffin, August 31, 1867 (second and third quotation), Microfilm Reel #10, BRFAL, RG 105, M821, NA (1973).

43. "Records of Criminal Offenses Committed in Texas," [September 2, 1867, and August 3, 1867], p. 87, Microfilm Reel #32; and Benjamin Brown to Charles Griffin, August 31, 1867 (quotations), Microfilm Reel #10, BRFAL, RG 105, M821, NA (1973).

County officials proceeded at a slow pace, mainly because Randall had difficulty finding qualified men to replace the current set of officeholders.[44]

Meanwhile, Azeline and Dock were absent from Robertson County. Out of concern for their safety, Hunsaker had taken them back with him to Galveston. Their arrival in the bustling boomtown of Bryan, the new northern terminus of the H&TC Railroad in neighboring Brazos County, must have been a stimulating prelude to their subsequent train trip through Houston and their final dramatic entrance over the bridge across the bay into Galveston. The cosmopolitan port offered many advantages not found in the Brazos River bottomlands, especially a chance to live comfortably on Dock's earnings generated by his inheritance in the growing black enclave known as "Saccarap" near the seashore in the eastern section of the city. In addition, the island had seven schools operated by the Freedmen's Bureau in which "Yankee teachers" taught between three or four hundred blacks.[45]

While Dock attended school, Azeline became involved with the African Baptist Church then being reorganized as the independent First Regular Missionary Baptist Church (today surviving as the Avenue L Baptist Church). Here she met Reverend Israel S. Campbell, the church's postwar founder. Campbell was a Kentucky-born slave who escaped to Ontario and became a Canadian citizen as well as an ordained Baptist preacher. As a literate and light-complexioned man who could pass for white, he claimed to have matriculated in the 1850s at an Ohio college then swept up in the abolitionist crusade. Near the end of the war, he performed missionary work in occupied Louisiana and subsequently came to Galveston. Campbell was the first person in Texas to ordain black Baptist clergymen, and in the wake of the advent of Congressional Reconstruction he became active in Republican Party politics. As the Galveston *Daily News* contemptuously put it, he was one of the "mongrels from Oberlin College" who collected from "real Southern blacks" their Union League dues.[46]

Upon his return to Galveston with Azeline and Dock, Hunsaker had recommended to headquarters that an attorney be employed by the Freed-

44. Moneyhon, *Republicanism in Reconstruction Texas,* pp. 68–69; and "Reconstruction," *TNHT,* 5: 477 (quotation).

45. [Unsigned Letter to Brevet Major General Joseph J. Reynolds], February 11, 1868, Microfilm Reel #39, COCADT, RG 393, M1188, NA (1981); and David G. McComb, *Galveston: A History* (Austin: University of Texas Press, 1986), pp. 68–69, 87 (first quotation), and 89 (second quotation).

46. "Campbell, Israel S.," *TNHT,* 1: 925; and Galveston *Daily News,* "The Negro Vote," November 17, 1869, p. 2 (quotations).

men's Bureau to represent Dock's interests. Otherwise, he claimed, Dock would be "cheated" out of his lawful inheritance. The very next day Hunsaker informed headquarters that he had been retained as Dock's lawyer for a legal fee of $1,500. Significantly, on this same day, August 1, 1867, Griffin revoked Hunsaker's appointment as a special field agent for the bureau and appointed him recorder of the City of Galveston—an important city police court position that Griffin had planned for Hunsaker to assume. Although Hunsaker now held no position in the bureau, he returned to Robertson County accompanied by Second Lieutenant Joel T. Kirkman, the Freedmen's Bureau's acting assistant adjutant general. Their purpose was to collect more money from Wash, Rasche, and Lorenzo for having improperly administered Sam's estate.[47]

When Hunsaker and Kirkman arrived in Sterling, they gave Randall a copy of the accounts connected with the estate, told him that the $2,206.41 settlement had been "disapproved at headquarters," and directed him to collect an additional $1,850 from Lorenzo and his sureties. Kirkman's justification for the increase was twofold: headquarters had rejected the validity of certain payments made or expenses claimed by Lorenzo, and the initial settlement had rested on the false assumption that he was administrating the estate "with the will annexed." It will be recalled that, although Lorenzo had applied to administer the estate strictly according to the provisions of will, the probate court had decided to make him administrator for only the time required to reach a final settlement of the lawsuit to set aside the will. Whether Lorenzo intentionally misled Hunsaker in this matter is not clear, but Lorenzo's status was a matter of public record clearly described in the copies of court documents initially handed over to Hunsaker.[48]

With Kirkman and Hunsaker present, Randall showed Wash, Rasche, and Lorenzo the accounts with certain items checked off as disapproved and the corresponding amounts of money owed to the estate. When Kirkman demanded an additional settlement, the Hearnes refused to pay, pro-

47. Oscar F. Hunsaker to Joel T. Kirkman, July 31, 1867 (quotation), Microfilm Reel #14, and Oscar F. Hunsaker to DTH, Microfilm Reel #3, and Charles Griffin to O. O. Howard, July 3, 1867, Microfilm Reel #1, BRFAL, RG 105, M821, NA (1973); SO No. 145, DTH, Galveston, Texas, August 1, 1867, [By authority of Major General Griffin], "Adjutant General Reconstruction Records," folder 6, [401–860], TSL-AD; and [Unsigned Letter to Brevet Major General Joseph J. Reynolds], February 11, 1868, Microfilm Reel #39, frames 0715–0721, COCADT, RG 393, M1188, NA (1981).

48. Joshua L. Randall to Joel T. Kirkman, November 4, 1867 (quotations), Microfilm Reel #14, BRFAL, RG 105, M821, NA (1973).

testing that they held Hunsaker's receipt indicating that they had made "a full and final settlement" of their management of the estate and averred that they could prove that the disallowed items were as valid as any contained in the accounts. Kirkman dismissed their objections, and ordered Randall to arrest them and take them to Austin to be tried before a military commission. Rather than being led off under gunpoint by a squad of soldiers from the Sixth U.S. Cavalry, Rasche negotiated on the spot a compromise payment of "fifteen hundred dollars in gold." He angrily referred to his payment as an "outrage" because he was essentially forced to pay it in exchange for his release. For the rest of his life, Rasche declared that this incident was "tantamount to robbery under color of military authority"—a claim that endorsed the sentiment of most southern whites that they were living under "Blackstone with a bayonet."[49]

Rasche actually paid $1,000, and not the $1,500 that he claimed, as a settlement. His second bureau receipt indicated that the additional amount, taken together with the amount previously paid, constituted a full payment of $3,206.41 for all demands of Sam's estate against the Hearnes. Randall then transferred the $1,000 to Dock. When requested to report on these particular proceedings, Randall never questioned Hunsaker's role as anything other than a special agent of the bureau who had handled everything "with much dignity and ability" and "in no instance departed from or exceeded the powers granted him." Yet Kirkman, not Hunsaker, had issued all the orders—a circumstance due to Hunsaker no longer possessing any official position with the Freedmen's Bureau.[50]

Word of Hunsaker's alleged misdeeds traveled fast. Bureau agents in nearby counties relayed to headquarters gossip about Hunsaker extorting large sums of money from the Hearnes, paying none of the debts attached to the Brazos River plantation, and subsequently gambling the money

49. Joshua L. Randall to Joel T. Kirkman, November 4, 1867, Microfilm Reel #14, BRFAL, RG 105, M821, NA (1973); and [Unsigned Letter to Brevet Major General Joseph J. Reynolds], February 11, 1868 (first and fourth quotations), Microfilm Reel #39, frames 0715–0721, Horatio R. Hearne to Thomas H. Norton, [undated] (second and third quotations), Microfilm Reel #39, COCADT, RG 393, M1188, NA (1981); and Interview with Norman L. McCarver Jr., August 14, 1999 (fifth quotation), Hearne, Texas.

50. "Receipt: from Horatio R. Hearne for $1,000.00," August 13, 1867, [signed by Joshua L. Randall], and Joel T. Kirkman to Joshua L. Randall, August 10, 1867, "Subassistant Commissioner Records filed under 'Sterling, Texas,'" BRFAL, [unmicrofilmed], RG 105, NA; Joshua L. Randall to J. P. Richardson, November 4, 1867 (quotations), Microfilm Reel #14, BRFAL, RG 105, M821, NA (1973).

away. Randall consistently defended Hunsaker against these "stories in circulation," declaring them "base and malicious fabrications." Yet, in point of fact, the Freedmen's Bureau had not paid any of the remaining estate debts with the money it received from the Hearnes. Moreover, $1,500 of the settlement money had wound up in Hunsaker's pocket as a result of his agreement with Dock for legal services—a situation demanding bureau accountability. When Hunsaker signed receipts "Agent and Attorney for D .S. J. Hearne," it sparked rumors that Dock had signed over to Hunsaker his entire interest in his father's estate, or sizable chunks of it, via a power of attorney or deed of trust. No such legal instruments exist on file in the courthouse records in Robertson, Brazos, or Galveston Counties. Nor do any surviving records indicate that Hunsaker took over management of Sam's estate or did anything of value that he was not legally obligated to do for Dock. The absence of documentation, however, does not prove that Hunsaker neglected the general welfare of Dock and his mother while they lived in Galveston.[51]

The Death of Doctor Samuel Jones Hearne

In October 1867 Lieutenant Louis V. Caziarc arrived in Robertson County to assume his appointment as "Government Agent" of the Sam Hearne estate. No extant letter or acknowledgment of any report from Caziarc regarding his assignment can be found in the correspondence of either the Office of Civil Affairs or the Freedmen's Bureau. All that can be surmised is that at some point he probably placed Dr. Farner in charge, with instructions to rent the plantation for a period not longer than three years and "to convert the stock into money"—a reference presumably to Sam's shares of stock in the H&TC Railroad. No mention of the estate's debts was made, although Farner signed copies of claims against the estate as its agent following his opinions regarding their validity. On the ledger of items purchased on credit by Sam from Green Brown's store, Farner wrote that an "allowed payment will be properly made as soon as sales of property is ordered sold." But neither Caziarc nor Farner, or anyone else associated with the Freedmen's Bureau or the federal government, paid this or any

51. Edward Miller to William Sinclair, September 23, 1867, Microfilm Reel #14, and Joshua L. Randall to J. P. Richardson, November 4, 1867 (quotations), Microfilm Reel #14, BRFAL, RG 105, M821, NA (1973); and [Unsigned Letter to Brevet Major General Joseph J. Reynolds], February 11, 1868, Microfilm Reel #39, frames 0715–0721, COCADT, RG 393, M1188, NA (1981).

other valid debt. There were, however, extenuating circumstances for the lack of activity in all matters in Robertson County during the last part of the year.[52]

In late summer of 1867 the lower Brazos River valley experienced a major yellow fever epidemic. At the time most people believed that noxious swamp vapors or bad stagnant air caused the disease, which modern medicine calls malaria. Randall survived an attack of malaria in Sterling, even though local doctors, believing the sweating and shivering symptoms of his fever to be highly contagious, would not come near him. Millican, located on the eastern edge of the Brazos County bottomlands, became a virtual ghost town and suffered a reported mortality rate of nearly 70 percent. Randall's counterpart stationed there described the town as "a thing that has been, everybody that would leave, left, and the rest are dead men of about 200 inhabitants." The disease showed no respect for race or status. In Galveston most of the population caught the disease, and a total of 1,150 died at a rate of twenty per day. In September the epidemic took the life of General Griffin, the commander of the Department of Texas, and in early 1868 it claimed the life of Doctor Samuel Jones Hearne, a Texas freedman who owned a splendid Brazos River cotton plantation.[53]

Dock died in his mother's care after lapsing into the well-documented and predictable final stages of internal hemorrhaging, vomiting blood, deliriousness, and drifting into a coma. Galveston Health Department records reveal scant information other than that Dock died in the early weeks of January. His name was scribbled hastily and out of usual alphabetic order as "Jones Hearne." The spaces for "race" and "cause of death" were left blank. His age was indicated by a "20" followed by a dash—suggesting he was over twenty, which was true but misleading. Dock was over twenty-one years of age at the time of his death—a nagging detail raising the possibility that Hunsaker deliberately misrepresented Dock's age to the

52. Joshua L. Randall to J. P. Richardson, November 4, 1867 (first and second quotations), Microfilm Reel #14, BRFAL, RG 105, M821, NA (1973); [Unsigned Letter to Brevet Major General Joseph J. Reynolds], February 11, 1868, Microfilm Reel #39, frames 0715–0721, COCADT, RG 393, M1188, NA (1981); Notation of William H. Farner on "Brown's Store. Robertson County, Texas [account of] Mr. S. R. Hearne Bo[ugh]t of Greenwood Brown," [undated] (third quotation), Re: Estate of Samuel R. Hearne, Docket #134, PF, CCO, Robertson County, Texas.

53. George T. Ruby to Joel T. Kirkman, July 26, 1867, Microfilm Reel #7, and Edward Miller to William H. Sinclair, September 23, 1867 (quotation), Microfilm Reel #14, BRFAL, RG 105, M821, NA (1973); and McComb, *Galveston: A History,* p. 94.

health department. Dock had inherited his father's sizable wealth, come of age, and died intestate. Under the laws of Texas, an administration of Dock's estate should have been opened either in Galveston or in Robertson County.[54]

Hunsaker was Dock's attorney. Yet he apparently decided that an administration of Dock's estate was unnecessary because Azeline was her son's solitary heir as established under Sam's will. Sam's entire estate now legally devolved exclusively to her. Moreover, every knowledgeable person remotely concerned about securing some degree of justice for Dock and Azeline had assumed that no other option existed beyond administrating, for a prolonged period of time, Sam's estate for their benefit because they would need considerable help managing its supervisory, financial, and legal matters. At the time of Dock's death, most assumed that Hunsaker was in charge, but with the demise of his client he washed his hands of the entire matter. What at this time constituted Lieutenant Caziarc's official responsibilities as an agent of Sam's estate remain unknown, and no reports from Captain Randall regarding the bureau's management of Sam's plantation have been located. What is known for certain is that Azeline decided to leave Galveston and return home to Robertson County to live on her plantation as its rightful owner. Once back in the house she had lived in for fourteen years, she learned that the Hearnes were attempting to put an end to the army's control of Sam's estate.

After learning of Dock's death and Azeline's return, Lorenzo Hearne petitioned the Robertson County Probate Court "to dislodge" Sam's estate from beneath the prohibition against litigating or handling in the civil courts any issues pertaining to it. Lorenzo requested the court to resurrect his administration of the estate in order to allow him to make a final settlement. However, he did not specify a closing date or whether he would carry out his duties with the will annexed. Lorenzo declared that, as the estate's prior administrator pending the outcome of the litigation over the will's validity, he had paid the 1867 county taxes on the Brazos River plantation, kept the probate court informed of his activities, and asked for approval to pay off all the estate's accumulated debts. He thus had diligently discharged his duties up until being, in his words, "forcibly discharged and ejected by Oscar F. Hunsaker," who claimed to be act-

54. Galveston Health Department, "Interment Record, 1866–1881," entry for "Hearne, Jones," #723, p. 317, [microfilm copy], Rosenberg Library, Galveston, Texas.

ing under orders from General Griffin. The court rejected Lorenzo's petition, ruling that military authorities had not lifted Hunsaker's July 15th interdict.[55]

Captain Joshua L. Randall's Unsigned Letter

When Captain Randall learned of Dock's death, his conscience was sufficiently troubled over the bureau's management of Sam's estate to cause him to vent his critical bile. During the past six months, his tenure as a bureau agent had been both disappointing and hazardous. Following his bout with yellow fever and continued threats on his life, he had tried unsuccessfully to force ex-Confederate army veteran Judge Robert S. Gould of the Thirteenth Judicial District to comply with an order from headquarters directing that only persons registered as voters under the Reconstruction Acts should be eligible as jurors. The order cleared away the legal confusion of a prior order that had required white voters to swear that they had never voluntarily aided the Confederacy before being allowed to serve as jurors. But even with a greatly enlarged pool of whites from which a jury could be drawn, Judge Gould declared that the new directive "rendered it impractical to empanel a jury" and thus refused to try any cases during the court's fall 1867 term. Consequently even a threadbare chance to secure convictions for the murder of blacks—or, more realistically, given the nature of the jury system, to at least prevent their being unjustly convicted for crimes or wrongly ruled against in civil cases—had remained an impossibility in Robertson County. At the same time Randall had watched the registration process for the balloting in the upcoming convention referendum degenerate into precisely the "humbug" predicted by Hunsaker.[56]

Upon completion of the revision of voter registration in Robertson County, blacks comprised nearly 65 percent of those enrolled on the voting lists. Only 38 percent of the county's adult white males had bothered

55. Horatio R. Hearne to Thomas H. Norton, [undated letter] (first quotation), Microfilm Reel #39, COCADT, RG 393, M1188, NA (1981); and "Application of Lorenzo Hearne Admin[istrator] *Pendente Lite* for power to buy debts," filed April 29, 1867, and "Amended petition," filed May 27, 1867, and "Petition," filed January 28, 1868 (second quotation), Re: Estate of Samuel R. Hearne, Docket #134, PF, CCO, Robertson County, Texas.

56. Charles William Ramsdell, *Reconstruction in Texas* (Austin: University of Texas Press, 1910; reprint 1970), pp. 155–60; "Fall Term 1867," Book "J [452–922]," p. 638 (first quotation), MDC, Robertson County, Texas; Oscar F. Hunsaker to Joel T. Kirkman, July 9, 1867 (second quotation), Microfilm Reel #6, BRFAL, RG 105, M821, NA (1973); and "Gould, Robert Simonton," *TNHT,* 3: 258.

to register, and of this group less than one-third turned out at the courthouse in Owensville during the February 10th to 14th balloting on calling a state constitutional convention and in a simultaneous election for choosing a convention delegate. Although the abysmal white voter participation can be largely explained by revulsion against black suffrage, it was also due to the election result having been predetermined. In order to minimize the likelihood of white violence directed at the newly enfranchised black voters, influential whites announced that the freedmen would be allowed to carry the referendum in favor of holding a convention, but they must accede to white demands that battle-scarred ex-Confederate soldier James B. Boyd, who had been elected on the Conservative Democratic ticket in June 1866 to represent Robertson County in the Texas Senate, would run unopposed as a candidate for delegate. In brief, to avoid dangerous confrontations at the polling place, the freedmen were freely allowed to vote for the candidate who their late masters chose. The overwhelming majority of whites judged this arrangement to be logical and fair because they believed that the ensuing convention, if unchecked by men like Boyd, would bring about an unacceptable "Africanization of the state."[57]

The vote on whether to call a convention was racially polarized: black voters favored holding a convention by a vote of 292 to 6; whereas whites voted against it by 47 to 7. The lone seven white men, including Captain Randall and Dr. Farner, constituted a pathetic measure of Republican Party strength among white voters. Not much had changed since the 1866 gubernatorial race, in which Union Republican candidate Elisha Pease had garnered an equally disappointing eight votes. The unchallenged Boyd, who got the votes of every freedman who voted for holding a convention, became the convention delegate. Although Boyd often cooperated during the 1870s with the county's radical Republican leaders, in 1868 he was not supportive of the aspirations and hopes of the freedmen who elected him.[58]

On the third day of the balloting, Randall penned an indictment of the

57. U.S. Army, Fifth Military District, State of Texas, General Order No. 73, *Tabular Statement Of Voters (white and colored) Registered in Texas at Registration in 1867, and at Revision of the Lists in 1867–'68–'69; showing also the number (white and colored) Stricken Off the Lists. Tabular Statement Of Votes (white and colored) cast at Election held in the State of Texas, under the authority of the Reconstruction Acts of Congress* (Austin: April 16, 1870), pp. 1–9; Baum, *The Shattering of Texas Unionism,* p. 170; Robert C. Robison to Charles A. Morse, February 15, 1868, Microfilm Reel #7, COCADT, RG 393, M1188, NA (1981); and Dallas *Herald,* February 8, 1868 (quotation).

58. U.S. Army, Fifth Military District, State of Texas, General Order No. 73, *Tabular State-*

bureau's handling of Sam's estate. He could not bring himself, however, to accuse Hunsaker, Kirkman, Caziarc, Farner, or Brown—the bureau agents who had been most involved—of any wrongdoing. Having relied on these men for the defense of his own life, Randall perhaps had no other choice. Never once in his correspondence to headquarters had he criticized other bureau agents, but neither would he be a witness to further bureau malfeasance. He thus took a roundabout way to pass judgment on Hunsaker's actions, which would provoke headquarters to investigate matters. He wrote an unsigned statement detailing everything that had ostensibly gone awry and enclosed it with a cover letter to Rasche Hearne, who had been the alleged victim of an illegal bureau shakedown during the previous summer.[59]

Randall's statement claimed that Hunsaker's actions had for the last seven months placed the plantation and other property in legal limbo, where accountability had been conspicuously absent. Although, after Dock's death, Azeline was the sole heiress of Sam's entire estate under his will, the title to the Brazos River plantation could not be "legally vested" in her because Sam's will had not yet been properly probated. A specific eightfold denunciation followed: first, no authority had existed for Hunsaker to withdraw from the docket the lawsuit to vacate Sam's will merely "for fear" that the courts would not validate or sustain it. Second, the first settlement made by Hunsaker with the Hearnes was a final one, and thus the additional $1,000 paid by Rasche had been "an arbitrary extortion." Third, when the bureau took possession of the estate's entire assets, it was "in common honesty bound to make some provision for paying the indebtedness of the estate." Fourth, Hunsaker had no right to charge $1,500 in legal fees "for attending to the business of a colored woman and boy." Fifth, if Dock made any conveyance of all or part of his interest in his father's estate to Hunsaker without receiving any consideration in return, it constituted criminal fraud. Sixth, the bureau's goal of providing basic jus-

ment Of Voters (white and colored) Registered in Texas at Registration in 1867, and at Revision of the Lists in 1867–'68–'69; showing also the number (white and colored) Stricken Off the Lists. Tabular Statement Of Votes (white and colored) cast at Election held in the State of Texas, under the authority of the Reconstruction Acts of Congress (Austin: April 16, 1870), pp. 1–9; and Manuscript Election Returns for 1866, Folder for Robertson County, Secretary of State Records, RG 307, TSL-AD.

59. [Unsigned Letter to Brevet Major General Joseph J. Reynolds], February 11, 1868, frames 0715–0721, and Joshua L. Randall to Horatio R. Hearne, February 12, 1868, Microfilm Reel #39, COCADT, RG 393, M1188, NA (1981).

tice to Dock and Azeline had been "defeated by the corruption and malfeasance of the subordinate officials of Gen'l Griffin." Seventh, Hunsaker ought to be compelled to provide a full accounting of the estate's property and turn the books over to whomever civil authorities appointed as an administrator to make a final settlement. Eighth and finally, all bureau agents involved in the management of the estate should "be duly investigated" and "such action taken as the facts and evidence will warrant."[60]

Randall's letter to Rasche suggested that the statement would bring about an investigation from headquarters. But Rasche ought to have his lawyer "put the document in his own handwriting" and send it to Major General Winfield S. Hancock, the commander of the Fifth Military District in New Orleans, who in turn would send it down the chain of command, where it would be referred for report either to Randall or to an officer appointed expressly to look into the case. But Randall's plan contained a couple of fatally wrong assumptions, namely, that Rasche cared about the internal problems of the Freedmen's Bureau and about the legal problems of his deceased cousin's former slave mistress. To the contrary, he believed that any military investigation would only enhance Azeline's title to Sam's plantation. The destruction of her inheritance was still Rasche's, along with Sam's other white lineal heirs', prime goal.[61]

Rasche's lawyer promptly filed Randall's unsigned statement away in a desk drawer and two years passed before he showed it to military authorities. By then the Freedmen's Bureau had left Texas, Randall and Hunsaker had moved to California and Louisiana, respectively, and the newly created railroad towns of Hearne and Calvert were bustling with activity. In addition, a radical Republican Party coalition of blacks, scalawags, and carpetbaggers controlled Robertson County politics. Yet Hunsaker's words, penned to headquarters in the summer of 1867, when he took Dock and Azeline to Galveston, eclipsed Randall's concerns with bureau malfeasance and were at once so uncomplicated, and yet so sadly prophetic: if the "legal, just, and rightful" heirs of Sam Hearne were not represented by an honest and competent attorney, they would be easily "cheated out of the entire estate."[62]

60. [Unsigned Letter to Brevet Major General Joseph J. Reynolds], February 11, 1868 (quotations), frames 0715–0721, Microfilm Reel #39, COCADT, RG 393, M1188, NA (1981).

61. Joshua L. Randall to Horatio R. Hearne, February 12, 1868 (quotations), Microfilm Reel #39, and Samuel J. Adams to Charles E. Morse, [undated] (January 1870?), Microfilm Reel #39, COCADT, RG 393, M1188, NA (1981).

62. Oscar F. Hunsaker to Joel T. Kirkman, July 31, 1867 (quotations), Microfilm Reel #14, BRFAL, RG 105, M821, NA (1973).

Chapter 4

Unheard of in Any System of Procedure

> The suit against her [Azeline Hearne] was unfounded and . . . the parties setting up title to her land were mere usurpers.
>
> —MOSES B. WALKER, TEXAS SUPREME COURT JUSTICE, TO JOSEPH J. REYNOLDS, APRIL 11, 1870

IN 1868 ROBERTSON COUNTY underwent a dramatic transformation. Lum Hearne's prewar offer of a gift of land to the H&TC Railroad ensured that its postwar continuation would bypass Wheelock and Owensville and run closer to the Brazos bottomlands containing his family's plantation lands. After Lum's death in 1867, his wife Mary Ellen Hearne deeded about seven hundred acres to the railroad, and the new town named in Lum's honor was laid out in anticipation of the arrival of the tracks from Bryan. Tent stores and saloons sprang up to serve the needs of construction workers, many of whom were Irish immigrants brought into Texas by the railroad in order to avoid interfering with "the agricultural labor." Camp followers "with ethics of their own" soon made their predictable appearances. Hearne, or "Hearne Station," as contemporaries of the period called it, became in April 1868 the northern terminus of the H&TC Railroad.[1]

1. Richard Denny Parker, *Historical Recollections of Robertson County, Texas, with Biographical & Genealogical Notes on the Pioneers & Their Families* (Salado, Tex.: Anson Jones Press, 1955), p. 79 (first quotation); Norman L. McCarver and Norman L. McCarver Jr.,

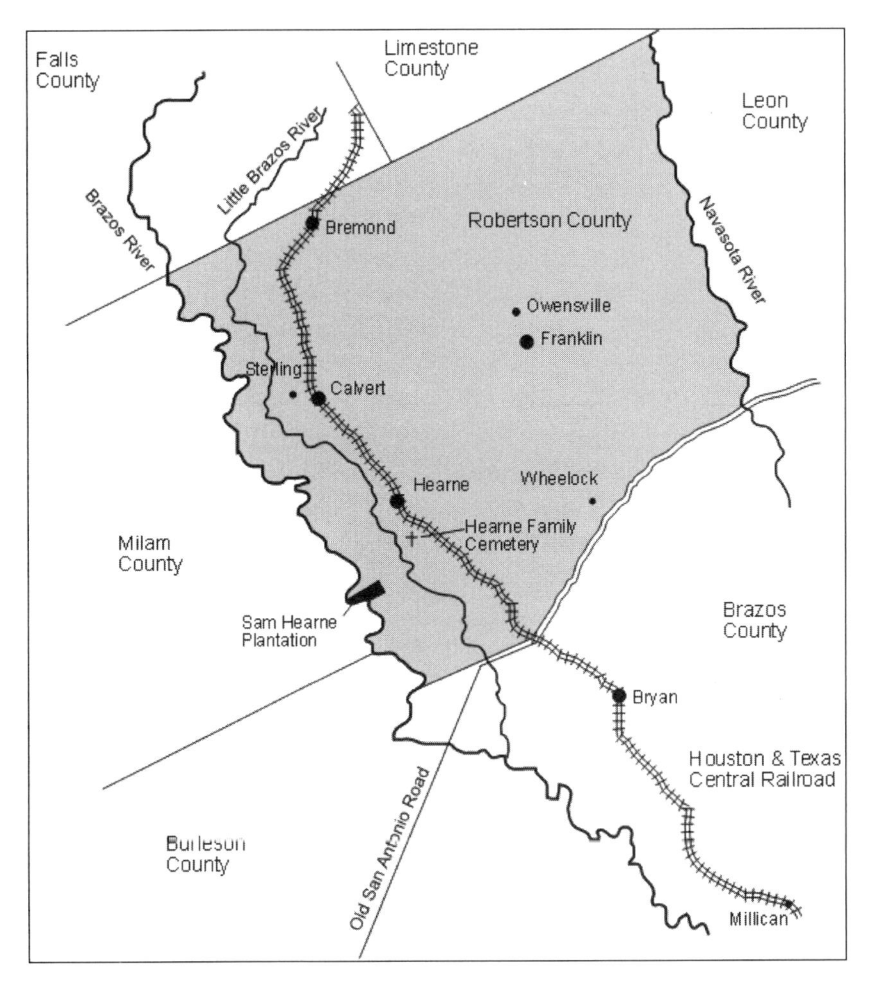

Robertson County, Texas, circa the Early 1870s

In a private venture, Robertson County planters, with involvement of a construction engineer for the railroad, mapped out to the north of Hearne another town site, deeded the railroad a right-of-way through it, and provided land for a depot. The town of Calvert was thus born, and speculation in lots began in the spring of 1868. Sterling and Owensville experienced a rapid decline when most of their residents moved to the new town

Hearne on the Brazos (San Antonio: Century Press of Texas, 1958), pp. 10–12; William R. Baker to Joseph J. Reynolds, November 3, 1869 (second quotation), Microfilm Reel #30, COCADT, RG 393, M1188, NA (1981); and Letter of Lizzie Abram, *Southwestern Christian Advocate,* June 3, 1880, p. 4 (third quotation).

site. Merchants from Galveston, Houston, and Hempstead started building stores on Calvert's Main Street in expectation of the economic explosion that came in the summer of 1869 with the arrival of the first train. The sounds of hammers and saws could be heard constantly for months, while grocery store merchants provided a free drink of whiskey to every paying customer. At the height of the subsequent cotton harvest, trains from Calvert carried in just one day, at one-third the cost, as many bales to Hempstead as one thousand ox teams had been able to haul in two weeks. By 1879 Robertson County produced over two and a half times as much cotton as in 1869, and into the beginning of the twentieth century Calvert remained the most important cotton market in central Texas.[2]

Later-day myths about the Reconstruction era in Robertson County ignore the economic prosperity sparked by the arrival of the H&TC Railroad, which obtained the financial backing of northern Republican investors and also received favorable treatment from the Republican-controlled Twelfth Texas Legislature. The county seat of Owensville, along with Sterling and Wheelock, did not go into a swift decline because they were "[d]espised by [federal] troopers, scalawags, and Negro freedmen." They deteriorated because they were bypassed by the railroad. More importantly, during the enormous economic development of Hearne and Calvert, which lasted throughout the 1870s—a period that corresponded to the zenith of local Republican Party dominance—the biggest problem confronting the county was how to deal with the unwanted accompaniments of rapid growth, including the vices of a large transient population comprised of workers, gamblers, and hucksters, of whom the overwhelming majority were white and not black.[3]

Military Appointments during the Winter of 1867–68

In November 1867 military authorities appointed Texas scalawags Nathaniel Hart Davis and Phidello ("Fidella") William Hall as district judge and district attorney, respectively. Davis served as district judge until 1870, but

2. J. W. Baker, *A History of Robertson County, Texas* (Waco, Tex.: Printed by Texian Press, 1970), pp. 162–63, 464–65, 467–80, and 484–500; Galveston *Daily News*, September 24, 1869, p. 3; Manford Eugene Jones, "A History of Cotton Culture along the Middle Brazos River" (M.A. thesis, University of New Mexico, 1939), p. 17; Ivory Freeman Carson, "Early Development of Robertson County" (M.A. thesis, North Texas State College, 1954), p. 46, and Carl H. Moneyhon, *Texas after the Civil War: The Struggle of Reconstruction* (College Station: Texas A&M University Press, 2004), p. 156.

3. Moneyhon, *Texas after the Civil War*, pp. 150–151; and Baker, *A History of Robertson County*, p. 139 (quotation).

Fidella Hall played a leading role in Robertson County Republican politics throughout most of the next decade. Hall had worked early in the war as a munitions specialist to avoid being drafted into the Confederate army. His antislavery views, however, compelled him to return to his family's home state, where in early 1863 he enlisted in the Eleventh Union Kentucky Volunteer Cavalry. He subsequently served with General William Tecumseh Sherman in the invasion of Georgia. After the war Hall returned to Texas, where his family had taken up residence in the new town of Bryan in neighboring Brazos County.[4]

Fidella Hall's family possessed an impeccable Lone Star State pedigree. His father, Thomas Jefferson Hall, an original Texas colonist who fought in the Texas Revolution, was an antisecessionist slaveholder before the war, a stalwart unionist during it, and after it held military appointments as the treasurer of Brazos County and an alderman in Bryan. In addition, he was a well-known inventor. In the late 1860s he received patents for a gangplow, a cultivator, and a coffee roaster, and previous patents were reissued to him for other profitable inventions. In the early twentieth century, his second wife and youngest sons, especially Edward, played prominent roles in the history of the city of Bryan. By then, however, the family's radical Republican antecedents had been either graciously forgiven or conveniently forgotten.[5]

Before the appointments of Fidella Hall and Judge Davis, indictments and convictions against whites who committed outrages against blacks had been virtually impossible to obtain. In 1867 twenty freedmen in the county had been "deliberately shot," but "not one of the criminals" had been brought to justice. Although most whites were unwilling to convict any white defendant for an offense against a black and the freedpeople's testimony still carried, in Hall's words, "no weight with Rebel jurymen,"

4. Houston *Post,* October 10, 1893; SO No. 206, DTH, Austin, Texas, November 18, 1867, [By authority of Brevet Major General Joseph J. Reynolds], "Adjutant General Reconstruction Records," box 860, folder 8, RG 401, TSL-AD; *Registers of Elected and Appointed State and County Officials, 1866–1870,* Microfilm Reel #4, pp. 566–567, RG 307, TSL-AD.

5. Ernest Emory Bailey, comp. and ed., *Texas Historical and Biographical Record: With a Genealogical Study of Historical Family Records* (Austin: By the Author, 1900), pp. 310–13; Elmer Grady Marshall, "The History of Brazos County, Texas" (M.A. thesis, University of Texas at Austin, 1937), p. 224; Glenna Fourman Brundidge, *Brazos County History: Rich Past—Bright Future* (Bryan, Tex.: Family History Foundation, 1986), p. 100; U.S. Department of Interior, Patent Office, *Annual Report of the Commissioner of Patents for the Year 1869,* United States Patents #89, 144 (April 20th), #95, 338 (September 28th), and #97, 083 (November 23rd), 41st Cong., 2nd sess., 1869. H. Exdoc. 102 vol. 1 Serial 1420.

packing a jury, false swearing, and blatantly unfair treatment of blacks by civil authorities became less common. When blacks were eventually included in jury pools, ruling unjustly against them in civil cases or convicting them for crimes they did not commit became more difficult, but a guaranteed chance at justice was far from assured. Discriminatory practices continued, even though the laws were, in theory, completely colorblind.[6]

At the end of 1867, Isaac B. Ellison replaced Alfred L. Brigance as county judge. Captain Joshua Randall, the local Freedmen's Bureau agent, had recommended Ellison, calling him a "fine lawyer" who had been "tried in an ordeal of fire" during the war because of his unbendable unionism. The search for a new sheriff, the next major appointment, generated considerable controversy. In the spring of 1868, Captain Randall endorsed William H. Wheelock. Former bureau agent Ben Brown and planters Dr. Benjamin F. Hammond and Rasche Hearne also endorsed Wheelock, but not a single member of the local bar recommended him, and District Attorney Hall and Judge Ellison's support was lukewarm. Ellison was "astonished" that Wheelock could take the "iron-clad" oath, not to mention that he could manage to qualify under the restrictions of the soon-to-be-ratified Fourteenth Amendment. Wheelock had been the county's sheriff during the 1850s and a unionist during the secession crisis, but during the war he had taken an oath to support the Confederacy when again sworn in as sheriff. During Presidential Reconstruction he had won election on the Conservative Union, or Democratic, ticket to represent Robertson and Burleson Counties in the Texas House of Representatives.[7]

Repeated efforts to find someone sensitive to the welfare of the freedpeople who could qualify to be appointed as sheriff exposed the tiny pool

6. Joshua L. Randall to J. P. Richardson, January 27, 1868 (first and second quotations), BRFAL, RG 105, M821, NA (1973); and Phidello W. Hall to Joseph J. Reynolds, March 15, 1868 (third quotation), Microfilm Reel #17, and Phidello W. Hall to Charles Griffin, n.d. [August 1867?], Microfilm Reel #6, COCADT, RG 393, M1188, NA (1981).

7. *Registers of Elected and Appointed State and County Officials,* Microfilm Reel #4, pp. 566–67, RG 307, TSL-AD; Joshua L. Randall to Joel T. Kirkman, August 31, 1867 (first and second quotations), box, 56, folder 9, and "Petition to Governor Pease," [signed by Joshua L. Randall, Robert C. Robinson, J. W. Maris, James I. Galloway, Charles P. Salter, and 38 others], April 14, 1868, box 57, folder 34, and "Anonymous letter against William H. Wheelock," April 24, 1868, box 57, folder 36, and Isaac B. Ellison to Elisha M. Pease, June 1, 1868 (third and fourth quotations), box 57, folder 39, Governors' Papers: Pease, RG 301, TSL-AD; Donaly E. Brice and John C. Barron, *An Index to the 1867 Voters' Registration of Texas,* Robertson County, "William H. Wheelock," Registration No.1348 (CD-ROM #1354; Bowie, Md.: Heritage Books, Inc., 2000); and *Registers of Elected and Appointed State and County Officials,* Microfilm Reel #3, p. 29, RG 307, TSL-AD.

of loyal or open-minded whites available locally to replace the old set of officeholders. Sheriff Wheelock's detractors failed to propose suitable alternative candidates, although one of them sarcastically wrote "a respectable freedman would be preferable." Carpetbagger Robert Porter replaced Wheelock in the fall of 1868. Military authorities, in turn, tried to replace Porter in the following year with another discharged Union soldier, but after local citizens refused to "go on his bond" Robertson County, in the fall of 1869, was without a sheriff—a situation temporarily crippling the operation of the civil courts.[8]

The Freedmen's Bureau's Mismanagement of Sam Hearne's Estate

When Azeline's son Doctor Samuel Jones Hearne died in early 1868, all the extraordinary legal arrangements made by the Freedmen's Bureau involving Sam Hearne's estate had proceeded with as much evenhandedness as one could have possibly expected. Even the much-maligned special bureau agent Oscar Hunsaker had taken, in the summer of 1867, the most reasonable course of action consistent in assuring basic fair play to Dock and Azeline. Before juries included blacks in the Robertson County District Court, disregard by whites of the facts and the law would have guaranteed Sam's will being vacated and set aside. But for Hunsaker's July 15th interdict prohibiting any action in the civil courts in regard to issues involved in settling Sam's estate and placing the Freedmen's Bureau in control of its administration, a miscarriage of justice would have occurred.

A review by the army's Office of Civil Affairs of the bureau's management of the estate acknowledged only one possible mistake, that a wrong "might have been done" to Rasche Hearne. The extra $1,000 allegedly "extorted" from him might well have been a fair settlement, but the wording on the initial receipt clearly suggested otherwise. This slipup, however, was eclipsed by a much larger unacknowledged mistake: the bureau, although admittedly undermanned and overextended, had failed to prop-

8. "Anonymous letter against William H. Wheelock," April 24, 1868 (first quotation), box 57, folder 36, and Phidello W. Hall to Elisha M. Pease, October 8, 1868, box 58, folder 48, Governors' Papers: Pease, RG 301, TSL-AD; *Registers of Elected and Appointed State and County Officials* Microfilm Reel #4, pp. 566–67, RG 307, TSL-AD; SO No. 61, DTH, Austin, Texas, October 19, 1868, [By authority of Brevet Major General Joseph J. Reynolds] quoted in Book "J [452–922]," pp. 770–71, MDC, Robertson County, Texas; Charles E. Morse to E. B. Turner, August 23, 1869 (second quotation), "Letters Sent: Volume 2," ledger #614, p. 305, Microfilm Reel #1, COCADT, RG 393, M1188, NA (1981).

erly administer Sam's estate during the second half of 1867—a breakdown of accountability that can be attributed partly to the advent of the yellow fever epidemic. During its "awful visitation," former bureau agent Dr. William Farner managed to accumulate sworn statements and corroborating evidence of claims against the estate, but the bureau never negotiated schedules of payments to clear these debts at the end of the harvest season, when it presumably had some cash on hand from the sale of cotton and other crops. Before ceasing its operations in the state at the end of 1868, the bureau was duty-bound, but unsuccessful, in arranging settlements of all outstanding claims, rendering a final report of its accountings, and finding an honest and qualified executor willing to be supervised by the probate court in carrying out the terms of Sam's will.[9]

The duties of an executor of a sizable estate, then as now, were seldom easy, and serving as the administrator of Sam's estate entailed additional problems. Legal challenges from the Hearne and Lewis families would be predictable, along with the appearance of claimants pretending ownership of the Brazos River plantation under Mexican land grants. In addition, management of the Brazos River plantation would have to be continued for a protracted period of time, due to the difficulty faced by Azeline, who had returned home from Galveston after Dock's death, in managing its financial affairs, not to mention negotiating, supervising, and enforcing by herself all rental, sharecropping, and hiring agreements. What efforts were taken by government authorities to find a suitable administrator are not known, but former bureau agents Dr. Farner and Ben Brown had to have been among the most likely candidates. Between the two of them, however, only Brown would have been able to post the required bond.

In the spring of 1868, during the constitutional crisis triggered by the impeachment and trial of President Andrew Johnson, Sam's brothers and cousins once again futilely petitioned civil authorities to lift the ban on litigating matters regarding Sam's estate and hear the case still lingering on the district court docket to set aside Sam's will. At the same time,

9. Statement written by Judge Advocate DeWitt Clinton on cover of a letter from Lieutenant John B. Guthrie, February 22, 1870 (first quotation), frame 0618, and Oscar F. Hunsaker, "1st receipt," [copy], July 15, 1867, frame 0712, and [Unsigned Letter to Brevet Major General Joseph J. Reynolds], February 11, 1868, frames 0715–0721, and Horatio R. Hearne to Thomas H. Norton, [undated] (second quotation), Microfilm Reel #39, COCADT, RG 393, M1188, NA (1981); Livingston Lindsay to Elisha M. Pease, October 9, 1867 (third quotation), box 56, Governors' Papers: Pease, RG 301, TSL-AD; [Unsigned Letter to Brevet Major General Joseph J. Reynolds], February 11, 1868, frames 0715–0721, Microfilm Reel #39, COCADT, RG 393, M1188, NA (1981).

well-known Galveston merchant Ebenezer B. Nichols announced that he would no longer try to prosecute his firm's lawsuit initiated a year earlier against Sam's estate to collect a debt. Cases against the estate filed by creditors presenting incontrovertible evidence of valid contracts had been routinely set aside under the existing bureau ban, but the lawsuits themselves were allowed to remain on the docket. When Nichols and Company dropped its lawsuit, most creditors holding claims against Sam's estate lost hope of ever collecting the money owed them. Many sold their claims to others at substantially discounted rates.[10]

Not until June 1868 was the problem of finding someone to assume a normal administration of Sam's estate resolved. In the Robertson County Probate Court, with scalawag county judge Ellison presiding, Ben Brown petitioned to be its administrator. Brown stated that he had been requested to apply "by those directly interested"—an assemblage that must have included Azeline, Captain Randall, Dr. Farner, Reverend Richard Sloan, and Azeline's well-respected neighbor Dred Dawson, who signed as a major surety on Brown's required bond. Brown claimed that there was a considerable amount of property, both real and personal, that was "going to distraction, waste, and decay." Although lawyers in similar petitions routinely used this sequence of words, this one most likely contained a candid description of bureau mismanagement over the past eleven months. Lorenzo Hearne, in his attempt in January to rescind the army's ban on litigating matters regarding the estate, had complained that the Brazos River plantation was "going to waste" because the bureau had placed it "in the hands of irresponsible parties"—a group that included two of the adversaries of the Hearnes in the probate court skirmishes immediately following Sam's death, James Cunningham and Enoch Aiken, and more significantly, most likely many freedmen who were subleasing from them.[11]

Renting or subleasing land to former slaves was controversial. The practice ran counter to the notion that the freedmen were incapable of work-

10. *A. L. Hearne, et al. vs. J. W. Cunningham, Administrator,* Case No. 978, [Spring Term, 1868], Book "J [452–922]," p. 668, and *E. B. Nichols & Co. vs. S. R. Hearne,* Case No. 930, [Spring Term, 1868], April 8, 1868, Book "J [452–922]," p. 656, MDC, Robertson County, Texas; and [Unsigned Letter to Brevet Major General Joseph J. Reynolds], February 11, 1868, frames 0715–0721, Microfilm Reel #39, COCADT, RG 393, M1188, NA (1981).

11. "B[enjamin] Brown Petition for Administration," June 10, 1868 (first and second quotations), filed June 18, 1868, and "Petition of L. D. Hearne," filed January 28, 1868 (third and fourth quotations), Re: Estate of Samuel R. Hearne, Docket #134, PF, CCO, Robertson County, Texas.

ing without close control over their daily activities. The vast majority of the freedmen worked on someone else's land for either wages or shares of the crop under conditions that allowed their employers to supervise them, squeeze more out of them, and cheat them at settlement time. Yet renting or subletting to freedmen was not unprecedented. In 1868 and 1869 ex-slave John C. Love rented two large plantations in the northern part of the county's bottomlands and sublet the lands to other freedmen for specified quantities of various crops. Upon Love's death in the fall of 1869, numerous tenants owed him some $4,000 in rents and debts. The absence of any written contracts yielded nothing short of a collection nightmare. A few incidents of broken contracts and renters planting "very indifferent crops" further complicated matters. Cunningham and Aiken's difficulty in paying their rents on time during the 1868 fall harvest suggests that similar circumstances existed on Azeline's plantation.[12]

Black Assertiveness and Racial Violence in the Summer of 1868

Brown had filed his petition to be the administrator of Sam's estate shortly after the wildly distorted news arrived of the humiliation of the Ku Klux Klan at the hands of the freedpeople living on the outskirts of Millican thirty-five miles to the south. The town's location on the edge of large cotton plantations in the Brazos County bottomlands mirrored most of the characteristics of the newly established town of Hearne. However, unlike in the vicinity around Hearne, the Republican Party Union League, an organization created to organize and enfranchise black voters, was well organized in the Millican area. Blacks were just slightly over two-fifths of Brazos County's total population, but the February military-supervised election had not been, as in Robertson County, a farce in which they voted for a candidate whom their late masters had selected. With the help of unionist ex-slaveholder Robert C. Myers, who had ridden with Brown's posse immediately after the war, Brazos County black Republicans had nominated and elected one of their own race to be a delegate to the state constitutional convention.[13]

12. "Report of W. L. Faulkner," October 25, 1869 (quotation), [October Term, 1869], vol. "T," pp. 2–4, Microfilm Reel #964210, PM, CCO, Robertson County, Texas; and Joshua L. Randall to Charles A. Vernon, October 31, 1868, frame 0955, COCADT, RG 393, M1188, NA (1981).

13. Barry A. Crouch, *The Freedmen's Bureau and Black Texans* (Austin: University of Texas Press, 1992), pp. 117–22; Joseph Allen Myers, "Life of Joseph Allen Myers: Written in

At the time of the balloting for convention delegates, the Galveston *Daily News* noted with alarm reports from Millican that the freedmen, having "imbibed from some source very high ideas of their own importance," intended to make themselves "independent of the whites and to attempt to inaugurate Negro supremacy." The incident triggering the newspaper's concerns was a speech by Alfred Venable, one of many freedmen attending a Republican political meeting at the town's "Freedmen's church." In response to some resolutions introduced by Myers and other scalawags, Venable exclaimed that, although most of his race was illiterate, "the same benign Providence that gave them liberty would inspire them with wisdom to govern themselves loose from the whites." He concluded by calling upon the freedmen in attendance "to subscribe two dollars each to establish a store in Millican for their own benefit and accommodation."[14]

In retribution against the growing political and economic independence of Brazos County blacks, the Ku Klux Klan marched through the center of the Millican freedpeople's settlement. When the Klansmen shot off their weapons in an intimidating display of force, the former slaves retaliated by firing back in self-defense. The terrified Klansmen rode off, "leaving the ground littered with masks, winding sheets, other wearing apparel, and two revolvers." White indignation over the incident generated rumors of hundreds of blacks preparing to launch armed warfare against whites or set fire to the town. Because the overwhelming majority of whites were determined to not back down again from any display of black solidarity, an inevitable confrontation occurred in mid-July. Whites used the opportunity to murder George Edward Brooks, one of the county's three military-appointed voter registrars and the black community's charismatic Methodist minister who had served in the Union army in the Seventh Louisiana Colored Infantry. A band of armed whites with bloodhounds chased him down, tortured him by stripping the flesh from his body, broke both his legs, and then hanged him by the neck.[15]

Only blacks died in the ensuing so-called Millican riot, which turned

the Month of November 1927" [typescript, taken from a ledger with the handwritten text of Joseph Allen Myers, by William Allen Myers, November 20, 2001], pp. 43–49, Bryan Public Library, Bryan, Texas.

14. Galveston *Daily News,* February 20, 1868 (quotations), p. 1.

15. Crouch, *The Freedmen's Bureau and Black Texans,* pp. 102–27; Melinda Meek Hennessey quoted in ibid., p. 117; and New Orleans *Advocate,* January 3, 1867, and October 24, 1868.

out to be the worst incident of racial violence in Texas during Reconstruction. At the time it received considerable attention throughout the nation. To underscore what would occur if the freedmen disobeyed white authority, most Texas newspapers exaggerated the dead and wounded figures for the blacks and falsely blamed them for having started the deadly incident. Although there were admittedly many "incalculable ramifications" of the killing of the "intelligent, courageous, powerfully built" Brooks and other Republican Party leaders, the withdrawal of Brazos County freedmen from political activity was *not* among them.[16]

Robertson County, like Brazos County, was saturated with white racism and violence and destined to witness an increase in the assertiveness of the freedmen. After the Millican episode some contemporaries of the period credited Myers and Brown with preventing further racial incidents. Because both had reputations for protecting blacks from whites who considered it "no crime to deceive, cheat, or murder a freedman," they were frequently denounced as "Negro lovers." In return they expected the freedmen to defer to them, rather than to carpetbaggers or even at times to their own leaders, for guidance and advice. Myers and Brown were among a small group of southern-born slaveholders whose postwar cooperation with the Freedmen's Bureau and the Republican Party offered some hope of introducing the freedpeople to the burdens and mysteries of freedom in extremely dangerous circumstances. A Democratic political opponent assassinated Myers in 1871, but Brown, who killed more than one of his enemies before they allegedly had a chance to kill him, died of natural causes.[17]

The new political militancy of the freedmen in the central Brazos River Valley surfaced dramatically when Hunsaker's friend George T. Ruby, an educated light-skinned carpetbagger who represented Galveston County in the state constitutional convention, successfully challenged white control of the Republican Party Union League. Discontent over military-appointed Governor Elisha M. Pease's record on prosecuting white terrorists and rewarding blacks with offices spilled over in August to the Republican state convention. In the pro-Ruby Republican Union League meeting held in Robertson County, blacks elected Randall and Fidella

16. Crouch, *The Freedmen's Bureau and Black Texans,* pp. 102 (first quotation) and 126 (second quotation); New Orleans *Advocate,* October 24, 1868, p. 5 (third quotation); and Dale Baum, *The Shattering of Texas Unionism: Politics in the Lone Star State during the Civil War Era* (Baton Rouge: Louisiana State University Press, 1998), p. 192.

17. Marshall, "The History of Brazos County," pp. 88–89; Freedmen's Bureau agent Nathan H. Randlett quoted in Crouch, *The Freedmen's Bureau and Black Texans,* p. 122 (first quotation); and Myers, "Life of Joseph Allen Myers," p. 9 (second quotation).

Hall to head up their delegation to the state convention, where Pease supporters prevailed but only at the expense of a serious rupture in their party. Republican bolters, or "Radicals," knowing that they could control the Union Leagues, formed a new party organization in opposition to the regulars, or Republican "conservatives." Hall and Randall were now "marked men," in the parlance of the day, because their careers in radical Republican politics could easily end in shallow graves. Such was the fate of George W. Smith, a former Union army captain and carpetbagger delegate to the state constitutional convention from Marion County. Participation in the Union Leagues by blacks was far more dangerous. So many blacks had been murdered in East Texas since congressional control of Reconstruction that the army could no longer keep track of the number.[18]

Thomas P. Aycock vs. Asaline Hearne

Amidst the attention generated by the approaching 1868 presidential election, in which Texans would not participate, Cunningham and Aiken failed, for unknown reasons, to pay the rent for Azeline's land upon which they were farming or subleasing. Brown, the executor of Sam's estate, held a power of attorney to act on Azeline's behalf. He made a complaint to the Freedmen's Bureau and threatened to file suit against Cunningham and Aiken in the district court. In an action signifying how small a chance Randall thought Azeline would have of collecting in the local courts the rents owed her, he intervened and ordered Sheriff Wheelock to take control of the cotton crop growing upon her plantation "together with the mules & gin & farming implements used thereon" until the bureau held enough security for the rent. Within two weeks Aiken and Cunningham gave Randall $590 in full payment for the overdue rent, which, in turn, Randall turned over to Brown. The total amount for which the bureau had rented out the plantation in 1868 is unknown, but containing at least 400 acres of cleared land, its rental value should have easily commanded up to $6 an acre, or at least $2,000.[19]

Besides collecting the rents, Brown limited his actions to protecting the

18. Carl H. Moneyhon, *Republicanism in Reconstruction Texas* (Austin: University of Texas Press, 1980), pp. 95–102; *The Free Man's Press* (Austin), August 15 and 22, 1868; *The Weekly Free Man's Press* (Galveston), October 24, 1868; and William L. Richter, *Overreached on All Sides: The Freedmen's Bureau Administrators in Texas, 1865–1868* (College Station: Texas A&M University Press, 1991), pp. 284–85.

19. Joshua L. Randall to Charles A. Vernon, October 31, 1868, frame 0955, COCADT, RG 393, M1188, NA (1981); and Joshua L. Randall to William H. Wheelock ("Sheriff Robertson County"), SO No. 98, September 22, 1868 (quotation), account page 64, and SO No. 99,

freedpeople working and living on or near Azeline's land, who would have been defenseless, in the absence of guaranteed retaliation from Brown's posse, against the lawlessness of the whites, who murdered freedpeople, in the words of one observer, "with the same indifference displayed in the killing of a snake or other venomous reptile." Otherwise, Brown disregarded many less vital duties as the administrator of Sam's estate. In the fall of 1868, when he had some cash on hand to pay off or reduce some of the estate's debts, he failed to do so. He also neglected to file his required reports with the probate court. Nor did he pay the estate's annual local and state taxes. Far more distressing was his failure to assist Azeline when she was served with her first ever court summons requiring her to respond to a lawsuit.[20]

Filing suit against her in the district court was Thomas Aycock, who was asking for payment of his attorney fees that she had assigned to him in December 1866 in exchange for his preventing Sam's will from being set aside in the district court. Brown presumably told Azeline to disregard the summons, because matters pertaining to the estate remained untouchable by any legal actions under the Freedmen's Bureau ban. Although Brown was correct, it remains a mystery why Judge Davis allowed Aycock's suit to circumvent Hunsaker's interdict and why Brown would let advance unchallenged a lawsuit having potentially devastating consequences to the estate of which he was the administrator. In the middle of October, at the same time that Cunningham and Aiken neglected to pay their rents, Azeline failed to appear at the courthouse to answer Aycock's claim against her.[21]

Aycock's contingency contract, it will be recalled, had set his fees at half the value of Sam's entire estate. The court minutes state that Azeline "wholly made default." The court accordingly ordered the sheriff, with the aid of a jury, to assess the precise dollar amount of Aycock's compensation. At this point Azeline had lost half of her entire net worth, which consisted of more than just the Brazos River plantation but also included a cotton gin and press, farm livestock, tracts of land in two other coun-

---

October 7, 1868, account page 64, "Subassistant Commissioner Records filed under 'Sterling, Texas'" BRFAL, [unmicrofilmed], RG 105, NA.

20. George T. Ruby to Joel T. Kirkman, August 12, 1867 (quotation), Microfilm Reel #4, BRFAL, RG 105, M821, NA (1973).

21. *Thomas P. Aycock vs. Asaline Hearne,* Case No. 1113, [Fall Term, 1868], October 15, 1868, Book "J [452–922]," p. 741, MDC, Robertson County, Texas.

ties, railroad stock, and all Sam's personal property. Fortunately, the order to the sheriff was afterward crossed out with an illegible explanation, preceded by the notation "*Error*" written in the margin. The unreadable words presumably reflected subsequent entries, that the case would be continued to allow Azeline time to demonstrate why Aycock's claim should be disallowed, and that he would have time to make amendments to his original lawsuit and have them duly served on her.[22]

Although Brown might have been the one who intervened to have the default judgment blotted out, far more likely it was Captain Randall. If Randall did not trust the district court with Azeline's claim against Cunningham and Aiken, then he also probably used the authority of his office to quash the award to Aycock. Not only would his action have been consistent with Hunsaker's interdict, but other evidence indicates that Randall, knowing that litigation involving the estate could not be postponed forever, wanted to put lawsuits regarding it on a path to a full and fair hearing in the civil courts. Moreover, because of the weakness of Aycock's case, Randall presumably believed that its resolution would be advantageous to Azeline and the estate. Aycock never strayed from arguing that Azeline and her son had assigned to him one-half interest in the estate for his *merely preparing* to go to trial on their behalf. In addition, and revealing for its additionally deficient legal reasoning, was Aycock's allegation that she had "disregarded" and "ignored" her obligations to him as her attorney by failing to notify him that she got the dispute over Sam's will removed from the civil courts and tried by a special military court.[23]

In January 1869, after Randall closed the Freedmen's Bureau office in Sterling, Brown made a provocative break with the past: he altered the rental arrangements on Azeline's plantation. While cotton stalks from the previous year were being pulled up and burned in preparation for the new crop, Brown leased, most likely on the wishes of Azeline, the entire plantation to two former slaves, Israel Campbell and Jim Wade. In the only known survival of her signature, Azeline signed the leasing agreements

22. *Thomas P. Aycock vs. Asaline Hearne,* Case No. 1113, [Fall Term, 1868], October 15, 1868, p. 741 (quotations), and [Spring Term, 1869], April 14, 1869, p. 824, Book "J [452–922]," MDC, Robertson County, Texas.

23. *Thomas P. Aycock vs. Asaline Hearne,* Case No. 1113, [Spring Term, 1871], February 20, 1871, Book "K," pp 57–58 (quotations), MDC, Robertson County, Texas; [Unsigned Letter to Brevet Major General Joseph J. Reynolds], February 11, 1868, frames 0715–0721, Microfilm Reel #39, COCADT, RG 393, M1188, NA (1981); and [Evidence of claims and some accounting of the S. R. Hearne estate], in *Asaline Hearne vs. H. D. Prendergast,* Case No. 3069, ODC, Robertson County, Texas.

using her nickname "Mrs. Press Hearne"—the moniker "Press" presumably stemming from her land boasting both a cotton gin and a press, but one cannot exclude her reputed skill at ironing clothes. Of her two black tenants, little is known about Wade other than he was originally from South Carolina and since emancipation had lived in Robertson County. Campbell was the well-known Baptist preacher and radical Republican leader who had befriended Azeline in Galveston.[24]

Campbell and Wade each rented one-half of Azeline's plantation. Both had the right to use the gin and press. Rent for each contract was $1,000—an amount not at all out of line with a reasonable rental fee. On the eve of the Civil War, Sam's plantation produced 175 ginned cotton bales, which at ten cents a pound, had been worth at least $7,500. At a price of around seventeen cents a pound in 1869, the 1860 cotton crop would have sold for over $13,000. Subtracting the usual expenses incurred by Campbell and Wade, their contracts either were potentially quite lucrative or reflected the neglected condition of the plantation while under the supervision of the Freedmen's Bureau. One thing was certain: Campbell had no intention of being a plantation manager. Throughout 1869 he dedicated himself to organizing the Regular Missionary Lincoln Baptist Association, which encompassed Houston and Galveston as well as the entire lower Brazos River Valley from Waco to the Gulf of Mexico. Reverend Campbell either hired a farm manager or sublet to other freedmen living on or near Azeline's land.[25]

Cayton Erhard and Others vs. Asaline Hearne

At some point during the spring of 1869, Brown decided to become an accomplice in a fraudulent scheme to cheat Azeline out of her rightful ownership of her Brazos River plantation. Although Brown's motives were never made clear, he might have concluded that fulfilling all his obligations as administrator of the estate for a lengthy and unknown duration

24. Joshua L. Randall to Charles Vernon, January 6, 1869, frame 0719, BRFAL, RG 105, M821, NA (1973); Contracts between Ben Brown and Jim Wade and between Ben Brown and Israel Campbell, January 21, 1869 (quotation), frames 0672–0673, Microfilm Reel #39, COCADT, RG 393, M1188, NA (1981); and "J. Wade," Registration No. 487, *Voter Registration Lists, 1867–1869*, p. 207, July 23, 1867, Microfilm Reel VR-10, Robertson County, Texas, TSL-AD.

25. Bureau of the Census, *Eighth Census of the United States, 1860*, Agricultural Census, Production of Agriculture, Robertson County, Texas, "Schedule 4," Microfilm Reel, #6, pp. 17–18, M653, NA (1967); "Campbell, Israel S.," *TNHT*, 1: 925; Galveston *Weekly News*, August 14, 1860, p. 2; and *Tri-Weekly State Gazette* (Austin), March 3, 1869, p. 3.

would be far too demanding. Perhaps he was bribed. All that is known for certain is that Brown held Azeline in low regard and did not approve of her possessing an amount of wealth putting her financially in a position superior to that of the vast majority of the white race. In spite of his prewar unionism, his stint, albeit it a brief one, as a Freedmen's Bureau agent and the respect given to him by Robertson County blacks, Brown came to the task of administrator of Sam's estate with his own unique set of racist predispositions, which easily could have been exacerbated by the pretentions of a former slave concubine to the ownership of a valuable cotton plantation.[26]

The occasion for Brown's betrayal was a lawsuit to contest Azeline's title to her plantation brought against her in April by Cayton Erhard and other heirs of Allen Reynolds. Spearheading the lawsuit was ex-Confederate veteran and prominent attorney William H. Hamman, who had a contractual interest in its outcome. Appallingly bad rulings made in the district court by Judge Davis aided Hamman's legal maneuvering—circumstances that either attested to Davis's incompetence or, worse yet, to his connivance with Brown and Hamman.[27]

By 1869 the thirty-nine-year-old Virginia-born Hamman had already led a remarkable life as a scholar, lawyer, orator, soldier, and oil prospector. After graduating from the University of Virginia, he earned a reputation during the 1850s as a gifted orator who spoke in praise of the glories of the American Union. In 1858 he migrated to Robertson County. The election of Abraham Lincoln altered the content of his public orations. Fearing the "perfidious fanatics" in the North who conspired to make slaves the masters of whites, Hamman spoke of the necessity for Texas secession. He subsequently enlisted as a private, fought in some forty battles, including Gettysburg, and rose from the rank of a regimental commissary sergeant to brigadier general only by virtue of a gubernatorial commission. Although subsequently referred to as "General Hamman," he was "in no credible sense," in the words of one Civil War scholar, a Confederate general. At the war's end Hamman became a bitter ex-Confederate

26. "Int[erro]g[atorie]s to B. F. Hammond, Ben Brown, and Crawford Allen," [Witnessed by A. M. Ruskin], June 22, 1882, [Interrogatories File], *Asaline Hearne vs. H. D. Prendergast,* Case No. 3069, ODC, Robertson County, Texas.

27. *Asaline Hearne vs. C. Erhard and others,* [No number in original (Case No. 3221)], Supreme Court of Texas, 33 Tex. 60; 1870 Tex. LEXIS 87, Decided 1870; Moses B. Walker to Joseph J. Reynolds, April 11, 1870, and Harvey D. Prendergast to Charles E. Morse and Joseph J. Reynolds, [undated and marked as "Exhibit B"], frames 0687–0690, Microfilm Reel #39, COCADT, RG 393, M1188, NA (1981).

diehard obsessed with the notion that the "noblest, the proudest, the most chivalrous" southern people would be "dragged down to the level of the [N]egro." He asked himself, as a consequence, whether he should go to a place "where there are no [Negroes]?"[28]

Hamman stayed in Texas. In 1866 he began searching for lignite, salt, coal, iron ore, and, most importantly, oil. He had "caught the oil fever" as a soldier invading Pennsylvania in the area of the Drake field. In East Texas he "blocked up land leases and options like a modern oil scout, hot on the trail of bonanzas." His ability to locate future rich pools of oil would, unbeknownst to him, later make his heirs fabulously wealthy. In the spring of 1867 Hamman began his successful courtship of Ella Virginia Laudermilk, whose family lived next door to Azeline. From the big porch of the Laudermilk house overlooking a bend of the Brazos River, Hamman gazed many times upon the adjacent "old Sam Hearne plantation." During this time he rekindled his prewar attention to the tangle of litigation over conflicting land claims to the Robertson County bottomlands.[29]

Hamman's intense antebellum searches in the deed books for imperfections in land titles paid him large dividends. By tracking down possible claimants and either purchasing their rights to the land or entering into agreements for his compensation in settling the conflicts of claims, he compiled files of "pretended claimants" holding valuable plantation lands under "various and different pretenses." These potential defendants included a veritable "Who's Who" of wealthy landowners in Azeline's immediate neighborhood, including Charles Lewis, Rasche Hearne, Titus C. Westbrook, and Lewis W. Carr. Hamman even targeted as a false owner his future father-in-law, George W. Laudermilk. Just prior to suing Azeline, Hamman had achieved a string of settlements among residents of the

28. Parker, *Historical Recollections of Robertson County,* pp. 156–60 (first, second, fourth, and fifth quotations on pp. 156–57); Harold B. Simpson, *Hood's Texas Brigade: A Compendium* (Hillsboro, Tex.: Hill Jr. College Press, 1977), p. 92; "W. H. Hamman's Speech—prepared when a candidate for the Senate of Texas 1865" (sixth quotation), box 2, William Harrison Hamman Papers, WRC-RU, Houston, Texas; and Bruce Allardice quoted in Ralph A. Wooster, *Lone Star Generals in Gray* (Austin, Tex.: Eakin Press, 2000), p. 246 (third quotation).

29. Parker, *Historical Recollections of Robertson County,* pp. 156–60; Ed Kilman writing for the Houston *Post* in 1943 in "Commissions, Speeches, Letters, etc.," vol. 2, p. 115 (first and second quotations), box AR29, William Harrison Hamman Papers, CAH-UT, Austin, Texas; W. A. Adair, "Early Days in Brazos Bottom," Bryan *Daily Eagle,* March 29, 1926, p. 4; "Road Overseer for Precinct 28," [March 1876–September 1879: Special Term, 1876], p. 94 (third quotation), CCM, Robertson County, Texas; and "Correspondence W. H. H. and Ella V. Laudermilk," box 1, folder 6, William Harrison Hamman Papers, WRC-RU, Houston, Texas.

southern half of the Brazos Bottoms, including a few with the Hearne and Lewis families. The largest was with brothers Rasche and Ebb Hearne for $8,500 in exchange for release of all claims on their and Charles Lewis's lands by a long list of individuals, most of whom were the heirs of Allen C. Reynolds. In this instance, Hamman's share was half of the compromise money.[30]

Perhaps Hamman performed a service to many in possession of valuable cotton lands who were thankful to eliminate, at often discounted compromise prices, the clouds cast over their titles, in most instances by heirs of earlier owners of the old Manchaca, Nixon, Martínez, and Ruiz grants. However, Hamman often used chains of titles as poker chips in a legal game of bluff. He never feared giving defendants or supposed claimants warranty deeds, because he knew that no one else could produce titles superior to the ones that he represented, assembled, or owned. Although no grand jury ever charged him with "common barratry"—the practice of initiating "exciting groundless suits" over land titles, Hamman nevertheless was typical of the widely disliked lawyers who made their living by stirring up litigation. "Who can be more nearly a fiend," wrote Lincoln as a young Illinois attorney, "than he who habitually overhauls the register of deeds, in search of defects in titles, whereon to stir up strife, and put money in his pocket."[31]

It will be recalled that the heirs of Allen Reynolds claimed a large portion of the Dred Dawson headright by virtue of inheriting it from an individual who could trace ownership directly back to José Antonio Manchaca—the original grantee of the Mexican state of Coahuila and Texas to six leagues of land along the Brazos River. The lawsuits of Reynolds's heirs against many of the alleged pretenders claiming the land were on the dis-

30. Power of Attorney, William A. Driskell & wife and Thomas C. Woodlief to William H. Hamman, dated June 12, 1868, Book "Q," pp. 15–17 (quotations), and warranty deeds to Horatio R. Hearne and Ebenezer Hearne from William H. Hamman signing for H. J. Jones, Cayton Erhard, H. M. Driskell, Thomas C. Woodlief, etc., August 18 and 26, 1868, Book "Q," pp. 1–4, Microfilm Reel #963281, RD, CCO, Robertson County, Texas; and Warranty Deed, William H. Hamman to George W. Laudermilk, August 7, 1869, *General Index to Deeds (Reverse), 1838–1901,* Book "L&M," p. 11, Microfilm Reel #963273, RD, CCO, Robertson County, Texas.

31. Henry Campbell Black, *Black's Law Dictionary,* 4th ed. (St. Paul, Minn.: West Publishing Co., 1951), p. 190 (first and second quotations); and Abraham Lincoln quoted in Lawrence W. McBride and Frederick D. Drake, "Abraham Lincoln and the Rule of Law," *National Council for History Education, Inc.: Ideas, Notes, and News about History Education* 14, no. 9 (May 2002): 7 (third quotation).

trict court docket in 1851, when Sam purchased his 903 acres from Britton Dawson. Most of the cases were dismissed three years later, prior to heirs or legal representatives of deceased plaintiffs and defendants being identified and added as litigants. Then in 1857 and 1858, William H. Cundiff and the Reynolds heirs, respectively, filed lawsuits against Sam Hearne.[32]

Cundiff was a large landowner from Houston County who apparently was not related to Reynolds. In December 1857, a full four years after Sam had begun actually living and paying taxes on his land under apparent title by his 1851 purchase of part of the Dawson headright, Cundiff filed a lawsuit against Sam for recovery of part of the Manchaca grant. He joined as defendants seven others in Sam's neighborhood, including Sam's brother Alley, and Sam and Alley's widowed sister-in-law Nancy Hearne. Cundiff had purchased the land from someone who had bought it from Manchaca in exchange for a "fine horse" and a "fine gold watch." Nine months later, in September 1858, the Reynolds heirs, none of whom ever actually lived on the lands in question, filed suit against Cundiff along with all those whom he was suing, including Sam, and others, including Charles Lewis, and Rasche and Ebb Hearne. Sam acknowledged both his 1857 and 1858 court summons and employed the same attorney as the other defendants to defend his title.[33]

The apparent separate chains of title emanating from Manchaca fueled an enduring local legend that "Manchaca was crooked." Nevertheless, a few defendants settled with Cundiff, including Charles Lewis and brothers Rasche and Ebb Hearne. Sam's cousin's husband Charles Lewis, who had not resided continually on his bottomland plantations for three years prior to Cundiff's 1857 suit, purchased for $550 Cundiff's rights in the parts of the Manchaca grant in which his Brazos Bottoms plantations were located. Subsequently, in the spring of 1860, Cundiff stated that he

32. *The Heirs of Allen Reynolds vs. Britton Dawson,* Case No. 180, [Fall Term, 1851], Book "I," pp. 43–44, MDC, Robertson County, Texas; "Statement of Facts," [undated], in *Eliza Cornelia Willett (Reynolds) vs. Charles Lewis, et al.,* Case No. 662, folder #2, ODC, Robertson County, Texas.

33. "Statement of Facts," [undated], and "Summons: Samuel R. Hearne and others," September 20, 1858, and "Statement of Fact" [by attorneys], and "H. J. Jones answers to interrogatories," March 16, 1860 (quotations), in *Eliza Cornelia Willett (Reynolds) vs. Charles Lewis, et al.,* Case No. 662, folder #2, ODC, Robertson County, Texas; *Asaline Hearne vs. C. Erhard and others,* [No number in original (Case No. 3221)], Supreme Court of Texas, 33 Tex. 60; 1870 Tex. LEXIS 87, Decided 1870; "Brief for the appellant filed by Ballinger, Jack, and Mott," March 9, 1870, *Asaline Hearne vs. Cayton Erhard and others,* Case file M-5761, Texas Supreme Court Records, RG 201, TSL-AD.

had recently purchased from the heirs of Rhoda Kennedy and John Boren the title to the land in question and would now rely instead on this new chain of title. He accordingly amended his suit against the remaining defendants, including Sam. Because of Sam's actual and continual possession of his land, he never considered at any time settling with Cundiff. Nor was Sam's title in conflict with the Kennedy and Boren claims. After Britton Dawson agreed in 1861, in his conveyance of a warranty deed to Sam, to defend the title that he had transferred to Sam ten years earlier, any compromise by Sam with Cundiff or, for that matter, with the Reynolds heirs was out of the question.[34]

The Cundiff case, along with the suit brought by Reynolds's heirs, lingered on the docket throughout the Civil War years. Not until the spring of 1868, when Hamman took over the handling of these cases, did the plaintiffs note for the first time Sam's death. Hamman accordingly and reasonably asked the court to replace Sam as a defendant with his legal representatives, who at this time, prior to Brown's June appointment as Sam's executor, were not readily known. Although these lawsuits fell under Hunsaker's interdict, they embodied old issues that would eventually have to be resolved in settling Sam's estate. They also were similar to the Aycock case, which Captain Randall, before shutting down the Freedmen's Bureau operations, had allowed to move forward. Because the lawsuits of Aycock, Cundiff, and Reynolds's heirs against Azeline and Sam's estate all rested on feeble legal grounds, litigating them unquestionably would be to her and the estate's considerable advantage.[35]

Almost a year later in March 1869, Hamman, on behalf of his client Cundiff, filed a petition with the district court stating that Azeline, by inheritance from Sam's son, was now the owner of part of the land in question and thus she should be named as a defendant. On the following day, Alley Hearne and Dred Dawson Jr., *who were defendants* in the Cundiff

34. Interview with Norman L. McCarver Jr., Hearne, Texas, August 16, 1999 (quotations); William H. Cundiff to Charles Lewis, November [?], 1859, "Deeds-Transcribed 1856–1860," Book "M," p. 502, Microfilm Reel #963278, RD, CCO, Robertson County, Texas; "Brief for the appellant filed by Ballinger, Jack, and Mott," March 9, 1870, *Asaline Hearne vs. Cayton Erhard and others,* Case file M-5761, Texas Supreme Court Records, RG 201, TSL-AD; and Warranty Deed, dated September 10, 1861, and filed for record on September 12, 1861, Book "N," pp. 299–300, Microfilm Reel #963279, RD, CCO, Robertson County, Texas.

35. "Brief for the appellant filed by Ballinger, Jack, and Mott," March 9, 1870, *Asaline Hearne vs. Cayton Erhard and others,* Case file M-5761, Texas Supreme Court Records, RG 201, TSL-AD; and *William H. Cundiff vs. Dred Dawson, et al.,* Case No. 594, [Spring Term, 1868], April 7, 1868, Book "J [452–922]," p. 643, MDC, Robertson County, Texas.

suit, for unknown reasons petitioned the court to add Azeline as a defendant. At this crucial point, Brown, under the cover of holding a power of attorney from Azeline, pretended to represent her as a defendant rather than, as his fiduciary obligations as Sam's executor required, petitioning to have himself made a defendant. Yet all parties knew, as did Judge Davis and every lawyer in Robertson County, that the court had no power to join Azeline as a defendant unless Cundiff demonstrated that there was no administration on either Sam's estate or that of Sam's son. In no other way could Cundiff have discovered whether the title that Azeline received from her son was valid. More bizarre twists and turns in the case occurred during the following week.[36]

Cundiff gave Azeline, but *no other defendants,* notice of the chain of title papers on which he would base his claim for her plantation. Law partners Davis and Beall, who represented the other defendants, made no objection to her being made a defendant—a fact suggesting that they were either unconcerned with her interests or in collusion with Hamman and Brown. On the same day, Cayton Erhard and other heirs of Allen Reynolds filed a petition through their attorney Hamman claiming that during the previous year they purchased the land in question from Cundiff and, as a consequence, they should be made plaintiffs in the case. Judge Davis then allowed Erhard and his wife Harriet, but none of the other Reynolds heirs, to make themselves plaintiffs *in place of Cundiff.* Then at the insistence of the Erhards, Judge Davis ordered that Azeline be made a defendant. Again, *nobody objected.* In effect, Azeline, who was cited in court to answer to Cundiff, discovered that she was litigating with Erhard and his wife—a situation brought about not due to Cundiff's consent, disappearance, or death but rather by his allegedly no longer owning the land at issue. Only the dullest of minds at the courthouse would have failed to recognize instantly that what transpired in Judge Davis's court was, as lawyers for Azeline later argued, "unheard of in any system of procedure, legal or equitable" and "simply absurd."[37]

36. Harvey D. Prendergast to Thomas H. Norton, [undated and marked "Exhibit A"], frames 0628–0632, Microfilm Reel #39, COCADT, RG 393, M1188, NA (1981); and "Brief for the appellant filed by Ballinger, Jack, and Mott," March 9, 1870, *Asaline Hearne vs. Cayton Erhard and others,* Case file M-5761, Texas Supreme Court Records, RG 201, TSL-AD.

37. *William H. Cundiff vs. Dred Dawson , et al.,* Case No. 594, [Spring Term, 1869], April 5 and 9, 1869, Book "J [452–922]," pp. 787 and 798, MDC, Robertson County, Texas; and "Brief for the appellant filed by Ballinger, Jack, and Mott," March 9, 1870 (quotations), *Asaline Hearne vs. Cayton Erhard and others,* Case file M-5761, Texas Supreme Court Records, RG 201, TSL-AD.

In point of fact, under the law the rights of Cundiff and the Erhards had been fixed against Sam at the commencement of Cundiff's suit filed in1857 against Sam and others. No sale of land to the Erhards by Cundiff, pending the outcome of his lawsuit, could have possibly entitled the Erhards to any right to be made plaintiffs in the case. Nor could their purchase have relieved Cundiff from the responsibilities of his suit. If he had title at the start of his case in 1857, and if he had prosecuted his claim to a successful recovery, then the judgment in his favor would have inured to the benefit of the Erhards. If the law were otherwise, plaintiffs could file lawsuits, and after years of costly litigation and realizing that outcomes would result unfavorably, they would only have to sell out to irresponsible or foolish persons who then would replace the original plaintiffs—a course of action making impossible any recovery of money to pay the officers of the court for their expenses or to compensate the defendants for their expenditures incurred in the course of litigation.[38]

The final act in this wholesale mockery of justice occurred eleven days later on April 16th, the day of the trial at the Owensville courthouse. Acting on behalf of Azeline, attorneys Davis and Beall asked for dismissal of the suit against her but offered only the token argument that even if the Erhards' statements were true, the facts they alleged failed to substantiate their claim to be legal owners of Azeline's plantation. Hamman, representing the plaintiffs, then *dismissed the lawsuit to all the other defendants,* leaving Azeline as the sole defendant. But in regard to the Erhards, the record on the day of the trial listed by some miraculous sleight of hand *all Reynolds's heirs* as plaintiffs. There was no bill of exception and no statement of facts in the jury trial that ensued. The jury ruled for the plaintiffs, whose claim was maintained without any presentation of evidence of Sam's adverse and continual possession for three years under color of title before the commencement of the lawsuit. It did not even matter that Hamman based his plaintiffs' claim to Azeline's plantation on a chain of titles that had been previously adjudicated as invalid by the Texas Supreme Court. After the trial's conclusion all the title papers prepared by Hamman mysteriously disappeared from the courthouse files. Not only was Azeline legally robbed of her land, but she was also burdened with the costs of a decade of litigation against half a dozen plaintiffs—four of whom she learned were suing her only on the day of the trial itself. These

38. "Brief for the appellant filed by Ballinger, Jack, and Mott," March 9, 1870, *Asaline Hearne vs. Cayton Erhard and others,* Case file M-5761, Texas Supreme Court Records, RG 201, TSL-AD.

last details demonstrated, in the subsequent opinion of the Texas Supreme Court, "the animus of the case" and the extent to which she was unfairly sacrificed and her rights were callously violated.[39]

The only surviving reaction of the Hearne and Lewis families to the judgment against Azeline appears in a letter that Rasche Hearne wrote to military authorities at Calvert. Rasche asserted that Judge Davis had been "badly deceived" in permitting Hamman to circumvent the Freedmen's Bureau's ban on litigating matters involving Sam's estate but only because, the year before, Davis had refused to hear the case (in which Rasche was one of the plaintiffs) to set aside Sam's will. In regard to Hamman's default judgment, Rasche stated that it was common knowledge that it was obtained by "fraud and collusion." He did not elucidate further but quickly added that "fraudulent proceedings" had been practiced in the entire matter "from its *infancy*." At this point he launched into a recounting of the wrongs done in 1867 to him by Hunsaker. It is doubtful that Rasche, who showed no concern for the wrongs done to Azeline in Judge Davis's court, helped Azeline find an attorney to appeal the decision rendered against her, but at various times after the war members of his family had hired Harvey D. Prendergast to conduct their legal business.[40]

Prendergast was a Tennessee native who had served in the war as an officer in the 10th Texas Infantry Regiment. He moved in the fall of 1866 to Robertson County from his home in neighboring Limestone County. In the following year he was among the first white men to register to vote under military supervision. In late 1867 and in 1868, he periodically served as sheriff *pro tem*—a position demonstrating that he enjoyed the confidence of County Judge Ellison. Few other members of the Robertson County bar cooperated so closely as Prendergast with the military-appointed Republican officeholders. To the contrary, many, including most notably Hamman and Alexander W. Terrell, denounced Fidella Hall and other Republican appointees as "incompetent and criminally negligent." In any event, three months after the April 16th default judgment, Azeline employed Prendergast as her legal counsel but, significantly, not until after

39. *William H. Cundiff vs. Dred Dawson , et al.*, Case No. 594, [Spring Term, 1869], April 16, 1869, Book "J [452–922]," p. 837, MDC, Robertson County, Texas; "Brief for the appellant filed by Ballinger, Jack, and Mott," March 9, 1870 (quotation), *Asaline Hearne vs. Cayton Erhard and others,* Case file M-5761, Texas Supreme Court Records, RG 201, TSL-AD.

40. Horatio R. Hearne to Thomas H. Norton, [undated] (quotations), frames 0664–0668, Microfilm Reel #39, COCADT, RG 393, M1188, NA (1981); *A. L. Hearne, et al. vs. J. W. Cunningham, Administrator,* Case No. 978, [Spring Term, 1868], Book "J [452–922]," p. 668, MDC, Robertson County, Texas.

military authorities arrested Ben Brown for murder and effectively removed him from affairs on her plantation.[41]

The Murder of Dr. Maxwell

Little is known about Dr. J. M. Maxwell other than that he was a well-respected doctor whose family had resided in the county since the mid-1850s. He and Brown developed a mutual dislike that simmered for over a year before it reached the boiling point. Newspaper accounts referred to Brown as "a notorious character" who rode into Calvert with a gang of about forty "desperados" armed "to the teeth" for the sole purpose of killing Maxwell. The H&TC Railroad tracks had just reached the outskirts of the bustling town of recently constructed stores, saloons, churches, and houses. Mordecai Boatner, a newly arrived merchant who witnessed the shooting, recounted that, upon seeing Maxwell mount his horse to make a getaway, someone under Brown's leadership had yelled, "Shoot him, kill him." Shotguns and six-shooters then opened fire at the hapless physician. Brown, the administrator of Sam Hearne's estate, and Dr. Hammond, one of the wealthiest landowners in the county, were at the head of the posse and fired the first shots. Maxwell "was shot all to pieces," his body "frightfully mangled" by thirty or forty bullets.[42]

The story of Dr. Maxwell's murder circulated widely throughout the nation. It made the second page of the July 7th edition of the New York *Times* under the headline "Tragedy at Calvert, Texas." No account offered an adequate explanation for it, although statements in the anti-Republican press cried out for clarification. If, as repeatedly claimed, "politics had nothing to do with the affair whatsoever," then a great deal had presumably been at stake among men for whom Democrats had little or no sympathy. Brown's reputation for protecting, in the words of one of his anonymous defenders, "all honest freedmen from fraud and oppression" was well known. Brown's friend and neighbor Hammond was the planter who had rented the large tracts of land to former slave John Love. And Max-

41. "H. D. Prendergast," Registration No. 43, p. 207, July 23, 1867, *Voter Registration Lists, 1867–1869,* Microfilm Reel VR-10, Robertson County, Texas, TSL-AD; List of the officers of the court, [Spring Term, 1868], vol. "S," p. 38, PM, CCO, Robertson County, Texas; and T. C. Moore, W. H. Hamman, E. G. S. Orear, M. L. Cooksey, J. A. Hill, C. L. Hill, and A. W. Terrell to Joseph J. Reynolds, August 10, 1869 (quotation), Microfilm Reel #15, COCADT, RG 393, M1188, NA (1981).

42. Galveston *Daily News,* June 29, 1869, p. 2 (first, second, and third quotations); and Mordecai S. Boatner quoted in ibid., July 8, 1869, p. 1 (fourth, fifth, and sixth quotations).

well, because of his uncompensated medical services to the freedmen, had earned the trust of Freedmen's Bureau agent Randall. When military authorities got involved in the prosecution of Maxwell's killers, the pro-Democratic press, which previously had denounced all military interference in local civil or criminal proceedings as wrong in principle, expressed exuberant praise for the army's intervention.[43]

Brown and Hammond knew that few men in Robertson County would express themselves against them, and so they took responsibility for killing Maxwell and gave themselves up to the sheriff. Tremendous excitement surrounded their arraignment and trial in Calvert before the local justice of the peace. The proceedings, however, degenerated into a charade when thirty of Brown's men occupied the courtroom armed with pistols and shotguns for the purpose of intimidating witnesses. Because Brown and Hammond hired most of the "able lawyers" in the county to handle their defense, no one could readily be found to prosecute the case for the state. At this point Lieutenant John B. Guthrie, the commanding officer at the Post of Calvert, cleared the courtroom and stopped the proceedings. He then filed charges against Brown's men as accessories to murder, issued summonses for witnesses, and searched for a prosecutor. When Brown and Hammond, who in custody of the sheriff had been allowed to return to their homes, learned that their cases were more serious than they initially believed, they refused to return to Calvert—a development that caused military authorities to decide that the "safety of society" required a military commission to prosecute all involved in Maxwell's murder. Speculation arose that "startling developments with regard to affairs in Robertson County," namely, the power and influence wielded by Hammond and Brown and "the crowd" that was always with them, would be revealed in the course of their trials.[44]

Federal soldiers captured Brown and eight of his men and took them

43. New York *Times,* July 7, 1869, p. 2 (first quotation); Galveston *Daily News,* June 29, 1869, p. 2 (second quotation), and July 7, 1869, p. 2; "Letter from Brazos County," signed "H. J. J." and dated July 18, 186[9], *Flake's Daily Bulletin,* July 21, 1869, p. 8 (third quotation); Joshua L. Randall to Joel T. Kirkman, June 29, 1867, "Subassistant Commissioner Records filed under 'Sterling, Texas,'" BRFAL, [unmicrofilmed], RG 105, NA; Phidello W. Hall to Edmund J. Davis, January 19, 1870, Microfilm Reel #29, COCADT, RG 393, M1188, NA (1981); Report of W. L. Faulkner, October 25, 1869, "Estate of John C. Love, fmc," [October Term, 1869], vol. "T," pp. 2–4, PM, CCO, Robertson County, Texas; Houston *Daily Times,* June 29, 1869, reprinted in the Galveston *Daily News,* June 30, 1869, p. 1.

44. Thomas H. Norton, Commanding Officer Post of Bryan, to HFMD, July 29, 1869, "Register of Letters Received," vol. 3, p. 74 (first quotation), Microfilm Reel #4, and Thomas H. Norton to Charles E. Morse, July 7, 1869 (second quotation), Microfilm Reel #29, and July 12,

to Bryan in neighboring Brazos County for incarceration. The emotional strain of Brown's arrest on members of his extended family set off a near deadly "gay old row" on the train station platform in Hearne. One of Brown's nephews tried to kill his brother-in-law, and when his father, Green Brown, prevented him from doing so, the son held a cocked pistol to his father's breast. Repeated blows to the head restrained another son who unwisely got between his brother and father. Frightened witnesses to the hostilities were amazed that nobody was killed by the family's violent conduct—a kinship behavioral trait that continued in subsequent years to generate deadly and legendary confrontations.[45]

Unlike Brown, Hammond escaped military arrest. Rumors circulated that he had fled to Mexico. Throughout Robertson County and adjacent counties the army posted handbills calling for his "apprehension and delivery" to military authorities and offering a reward to be paid upon his conviction for Maxwell's murder. William H. Hamman, whose last name was often confused by contemporaries of the period with Hammond's, did not appear among the list of lawyers employed to represent either Hammond or Brown. Nor was Prendergast's name on the list. Yet both materialized as leaders of a large "law and order meeting" pledging assistance to the county's Republican officeholders. More importantly, the distraction caused by Maxwell's murder determined the timing of Hamman and Prendergast's extensive intrusions into Azeline's life.[46]

Setting Aside the April 16th Default Judgment

No evidence exists that Azeline ever developed any distrust of Brown prior to the default judgment against her in the Erhard case. When she hired Prendergast to set it aside, he had just completed serving during the tem-

---

1869, "Register of Letters Received," vol. 2, p. 55 or #143 (third quotation), Microfilm Reel #3, and George K. Sanderson to Charles E. Morse, March 30, 1870 (fourth quotation), Microfilm Reel #29, COCADT, RG 393, M1188, NA (1981); and Galveston *Daily News,* July 7, 1869, p. 1.

45. Bryan *News-Letter* (quotation) cited in the Galveston *Daily News,* July 11, 1869, p. 4; Charles E. Morse to H. Clay Wood, August 2, 1869, "Letterbook Volume 2," p. 212, or #415, Microfilm Reel #1, COCADT, RG 393, M1188, NA (1981); Houston *Daily Times,* July 9, 1869, p. 2; and Chuck Parsons and Marianne E. Hall Little, *Captain L. H. McNelly—Texas Ranger: The Life and Times of a Fighting Man* (Austin, Tex.: State House Press, 2001), pp. 88–89.

46. "One Thousand Dollars Reward!" [Handbill for arrest of B. F. Hammond], Headquarters Post of Bryan, August 11, 1869 (quotation), signed by Thomas H. Norton, Microfilm Reel #19, and Thomas H. Norton, Commanding Officer Post of Bryan, to HFMD, July 29, 1869, "Register of Letters Received," vol. 3, p. 74, Microfilm Reel #4, COCADT, RG 393, M1188, NA (1981); and Galveston *Tri-Weekly News,* July 23, 1869, p. 4.

porary absences of District Attorney Hall as an "attorney of the court" to prepare bills of indictments that a grand jury might recommend. The best guess is that Hall and Ellison, while enduring bitter criticism for conducting the county's legal business in the bustling new town of Calvert rather than in the all-but-evacuated county seat of Owensville, urged Azeline to hire Prendergast or suggested to him that he represent her. With the Freedmen's Bureau withdrawn from the state, with Brown unable to function as the estate's administrator, and with only members of the local bar from which to select an attorney to represent her, Prendergast was a reasonable choice.[47]

In the late nineteenth century no state bar association with an enforceable professional code of responsibility existed to hold lawyers accountable for their behavior. To become a member of the bar of the Robertson County District Court, one merely filed a petition asking to be admitted to practice law. A candidate might present a previous license from another court to use in support of his application, in addition to evidence of good moral character, which often took the form of letters of recommendation. A committee of at least three bar members then examined the applicant regarding his qualifications to practice law. If one passed, he took an oath and received a license. Subsequent instances of legal malpractice, at least as defined by modern-day standards, rarely affected one's status at the bar. The case of Owensville lawyer M. L. Cooksey provides a case in point.[48]

Cooksey was one of the local attorneys who had criticized Fidella Hall for handling most of the county's legal business away from the county seat. Yet Cooksey, while a practicing member of the bar, had obstructed justice by sheltering his brother from arrest for shooting an unarmed freedman and firing on federal soldiers. In addition, while defending white men who killed blacks, Cooksey had procured false testimony at nominal prices in order to guarantee acquittals if the cases were tried in the civil courts. Finally, he had shamefully asked for thousands of dollars in phony damages for an irresponsible freedman who had violated his contractual

47. Notation dated April 13, 1869 (first quotation), [Spring Term, 1869], Book "J [452–922]," p. 821, MDC, Robertson County, Texas; and T. C. Moore, W. H. Hamman, E. G. S. Orear, M. L. Cooksey, J. A. Hill, C. L. Hill, and A. W. Terrell to Joseph J. Reynolds, August 10, 1869, Microfilm Reel #15, COCADT, RG 393, M1188, NA (1981).

48. "Resolutions of members of the bar, April 20, 1855," [Spring Term, 1855], Book "I," p. 340, "Application of George A. Watts," [Spring Term, 1869], Book "J [452–922]," p. 840, MDC, Robertson County, Texas; and *Burrow vs. Arce,* No. 98–0184, Supreme Court of Texas, 997 S.W.2d 229; 1999 Tex. LEXIS 86; 42 Tex. Sup. J. 932; Decided July 1, 1999.

agreements with a reputable employer. Cooksey's colleagues never reprimanded him for harboring a wanted fugitive, purchasing false testimony, or drafting frivolous lawsuits. Cooksey, whom Captain Randall characterized as one of the local "Jackels of the Law," was a member of the bar in good standing when Azeline hired Prendergast.[49]

In general, setting aside and reversing a default judgment, then as now, was often quite difficult. But in this instance the odds of Prendergast getting it set aside were all but guaranteed, and, more importantly, the chances of having it eventually overturned on appeal were extremely high. A successful petition to first get it set aside required a minimal amount of legal work: only a brief recapitulation of the grounds for appeal and the posting of a sufficient bond were required. Azeline had to raise two basic legal points: (1) she had been improperly made a defendant because the court never concluded that there was no administration upon Sam's estate or upon the estate of Sam's son; and (2) the Erhards had been improperly made plaintiffs because the rights of the parties were fixed at the institution of the lawsuit and no sale of the land pending the litigation by the original plaintiff could entitle his buyers to be made plaintiffs.[50]

Compensation for an attorney's hours to set aside the default judgment in the district court and handle the case on appeal to the Texas Supreme Court could have arguably reached as high as $2,000—$500 or less for securing the writ of error and $1,500 or more for managing the appeal. Prendergast, however, was in a position to convince Azeline that, if the case was lost and she failed to regain possession of the Brazos River plantation, she would be unable to pay him if he billed her for hours worked. He thus did not receive his fee in the normal form of taking a note in advance or agreeing on some form of an hourly-fee arrangement. His July

49. *The State of Texas vs. B. Cooksey,* Case No. 471, [Spring Term, 1867], Book "J [452–922]," p. 581, MDC, Robertson County, Texas; T. C. Moore, W. H. Hamman, E. G. S. Orear, M. L. Cooksey, J. A. Hill, C. L. Hill, and A. W. Terrell to Joseph J. Reynolds, August 10, 1869, Microfilm Reel #15, and M. L. Cooksey to Winfield Scott Hancock, December 15, 1867, frames 0799–0800, and Joshua L. Randall to J. P. Richardson, January 27, 1868, frames 0827–0833, Microfilm Reel #10, BRFAL, RG 105, M821, NA (1973); and A. W. Evans to "Subassistant Commissioner BRF&AL Robertson County," August 13, 1867, and Joshua L. Randall to Joel T. Kirkman, May 27, 1867 (quotation) and June 29, 1867, "Subassistant Commissioner Records filed under 'Sterling, Texas,'" BRFAL, [unmicrofilmed], RG 105, NA.

50. "Bond," Assaline Hearne to Harvey D. Prendergast, dated July 22, 1869, filed for record on October 18, 1869, Book "Q," p. 496, RD, CCO, Robertson County, Texas; and *Asaline Hearne vs. C. Erhard and others,* [No number in original (Case No. 3221)], Supreme Court of Texas, 33 Tex. 60; 1870 Tex. LEXIS 87, Decided 1870.

22nd agreement with her was a contingency-fee agreement contained in a bond.[51]

Under the presumably nonnegotiable terms of the agreement, Azeline stated that she understood that there was a lawsuit by Cundiff in the district court over the title to her Brazos River plantation, which she had inherited via her son. Because Cundiff, or other persons representing his claim, obtained a ruling against her, she had hired Prendergast to set aside the judgment, and because she had "no other property with which to remunerate him" for his legal services, she obligated herself to make him and his heirs a deed for ownership of one-half of her plantation. A legal description of the land followed that described Prendergast's half as "the south half" and specified that she would make the deed out to him upon his demand but allow him from the date of the agreement "to get into immediate possession" and "to receive half of all rents falling due." The detail that the south half contained the cotton gin and press, as well as Azeline's home, the old log cabin mansion house built by Sam in 1853, was not mentioned.[52]

Nor did the agreement state the total amount of rental fees currently due or the current market price of $20 an acre for cleared bottomland. The calculations would have revealed that Prendergast had established his fee for setting aside the default judgment at a total of about $9,000 worth of Robertson County bottomland plus $1,000 in rents due from Wade and Campbell. Prendergast's legal fees would equal, on the day he won the case on appeal, not less than $10,000—an amount equal to ten times the annual wage of a skilled carpenter working in the railroad boomtown of Calvert. In today's money the amount would represent a compensation package for his legal services worth around $124,000. In addition, because bottomland rented for no less than $3 an acre per year, Prendergast could look forward to receiving a substantial annual rental income for the rest of his life.[53]

It would be difficult to believe that Prendergast did not know that his legal fees were, by any moral or ethical compass, excessive. His agreement

51. "Bond," Assaline Hearne to Harvey D. Prendergast, dated July 22, 1869, filed for record on October 18, 1869, Book "Q," p. 496, Microfilm Reel #963281, RD, CCO, Robertson County, Texas.

52. Ibid., p. 496 (quotations).

53. "Warranty Deed," Richard J. White to Decimus et Ultimus Barziza, August 23, 1868, Book "Q," pp. 143–44, Microfilm Reel #963281, RD, CCO, Robertson County, Texas; Houston *Daily News,* June 2, 1869, p. 1, and June 10, 1869, p. 2; and *The Inflation Calculator,* www.westegg.com/inflation (accessed Oct. 26, 2003).

with Azeline obligated him to do nothing more than set aside the default judgment. The expense, time, effort, and risk of his posting a bond and filing a petition summing up a couple of basic legal points, were nonexistent or minimal. Of course, in order to secure good title for himself to the south half of the plantation, he would have to prevail on the ensuing appeal. But once he acquired, via his agreement with Azeline, Sam Hearne's virtually unassailable legal position in regard to the south half, Prendergast knew that no knowledgeable person, including Hamman or whoever else would be his legal antagonist during an appeal, believed that his ownership rights were defective or vulnerable to a lawsuit contesting his title.

Moreover, Prendergast had to have known that his agreement with Azeline violated the fundamental principle justifying the handling of a case on a contingency-fee basis, namely, that the smaller the risk of losing assumed by him, the smaller the percentage he should claim if he won. Prendergast did not have to accept the risk of all-but-certain jury nullification faced in 1866–67 by Aycock in his contingency contract with Azeline to defend the validity of Sam's will. In addition, Prendergast unconscionably put himself in a position to further bill Azeline for handling the appeal. His agreement with her offered no sliding scale pegging the percentage of the plantation that he would take as compensation for his legal services either to the stage at which the case might be settled or a possible compromise settlement agreed upon with the Erhard plaintiffs. Finally, the agreement contained a significant falsehood of which Prendergast was without doubt aware but chose to ignore, Azeline's claim to have "no other property with which to remunerate" him.[54]

Although Azeline might have believed that she had no other property than the Brazos River plantation, this was not true. She owned land in Limestone and Young Counties and stock in the H&TC Railroad Company, and Campbell and Wade owed her rental fees. Even assuming Azeline had no other property with which to pay an attorney, Texas law provided that, in cases where appellants were unable to pay the costs of an appeal or give security for bond for a writ of error, they had the right to prosecute the appeal by making strict proof of their inability to pay the costs. Azeline could have signed an affidavit stating her inability to pay costs before either the county judge or Judge Davis, who had tried the case. If she

54. "Bond," Assaline Hearne to Harvey D. Prendergast, dated July 22, 1869, filed for record on October 18, 1869, Book "Q," p. 496 (quotation), Microfilm Reel #963281, RD, CCO, Robertson County, Texas.

had been unable to give bond leading to the issuance of a court order forcing the sheriff to stop the enforcement of the execution of Hamman's writ of possession, she could have posted just enough bond to cover the costs and damages of the appeal—a situation that would have put the sheriff and not her in possession of her plantation, or as much of it as would protect Hamman's possible interest in it, until the resolution of the case by the Texas Supreme Court.[55]

Prendergast never considered any option other than placing his personal interests over those of his client. If he had zealously represented her with undivided loyalty, he would have filed a motion in federal district court to get Hamman's writ of possession quashed on the grounds that Judge Davis had wrongfully allowed Cundiff and Reynolds's heirs to defy the U.S. Army's ban on litigating matters regarding Sam's estate. This option would have entailed the least risk of his losing and would have justified his billing her for a small portion of the 1869 rent money to cover his hours worked. After Brown's complicity with Hamman brought about the miscarriage of justice in the Robertson County District Court, Azeline's inability to find someone who would be Sam's executor, her attorney, and her genuine advocate all rolled into one, made her, for the next decade, merely an obstacle in the way of Prendergast's achieving, through legal malpractice and breach of fiduciary duty, his own interests at her expense.

55. *A. P. Wooldridge, assignee, vs. George Roller,* Supreme Court of Texas, 52 Tex. 447; 1880 Tex. LEXIS 13, Decided January 29, 1880.

Chapter 5

A Most Wanton Violation of Private Rights

> [T]he attempt . . . on the part of W. H. Hamman to go onto the farm of Assaline Hearne and control the labor and collect the rents in defiance of the writ of error and the injunction is unprecedented and is a most wanton violation of private rights.
>
> —HARVEY D. PRENDERGAST, TO CHARLES E. MORSE AND JOSEPH J. REYNOLDS, UNDATED LETTER [NOVEMBER 1869]

THE 1869 COTTON CROP in the Brazos Bottoms was by all accounts excellent. One observer predicted that, in the absence of bad weather, cotton worms, or some other unforeseen event, planters would make so much money that they would not know what to do with it. He alluded to "a great deal of sunk-money" being buried in the ground because of the reluctance of planters to spend it "when *ab initios* are hanging over them." This pervasive notion—that a radical Republican victory in the forthcoming elections would initiate a diabolical reign of carpetbagger rule—gave rise to one of the most enduring Robertson County legends. Ebb Hearne allegedly buried on the grounds of his plantation the proceeds from the sale of his cotton crop and then unexpectedly died shortly afterward without telling anyone precisely where the money, believed to be in gold specie, was hidden. The apocryphal story of Ebb's buried gold contrasts sharply with the simultaneous financial devastation suffered by Azeline Hearne.[1]

Hamman as a Trespasser on Azeline's Plantation

Sometime during the late summer of 1869, while Ben Brown was in jail, Hamman rode out onto Azeline's plantation and pronounced to the inquisitive freedpeople who surrounded him that he was its new owner. With his gifted flow of speech, he observed what he had often referred to as the inevitable "retrogradation" of the former human chattels, who were "at best not above a half savage." Hamman believed that their decline, which had "commenced at the moment of their liberation," would continue due to their "idleness" and other bad character traits until they finally became, as he expressed it, "exterminated." Whatever plans he had in mind, Hamman knew that his venturing onto Azeline's plantation would throw its links of authority and divisions of labor into complete chaos.[2]

Hamman was a mere trespasser on Azeline's land. Through her attorney Harvey Prendergast, she had filed a petition and posted a bond to set aside the judgment won in April by the Erhards and others for her plantation. Her sureties were Buck Watts, John H. Drennan, and Richard J. White. The latter two were large landowners easily worth the $75,000 required for the bond. The court's approval of the bond returned the plantation to Azeline's legal possession, just as it was before the institution of Hamman's lawsuit. Moreover, when Prendergast got the default judgment set aside, the clerk of the district court ordered the sheriff to stop enforcement of the execution of Hamman's writ of possession. In other words, Azeline had obtained a suspension of the judgment against her until the Cayton Erhard case was decided on appeal to the Texas Supreme Court.

1. A "Fine Arkansas Gentleman" quoted in the Galveston *Daily News,* July 3, 1869, p. 2; Norman L. McCarver and Norman L. McCarver Jr., *Hearne on the Brazos* (San Antonio: Century Press of Texas, 1958), p. 28. Ebenezer Hearne died in 1869, not in 1859 or 1860 as is often mistakenly stated in secondary sources. See "Ebenezer Hearne Cemetery," Robertson County TXGenWeb Site, www.rootsweb.com/~txrober2/EBENEZERHEARNECEMETERY.htm (accessed June 20, 2006).

2. William H. Hamman, "Commissions, Speeches, Letters, etc.," vol. 2, p. 82 (first and second quotations), box AR29, William Harrison Hamman Papers, CAH-UT, Austin, Texas; Ada Margaret Smith, "The Life and Times of William Harrison Hamman" (M.A. thesis, University of Texas, 1952), p. 37; and William H. Hamman to "My Dear Caroline," November 18, 1865 (third, fourth, and fifth quotations), William Harrison Hamman Papers, box 2, folder 26, WRC-RU, Houston, Texas.

In the meantime she enjoyed full ownership of her land and was entitled to the rents owed her by her tenants Israel Campbell and Jim Wade.[3]

Hamman ignored the order suspending enforcement of his judgment and proceeded with his unwarranted meddling into Azeline's affairs. As the most prominent attorney in Robertson County, the "tall, straight, and handsome" ex-Confederate war hero had to have made an imposing presence among the tenants and farm laborers on her land, not to mention on Azeline herself, who was still living in the prewar log cabin manor house, around which now sprouted the cabins of many of her black residents. Hamman lent horses to field hands to help raise the cotton and corn crops, advanced small amounts of money to others, and convinced many to defer to his judgments on plantation matters. By harvest time he insinuated that he would handle all sales of cotton bales piled up at the plantation's gin. Predictably, cotton began mysteriously disappearing off the plantation. Field hands, fearing that they would get nothing for their labor, cut deals with whoever offered cash for the cotton and corn crop, or for probably anything else of value on the plantation that they could get their hands on. Their surreptitious transactions no doubt confirmed Hamman's notions concerning their natural tendencies toward, in his words, "villainy" and "theft." Yet Campbell and Wade were legally obligated to pay their rent in full to Azeline by January 1, 1870. Wade decided to do what by law he could not do, defer to Hamman and not pay Azeline any of the rent money. Whoever was acting as Campbell's manager or agent most likely followed in Wade's footsteps.[4]

3. Harvey D. Prendergast to Thomas H. Norton, [undated and marked "Exhibit A"], frames 0628–0632, Microfilm Reel #39, COCADT, RG 393, M1188, NA (1981).

4. Harvey D. Prendergast to Thomas H. Norton, [undated and marked "Exhibit A"] , frames 0628–0632, and Harvey D. Prendergast to Charles E. Morse and Joseph J. Reynolds, [undated and marked "Exhibit B"], Microfilm Reel #39, Petition on behalf of Asaline Hearne submitted by Hollingsworth and Broaddus, October 15, 1869, and affidavit of William H. Hamman witnessed by George D. Beale, J.P., Robertson County, October 22, 1869, Microfilm Reel #39, COCADT, RG 393, M1188, NA (1981); Smith, "The Life and Times of William Harrison Hamman," p. 37 (first quotation); William H. Hamman, "Commissions, Speeches, Letters, etc.," vol. 2, p. 82 (second and third quotations), box AR29, William Harrison Hamman Papers, CAH-UT, Austin, Texas; William H. Hamman to "My Dear Caroline," November 18, 1865, William Harrison Hamman Papers, box 2, folder 26, WRC-RU, Houston, Texas; "Answers of Ophilia Holliday," a deposition witnessed on February 19, 1873, in *F. M. Hall vs. Assaline Hearne,* Case No. 1639, ODC, Robertson County, Texas; and S. P. Hollingsworth to Lieutenant William V. Wolfe, October 22, 1869, Microfilm Reel #39, COCADT, RG 393, M1188, NA (1981).

Prendergast refused to offer any advice or assistance for his client. Beyond preventing enforcement of Hamman's writ of possession and handling the appeal of the default judgment, he felt no obligation to further help her or be involved with the administration of Sam Hearne's estate or with the details of managing her plantation. Although suspicious of Hamman's behavior, Prendergast wanted to conceal his own interest in the plantation and the rent money. He was, as matters stood, a circuitous beneficiary of Brown's courtroom collusion with Hamman. Prendergast thus postponed filing for record his agreement with Azeline that legally obligated her to give him, upon his demand, a deed to one-half of her plantation. The agreement also granted him privileges prior to any conveyance of a title: his immediate use of the south half and his ownership of the rent that it would generate from Campbell and Wade. Prendergast, for the time being, watched from the sidelines the unfolding struggle between the legitimate renters, Campbell and Wade, on one side, and Hamman, a pretender claiming the rent money, on the other. Caught in the middle were his client Azeline and the large black community on her plantation. Absent altogether from the landscape was Brown, the jailed administrator of Sam's estate.[5]

Azeline had to have experienced discomfort caused by the behavior of many subaltern freedmen lessees, croppers, and hired hands who caved in before Hamman's spurious authority. Day after day she watched them cheating her tenants. Given the indifference of Prendergast to the disorder around her, she understandably looked elsewhere for advice. She turned for help to Reverend Richard Sloan, the octogenarian carpetbagger preacher serving as the military-appointed Brazos County precinct commissioner for Millican, where he also was in charge of the local African Methodist Episcopal Church. Azeline had known Sloan for the past three years as a compassionate man who preached, taught, and lived among her people. He most likely lent a kind ear and tried to counsel her, especially after Prendergast had forfeited her trust by ignoring her plight. But her decision to put her faith in Sloan set into motion her participation in a dangerous succession of activities regarding powers of attorney, real property deeds, and land leases.

In late September, while in Bryan in neighboring Brazos County, Azeline made a terrible mistake: she appointed Reverend Sloan to be her agent to

5. "Bond," Assaline Hearne to H. D. Prendergast, dated July 22, 1869, and filed for record on October 18, 1869, and recorded on November 17, 1869, Book "Q," p. 496, Microfilm Reel #963281, RD, CCO, Robertson County, Texas.

transact all her business, collect all money and rent due her, "and to perform all things necessary" to be done by her. Her signature, "her mark" of an "X" through her name, was witnessed by notary public William J. Pierce, who held military appointments as a city alderman and a county surveyor. Shortly thereafter, as if a bad omen of things to come, a fire of suspicious origin broke out in downtown Hearne, about six miles to the northeast of her plantation. A vigilante group, claiming that blacks started the fire as a pretext for looting the downtown stores, threatened retaliation. In early October, with racial tensions running high, Azeline, accompanied by Sloan, appeared again in Pierce's office in downtown Bryan.[6]

What transpired was controversial and problematical, but if Pierce's sworn recollections years later can be believed, Azeline reiterated her faith in Sloan to attend to all her business. In testimony that proved later unsupportive, if not fatally damaging, to her, Pierce claimed that she wanted to sign and acknowledge before him a general power of attorney from her to Sloan. According to Pierce, she stated that Sloan was "a good man" who had given her "good advice," which if taken would have been greatly to her advantage—a reference probably to the fiasco of the default judgment secured against her in the Erhard case. Azeline wanted to sell the plantation, in Pierce's words, in order "to get available means or other property" to live elsewhere because if she stayed in Robertson County she would "loose [*sic*] what she had there." Her intention, Pierce recollected, "was to enable Sloan her agent to sell the land in controversy" and get in exchange "other property out of the neighborhood" where her plantation was located.[7]

Azeline revoked any previous power of attorney granted to Brown and drafted another power of attorney to Sloan, appointing him her attorney to represent her "in all matters in anywise connected with [her] interest—as widow and legatee under the will of Samuel R. Hearne deceased." If "all matters" included the selling, buying, or renting land on her behalf, then the scope of her second power of attorney to Sloan was as all encompassing as the prior one, which she had just recently signed. Subscribing

6. Power of Attorney from Assaline Hearne to Richard Sloan, dated September 27, 1869 (quotations), and filed for record on March 30, 1870, Book "K," p. 251, RD, CCO, Brazos County, Texas; Galveston *Daily News*, October 6, 1869, p. 2; and *Flake's Daily Bulletin* (Galveston), October 6, 1869, p. 5.

7. "Answers to Interrogatories and Cross Interrogatories made by William J. Pierce," October 14, 1872 (quotations), in *F. M. Hall vs. Assaline Hearne*, Case No. 1639, ODC, Robertson County, Texas.

witnesses were Charles Stewart, an attorney from Falls County who later served in the U.S. Congress, and Samuel P. Hollingsworth of the Bryan law firm of Hollingsworth and Broaddus.[8]

While in Pierce's office Azeline learned that nothing could be done to stop Hamman from boasting that he was the new owner of her plantation or lending equipment or money to the workers in the fields, but the law did afford a way to protect her from the wrongdoers who deprived her or Sam's estate of the rent money. Even if the civil authorities proved unable or unwilling to act, there was the chance that the army might be induced to forbid removal of any more cotton from the plantation until the rental claims were properly sorted out and adjusted. On Sloan's recommendation, she hired Hollingsworth and Broaddus to recover rents that her tenants were refusing to pay in compliance with the contracts they had made with Ben Brown. The fee for the collection effort laid claim to half of any money recovered.[9]

On the following day, Brown, while being held in downtown Bryan in a jail built on poles fifteen feet off the ground and referred to as the "Yankee Sky Parlor," assigned to Azeline all his interest in the rental contract with Campbell. The next day, October 10th, Brown's guards again raised up the removable ladder to his elevated jail quarters to allow him to sign away to her his interest in the contract with Wade. Brown wrote both his endorsements on the original contracts. Five days later Hollingsworth and Broaddus submitted a petition full of spelling errors to the commander of the military post of Bryan, requesting his assistance in helping Azeline recover the rents owed her by Campbell and Wade.[10]

The petition filed on Azeline's behalf argued for granting her a way to obtain from civil authorities a "distress warrant" empowering the sher-

8. Untitled Instrument, [revocation of power of attorney to Ben Brown], dated October 8, 1869, and filed for record on January 9, 1870, Book "Q," p. 566, and Power of Attorney from Assaline Hearne to Richard Sloan, dated October 8, 1869 (quotations), and recorded for record on January 9, 1870, Book "Q," p. 566, Microfilm Reel #963281, RD, CCO, Robertson County, Texas.

9. *S. P. Hollingsworth and A. S. Broaddus vs. Assaline Hearne,* Case No. 1402, October 19, 1871, Book "K," p. 310, MDC, Robertson County, Texas.

10. Contracts between Ben Brown and Jim Wade and between Ben Brown and Israel Campbell, January 21, 1869, frames 0672–0673, Microfilm Reel #39, and Petition on behalf of Asaline Hearne by S. P. Hollingsworth and A. S. Broaddus, undated [October 15, 1869?], Microfilm Reel #39, COCADT, RG 393, M1188, NA (1981); and Glenna Fourman Brundidge, *Brazos County History: Rich Past—Bright Future* (Bryan, Tex.: Family History Foundation, 1986), p. 29 (quotation).

iff to seize cotton bales or other assets belonging to Campbell and Wade. Although distress for rent was an unsettled remedy under considerable legal clouds, her petition stated that as a landlord she knew or feared that her tenants had left or would leave without paying her the rent and therefore she was entitled to have the court seize their possessions pending a trial against them to determine or adjust the rents owed her. The petition noted that there was currently no sheriff in Robertson County, and, as a consequence, the civil courts were for the moment adjourned. This "slow process of laws" placed Azeline "in great danger of loosing [*sic*] her rights," and thus the necessity for military authorities to take immediate "conisansce [*sic*] of the case." Copies of rental contracts witnessed by Brown's agents, signed by Campbell and Wade, and endorsed by Brown to Azeline were attached to the petition. Within another week, Hollingsworth applied for a distress warrant from the district court. Sloan accompanied the application with his affidavit confirming that Campbell and Wade were "justly indebted" to Azeline and that they each owed her $1,000 for renting her land.[11]

Azeline's hope to collect her rents hinged on the decision of the commanding officer at the Post of Bryan, who in mid-October ordered his subordinates to provide the necessary safeguards she requested, if and only if the usual process of law could not provide her with the protection that she was asking for. When the news of this directive arrived at the army post in Calvert, Prendergast discovered that he had lost Azeline's confidence and that she had turned for assistance to Sloan and the law firm of Hollingsworth and Broaddus. He decided that the time had arrived for him to protect his own interests in Azeline's plantation. Three days later, on October 18th, Prendergast filed for record his July 22nd agreement with her, which allowed him to be in immediate possession of the southern half of her plantation and own the current rents accruing to it.[12]

11. Petition on behalf of Asaline Hearne submitted by S. P. Hollingsworth and A. S. Broaddus, undated [October 15, 1869?] (first, second, third, and fourth quotations), Microfilm Reel #39, and affidavit of Richard Sloan, "Agent and Attorney for Adaline Hearne," dated October 21, 1869 (fifth quotation), and witnessed by George D. Beale, J.P., Robertson County, Microfilm Reel #39, COCADT, RG 393, M1188, NA (1981).

12. Endorsement [dated October 15, 1869] of Thomas H. Norton on the cover of Petition on behalf of Asaline Hearne submitted by S. P. Hollingsworth and A. S. Broaddus, undated [October 15, 1869?], Microfilm Reel #39, COCADT, RG 393, M1188, NA (1981); and "Bond," Assaline Hearne to H. D. Prendergast, dated July 22, 1869, and filed for record on October 18, 1869, and recorded on November 17, 1869, Book "Q," p. 496, Microfilm Reel #963281, RD, CCO, Robertson County, Texas.

Within the following week, Lieutenant William V. Wolfe, the military commander at Calvert, issued orders forbidding "the persons in charge" of Azeline's plantation from further removing any portion of the crops until there was an investigation into the apparent defrauding of the proper owners of the rents. If his order were "in any way, directly or indirectly, disobeyed," then he would arrest and confine the guilty parties. Wolfe neglected, however, to order the seizure of any cotton bales. His orders were highly unusual, usurping as they did the normal authority of the civil courts and local officials. Their issuance, however, did not stop the continuing disappearance of cotton off Azeline's plantation.[13]

A few days later, after Wolfe's directive that all crops must remain on Azeline's plantation pending payment of the rents, Hamman produced an affidavit in which he summarized the litigation over the title to "the Sam Hearne place." He discussed the legal procedures in the recent spring term of the district court that had made Azeline, whom Hamman referred to as "a free [N]egress," a defendant to the litigation. After a judgment had been entered against her for the ownership of her plantation, he, in his capacity "as the attorney and agent of the plaintiffs" and "for himself," had taken its possession by making Azeline's tenants and field hands "then on the place" defer and "attune" to him. Having furnished supplies and money to help them raise the cotton and corn crops, Hamman further argued, they were now indebted to him. At this point Hamman drafted two of the most outrageous documents ever witnessed in the legal history of Robertson County.[14]

Hamman was not a sharecropper, renter, or tenant on Azeline's land. Nevertheless, he volunteered to provide the military authorities with surety bonds allowing his misappropriation of the entire cotton and corn crop on her plantation. With himself as principal and two local cotton commission agents as sureties, Hamman promised to pay Azeline $2,000, the total amount of the rents, if she won the Erhard case on its appeal to the Texas Supreme Court. If she lost, his obligation to pay would disappear.

13. Endorsement [dated October 15, 1869] of Thomas H. Norton on the cover of Petition on behalf of Asaline Hearne submitted by S. P. Hollingsworth and A. S. Broaddus, undated [October 15, 1869?], and "Statement at length in the Adeline Hearne case" written by "Hollingsworth and Broaddus, Attorneys," to Major Thomas H. Norton, undated, and "To the persons in charge of the Adeline Hearne farm" [Order from Headquarters Post of Calvert], October 23, 1869 (quotations), signed by William V. Wolfe, Microfilm Reel #39, COCADT, RG 393, M118, NA (1981).

14. Affidavit of William H. Hamman, dated October 22, 1869 (quotations), and witnessed by George D. Beale, J.P., Robertson County, Texas, Microfilm Reel #39, COCADT, RG 393, M118, NA (1981).

He drafted an identical bond with a mercantile firm as a surety. In effect, he was posting bonds to allow him to do something that he had no lawful right to do. Yet his gambit worked. Hamman, who had no more legal right to the rents than a perfect stranger, bamboozled the U.S. Army to let him take possession of the crops on Azeline's plantation until the result of the appeal of the Erhard case was handed down.[15]

Although Hamman was one of the most successful attorneys in East Texas, his malice toward Azeline in the fall of 1869 was extreme. He knew that he was not entitled to any of the rent money due her and that any questions surrounding its payment were entirely between her and her tenants. Moreover, he knew that even if she won the Erhard case on its appeal, no court in the land would subsequently force him to pay her the promised $2,000. The bogus bonds that Hamman drafted were mean-spirited ploys designed to harass Azeline and create confusion on her plantation. Azeline's chances of collecting the rents due her were all but destroyed the moment Lieutenant Wolfe had allowed him to take control of the crops on her land.[16]

Azeline's attorneys Hollingsworth and Broaddus immediately fired off volleys of protest to Lieutenant Wolfe's superior officers, providing them with detailed legal documentation demonstrating why Hamman never should have been allowed into the controversy between Azeline and her tenants. Because the default judgment that Hamman had obtained for her land had been properly appealed, her action on a writ of error to the Texas Supreme Court legally superceded Hamman's judgment, which could not now have any "force or effect" until the state supreme court heard the case. Then, putting all legal arguments aside, Hollingsworth and Broad-

15. Bond of William H. Hamman, John C. Roberts, and John Lloyd, dated October 22, 1869, and bond of William H. Hamman, J. G. Wilkerson, and Greenwood Brown, dated October 23, 1869, and Harvey D. Prendergast to Thomas H. Norton, undated letter marked as "Exhibit A," Microfilm Reel #39, COCADT, RG 393, M118, NA (1981). Hamman made use of an exceptionally flexible common law remedy, known as *replevin,* to post his bogus bonds and destroy Azeline's right to the rents. *Replevin* was understood as an action taken to redeliver goods that were controlled by another to the original possessor of them, on the condition that the latter give security to bring an action against the "distrainor" for the purpose of trying the legality of the "distress." The related writ of *de homine replegiando,* or personal *replevin,* had been used in the northern states during the antebellum period as a way to obstruct the recovery by slaveholders of fugitive slaves. See Henry Campbell Black, *Black's Law Dictionary,* 4th ed. (St. Paul, Minn.: West Publishing Company, 1951), pp. 1463–64.

16. Harvey D. Prendergast to Thomas H. Norton, October 31, 1869, Microfilm Reel #39, and Harvey D. Prendergast to Thomas H. Norton, undated [and marked Exhibit "A"], Microfilm Reel #39, frames 0628–0632, and S. P. Hollingsworth and A. S. Broaddus to Thomas H. Norton, November 5, 1869, Microfilm Reel #39, COCADT, RG 393, M118, NA (1981).

dus addressed a far more pressing concern: in the wake of the army's mistake in accepting Hamman's bonds, the cotton on Azeline's plantation had started once again to disappear at an alarming rate. They pleaded with military authorities to take "speedy action" because "in a very short while there will be nothing left on the Farm out of which to make the suit." In other words, their chances to collect their legal fees were disappearing along with the cotton.[17]

The gossip ignited by the contest between Hamman and Azeline over the rent money angered Rasche Hearne. Although his repetitive assertion that Hamman's demand for the rent was at most a "pretended claim," Rasche's complaints to military authorities still emanated from his inability to let go of his bitterness over perceived injustices done to him long ago by the Freedmen's Bureau. Rasche reasoned that Azeline's tenants owed *him* most of the rent money! If special bureau agent Oscar Hunsaker had possessed the right in 1867 to act as an agent for Azeline, then, claimed Rasche, "I am certainly entitled to the fifteen hundred dollars from her which was wrongfully extorted from me."[18]

Prendergast now surfaced to demand that the army take immediate action to prevent Azeline from being "disturbed or molested in possession [of her plantation] until her rights can be adjudicated in the civil courts." According to Prendergast, Hamman's intrusion upon her land and his attempt to supervise the workers and collect the rents was an "unprecedented" and "most wanton violation of private rights." Through the mere force of his high-handed behavior, Hamman had persuaded Azeline's tenants, who were no more than "ignorant freedmen" (a description that included Reverend Campbell!), to avoid paying their rents. Because of the complexity of the legal issues involved, Prendergast requested to meet personally with military authorities at Calvert in order to explain in detail how Hamman had misapplied Texas law to hoodwink them into believing that he had an interest in the rents.[19]

Resolving the turmoil over who controlled the cotton on Azeline's plantation devolved ultimately upon Lieutenant Max Wesendorff, a Prussian-born Jew who had joined the Washington Territory Infantry at the out-

17. S. P. Hollingsworth and A. S. Broaddus, to Thomas H. Norton, November 5, 1869 (quotations), Microfilm Reel #39, COCADT, RG 393, M118, NA (1981).

18. Horatio R. Hearne to Thomas H. Norton, [undated letter] (quotations), Microfilm Reel #39, COCADT, RG 393, M118, NA (1981).

19. Harvey D. Prendergast to Thomas H. Norton, October 31, 1869 (quotations), and undated letter [marked "Exhibit A"], and Harvey D. Prendergast to Charles A. Morse and Joseph J. Reynolds, undated letter [marked as "Exhibit B"], [November 1869], Microfilm Reel #39, COCADT, RG 393, M118, NA (1981).

break of the war. After deconstructing Hamman's arguments, Wesendorff curtailed the damage done by prior military directives. His November 10th circular printed the applicable parts of Texas state law, because, in his words, "considerable misunderstandings and ignorance of law" had prevailed in regard to "the priority of liens upon crops cultivated by freedmen" who were under contracts with planters and landowners. On the next day Wesendorff executed the original distress warrant requested by Azeline almost a month earlier. It directed the sheriff to seize enough cotton on her plantation as would equal in value the rents and to take the cotton in equal quantities from Campbell and Wade. The hullabaloo over the rents finally ended, at least for the rest of the year, and attention shifted to an event rivaling emancipation as the single most revolutionary event in the history of Robertson County and the state of Texas.[20]

The 1869 Gubernatorial Election

From November 30th to December 3rd, Texas voters, including thousands of newly enfranchised African Americans, went to polling places to participate concurrently in two critical elections: a ratification of the proposed state constitution and a selection, should the constitution be approved, of state and local officials. Registration had reopened for ten days just before the election. Blacks comprised slightly less than half the population of Robinson County, but by the close of the revision of registration, they comprised over 60 percent of the county's registered voters. The percentage of registered adult black males rose from 81 to 99 percent, but the percentage of adult white males issued voter registration certificates increased only from 38 to 53 percent. In other words, virtually every eligible black had been registered, which was not surprising, given the work of the Union League and the guidelines given to the local registration boards, but the rate at which the county's whites had registered lagged considerably behind the statewide average.[21]

20. "The Max Wesendorff file," Bloom Southwest Jewish Archives, University of Arizona Manuscript Collection, The University of Arizona Library, Tucson, Arizona; GO No. 5 [Calvert, Texas: November 10, 1869] (quotations), signed by Max Wesendorff, 1st Lieutenant, U.S.A., Post Adjutant, Headquarters Post of Calvert, Department of Civil Affairs, and Lieutenant Max Wesendorff to "Sheriff of Robertson County," November 11, 1869, Microfilm Reel #39, and "Statement of Cotton sold & expenses incurred in the sale of cotton seized on the Sam Hearne place," signed by Robert Porter, [undated receipts], Microfilm Reel #39, COCADT, RG 393, M118, NA (1981).

21. Dale Baum, *The Shattering of Texas Unionism: Politics in the Lone Star State during the Civil War Era* (Baton Rouge: Louisiana State University Press, 1998), p.187; and U.S. Army, Fifth Military District, State of Texas, GO No. 73, *Tabular Statement Of Voters (white and*

During the revision of voter registration, Ben Brown's lawyers in Washington, D.C., had discussed, to no avail, his case with President Ulysses S. Grant with the hope of getting it transferred to civil authorities for prosecution and trial. While awaiting sentencing from a military commission, Brown learned the news that the U.S. Supreme Court had denied hearing his petition for a writ of habeas corpus. He bribed a guard and escaped from prison. Standing military orders regarding him never changed: he was to be either taken back into custody or killed. Speculation regarding possible legal deals between federal authorities and Brown's many friends and lawyers negotiating on his behalf while he remained a fugitive at large, along with the commotion over control of the cotton crop on Azeline's plantation, were—next to the cold weather—the most commonly discussed topics when Robertson County citizens went to the Owensville courthouse to vote.[22]

Most whites believed that the new Republican-drafted constitution would someday be "cleansed of its venom" of black suffrage, but they acknowledged that its approval at the polls was unavoidable. Therefore, the actual battle was for control of local offices as well as of the state administration, which would guide Texas back into the Union. Because the Democrats fielded no consequential statewide ticket, the majority of whites regarded the gubernatorial race as a "choice of evils" between former governor Andrew J. Hamilton, who had the support of moderate or conservative Republicans, and Edmund J. Davis, who was the candidate of the radical Republicans. Blacks tended to enthusiastically support Davis, but the large majority of whites preferred Hamilton, who in most coun-

---

colored) Registered in Texas at Registration in 1867, and at Revision of the Lists in 1867–'68–'69; showing also the number (white and colored) Stricken Off the Lists. Tabular Statement Of Votes (white and colored) cast at Election held in the State of Texas, under the authority of the Reconstruction Acts of Congress. Austin: April 16, 1870, pp. 1–9.

22. Galveston *Daily News,* November 25, 1869, p. 3; *Ex parte Yerger,* Supreme Court of the United States, 75 U.S. 85, 19 L. Ed. 332, U.S. LEXIS 1085; 8 Wall. 85 (decided October 25, 1869); *In the Matter of Benjamin Brown, et al.,* Petition (File Date: October 8, 1869), 11 pp., Term Year: 1869, *U.S. Supreme Court Records and Briefs, 1832–1978,* Thomson Gale, Texas A&M University, College Station, http://galenet.galegroup.com/servlet/SCRB?uid=0&srchtp=a&ste=14&rcn=DW111215861 (accessed April 3, 2007); Thomas H. Norton to HFMD, October 20, 1869, "Register of Letters Received," vol. 3, p. 309, Microfilm Reel #4, and Telegram from Calvert, Texas, dated December 13, 1869, Thomas H. Norton to Charles E. Morse, Microfilm Reel #29, and Telegram, [copy], from Calvert, Texas, dated November 22, 1869, Thomas H. Norton to H. Clay Woods, Microfilm Reel #30, COCADT, RG 393, M118, NA (1981).

ties headed up tickets laden with conservatives and anti-Reconstruction Democrats. In Robertson County it was well known that an electorate comprised of 1,169 blacks and 714 whites would decide the races for local offices, and barring the unlikely possibility of a dismally low turnout among black voters, the registration results alone caused despair among whites hoping to prevent the radical Davis ticket from winning a sweeping victory of local offices.[23]

Contrary to one of the most commonly perpetuated historical myths about Reconstruction days in Robertson County, the Davis faction neither "deprived the whites who fought in the rebel army from voting" nor "made [Negroes] all eligible while refusing the ballot to most white people." Even the rabidly antiradical Galveston *Daily News* complimented the military authorities "for the impartial manner" with which they handled the registration process. Moreover, because no Texas slave ever held public office during the antebellum period and then freely joined the rebellion, the Robertson County freedmen were not among the groups of Texans who had taken an oath that they did not expect to honor or had added perjury to treason. Although the extent to which the county's white men tried to register but were denied voting certificates will never be known, they could not possibly have accounted for the large percent of the adult white males who were not on the voting lists. Hundreds of them were typical of Hamman, who, although eligible to vote, deliberately chose not to register. They stayed away from the registration tables out of false pride, animosity to black suffrage, or lack of enthusiasm for Hamilton's candidacy.[24]

In Robertson County an assorted group of no more than a dozen white men voted the radical Republican ticket. Recruitment of black voters, upon which a radical victory depended, fell on the shoulders of Fidella Hall and scalawag John R. Harlan, who was the military-appointed county tax assessor and collector and a longtime friend of fugitive-at-large Ben Brown. A year earlier a jury had acquitted Harlan of murdering the miscegenationist John Deveraux, whose allegations during the war had led a grand jury to hand down charges of horse stealing against Sam Hearne. Harlan

23. Galveston *Daily News*, July 1, 1869, p. 1, and November 30, 1869 (quotations); and *Tabular Statement Of Voters (white and colored) Registered in Texas*, pp. 1–9.

24. Galveston *Daily News*, December 7, 1869 (first quotation); "Interview with Mrs. Emma Falconer, [interviewed by Miss Effie Cowan, P. W.], in *American Life Histories: Manuscripts from the Federal Writers' Project, 1936–1940*, http://memory.loc.gov/ammem/wpaintro/wpahome.html (accessed July 6, 2008), File No. 240, p. 1 (second quotation); J. W. Baker, *A History of Robertson County, Texas* (Waco, Tex.: Printed by Texian Press, 1970), p. 163 (third quotation); and Baum, *The Shattering of Texas Unionism*, pp. 172–73.

and Hall were candidates for county sheriff and the state senate, respectively. To a lesser extent the responsibility for getting out the black vote fell upon a recently arrived Alsatian immigrant, Conrad ("Chicks") Anschicks, who owned a grocery store that catered to a black clientele. Anschicks was running for clerk of the county court. County Judge Isaac Ellison would retain his office no matter the outcome of the election because his position was not on the ballot. D. W. Burley, a young black carpetbagger, and Giles ("Jiles") Cotton, an older, illiterate ex-slave, were candidates, like Hall, for the state legislature—offices that notably did not require the posting of any bonds.[25]

Fidella Hall, as the leader of the powerful local Republican Party Union League, was the most despised of all the radical candidates. His detractors described him as a "rip-roaring young varmint" who had "somewhat the appearance of being descended from mankind." Yet after personally interviewing Hall, the Calvert correspondent for the pro-Democratic Galveston *Daily News* was unwilling to speculate why the affable Hall was so "exceedingly unpopular" among most Robertson County whites. Besides the obvious dislike of Hall's endorsement of the revolutionary agenda of Congressional Reconstruction, many local attorneys complained that he had illegally presided over official county business in Calvert, where he served as postmaster, rather than in the county seat of Owensville. Much unfinished business in the district court had, in fact, become "inextricably confused" during the summer of 1869 as a consequence of Hall's prolonged absences from the courthouse.[26]

Hall was aware that the possible margin of victory for the local Davis ticket could reach as high as four hundred votes, but the actual margin would depend on successful mobilization of black voters to the polls—a task complicated by the fact that most blacks lived in the extreme western

25. *The State of Texas vs. John R. Harlan,* Case No. 494, October 20, 1868, [Fall Term, 1868], Book "J [452–922]," pp. 754–55, MDC, Robertson County, Texas; Elisha M. Pease to Joseph J. Reynolds, April 14, 1869, [copy of a letter], Letterbook, p. 225, box 59, Governors' Papers: Pease, RG 301, TSL-AD; Bureau of the Census, *Population Schedules of the Ninth Census of the United States, 1870, State of Texas,* Microfilm Reel #1602, M593, printed pp. 174 and 204, M593, NA (1965); "Burley, D.W." and "Cotton, Giles," *TNHT,* 1: 845 and 2: 351.

26. Houston *Daily Times,* June 13, 1869, p. 1 (first, second, and third quotations); and "Special Correspondence from Calvert," by D.R., Jr., Galveston *Daily News,* September 24, 1869, p. 3 (fourth quotation); T. C. Moore, W. H. Hamman, E. G. S. Orear, M. L. Cooksey, J. A. Hill, C. L. Hill, and A. W. Terrell, Citizens of Robertson County, to Major General Joseph J. Reynolds, August 10, 1869, Microfilm Reel #15, COCADT, RG 393, M1188, NA (1981).

side of the county, at least twenty miles from the one and only mandated polling place at the county seat of Owensville. Moreover, Hall, Harlan, Anschicks, Burley, and Cotton would have to make sure that black voters, who were virtually all illiterate, had in their hands the unadulterated, or straight, Davis tickets when they were led up the steps of the county courthouse to vote. One can imagine Hall's frustration when a series of unexpected events worked against his determination to have the entire radical slate of candidates elected.

The first bit of bad luck came in the form of a cold front that moved into the state at the start of the four-day election. Hall had arranged for blacks transported from the Brazos Bottoms to the courthouse to have the option of camping overnight on the outskirts of Owensville before returning home, but the unseasonably cold weather dampened enthusiasm for encampments. A greater misfortune occurred when Harlan died on the second day of the election. Rumors arose that his political enemies had poisoned him, but an inquiry into his death concluded that he had died suddenly from natural causes. If Hall had had Harlan's help for the four full days of the balloting, the Davis ticket would have probably garnered more votes. Finally, Hall failed to foresee that Lieutenant Wolfe's authority would be thrown in support of Samuel J. Adams, a Democratic candidate for the Texas House of Representatives who was Rasche Hearne's business partner and son-in-law.[27]

Davis carried Robertson County by ninety-four votes. Hall was elected state senator by a smaller margin; Burley and Anschicks won by extremely narrow margins; and the deceased Harlan prevailed only because he received a plurality of votes in a four-way sheriff's race. Throughout the state, less than 4 percent of the registered blacks had voted for Hamilton, but in Robertson County at least 8 percent of the county's registered blacks had voted for him. Hall could have accepted a small black defection rate to the antiradical ticket, but when the conservative Adams received more black votes than Davis to lead all candidates in votes polled, Hall was understandably outraged. He publicly accused Lieutenant Wolfe of having been "bought off" by the wealthy Hearne and Lewis families—a circumstance Hall claimed accounted for Wolfe's unresponsiveness when

27. Marks Wilson to Edmund J. Davis, February 20, 1870, Governors' Papers: Davis, TSL-AD; William V. Wolfe to Max Wesendorff, December 4, 1869, Microfilm Reel #20, and "Letter from P. W. Hall to a Friend," December 10, 1869, undated newspaper clipping [Houston *Union,* December 16, 1869?], Microfilm Reel #20, COCADT, RG 393, M1188, NA (1981); and "Bryan Business Directory," Houston *Daily Times,* June 1, 1869.

Davis tickets were snatched from the hands of freedmen waiting to vote by an abusive "armed mob" of white men. Wolfe also allowed, according to Hall, "Adams and his crowd of roughs and gamblers" to open the ballot box and make alterations to the freedmen's tickets—an irregularity giving Adams some votes as state representative that had been suspiciously cast for him as senator.[28]

Hall's repeated reference to "roughs and gamblers" was revealing, in that it reflected the widespread dislike of the influx of many unruly transients accompanying the extension of the railroad. Far more importantly, Hall's indignation over Adams's election was justifiable, unless one is willing to believe that Robertson County blacks freely voted for a candidate who was their sworn political enemy. What actually occurred is not difficult to reconstruct. Many Davis tickets with Adams's name either substituted or written in for state representative were handed out or traded for "straight" radical tickets. Hall simply had not been able to stop the flow of adulterated Davis ballots being pressed into the hands of illiterate black voters by Adams's supporters. With two black radical Republicans, Burley and Cotton, leading in the balloting for state representatives from the Eighteenth District (Leon, Freestone, and Robertson Counties), Wolfe justified turning a blind eye at the bulldozing efforts on behalf of Adams as counterbalancing an otherwise radical sweep of the legislative offices. When Hall and Burley subsequently contested Adams's election, an angry Lieutenant Wolfe unsuccessfully demanded that a military court of inquiry be convened to clear him of any wrongdoing. In June 1870 the Republican-dominated Twelfth Texas Legislature declared Adams's seat vacant after holding its own investigation.[29]

28. *Tabular Statement Of Voters (white and colored) Registered in Texas,* pp. 1–9; U.S. Army, Fifth Military District, State of Texas, GO No. 19, *Tabular Statement, Showing the Number of Votes Cast in Each County For and Against the Constitution, and for State Officers,* and *Tabular Statement, Showing Number Votes Cast in Each County for Members of Congress,* and *Tabular Statement, Showing the Votes Cast in Each District for Senators and Representatives,* and *Statement, Showing Vote by Counties for Clerks of District Courts, Sheriffs, and Justices of the Peace* (Austin: February 1, 1870), pp. 1–46; and James M. Thurmond to Charles E. Morse, December 12, 1869, "Register of Letters Received," vol. 4, p. 30, frame 0468, Microfilm Reel #4, and "Letter from Calvert," signed by P. W. Hall, December 10, 1869 (quotations), newspaper clipping from the Houston *Union,* December 16, 1869, Microfilm Reel #20, COCADT, RG 393, M1188, NA (1981).

29. Thomas H. Norton to HFMD, December 18, 1869, "Register of Letters Received," vol. 3, p. 326, Microfilm Reel #4, and James P. Butler to Joseph J. Reynolds, February 8, 1870, Microfilm Reel # 38, COCADT, RG 393, M1188, NA (1981); and *Registers of Elected and Appointed State and County Officials,* Microfilm Reel #5, p. 14 (quotation), RG 307, TSL-AD. In

At the end of his outburst against Lieutenant Wolfe, Hall became more philosophically resigned to the election outcome. After all, he had helped win radical victories under difficult conditions caused by the miserably cold weather, Harlan's untimely death, and Wolfe's studied indifference to the strong-arm tactics used against the freedmen by Adams's supporters. In addition, 343 more blacks had voted than in 1868—the second highest increase in black voting in counties throughout the state. And although voting irregularities had occurred, far worse ones had plagued surrounding areas. In Freestone County (to the east), intimidation of the freedmen, who outnumbered whites on the voter registration lists, caused the defeat of the local radical candidates. In neighboring Falls County (to the north), with nearly 350 more blacks than whites on the registration lists, the Davis ticket went down to defeat when the military post commander, who also served as the president of the board of registration, ignored massive frauds perpetrated against the freedmen. Finally, in Milam County (to the west), which enjoyed a reputation for unremitting lawlessness, the balloting had to be shut down when an army officer was shot and wounded while escorting about one hundred blacks traveling to the county seat and when, to prevent the arriving blacks from voting, a mob stormed the polling place. Hall thus concluded that he had done quite well under the circumstances: in his words, he had managed "to live and be elected."[30]

To further lift Hall's spirits, the radical Republicans had captured the statehouse. The South Texas scalawag Davis won the governorship, albeit by a razor-thin majority of 800 votes out of nearly 80,000 cast. In addition, radicals swept the races for the other principal state executive offices, and their ticket won three of four congressional seats, including the Third Congressional District, containing Robertson County. Davis, Hall, and the Union Leagues had, in fact, engineered a stunning triumph. With little financial assistance and the backing of a mere fraction of the newspapers in the state, Davis had won an election that many had considered

---

a special election held for four days from November 28 to 31, 1870, scalawag Republican John W. Robertson defeated three opponents for Adams's vacant seat. See: Manuscript Election Returns for 1870, Folder for Robertson County, Secretary of State Records, RG 307, TSL-AD.

30. Baum, *The Shattering of Texas Unionism,* table 35, p. 195, and pp. 197–226; A. M. Attaway to Nathan Patten, December 6, 1869, Microfilm Reel #39, and Report of Brevet Major W. O. Connell to Theodore J. Wint [in L. P. Graham to Charles E. Morse], August 1, 1869, Microfilm Reel #18, and "Letter from Calvert," signed by P. W. Hall, December 10, 1869 (quotation), newspaper clipping from the Houston *Union,* December 16, 1869, Microfilm Reel #20, COCADT, RG 393, M1188, NA (1981).

impossible. When the news reached Azeline and her neighbors in the Brazos Bottoms that Matthew Gaines, a rebellious former slave preacher on Lum Hearne's plantation, had been elected to the Texas state senate, they were astonished at how much the world had changed. Gaines spoke for all African Texans when, in the capitol building, he rejoiced at the death of the "old state of affairs" and welcomed the coming of a "new day" for black Texans, who had long been the victims of oppression.[31]

Reverend Sloan's Conveyance of Azeline's Plantation to Frank Hall

In neighboring Brazos County the radicals carried the countywide offices and elected their candidate as justice of the peace in the Millican District to replace Reverend Sloan. Although an unwavering Davis supporter, Sloan had been purged from the local radical ticket. The formal request for Sloan's removal from office for incompetence was not made until March 1870, but the rumors of his neglect of his duties and misappropriation of county funds most certainly reached Azeline's neighborhood. Like many other former slaves in the Brazos Bottoms, she nevertheless continued to trust the elderly preacher, who lived at times exclusively in their homes and who had a reputation for working tirelessly among them to establish churches and schools. With devastating consequences, Sloan, under a cloud of public controversy but acting as Azeline's attorney, conveyed in early January 1870 her entire plantation to Francis ("Frank") Marion Hall, the younger half-brother of state senator-elect Fidella Hall. No disclosure of her prior conveyance of half of it to Prendergast was indicated in the deed—an indication of Sloan's ignorance or sheer stupidity rather than his intent to deceive.[32]

The declared purchase price of the Brazos River plantation was Frank Hall's payment to Azeline of $2,000. The actual amount consisted of Hall's note for about $1,200, some goods out of his store, and "some land lying in [the] suburbs of Bryan." The discounted price reflected Hall's

31. Baum, *The Shattering of Texas Unionism,* p. 191; Ronald N. Gray, "Edmund J. Davis: Radical Republican and Reconstruction Governor of Texas" (Ph.D. diss., Texas Tech University, 1976), p. 178; and Matthew Gaines quoted in Charles Virgil Keener, "Racial Turmoil in Texas, 1865–1874" (M.S. thesis, North Texas State University, 1971), p. 69 (quotations).

32. "Petition by civil officers of Brazos Co. requesting removal of Richard Sloan (Co. Commissioner) for malfeasance in office," signed by Hiram T. Downard, Thomas J. Hall, W. L. Neall, W. B. Forman, Charles F. Moore, Benjamin F. Boldridge, William J. Pierce, Robert N. Mills, William Haverman, and Henry Mordecai, March 24, 1870, Microfilm Reel #29, COCADT, RG 393, M1188, NA (1981); and Mary Collie-Cooper, *Brazos County Texas 1870 Census* (Bryan, Tex.: Collie-Cooper Enterprises, 1987), p. 99.

knowledge of three encumbrances on her title: (1) Thomas Aycock's lawsuit for half the value of Sam's entire estate was still pending on the district court docket; (2) Azeline's conveyance of the south half of the plantation to Prendergast; and (3) both Aycock and Prendergast's claims to the plantation would be worthless if the Texas Supreme Court sustained the district court judgment against Azeline in the Erhard case. Nevertheless, Hall received from her not a mere quitclaim deed but rather a general warranty deed. It is not known if the validity of Hall's note was contingent upon his receipt of a good title, but otherwise all the formalities necessary to convey title to the land from Azeline to him were observed. She had apparently sold her Brazos River plantation. But had she? Years later while still residing on the plantation, Azeline denied under oath ever intending to sell it to Frank Hall.[33]

The news that Azeline had sold the plantation came as a bombshell to Prendergast. He learned about it soon after the deed was timely recorded on January 6th and her power of attorney to Sloan was filed for record three days later. As a frequent visitor to the Owensville courthouse, Prendergast most certainly had someone call these transactions to his attention. Not only would he have been annoyed with Azeline for putting additional legal obstacles in his path of acquiring uncontested ownership of the south half of her plantation, but because he had lost all rapport with his client he had to consider, as most attorneys would under similar circumstances, withdrawing as her legal counsel. Prendergast, however, could not allow himself to believe that his own behavior could have caused Azeline to seek Sloan's guidance and advice.[34]

Not only had Prendergast failed to talk with Azeline about the status of her appeal of the Erhard case, but he had initially ignored her plight when Hamman rode out upon her plantation as though he owned it—a circumstance that certainly helped in mistakenly convincing her that Hamman had prevailed against her for the ownership of her plantation. In retrospect, such a conviction on Azeline's part reveals the extent to which Prendergast had kept her completely uninformed of her legal affairs, especially considering that he was well aware of her excellent chance to win the

33. Deed from Asaline Hearne to F. M. Hall, dated January 4, 1870, and recorded January 6, 1870, Book "Q," p. 563, Microfilm Reel #963281, RD, CCO, Robertson County, Texas; Deed from Asaline Hearne to F. M. Hall [original], William Harrison Hamman Papers, box 3, folder #1, WRC-RU, Houston, Texas; and "Answers to Interrogatories and Cross Interrogatories made by George I. Goodwin," October 14, 1872 (quotation), in *F. M. Hall vs. Assaline Hearne,* Case No.1639, ODC, Robertson County, Texas.

34. "Interrogatories and Cross Interrogatories to John B. Rector," June 17, 1882, *Asaline Hearne vs. H. D. Prendergast,* Case No. 3069, ODC, Robertson County, Texas.

Erhard case on appeal. In terms of Prendergast's choice not to disclose to her information that could have avoided her loss of confidence in him, his decision to remain her lawyer was all the more shocking in light of his rationalization for his behavior: he blamed *her* for never consulting *him* about her decision to sell the plantation to Frank Hall. Azeline, Prendergast claimed, had made it "impossible" for him "to take care" of her.[35]

Prendergast had a significant weakness clouding his sense of right and wrong. He possessed an insatiable desire to acquire, own, and retain real estate. Upon his death in 1886 he had amassed more than twenty-three parcels of land spanning twelve counties and varying in size from city lots to a 3,800-acre tract. His decision to remain Azeline's attorney, and thus further complicate his relationship with her, was driven by his desire to protect his claim to the ownership of 452.5 acres of Robertson County bottomland, the south half of her plantation. Whatever persuasive powers he used on her will never be known, but he convinced her that she had made a bad decision to sell the plantation to Hall. Less than three weeks after the sale, Azeline, acting under Prendergast's guidance, revoked all powers of attorney that she had given to Sloan.[36]

The filing for record of Azeline's sale of the plantation to Frank Hall also caught the attention of Rasche Hearne and the law firm of Hollingsworth and Broaddus. They wanted to know what disposition had been made by the army regarding the contest between Azeline and Hamman over ownership of the rents. When the sheriff asked for permission to sell the cotton on Azeline's plantation to curtail expenditures for guarding it and avert dangers of it rotting, Lieutenant Guthrie at the Post of Calvert finally ordered that it be sold, necessary expenses incurred deducted, and the remainder of the money handed over to him. The seized cotton bales sold for $1,224.57, or $775.43 short of the total rental money. Guthrie then made the mistake of asking headquarters where he should deposit the money. Demonstrating neither any collective memory of the case nor common sense regarding it, headquarters proclaimed that Guthrie's actions

35. "Interrogatories and Cross Interrogatories to John B. Rector," June 17, 1882 (quotations), *Asaline Hearne vs. H. D. Prendergast,* Case No. 3069, and "Answers to Interrogatories and Cross Interrogatories made by William J. Pierce," October 14, 1872, *F. M. Hall vs. Assaline Hearne,* Case No. 1639, ODC, Robertson County, Texas; and Joe G. Bax, "A Summation of the Proceedings of the Probate and District Courts of Robertson County Relative to Asaline Hearne," [typescript manuscript in possession of the author, June 5, 2000], p. 73.

36. Re: Estate of H. D. Prendergast, Docket #553, PF, CCO, Robertson County, Texas; and Instrument, [revocation of power of attorney to Richard Sloan], dated January 25, 1870, and filed for record February 4, 1870, Book "Q," p. 579, Microfilm Reel #963281, RD, CCO, Robertson County, Texas.

were "disapproved" because he had shown "no grounds" for military interference in these matters. When Guthrie's successor, Captain James K. Sanderson, *demanded* to receive a direct order as to what to do with the money, headquarters instructed him on March 1, 1870, to deposit it with a reputable bank on his own account and subject to the disposition of the Robertson County District Court. Two weeks later, when the Texas Supreme Court reversed and dismissed the case of *Asaline Hearne vs. C. Erhard and others,* the matter of who owned the rents finally ended.[37]

Prendergast had all but eliminated any chance of losing the Erhard case on appeal. He hired the prestigious Galveston law firm of Ballinger, Jack, and Mott to argue the case before the high court. The added impressive legal firepower, however, proved unnecessary. The court, as expected, ruled that Erhard and his wife, along with the other heirs of Allen Reynolds, were not proper parties to the lawsuit initially filed against Sam over twenty years earlier by William H. Cundiff. As though the procedural absurdities in the district court were not enough for an easy reversal, Azeline also won her reversal on the basis of a derisory technicality. Claiming that the lack of a detailed description of the 903 acres prevented the sheriff from being able to put "a party in possession of that particular part of the six-league [Manchaca] grant," the justices voided the case for "uncertainty." When the court made its ruling, Frank Hall was the newly appointed sheriff of Robertson County, and he certainly knew where the plantation that he had just recently purchased was located. Although Azeline recovered her court costs against the phantom plaintiff Cundiff, who was the only plaintiff that the court possibly could have recognized, she was predictably not awarded to take from Erhard, his wife, and others, any compensation for her legal fee extracted from her by Prendergast, which consisted of the south half of her plantation.[38]

37. Samuel J. Adams [Office of Adams & Hearne, "Bankers, and Dealers in Exchange"] to Thomas H. Norton, January 8, 1870, and Thomas H. Norton to John B. Guthrie, January 9, 1870, and Max Wesendorff to "the Sheriff of Robertson County," January 21, 1870, and Robert Porter, "Statement of Cotton sold & expenses incurred in the sale of cotton seized on the Sam Hearne place," [undated], frames 0620–0627, and John B. Guthrie to Charles E. Morse, January 25, 1870, and statements on cover of ibid. by DeWitt Clinton (Major and Judge Advocate of the Fifth Military District), February [13?], 1870, and Charles E. Morse to Commanding Officer, Post of Calvert, March 1, 1870, ledger #2294, p. 500 (quotations), Microfilm Reel #39, and James K. Sanderson to HFMD, March 7, 1870, "Register of Letters Received," p. 138, Microfilm Reel #4, COCADT, RG 393, M1188, NA (1981).

38. "Brief for the appellant filed by Ballinger, Jack, and Mott," March 9, 1870, *Asaline Hearne vs. Cayton Erhard and others,* Case file M-5761, Texas Supreme Court Records, RG 201, TSL-AD; and *Asaline Hearne vs. C. Erhard and others,* [No number in original (Case

News that Azeline had won the case quickly filtered back to Robertson County and set off the final episode in the story of the army's awkward handling of the rental claims. Captain Sanderson, who was personally responsible for the money received from the sale of Wade and Campbell's cotton, implored headquarters to order him to return it to the sheriff because the reversal of the Erhard case had at last, in his words, placed "the matter beyond cavil." But Prendergast objected, because if anything were to happen to Sheriff Hall the question might arise "whether or not the receipt to the money by [him] could be an official act for which he would be responsible." Prendergast's quibble, which took another month to resolve, was self-serving, because he was entitled to half of the rent money and the Bryan law firm of Hollingsworth and Broaddus claimed the other half in legal fees. Mercifully, headquarters ordered Sanderson to "send for Assaline Hearne, and in person deliver to her the money."[39]

Soldiers accompanied Azeline from her home in the bottomlands to the Post of Calvert. After arriving downtown on Main Street, they escorted her past folding lottery tables and impromptu games of chance played outdoors and frequently blocking the public sidewalks with their motley crowds. They traveled through a residential area boasting some impressive new cypress houses and leading to the federal encampment (present-day Virginia Field Park), where she received the rental money directly from Sanderson. What she did with it is not known. She most likely kept it, in spite of her subsequent sworn statements suggesting the contrary. When she neglected to pay her legal fees to Hollingsworth and Broaddus, the Bryan attorneys sued her for half of the rent money they had recovered for her. Because her agreement with Prendergast entitled him as well to half of the rent money, they, as a consequence, were permitted to only one-fourth of it, or around $300.[40]

No. 3221)], Supreme Court of Texas, 33 Tex. 60; 1870 Tex. LEXIS 87, Decided March 1870 (quotations).

39. James K. Sanderson to Charles E. Morse, March 20, 1870 (first quotation), frame 0611, and Harvey D. Prendergast to Joseph J. Reynolds, undated letter [April 1870] (second quotation), frame 0607, Microfilm Reel #39, and Charles E. Morse to Commanding Officer, Post of Calvert, April 12, 1870, vol. 4, ledger #2593, p. 88 (third quotation), Microfilm Reel #2, COCADT, RG 393, M1188, NA (1981).

40. Galveston *Tri-Weekly News,* February 4, 1870, p. 3; *S. P. Hollingsworth and A. S. Broaddus vs. Asaline Hearne* Case No. 1402, October 19, 1871, Book "K," p. 310, MDC, Robertson County, Texas; and grand jury indictments, [Spring Term, 1870], Book "J [452–922]," pp. 872–74, MDC, Robertson County, Texas.

Nothing is known about the relationships among Aycock, Hamman, Prendergast, Hall, and Sloan after the army's deliverance of the rent money to Azeline. Aycock was waiting to have his day in court against her. His case for half the value of Sam's estate, if successful, would necessitate additional divisions or apportioning of the Brazos River plantation. Hamman was fanning the burned-out coals of his virtually futile lawsuit to contest the title to her plantation. His goal was to preempt the claims of all others to it except himself and perhaps the heirs of Allen C. Reynolds. Prendergast and Frank Hall were vying for the position to be the first to have the right to evict Azeline from her home of seventeen years—a course of action neither would have taken given the numerous other freedpeople squatting on the Brazos River plantation. And finally, in regard to Sloan, nobody bothered to inform him that, soon after Prendergast convinced Azeline that it had been a mistake to sell her plantation to Hall, she revoked the powers of attorney that she had given him. Sloan, acting without her knowledge or consent, sold her tract of land on the edge of Bryan to two different buyers.[41]

Azeline's Land Adjacent to "Hall's Town"

Frank Hall, acting with a power of attorney for his half-brother, William N. Hall, had transferred to Azeline twenty-three acres described as "adjoining the town of Bryan." The deed stated that he received $230 directly paid to him by Azeline. The real inducement to the conveyance a far more valuable cotton plantation in neighboring Robertson County—was not mentioned. The cash payment and the unstated consideration were not the only deceptions contained in the deed. Although it included no detailed metes and bounds of the land's precise location, a crucial part of the description of the land site was incorrect. The land conveyed to Azeline was part of a larger parcel purchased from William Joel Bryan, a nephew of Stephen Fuller Austin, the legendary leader of the first successful American-Mexican colony in Coahuila and Texas. It was part of a league of land commonly known as "Stephen F. Austin No. 10." It was

41. Revocation of a power of attorney dated January 25, 1870, and filed for record on February 4, 1870, Book "Q," p. 579, Microfilm Reel #963281, RD, CCO, Robertson County, Texas; and "Petition by civil officers of Brazos Co. requesting removal of Richard Sloan (Co. Commissioner) for malfeasance in office," signed by Hiram T. Downard, Thomas J. Hall, W. L. Neall, W. B. Forman, Charles F. Moore, Benjamin F. Boldridge, William J. Pierce, Robert N. Mills, William Haverman, and Henry Mordecai, March 24, 1870, Microfilm Reel #29, COCADT, RG 393, M1188, NA (1981).

not part of another nearby league of land described in the deed as "No. 9, granted [the] heirs of S. F. Austin." Nor was it exactly "adjoining" the city of Bryan. These unintentional, yet careless, mistakes involving the twenty-three acres prefaced a series of outlandish occurrences, all of them traceable to Sloan's incompetence, resulting in the fraudulent divestiture of Azeline of her ownership of her Brazos County land, where she allegedly had at one time decided to make her new home.[42]

The investigation during the winter of 1869–70 of Sloan's embezzlement of county funds was known to Frank Hall at the time he purchased Azeline's plantation. Hall's father, Thomas Jefferson Hall, served with Sloan on the county commissioners' court. In retrospect, how Sloan ever managed to acquire his position of precinct commissioner for the Millican district defies explanation. Although a member of the U.S. Christian Commission (present-day YMCA) and the American Missionary Association, he had falsely sworn that he was a registered voter upon accepting his appointment. Had military authorities checked, they would not have found Sloan's name on the voter registration lists. Otherwise, in all other respects he would have been able to qualify. His disingenuousness in accepting the appointment was overshadowed by his perpetration of a series of far greater unlawful acts that led to his public disgrace.[43]

Republican Party officials "ascertained indisputably" that, during his entire time in office, Sloan had failed to make use of county funds allocated to him to help the "indigent colored population." He had instead converted the money to his own use. In a bluntly worded formal request sent to headquarters, Brazos County's most prominent Republicans demanded Sloan's immediate removal from office and welcomed recommendations for possible punitive measures against him. Signing their petition were the newly elected sheriff and clerk of the district court, the chairman

42. Deed from W. N. Hall to Asaline Hearne, dated January 4, 1870 (quotations), and filed for record on January 26, 1874, Book "O," pp. 286–87, RD, CCO, Brazos County, Texas; "Bryan, William Joel," *TNHT,* 1: 793; Deed from William J. Bryan to William N. Hall, dated August 22, 1866, and filed for record on March 16, 1867, Book "H," pp. 88–89, RD, CCO, Brazos County, Texas.

43. Richard Sloan to E. M. Wheelock, December 4, 1866, Records of the Superintendent of Education for the State of Texas, 1865–1870, Microfilm Reel #4, BRFAL, RG 105, M822, NA (1973); *Voter Registration Lists, 1867–1869,* Microfilm Reels VR-1 through VR-12, TSL-AD; Donaly E. Brice and John C. Barron, *An Index to the 1867 Voters' Registration of Texas,* CD-ROM #1354 (Bowie, Md.: Heritage Books, Inc., 2000); Collie-Cooper, *Brazos County Texas 1870 Census,* p. 99, printed p. 50; and SO No. 111, HFMD, State of Texas, Austin: May 11, 1869, [By authority of General J. J. Reynolds], "Adjutant General Reconstruction Records," TSL-AD.

of the Brazos County Republican Committee and other Republicans, including Fidella and Frank Hall's father, along with others who had served with Sloan on the commissioners' board and police court. Military authorities, by the end of March 1870, removed Sloan from office.[44]

In spite of her title being legally, but not necessarily fatally, defective, Azeline's title to the twenty-three acres in suburban Bryan was superior to any other claim. Descriptive errors in the deed could have easily been corrected upon filing it for record at the courthouse, where officials would have recognized the land's location on the back edge of what was referred to as "Hall's Town," or Bryan's original "Freedman Town." In the fall of 1867 the scalawag Hall family made the first conveyances of land in the area to former slaves. Lots sold for as low as $12.50—a sum equivalent to what skilled workers could make in one week in Bryan's construction boom. The H&TC Railroad solidified the location of Freedman Town when its agents sold quitclaim deeds in a stretch of city blocks, initially called "Lower Freedmantown," extending alongside suburban Hall's Town. This combined set-apart area just under a mile from the downtown railroad passenger depot was centered to the east of the railroad tracks as they left the northern tip of the city and was only a few blocks from the disreputable north end of Bryan's downtown business district. By the summer of 1869, Sloan reported from Millican that "mostly all the Freedmen belonging to our church and forming our school, will move to Bryan, or near there, where they are buying land and settling."[45]

44. "Petition by civil officers of Brazos Co. requesting removal of Richard Sloan (Co. Commissioner) for malfeasance in office," signed by Hiram T. Downard, Thomas J. Hall, W. L. Neall, W. B. Forman, C. F. Moore, Benjamin F. Boldridge, William J. Pierce, Robert N. Mills, William Haverman, and Henry Mordecai, March 24, 1870, Microfilm Reel #29, COCADT, RG 393, M1188, NA (1981); SO No. 69, HFMD, State of Texas, Austin: March 29, 1870, [By authority of General J. J. Reynolds], "Adjutant General Reconstruction Records," TSL-AD.

45. Richard Sloan, "Report of August, 1869" (quotation), Records of the Superintendent of Education for the State of Texas, 1865–1870, Microfilm Reel #15, BFRAL, RG 105, M822, NA (1973); and *Sanborn Fire Insurance Maps,* Bryan, Texas, June 1912, Microfilm ed., Reel #6 (Teaneck, N.J.: Chadwyck-Healey, 1990). For $37.50 Hannibal [Harrison?] R. Hall sold lots 9, 10, and 12 in block 3 of Hall's Town to Thomas Bryan, "a man of color," and for $35 he sold lots 15 and 16 in block 6 to Mack Nolan [J. McNolan?] "a man of color." See: Warranty Deeds, dated November 1, 1867, Book "I," pp. 81 and 86, RD, CCO, Brazos County, Texas. The reference to "Lower Freedmantown" is found in Brundidge, ed., *Brazos County History,* pp. 151. For mention in conveyances to "Hall's Addition to the town of Bryan & known as Freedman Town," see: Warranty Deed, [undated], Guy M. Bryan to Charles C. Moore, recorded January 6, 1873, Book "N," p. 276b, RD, CCO, Brazos County, Texas. For notations on "Freedman Town" or "Freedmantown," see Book "L," pp. 215 and 268, RD, CCO, Brazos

Azeline made many trips to Bryan to visit her sister, who had moved there sometime after emancipation. In the wake of the election of Republican radicals to the most important local offices in Brazos County, Hall's Town must have been an alluring place to visit. Its distinctive street names were chosen by freedom's first generation of female residents: "Kalura" (present-day Preston), "Jewell" (Orleans), "Elpis" (Houston), and "Ena" (Justine). When Azeline traversed "Oneida Street" (Military Street), where the federal government schoolhouse was located, she looked directly upon the southwestern property line of her tract of land, which was twice the size of the sixty lots comprising Hall's Town. As notary public Pierce later recollected, perhaps she briefly considered moving here from her home in Robertson County, but she did not do so for long.[46]

In the summer of 1870, Sloan, acting without Azeline's approval but after discovering that she had decided to remain on her Brazos River plantation, conveyed away her interest in the twenty-three acres to Mary A. Moore, an illiterate white mother of six children and the wife of John S. Moore, a "saddler" in Millican. Sloan sold it to her for the same price that Azeline had supposedly paid for it. The reasons why Mrs. Moore wanted to own land adjacent to Hall's Town and why she trusted a discredited county official from her own district to sell it to her is not known, but possibly she was fooled by Sloan's misrepresentations of who he was. Sloan repeatedly followed his signature with "P.C.B.C"—the acronym for "precinct commissioner Brazos County"—the very office from which he had been ignominiously removed.[47]

Azeline's deed to Frank Hall for the Brazos River plantation was filed for record almost before the ink on it had dried, but inexplicably, nobody

---

County, Texas, and Brazos County Tax Rolls, 1842–1888, Tax Rolls for 1871, Microfilm Reel #1021-01, passim, TSL-AD.

46. Warranty deeds to Evaline Cipers, Emma Brown, Rose Williams, M[allera?] Manley, Bettie Mitchell, Matilda Brown, Margaret Johnson, and Laura Lumpkins, Book "I," pp. 61, 65, 76, 137, 422, Book "K," p. 148a, and Book "M," pp. 67 and 222, RD, CCO, Brazos County, Texas; *Sanborn Fire Insurance Maps,* Bryan, Texas, June 1912, Microfilm ed., Reel #6 (Teaneck, N.J.: Chadwyck-Healey, 1990); and "Answers to Interrogatories and Cross Interrogatories made by William J. Pierce," October 14, 1872, *F. M. Hall vs. Assaline Hearne,* Case No. 1639, ODC, Robertson County, Texas.

47. Warranty Deed from Asaline Hearne to Mary A. Moore, July 15, 1870, and filed for record on March 14, 1871, and recorded on May 26, 1871, Book "M," p. 109, RD, CCO, Brazos County, Texas; Collie-Cooper, *Brazos County Texas 1870 Census,* p. 96, printed p. 48A (first quotation); and To "Senators and Rep[resentatives]: [Recommended] Municipal Officers for Millican, Brazos Co.," [and marked as "No. 926"], July 12, 1870 (second quotation), box 65, folder 76, box 69, Governors' Papers: Edmund J. Davis, TSL-AD.

had bothered to file in timely fashion the deed from Frank Hall's brother to Azeline for the land adjacent to Hall's Town. Sloan probably kept it in his possession for safekeeping. Why Prendergast made no effort to recover it for Azeline defies all logic but would be perfectly consistent with his indifference toward her best interests. Nevertheless, by the end of 1870, W. N. Hall's deed to Azeline remained unfiled and unrecorded, and Sloan, acting improperly as Azeline's agent, had written a worthless deed from Azeline to Mary Moore.

Sloan waited six months to have his draft of the warranty deed from Azeline to Moore notarized. Perhaps he was waiting for her to pay him the total purchase price before giving her both papers, the original deed from W. N. Hall to Azeline and the one from Azeline to her, but the fact that he traveled to neighboring Grimes County to have the transaction notarized suggests that he knew that no notary public in Brazos County was willing to authenticate any document that involved his act or deed. Up to this point Sloan's behavior might not have involved premeditated wrongdoing, but his next transaction as Azeline's unauthorized agent was, by any moral compass, unpardonable. Sloan sold the same twenty-three acres to another person. In April 1871, almost a month after his bogus deed from Azeline to Mary Moore was finally filed for record, Sloan conveyed away for the second time all of Azeline's rights to the twenty-three acres to Douglas Dionycious ("Nish") Burkhalter.[48]

Nish Burkhalter was a thirty-three-year-old white South Carolina–born farmer who had arrived with his family in Brazos County sometime between 1866 and 1868. He purchased a farm some distance from the fertile Brazos River bottomlands near Millican, where he and his wife settled down to a hardscrabble existence. Burkhalter's reason, like Mary Moore's motive, for wanting to own land behind Hall's Town remains a mystery. His association in the spring of 1871 with Sloan implies that he was either extraordinarily naive or woefully uninformed of local political affairs. Presumably, Sloan once again collected the $230 stated as the purchase price, and in exchange Burkhalter secured a worthless piece of paper giving him only one asset: a right to sue for recovery of the money that he had paid to Sloan.[49]

48. Warranty Deed from Asaline Hearne to Mary A. Moore, July 15, 1870, and filed for record on March 14, 1871, and recorded on May 26, 1871, Book "M," p. 109, RD, CCO, Brazos County, Texas; and Deed from Asaline Hearne to D. D. Burkhalter, dated April 12, 1871, and filed for record on January 26, 1874, Book "O," p. 286, RD, CCO, Brazos County, Texas.

49. Brundidge, *Brazos County History,* pp. 257–58; and Brazos County Tax Rolls, 1842–1888, Tax Roll for 1873, Microfilm Reel #1021–01, TSL-AD.

By the end of June 1871, circumstances forced Sloan to acknowledge that both Nish Burkhalter and Mary Moore could not simultaneously own the same twenty-three acres. Rather than refunding the money to his buyers and tearing up the worthless deeds, Sloan expanded his chain of mistakes and frauds. Proceeding on the false premise that Mary Moore had a good and valid title, Sloan worked out a deal resulting in Mary and her husband selling the twenty-three acres to Burkhalter. In effect, the Moores conveyed away all their rights to land now described as previously sold by W. N. Hall to Azeline and then by her by deed via Sloan to Mary Moore. This sham transaction from the Moores to Burkhalter, like the one from Azeline to Mary Moore, also had to be notarized outside Brazos County. If Burkhalter assumed that, with the deed from the Moores, he possessed a valid title, he was dead wrong. Threaded through this chain of deeds there remained the repeated mistake in the description of the land, the misrepresentation by Sloan that he was Azeline's agent at the time of the conveyance to Mary Moore, the bizarre occurrence that Sloan had sold the same property twice to two different people, and the indispensable warranty deed from W. N. Hall to Azeline had still not been filed for record.[50]

In exchange for their warranty deed to Burkhalter, John and Mary Moore most likely received the money that Sloan had taken a few months earlier from Burkhalter. Evidence in the fall of 1871 that the Moores received some cash from the transaction was John's purchase of an improved lot in the town of Hearne and a lawsuit against him filed, but then quickly dismissed, by Burkhalter. Three years and a couple months later, Burkhalter successfully sold his worthless rights to the twenty-three acres to yet another buyer. By then, the Moores had defaulted on making their payments on their lot in Hearne, William N. Hall had declared bankruptcy, Richard Sloan had died or moved away, and Azeline had become embroiled in a battle over the title, possession, and ownership of what was still commonly referred to as "the old Sam Hearne plantation."[51]

50. Deed from John S. Moore and Mary A. Moore to D. D. Burkhalter, dated June 30, 1871, and filed for record January 26, 1874, Book "O," pp. 286–87, RD, CCO, Brazos County, Texas.

51. D. D. Buckhalter [*sic*] vs. John S. Moore and W. J. Lewis, Case No. 821, *Civil Minutes of the District Court,* Book "E," November 7, 1871, p. 3, Brazos County, Texas; "State of Texas, Order of Sale," [issued against John S. Moore, August 17, 1875], in *John E. Houghton vs. John S. Moore,* Case No. 1860, ODC, Robertson County, Texas; *Daily State Journal* (Austin), July 9, 1872, p. 2, and March 19, 1873, p. 2; and "Road Overseer for Precinct 28," [March 1876–September 1879: Special Term, 1876], p. 94 (quotation), CCM, Robertson County, Texas.

Chapter 6

It Seems Mighty Queer to Me, Lawyer

I never touched the pen in any way or signed the paper, nor did I authorize anyone to do so for me.

—Azeline Hearne, "Answers to Interrogatories," *F. M. Hall vs. Assaline Hearne*

At the beginning of 1870, there were good reasons for Azeline Hearne to believe that if she stayed in Robertson County she would lose everything. The unaccountability of the Freedmen's Bureau in managing Sam Hearne's estate had culminated in Ben Brown's ruinous executorship. Brown never paid the estate's taxes, filed any financial reports, or made any effort to pay any of the estate's debts. His complicity with William Hamman in the Cayton Erhard case put in motion the destruction of her ownership of the estate's principal asset, the Brazos River plantation. To appeal the judgment unfairly obtained against her, she had hired Harvey Prendergast, who put his own interest in acquiring half of her plantation ahead of her best interest in preserving it. The subsequent legal imbroglio over its annual rents had led the army to botch the execution of her distress warrant and had briefly allowed Hamman to wrongfully take control of her tenants' cotton and corn crop. These injustices had occurred at a time when military appointments had placed officeholders sympathetic to the Congressional Reconstruction Acts in firm control of the county government—a situation that paradoxically had made it possible in the first place to sustain Sam's will and provide a chance for his estate to be administered according to his wishes.

In December of 1869, when the time arrived for making rental or sharecropping and hiring contacts for the next season, nobody was willing, given the chaos in harvesting the prior crops, to sign written agreements with Azeline or with her agent, the Reverend Richard Sloan. Because the Erhard case was still on appeal, prospective renters or sharecroppers did not know with whom they could sign valid leases or agreements. Sloan, who was under investigation by the Brazos County sheriff for embezzlement, was not equal to the task of handling her interests in renting out the plantation or supervising its sharecropping arrangements. Yet he sensed that once federal military occupation ended and Texas was restored to the Union—an overdue event that was on schedule for the middle of April 1870—physical protection for Azeline would fade away and the floodgates for lawsuits against an administrator of Sam's estate would be thrown open. To represent her interests in the civil courts and manage her plantation's affairs, or perhaps just to enable her to start a new life in Bryan's Freedman Town, Sloan decided to pin her hopes for protection and assistance on the influential scalawag Hall brothers, Frank and Fidella.

Fidella Hall was a member of the Executive Committee of the Texas Republican Party. As the state senator-elect from Robertson, Leon, and Limestone Counties, he controlled, due to the death of the winning radical Republican candidate, the appointment of the next sheriff of Robertson County. His intention to appoint his twenty-two-year-old brother was well known. Frank Hall would not face an election until 1872, and barring a massive shift in the racial composition of the voting population he and other local Republicans would retain their offices. As the owner of the old Sam Hearne plantation, Sheriff Hall would be uniquely able to guarantee Azeline, and those subleasing under her, assurance that all financial rental or sharecropping arrangements were fair and equitable to all involved. He owed her such additional consideration because Sloan, acting as her agent, had sold him her valuable plantation for a considerably discounted price. This assumption puts Sloan and the Hall brothers' intentions in the best possible light. It presumes that Frank Hall bought the plantation essentially to be held in trust for Azeline and planned to act more or less as her legal trustee and, accordingly, she would be a beneficiary to a considerable extent of her own subleasing agreements.[1]

1. Phidello W. Hall to Charles E. Morse, January 1, 1870, Microfilm Reel #20, COCADT, RG 393, M1188, NA (1981); Bureau of the Census, *Population Schedules of the Eighth Census*

Frank Hall did not, however, draft a trust agreement with Azeline. Nor did he ask the probate court to be appointed administrator of Sam's estate—an appointment that would have allowed him to take over Brown's uncompleted and, since his arrest and escape from jail, abandoned duties. Hall neither demanded that military authorities render a full financial accounting of their management of the estate during the period when the Freedmen's Bureau had immunized it against legal actions, nor did he make an effort to take responsibility for managing the plantation, or any part of it, for the coming new planting season. Not surprisingly, the first documented interaction between Azeline and Frank Hall proved not only inhospitable but also disheartening.

Azeline Again "Touches the Pen"

The lawyer who had handled the preparation of closing documents for Frank Hall during the first week of January neglected to have Sloan sign and Azeline acknowledge a leasing agreement. To allow any seller of real estate to remain on it after its sale was risky because, unless there was some additional agreement on the part of the buyer and seller, such an action would violate the basic concept of a purchase. Not surprisingly, a subsequent document was filed for record describing a tenancy agreement between Azeline and Hall. It reiterated that she had conveyed away her interest in the plantation to him, placed him in possession of it, and acknowledged him as its owner. She further recognized that she would be his tenant under his charge and control for an unstipulated "said term"—meaning that she was at most a tenant at will. The leasing agreement achieved little or nothing for her, but Hall received precisely the documentation he needed as a buyer of land who was allowing a seller to remain in possession.[2]

The agreement was in Frank Hall's saddlebags when he rode out to Azeline's Brazos River plantation in January 1870. Hall wanted her to sign it in front of witnesses. She recalled seeing him three times at her home shortly after New Year's Day but refused to speak to him on the first

of the United States, 1860, Microfilm Roll #1300, "Limestone County, Texas," p. 64 [printed p. 345], M653, NA (1967); and Ernest Emory Bailey, comp. and ed., *Texas Historical and Biographical Record: With a Genealogical Study of Historical Family Records* (Austin: By the Author, 1900), pp. 310–13.

2. "[Tenancy] Agreement between Assaline Hearne and F. M. Hall," dated January 6, 1870 (quotation), and recorded February 16, 1872, Book "V," p. 131, Microfilm Reel #963284, RD, CCO, Robertson County, Texas.

visit. On the second occasion, Hall entered her house and informed her that he had purchased her plantation. She told him that she knew nothing about selling it to him, and they quarreled, and Hall soon left. The first and second visits were of short duration, but the third visit was an all-day affair.[3]

Hall, in Azeline's words, "had a paper" that he wanted her to sign, and his brother, William N. Hall, accompanied him. She did not know what the paper was, nor did she know whether it was a lease or a deed. Hall and his brother repeatedly begged her to "just touch the pen," but she steadfastly refused. She then left her house and walked to Jane Bentley's nearby residence and then went to Nelda Allen's cabin. Frank Hall followed her, constantly insisting that she should sign the paper, which he held in his hand. According to Azeline, Jim Wade, one of her tenants from the previous year, was not "then on the place." Unfortunately for her credibility, Wade was present at the time of Hall's visits. In Calvert in front of a notary public, Wade subsequently swore that he was the subscribing witness to her signing of the lease.[4]

According to Azeline, Frank Hall never read to her what was written on the folded paper he always had in his hand, nor did he explain to her what it said or what it was. She was adamant in her certainty that she "never touched the pen in any way, or signed the paper," nor did she ever authorize anyone to sign it on her behalf. The recollections of Ophelia Holiday, another freedwoman living in the immediate neighborhood, substantiated Azeline's testimony, at least for the most part. Holiday claimed that on the first visit Frank Hall announced that he had purchased her plantation from Reverend Sloan, whereupon Azeline denied that she had given Sloan any control over it. Azeline then asked how Sloan could have sold her place without her consent; she argued with Hall, and he left soon after. Hall's second visit was also brief and uneventful, but Holiday contradicted Azeline in one important detail, that Dred Dawson, Azeline's longtime neighbor in the bottomlands, accompanied Frank Hall and his brother William. Jane Bentley also recalled the three men being present together at the "gallery" of Azeline's house.[5]

3. "Answers [to Interrogatories] of Assaline Hearne," recorded by Wyndham Kemp, February 19, 1873, *F. M. Hall vs. Assaline Hearne,* Case No. 1639, ODC, Robertson County, Texas.

4. Ibid. (quotations); and "[Tenancy] Agreement between Assaline Hearne and F. M. Hall," dated January 6, 1870, and recorded February 16, 1872, Book "V," p. 131, Microfilm Reel #963284, RD, CCO, Robertson County, Texas.

5. "Answers [to Interrogatories] of Assaline Hearne," February 19, 1873 (first quotation),

Dawson had accompanied the Hall brothers to help them convince Azeline to sign the leasing agreement. Since Sam's death, he had often intervened at crucial junctures in Azeline's affairs by agreeing to the lesser of risks to her welfare. For example, he acted with James Cunningham and others in the winter of 1866–67 to probate Sam's will in opposition to the determination of Sam's cousins and brothers to have it set aside. He also was a major surety in 1868 on Brown's bond as administrator of Sam's estate, and, in the wake of Prendergast's indifference to Hamman's unwarranted intrusion onto her land, Dawson advised Azeline to hire another lawyer to help her collect the rents due her. Frank Hall, his brother William, and Dawson, according to Holiday and Bentley, had repeatedly urged Azeline to sign the paper, "telling her that it was for her benefit."[6]

Jane Bentley recalled how Hall offered Azeline "some money" if she would sign, but Azeline told him that she "did not want any of his money." Bentley also described how Hall persistently pursued Azeline: "I saw Assaline leave her house and she came over to mine . . . *to get shet [sic] of him.*" Hall followed her into Bentley's cabin but had to leave to chase his horse after it escaped from its hitching post. What occurred next was quite out of the ordinary. Azeline came "in a run" to Nelda Allen's house, which shared the same yard with the Holiday and Bentley residences. According to Allen, Hall had a paper, "which he wanted her to look at and kept *toomantin* [*sic*] her about it, but she wouldn't have anything to do with it." Hall and Azeline then went off together, but about thirty minutes later she came "*tearing* back" with him running after her. She ran into Allen's cabin and, in Allen's words, "jumped in my bed & covered herself up, *head and ears,*" but "Hall kept *fooling with her* and made her get up."[7]

During the emotionally exhausting day, Azeline at some point did eventually "touch the pen." This is likely not only because Wade swore that she

---

"Answers [to Interrogatories] of Ophelia Holiday," February 19, 1873, and "Answers [to Interrogatories] of Jane Bentley," February 19, 1873 (second quotation), recorded by Wyndham Kemp, *F. M. Hall vs. Assaline Hearne,* Case No. 1639, ODC, Robertson County, Texas.

6. "Adm[inistrato]r with the Will Annexed, Bond [of John W. Cunningham]," filed January 11, 1867, Re: Estate of Samuel R. Hearne, Docket #134, PF, CCO, Robertson County, Texas; and "Answers [to Interrogatories] of Ophelia Holiday" (quotation), and "Answers [to Interrogatories] of Jane Bentley," recorded by Wyndham Kemp, February 19, 1873, *F. M. Hall vs. Assaline Hearne,* Case No. 1639, ODC, Robertson County, Texas.

7. "Answers [to Interrogatories] of Jane Bentley" (first, second, and third quotations), and "Answers [to Interrogatories] of Nelda Allen" (fourth, fifth, six, seventh, and eighth quotations), recorded by Wyndham Kemp, February 19, 1873, *F. M. Hall vs. Assaline Hearne,* Case No. 1639, ODC, Robertson County, Texas.

did but also because the highly respected Dawson would not have knowingly been a party to a deliberate falsehood. In addition, Azeline's denials that she never gave Sloan the power to sell the plantation to Hall did not make believable her denial of acknowledging the leasing agreement. Admittedly, her recollections could have reflected her failure to comprehend the full extent of the legal authority she gave Sloan, who did not need to secure her signature or permission to sell the plantation to Hall or, for that matter, to anyone else. Sloan's deed to Hall—a transaction executed prior to Azeline's revocation of Sloan's authority—triggered permanent relinquishment of any residual interest that she might have had in the plantation. She had little to lose by putting her mark on the lease in accord with Hall's subsequent, persistent urging.[8]

By early February 1870, just after 250 Chinese contract laborers captivated attention by arriving in Calvert to work on the continuation of the H&TC Railroad, Frank Hall received his military appointment as sheriff. Six months later he received his civil commission by posting a required bond for $25,000—a considerable amount that had proven to be an insurmountable obstacle for a couple of previously military-approved candidates, not to mention all African Texans. The most important surety on Hall's bond was wealthy planter and landowner Dr. Benjamin Hammond, who, along with Ben Brown, was awaiting trial by civil authorities for the murder of Dr. Maxwell. Because the Republican-dominated commissioners' court controlled the pool of men selected for jury service, signing on as a surety on Hall's bond represented an investment on Dr. Hammond's part in facilitating his and Brown's acquittal. During this period Prendergast held a position at the pleasure of the probate court as a "special sheriff"—a circumstance testifying to the confidence that he continued to enjoy from the county's Republican officeholders. Even if Hammond, Brown, and Prendergast had not voted the complete, or "straight," radical ticket in the 1869 gubernatorial election, their cooperation with Robertson County's radical Republicans tainted them in the eyes of anti-Reconstruction Democrats.[9]

8. "Answers [to Interrogatories] of Assaline Hearne," recorded by Wyndham Kemp, February 19, 1873 (quotation), *F. M. Hall vs. Assaline Hearne,* Case No. 1639, ODC, Robertson County, Texas; and Deed from Asaline Hearne to F. M. Hall, dated January 4, 1870, and recorded January 6, 1870, Book "Q," p. 563, Microfilm Reel #963284, RD, CCO, Robertson County, Texas.

9. "Chinese," *TNHT,* 2: 86–87; Telegram from HFMD to CO Post of Calvert, [copy], February 7, 1870, vol. 3, p. 405, ledger #2092, Microfilm Reel #2, COCADT, RG 393, M1188, NA (1981); [January 1870], vol. "S," p. 86, PM, CCO, Robertson County, Texas; *Registers*

Throughout the remainder of 1870, the record regarding Hall's relationship with Prendergast is silent, although the conveyance of Azeline's plantation to Hall following the conveyance of the south half to Prendergast revealed a conflict over rights of ownership. If Prendergast's subsequent statements are accurate, no one in 1870 rented any part of the plantation. Previously cleared or improved acreage on what had been one of the county's finest antebellum plantations became, if Prendergast can again be believed, "overgrown with briars and bushes." Throughout the remainder of the year, the record is silent about Azeline and her plantation, but she must have gazed upon her surroundings with disbelief, sadness, and trepidation.[10]

The Early Days of "Radical" Reconstruction in Robertson County

On the eve of the army's exit in the spring of 1870, complaints "of the most outrageous and unjust swindling" of the freedmen were reported to the commander of the Post of Calvert so often that he still felt compelled to act in most cases by seizing a planter's cotton until agreements were fairly settled. Post commanders in neighboring counties on the eve of their departures described even more dispiriting situations. In Milam County (to the west) snipers still made it "unsafe for any [uniformed] person connected with the army to go outside of [the county seat of Cameron] alone." Elsewhere came predictions of a likely resurgence of Ku Klux Klan activity once federal troops were gone. Although many whites in Robertson County belonged to an imitation of the Klan under the guise of various "notorious social clubs," the degree of violence against blacks had subsided from levels reached in the immediate postwar years.[11]

The year 1870 in Texas political history would be deprecated for generations as having put "the pyramid upon its apex," because the "most igno-

---

of Elected and Appointed State and County Officials, Microfilm Reel #5, pp. 510–11, TSL-AD; and "Order of County Court Bonds," September 3, 1870, p. 236, and October 27, 1870, pp. 241–46, RCC, CCO, Robertson County, Texas.

10. "Answers of H. D. Prendergast, Adm[inistrato]r, to Motion of F. M. Hall," filed March 26, 1875 (quotation), Re: Estate of Samuel R. Hearne, Docket #134, PF, CCO, Robertson County, Texas.

11. George K. Sanderson to Charles E. Morse [and endorsement by J. P. Richardson], March 7, 1870 (first quotation), Microfilm Reel #29, Lynde Catlin to H. Clay Woods, March 14, 1870 (second quotation), Microfilm Reel #30, COCADT, RG 393, M1188, NA (1981); Alderman of Hearne [Charles Ernest Brandice, Dan Keegan, and Stephan S. Kurtan (?)] to Edmund J. Davis,

rant and incapable" ruled by carpetbaggers and scalawags, unnaturally ruled over the white majority. Robertson County folklore holds that the moving of the county seat by Republicans from Owensville to "their black precinct" of Calvert was one of the most notorious misdeeds of the entire Reconstruction era. Yet most large planters, including Rasche Hearne, along with virtually all the county's prominent lawyers—a group including many anti-Reconstruction and racist Democrats such as Alexander W. Terrell—favored the move.[12]

The handful of white Republican radicals in Robertson County constituted a flawed, albeit courageous and tough, group of newcomers. As political colleagues of the Hall brothers, all of them were well acquainted with Azeline. Carpetbagger brothers-in-law M. A. Connolly and Marks Wilson held military-appointed positions as mayor of Calvert and justice of the peace, respectively. This "sort of a family arrangement" by uneducated Irish immigrants annoyed most members of the city's legal fraternity, who constantly complained about their incompetence. After Connolly fined an inebriated attorney for contempt in the Mayor's Police Court, the attorney waylaid Connolly outside the building, hitting him with enough force to knock him down "to the grass." In the midst of the ensuing fisticuffs, a second attorney intervened, seized Connolly by "the nape of the neck" and "slung him" again down on the ground. When Connolly drew his six-shooter, aimed it point blank at the second attorney and threatened to kill him, policemen arrived and took the terrified lawyer to the safety of the city jail. Justice of the Peace Wilson then arrived waving his six-shooter in a determined search for the first attorney, who had started the fighting by having, in Wilson's words, "struck me brother-in-law." Wilson tracked down the first attorney and summarily administered retaliatory punishment.[13]

March 9, 1872 (third quotation), box 78, folder #234, Governors' Papers: Davis, RG 301, TSL-AD; and Statements of Louis Young in George P. Rawick, ed., *The American Slave: A Composite Autobiography,* vol. 5, [pt. 3 & 4], pt. 4 (Westport, Conn.: Greenwood Press, 1979), p. 234.

12. Charles William Ramsdell, *Reconstruction in Texas* (Austin: University of Texas Press, 1910, reprinted., 1970), p. 292 (first and second quotations); J. W. Baker, *A History of Robertson County, Texas* (Waco, Tex.: Printed by Texian Press, 1970), p. 164 (third quotation); Alexander W. Terrell to Charles E. Morse, January 17, 1870, frame 0449, and Samuel J. Adams to Charles E. Morse, February 26, 1870, Microfilm Reel #35, COCADT, RG 393, M1188, NA (1981).

13. "Marks Wilson," Registration No. 1382, and "M. A. Connolly," Registration No. 1389, p. 240, *Voter Registration Lists, 1867–1869,* Robertson County, Texas, Microfilm Reel VR-10,

Connolly and Wilson's brandishing of deadly weapons within the city limits resulted in a Robertson County grand jury indicting them for "assault with intent to murder." Two years later the district attorney dropped the charges against Connolly, but a jury fined Wilson for being guilty of "aggravated assault." After a brief appointment as mayor of Calvert, Connolly served as an elected justice of the peace for the Hearne district and then was appointed mayor of Hearne. Wilson was elected in 1869 as the justice of the peace for the Calvert district, but reputedly possessed "neither a knowledge of the law nor the capacity to acquire it." In late 1871, when the district court removed him for "incompetency in office," a dozen other separate cases were pending against him, including "embezzlement," "extortion as an officer," and "failure to pay over fines collected." Most, if not all, of these charges were subsequently dropped when Wilson arranged to settle his accounts.[14]

The overwhelming majority of the county's black residents strongly supported Connolly and Wilson. Serving as a notary public, real estate agent, and employment broker, Wilson had welcomed the freedmen into his downtown Calvert office, located near the black-patronized grocery store of Anschicks & Lieberman. Anschicks (the duly elected clerk of the district court) and Lieberman's store was sandwiched between two saloons, one of which was operated by a black barkeeper whose establishment, in turn, was next to a house of prostitution. In the spring of 1870,

---

TSL-AD; George K. Sanderson, Captain of the Post of Calvert, to Charles E. Morse, February 11, 1870 (first quotation), Microfilm Reel #29, and Mordecai S. Boatner, James Pruess, Peter Franz, and E. Allard ("The Board of Alderman for Calvert"), to George K. Sanderson, February 7, 1870, Microfilm Reel #2, and *The Calvert Enterprise,* March 8, 1870 (second, third, fourth, and fifth quotations), newspaper clipping contained in O. D. Thatcher to Joseph J. Reynolds, March 10, 1870, frame 0324, Microfilm Reel #35, COCADT, RG 393, M1188, NA (1981).

14. *The State of Texas vs. Marks Wilson,* Case No. 617, and *The State of Texas vs. M. Conley [sic],* Case No. 659, [Spring Term, 1870], April 20 and 23, 1870 (first quotation), Book "J," pp. 896 and 918, and [June Term, 1872], Book "K," pp. 536 (second quotation) and 571, MDC, Robertson County, Texas; Phidello W. Hall to Edmund J. Davis, September 14, 1870, box 61, folder 106, and M. A. Connolly to Edmund J. Davis, July 17, 1872, box 80, folder 251, Governors' Papers: Davis, RG 301, TSL-AD; Endorsement of Thomas H. Norton on cover of "Petition of D. W. Lewis and others to Thomas H. Norton," [received at HFMD on January 2, 1870] (third quotation), Microfilm Reel #20, COCADT, RG 393, M1188, NA (1981); *The State of Texas vs. Marks Wilson,* Case No. 757, October 24, 1871 (fourth quotation), Book "K," p. 320, and *The State of Texas vs. Marks Wilson,* Cases Nos. 624, 625, 626, 627, 628, 642, 643, 644, 645, 646, 647, 648, 649, 651, [Spring Term, 1870], April 23 and 25, 1870 (fifth, sixth, and seventh quotations), Book "J [452–922]," p. 905, and [Fall Term, 1871], November 7, 1871, Book "K," p. 355, MDC, Robertson County, Texas.

District Court Clerk Anschicks, Justice of the Peace Wilson, Mayor Connolly, County Judge Isaac Ellison, and postmaster and state senator-elect Fidella Hall were the most influential officials in the thriving new town of Calvert. Insults, threats, and the possibility of physical violence plagued them every minute of the day for no reason other than their affiliation with the Republican Party. Nor were they targeted by mere roughs and rowdies. When Hall had avowed in the fall of 1868 that he would "leave the United States if Semur [*sic*] and Blair" were elected, former county judge Alfred L. Brigance abruptly assaulted him. In the wake of the referendum decision to move the county seat to Calvert, a prominent resident of Owensville attacked Ellison while he was transporting county records. Such uncalled-for confrontations were routine.[15]

The Democratic claim that the Republican set of officeholders was "overly sympathetic to the Negroes," supposedly gave Calvert a reputation for being a "Yankee Hell Hole." But only much later was the word "Hell" inserted between "Yankee" and "Hole," because contemporaries of the period used the word "hole" to describe the surface water tank built by federal soldiers encamped on the edge of town. In any case, the pejorative label was not warranted by what took place. Even after factoring in Wilson's difficulty in interpreting the law and Anschicks's distressing propensity to break it, Robertson County Republicans were, at least in contrast to their predecessors, firmly committed to the principles of the Thirteenth, Fourteenth, and Fifteenth Amendments to the U.S. Constitution. Moreover, they represented a disconnection from a prior leadership that had caused more death, misery, and ruin to a generation of Texans than any other, if only by its disastrous decision to secede from the Union and provoke an inevitable civil war. After physically attacking Fidella Hall, Brigance won forgiveness when Congress removed his political disabilities. He was subsequently appointed a county road overseer with a salary

15. Baker, *A History of Robertson County,* p. 501; Phidello W. Hall to Edmund J. Davis, September 14, 1870, box 61, Governors' Papers: Davis, RG 301, TSL-AD; Bureau of the Census, *Population Schedules of the Ninth Census of the United States, 1870,* Microfilm Reel #1602, "Robertson County, Texas," p. 174, M593, NA (1965); *State of Texas vs. Conrad Anschicks,* Case No. 622, [Spring Term, 1870], April 22, 1870, Book "J [452–922]," p. 900, MDC, Robertson County, Texas; Dallas *Weekly Herald,* November 10, 1881, p. 4; "Office of M. Wilson, Justice of the Peace, Notary Public, Employment and Real Estate Agency" [Letterhead], Marks Wilson to Edmund J. Davis, October 27, 1871, box 76, folder 217, Governors' Papers: Davis, RG 301, TSL-AD; Phidello W. Hall to Elisha M. Pease, October 8, 1868 (quotation), box 58, folder 48, Governors' Papers: Pease, RG 301, TSL-AD; and Lawrence Ward St. Clair, "History of Robertson County, Texas" (M.A. thesis, University of Texas, 1931), p. 97.

of $500 per year. Other prominent opponents of the Republicans were likewise not excluded from local governance.[16]

Nor was there evidence of extensive mismanagement of county finances. The Republican-dominated county commissioners' court ordered former secessionist and anti-Reconstruction Democrats to examine the books of the treasurer and tax assessor-collector in order to find any discrepancies between "amounts ascertained to have been collected and those reported." It charged other leading anti-Republicans to review laws assessing taxes for a courthouse and a badly needed new jail. In the spring of 1871 the Robertson County Grand Jury, comprised mostly of anti-Republicans with the power to hand down any indictment they desired, praised two Republican radicals, former county judge and now district attorney Ellison and the newly appointed district judge James M. Thurmond, for their "fearless manner" in charging them to examine the actions of all county officers. It expressed its "indebtedness" to the "efficiency" with which Ellison and Thurman provided them with records and documents. Joining the Ku Klux Klan was hardly, as one oft-quoted local history book argues, the only alternative for anti-Republicans desiring to influence governmental policies during this period.[17]

Republicans proved at times to be their own worst enemies by engaging in disastrous internecine quarrels, often of a purely personal nature. Although the most serious early instance of factionalism in their ranks occurred in 1871 and 1872, the behavior of County Clerk Anschicks in 1870 foreshadowed the beginning of frequent internal party disputes—disagreements that were luxuries Robertson County Republicans could ill afford. After Anschicks was fined for a breach of the peace in the police court, he mobilized black voter disapproval of Mayor Connolly. Anschicks made bets that he could dictate, through his influence with black voters, the next appointment of any mayor or local official. In this regard he sup-

16. Baker, *A History of Robertson County,* pp. 164 (first quotation) and 467 (second quotation); [July 1870], p. 335, and [February 1871], p. 413, CCM-PM, Robertson County, Texas; and Richard Denny Parker, *Historical Recollections of Robertson County, Texas, with Biographical & Genealogical Notes on the Pioneers & Their Families* (Salado, Tex.: Anson Jones Press, 1955), p. 46.

17. [August 18, 1870], pp. 357–58 (first quotation), and [December 1, 1870], p. 392, CCM-PM, Robertson County, Texas; and "Report of the Grand Jury," [signed by John Orr, Foreman], February 28, 1871, Book "K," pp. 80–81 (second, third, and fourth quotations), MDC, Robertson County, Texas; and Norman L. McCarver and Norman L. McCarver Jr., *Hearne on the Brazos* (San Antonio, Tex.: The Naylor Company, 1936), p. 25.

ported the legitimate demand of blacks, who comprised a vast majority of the county's Republicans, for more political offices and positions.[18]

Growing black militancy exacerbated Republican divisions, as did the frequent failure of an assorted handful of white Republicans to be unified by any shared agenda, traditional party allegiance, or even class status. Governor Edmund J. Davis's extensive powers of appointment to the governing bodies of cities and towns additionally guaranteed that party factionalism would endure. Seeking the governor's favor interfered with trying to work out differences at the local level. At one point, sixty-three "German & Jewish Merchants" in Calvert petitioned Davis to replace the current Republican-appointed city marshal with another Republican, whom they claimed possessed more "force and fitness" for the office. Davis readily agreed, unleashing the complaint of supporters of the ousted officeholder that it was difficult enough "to stand the jibes, scorn, and persecution of the Ku-klux," without having to deal with "underworking, serpentine, base malignant falsifications of so-called Republicans." Republican factionalism plagued not only Robertson County but also affected the party throughout the state, in which white votes for Davis accounted for no more than 12 percent of his total.[19]

Prendergast Takes Over the Administration of Sam Hearne's Estate

At the end of 1870 Prendergast further complicated his relationship with Azeline. He decided to spare her Brazos River plantation from neglect for a second subsequent year. He filed an application in early January 1871 to become the administrator of Sam's estate. Because the previous administrator had left the estate unsettled, Prendergast asked the court to grant him an administration *de bonis non,* or administrator "of the goods not already administered." Avoiding any mention of Brown, who was await-

18. "Colored Men of the Town of Calvert" to Edmund J. Davis, July 9, 1870, box 65, and Petition of thirty-two Robertson County voters to Edmund J. Davis, July 12, 1870, box 65, Governors' Papers: Davis, RG 301, TSL-AD.

19. Ramsdell, *Reconstruction in Texas,* p. 298; Carl H. Moneyhon, *Republicanism in Reconstruction Texas* (Austin: University of Texas Press, 1980), p. 128; "Petition of 63 German & Jewish Merchants of Calvert," enclosed in Isaac Schmeidler to Edmund J. Davis, December 11, 1871 (first and second quotations), box 77, folder 228, and Charles S. Gillespie to Edmund J. Davis, December 8, 1871 (third quotation), box 77, folder 226, Governors' Papers: Davis, RG 301, TSL-AD; and Dale Baum, *The Shattering of Texas Unionism: Politics in the Lone Star State during the Civil War Era* (Baton Rouge: Louisiana State University Press, 1998, pp. 191–97.

ing trial for murder, Prendergast explained that after Sam's will had been probated, the Freedmen's Bureau had "disrupted from the docket" its administration, and since that time no completed administration upon the estate had occurred. Arguing that outstanding debts and unsettled business made administration indispensable, he revealed that he was "interested in the land" of the estate "by purchase" from Azeline, who owned it by "legacy and by inheritance." He added that he was also "a creditor" of the estate—a reference to Azeline's failure to pay him his share of the 1869 rent money. Nobody, including most noticeably Sheriff Hall, came forward to challenge Prendergast's appointment—a situation that exposed the limited, if virtually nonexistent, alternatives obtainable to Azeline.[20]

Prendergast was the principal signer on his required $20,000 bond, but his surety was somewhat of a surprise. Buck Watts had been managing plantations in the southern half of the county's Brazos Bottoms since the last years of the Civil War. Although Watts declared to the voter registration board that he arrived in the county in 1865, his name appears on an 1863 list of local men in the Texas Home Guards. At the beginning of 1867, he petitioned the Freedmen's Bureau for help in procuring transportation of freedmen to Robertson County from other states—an admission that he either had difficulty renegotiating contracts with local freedmen for another year or was acting as a labor broker for other planters. During the yellow fever epidemic, in which he nearly died, he asked permission from the bureau to buy from Azeline, whom he courteously referred to as "Mrs. Hearn[e]," the "old ambulance" used by Sam during his illness. In 1869, when Azeline filed her petition for a writ of error to the Texas Supreme Court to reverse the judgment against her in the Erhard case, Watts had been one of the three sureties on her bond. Yet he did not appear on the county's tax rolls until 1870, when he paid taxes on only fourteen horses and a few lots in Calvert—assets valued at an amount that would have made him, as was later alleged, "not pecuniarily responsible" for the amount of either the bond posted for the writ of error or for Prendergast's bond as administrator.[21]

20. Henry Campbell Black, *Black's Law Dictionary,* 4th ed. (St. Paul, Minn.: West Publishing Co., 1951), p. 476 (first quotation); and "Application for Letters *De Bonis Non,*" filed for record January 7, 1871 (second, third, fourth, and fifth quotations), Re: Estate of Samuel R. Hearne, Docket #134, PF, CCO, Robertson County, Texas; and "Original Notice: To All Whom It May Concern," January 9, 1871, and filed for record April 10, 1876, vol. 2, p. 130, PM, CCO, Robertson County, Texas.

21. "Application for Letters *De Bonis Non,*" [Spring Term, 1871], February 28, 1871, Book "K," p. 70, MDC, Robertson County, Texas; 134 "Letters of Adm[inistrato]r," February 28,

In early 1871 Prendergast made Watts the manager of the Brazos River plantation—a position he subsequently held for the next decade. The estate's property, Prendergast claimed, was then "in a state of complete dilapidation" and only a hundred acres of the plantation land could be cultivated. Yet the following year the plantation had "*five or six hundred acres of land in cultivation*." Assuming all previously cultivated acreage had been left to pasture during 1870, only a native prairie grass, little bluestem, would have posed minor problems in 1871. Using teams of mules dragging chains, workers could easily have ripped up the "briars and bushes." To further denigrate the estate's worth, Prendergast declared that its lawfully incurred debts had never been fully paid off and that the plantation's title had been in litigation since the late 1850s. At no time did he mention that schedules to pay off the debts could have been easily worked out, and the 1857 and 1858 lawsuits filed by William H. Cundiff and Eliza C. Willett, respectively, had no chance, at least under normal circumstances, of divesting Azeline of the plantation's title. During their long association and partnership, Prendergast, in his role as the estate's administrator, and Watts, as a putative agent or manager, were unashamedly in league to defraud the estate of the full amounts of yearly rent, which could otherwise have been routinely collected. Prendergast convinced the probate court that he could more "advantageously rent [the plantation] out at private rather than public renting." The benefit of this arrangement went to himself and Watts and never to the estate or Azeline.[22]

Shortly after Prendergast filed for his letters of administration, he man-

---

1871, and filed with notation "Filed/74," and "Bond of Adm[inistrato]r," filed March 9, 1871, Re: Estate of Samuel R. Hearne, Docket #134, PF, CCO, Robertson County, Texas; "W. W. Watts," Registration No. 1586, p. 245, *Voter Registration Lists, 1867–1869,* Microfilm Reel VR-10, Robertson County, Texas, TSL-AD; "Muster Roll of State Troops of Beat No. 2, 3 & 6 of Robertson Co. Tex. For July 1863," Josephus Cavitt Papers, box 3S167, CAH-UT, Austin, Texas; W. W. Watts to HFMD, January 14, 1867, "Register of Letters Received," vol. 1, p. 550 and W. W. Watts to Oscar F. Hunsaker, Letters Received (Entered in Register 1) "T–Z 1866–1867," August 25, 1867 (first and second quotations), frame 545, and Harvey D. Prendergast to Thomas H. Norton, [undated and marked "Exhibit A"], frames 0628–0632, Microfilm Reel #39, COCADT, RG 393, M1188, NA (1981); "Application of F. M. Hall to require return & etc.," filed for record February 3, 1875, [first complaint written by William H. Hamman] (third quotation), Re: Estate of Samuel R. Hearne, Docket #134, PF, CCO, Robertson County, Texas; Robertson County Tax Rolls, 1838–1882, Tax Rolls for 1863, 1864, 1865, 1866, 1869, 1870 & 1871, Microfilm Reel #1198–01, TSL-AD.

22. "Answer of H. D. Prendergast Adm[inistrato]r to Motion of F. M. Hall," filed on March 26, 1875 (first, second, and third quotations), and "Petition to rent out farm for 1872," filed on

aged to set aside in the district court two default judgments that had been entered against Azeline. The first case involved Sam Hearne's prewar promissory note to a man named William A. Van Alstyne. The Van Alstyne note is of significance because no creditor more aggressively sought payment from Sam's estate than the note's purchaser, Houston businessman William Marsh Rice. Although years later, when Rice ultimately prevailed by winning a judgment in the district court against Prendergast as Sam's administrator, Rice had to file a motion in the probate court to force payment of the money and interest due. When Prendergast's excuses for his failure to pay won over the probate judge, the relentless Rice gave notice of his appeal of his denied motion. Prendergast's successful stonewalling efforts not only exasperated Rice but also frustrated other creditors of Sam's estate, whose notes should have been routinely paid under due course of its administration.[23]

The second judgment against Azeline was far more serious because it was loaded with devastating legal implications for anyone having an interest in the Brazos River plantation. After the case had lingered on the docket for many years, the district court handed down a default judgment in favor of Thomas Aycock. As had happened in 1868, when Brown was Sam's executor, Azeline made no effort to appear in court or answer any subsequent amendments duly served upon her. Aycock produced the contract that she and her son had signed shortly after Sam's death. In exchange for his legal services in sustaining Sam's will, they gave him one half of their interest in Sam's estate. Aycock claimed that Azeline, after the Freedmen's Bureau had intervened in the controversy over Sam's will, ignored him as her attorney and gave him "no notice" of special agent Oscar Hunsaker's actions taken in the case. Once again, similar to the situation in 1868, all that remained to be performed was a jury's assessment of the

February 6, 1872 (fourth quotation), Re: Estate of Samuel. R. Hearne, Docket #134, PF, CCO, Robertson County, Texas.

23. *William M. Rice vs. Samuel R. Hearne,* Case No. 971, [Spring Term, 1871], February 21, 1871, Book "K," p. 57, and [renumbered] Case No. 791, [Fall Term, 1875], October 22, 1875, Book "O," p. 223, MDC, Robertson County, Texas; "Motion to have money loaned out & etc.," filed November 9, 1875, Re: Estate of Samuel R. Hearne, Docket #134, PF, CCO, Robertson County, Texas; "Answer of Adm[inistrato]r to Motion of Wm. M. Rice," November 9, 1875, vol. "W," pp. 78–79, PM, CCO, Robertson County, Texas. At the turn of the century William Marsh Rice bequeathed the largest educational endowment ever, and after years of litigation the bulk of his multimillion-dollar estate went to Rice Institute (present-day Rice University). See: Calvert *Picayune,* March 7, 1912, p. 2.

specific amount of money to be awarded him in damages—a task accomplished by adding up the value of Sam's estate, including all real and personal property at the time of Sam's death in November 1866, and dividing it in half.[24]

Aycock's suit had been brought *prior* to Azeline's conveyance of the south half of the plantation to Prendergast and to her selling the entire plantation to Frank Hall. It remains beyond comprehension why, with so much at stake, Prendergast and Hall, a prominent local attorney and the county sheriff, respectively, allowed the court to render a default judgment against Azeline. Hall and Prendergast, knowing that Aycock's claim was based on extremely flimsy legal grounds, unexplainably failed to demand to have the case tried. What occurred next also was perplexing: Judge Thurmond set aside the default judgment. In an atypical notation, reminiscent of the one scrawled in the margins of the court minutes in 1868, Thurmond set it aside "*by agreement of counsel.*" Prendergast represented Azeline, but Aycock, representing himself, would have had no reason to agree to such a ruling. Only years later would Aycock have his day in court.[25]

Political Turmoil and Republican Party Factionalism in 1871

During the time Prendergast initially applied to be the administrator of Sam's estate and finally received his letters of administration, a few local events of considerable interest transpired. Azeline had to have been aware of them, for they would have been subjects of the local news grapevine. First, in late February 1871, Hammond and Brown in separate trials on the same day were acquitted on charges of murdering Dr. Maxwell. Second, Calvin Brown, who was Ben Brown's nephew and a small creditor of Sam's estate, shot a state policeman in a Hearne saloon, shot him again while he lay dying on the floor, and then fled the scene. Although the killing of a "Negro State Policeman" became a celebrated local legend, not only was the slain policeman white, but the so-called Carpetbag Government state police force was a praiseworthy attempt to deal with the problem of recurrent lawlessness, especially white violence against

24. *Thomas P. Aycock vs. Asaline Hearne,* Case No. 1113, [Spring Term, 1871], February 21, 1871, Book "K," pp. 57–58 (quotation), MDC, Robertson County, Texas.

25. *Thomas P. Aycock vs. Asaline Hearne,* Case No. 1113, [Spring Term 1871], February 21, 1871, Book "K," pp. 57–58 (quotation), and [Fall Term, 1868], October 15, 1868, Book "J [452–922]," p. 741, and [June Term, 1875], June 18, 1875, Book "O," p. 718, MDC, Robertson County, Texas.

blacks. In the wake of the refusal of two constables to track down and apprehend Calvin, the Davis-appointed mayor of Hearne complained of Democratic intimidation. Although the mayor was whipped in the street with "a loaded cane" while a crowd yelled, "Kill-shoot-hang the damned Radical son of a bitch," Phidello Hall was unsympathetic. He dismissed the mayor as "a man of no influence" and demanded that Connolly be appointed as his replacement.[26]

Much more hinged on the outcome of the 1871 fall election than choosing a U.S. congressman. Control of the court of county commissioners was at stake. Republican unity was shaken when Lum Hearne's former slave, outspoken state senator Matthew Gaines of Washington County, together with Azeline's former tenant, Baptist preacher Israel Campbell of Galveston County, failed as the leading black candidates to receive the Republican nomination for congress from the Third Congressional District, which included Robertson County. A heightened sense of urgency to achieve harmony in Republican ranks ensued after the white Republican incumbent congressman narrowly lost his bid for reelection and Robertson County Democrats won two of the five positions on the commissioners' court, where, if they gained complete control, they could select future grand juries. White Republicans talked of future local election outcomes as constituting "a life and death struggle" through which they were about to pass, whereas blacks, knowing that they "after all are *the* Republican party," increased their demands for a greater share of political nominations and patronage.[27]

It is not known how many bales of cotton and bushels of corn were

26. "Bond of Adm[inistrato]r," filed for record March 9, 1871, and "Administrator's Bond," filed November 8, 1871, Re: Estate of Samuel R. Hearne, Docket #134 PF, CCO, Robertson County, Texas; *The State of Texas vs. Ben Brown and B. F. Hammond,* Case No. 661, February 24, 1871, [Spring Term, 1871], Book "K," pp. 64, 66–68, MDC, Robertson County, Texas; Chuck Parsons and Marianne E. Hall Little, *Captain L. H. McNelly—Texas Ranger: The Life and Times of a Fighting Man* (Austin, Tex.: State House Press, 2001), pp. 88–89, and n. 21 on p. 323; [Evidence of claims and some accounting of the S. R. Hearne estate], in *Asaline Hearne vs. H. D. Prendergast,* Case No. 3069, ODC, Robertson County, Texas; McCarver and McCarver, *Hearne on the Brazos,* p. 25 (first and second quotations); C. F. Putnam to Edmund J. Davis, November 4, 1871 (third and fourth quotations), box 77, folder 220, and Phidello W. Hall to Edmund J. Davis, November 6, 1871 (fifth quotation), box 77, folder 220, Governors' Papers: Davis, RG 301, TSL-AD.

27. Thomas J. McHugh to Edmund J. Davis, January 2, 1872 (first quotation), box 78, folder 231, and Isaac Schmeidler to Edmund J. Davis, September 18, 1871, box 75, folder 210, Governors' Papers: Davis, RG 301, TSL-AD; and Frank Webb, the African Texan editor of the *Galveston Republican,* quoted in Moneyhon, *Republicanism in Reconstruction Texas,* p. 157 (second quotation).

produced on the Brazos River plantation under the initial year of Prendergast's administration and Watts's management. In an incomplete report for 1871, which incorrectly listed the plantation as the only asset of the estate and failed to acknowledge any of the estate's debts, Prendergast declared that he collected only $241 for renting out a portion of the plantation and paid out $71 for necessary repairs, leaving a balance on hand of $170. For the year 1872 he again petitioned the court to be allowed to conduct a private rather than public renting of the plantation—an action that angered Sheriff Hall, who now recognized that Prendergast and Watts were in collusion to mismanage the estate.[28]

The year 1872 began with a flare-up of local political turmoil. In a special election in January to elect three justices of the peace, a talented and popular, albeit somewhat opportunistic, light-skinned former slave named Harriel ("Hal") G. Geiger kept about two hundred blacks from voting. Geiger's influence was greatest in the Hearne precinct, where Azeline's house and the black community on her plantation were located. In an act of defiance reflecting state senator Gaines's declaration that blacks "do all the voting and are entitled to the offices," Geiger, who had sided against Gaines and Campbell's nominations in the fall congressional race, was overheard to say that "as the Republicans wouldn't give him an office he meant to be a d[amne]d stumbling block in their way." In addition, he announced that all blacks voting a straight Democratic ticket would receive free drinks in Green Brown's saloon, and "the money to pay for [their] hash" had already been made available by William Hearne. Geiger, who years later represented Robertson County in the state legislature, worked out political deals with at least one or two of the three Democrats, who, due to his influence, won election to the commissioners' court. Nevertheless, among the county's Democratic voters, the Hearnes and Lewises, who were in league with Geiger, received the credit for having kept the blacks away from the polls.[29]

28. "Inventory & Appraisement," November 8, 1871, and "Report of Money Rec'd," February 6, 1872, vol. "W," pp.135–37, PM, CCO, Robertson County, Texas; and "Petition to rent out farm for 1872," filed on February 6, 1872, Re: Estate of Samuel R. Hearne, Docket #134, PF, CCO, Robertson County, Texas.

29. Merline Pitre, *Through Many Dangers, Toils, and Snares: The Black Leadership of Texas, 1868–1900* (Austin, Tex.: Eakin Press, 1985), pp. 84–98; Matthew Gaines quoted in the Brenham *Banner,* August 18, 1871 (first quotation); Barry A. Crouch, "Hesitant Recognition: Texas Black Politicians, 1865–1900," *East Texas Historical Journal* 31, no. 1 (1993): 56; Affidavit of Jerry [his mark] Landers, January 15, 1872, and Affidavit of Richard [his mark] Perry, January 15, 1872 (second and third quotations), and Affidavit of J. L. Moore, January 13,

Although Geiger was a special policeman during the election, he and his allies used bribes, threats, and violence against freedmen distributing the regular Republican ballot, which was marked with yellow polka dots to help illiterates identify it. The division in Republican ranks, in turn, unleashed considerable pent-up Democratic anger against black voters. William Hearne, eulogized years later as "warm-hearted, and generous to a fault," punched the face of a black voter who admitted voting the Republican ticket and screamed at him: "You God d[amne]d black son of a b[itc]h I can whip you and all your protectors." Nobody dared to arrest William on assault and battery charges after his companions issued warnings that in retaliation they would "clean up the whole town [of Calvert]." Geiger and his followers got their punches in as well, but only against members of their own race. They forced one voter to tear up his Republican ticket, claiming that "it wasn't worth a God d[am]n," and handed him another. They beat up at least two other freedmen intending to cast Republican ballots, one of whom worked on William's plantation for shares. He was, in the words of his wife, "hit over de head wid a blackjack" when approaching the polling place. He never tried to vote again in his life.[30]

The results of the 1871 statewide election, in which every Democratic candidate for Congress had been victorious, and the disastrous circumstances surrounding the January 1872 local election worried Robertson County Republicans. Geiger had demonstrated that black voters could not be taken for granted in future elections. Not only would a presidential election take place in the fall, but every seat in the state house of representatives would be simultaneously contested. In addition, Sheriff Hall, who

---

1872, box 2–12/572, Manuscript Election Returns for 1872, Folder for Robertson County, Secretary of State Records, RG 307, TSL-AD.

30. Chandler, Carleton, and Robertson [lawyers for William Kemp], to Edmund J. Davis and James P. Newcomb, and William Alexander, March 1, 1872, and affidavit of M. A. Connolly [Mayor of Hearne], January 16, 1872, and affidavit of D. W. Burley, [undated], sworn before Phidello W. Hall, Notary Public, and affidavit of Charles [his mark] Jefferson, January 13, 1872 (second and third quotations), and affidavit of Ned Butler, January 15, 1872 (fourth quotation), and affidavit of Humphrey [his mark] Johnson, January 15, 1872, box 2–12/572, Manuscript Election Returns for 1872, Folder for Robertson County, Secretary of State Records, RG 307, TSL-AD; William T. Hearne, *Brief History and Genealogy of the Hearne Family: From A.D. 1066, when they went from Normandy with William the Conqueror over to England, down to 1680. [sic] when William Hearne the London Merchant came to America, and on down to A.D. 1907* (Independence, Mo.: Press of Examiner Printing Company, 1907), p. 631 (first quotation); and Statement of Hattie (Hearne) Cole in Rawick, ed., *The American Slave*, supp., ser. 2, vol. 3: "Texas Narratives," pt. 2, p. 776 (fifth quotation).

along with Prendergast was scornfully considered by anti-Reconstruction Democrats as one of Azeline's guardians, faced what would unquestionably be a bitterly contested election. Visions of an impending electoral catastrophe for the Texas Republicans, including his own political demise, refocused Hall's interest in the Brazos River plantation.

Frank Hall Sues Azeline Hearne, Prendergast, and Watts

In late January 1872 Hall sued Azeline, Prendergast, and Watts in the district court, alleging that possession and control of the plantation by the latter two were designed to "convert the fruits and the income produced by [it] to their own use." Hamman was the attorney in charge of handling Hall's lawsuit. Although the original petition is missing or misplaced in the courthouse files, the extant pleadings make it clear that the suit was for the recovery and title to and possession of the Brazos River plantation. Hamman, on Hall's behalf, asked the sheriff for a court order separating the plantation from the possession of those who were contending for it and posted a required $25,000 bond. Hall, of course, was the sheriff—a fact that Prendergast tried to exploit because Hall was also the plaintiff in the case. In actuality, a county constable, not Sheriff Hall, executed a return the following day, indicating that he had levied upon the property. By early March the court ordered that both sides give security for expenses charged by the court. All of the foregoing constituted statutory formalities. The dominant issue of ownership would necessitate a district court trial.[31]

Based on the pleadings filed in the Hall case, the grand jury handed down an indictment against Azeline for perjury—the first indictment for lying under oath brought by the Robertson County District Court against a former slave. Details surrounding the perjury charge remain unknown, but court records indicate a summons was issued for a court appearance by Jim Wade, the ascribing witness to Azeline signing the leasing agreement with Hall. After examining Azeline's sworn statements, in which she denied ever agreeing to sell the plantation to Hall, and in light of other evidence, the grand jury deemed the contradictions in her statements taken

31. "Writ of Sequestration," January 26, 1872 (quotations), *F. M. Hall vs. Assaline Hearne,* Case No.1639, ODC, Robertson County, Texas; and "Motion for Costs," *F. M. Hall vs. Assaline Hearne,* Case No. 1639, [Spring Term, 1872], March 2, 1872, Book "K," p. 455, MDC, Robertson County, Texas.

under oath to be criminally indictable. A year and a half later, however, the district attorney decided, for unknown reasons, to drop the perjury charge against her.[32]

At the same time the grand jury indicted Azeline, it also indicted Anschicks, the clerk of the district court, for carrying a pistol within the city limits of Calvert. Anschicks pleaded guilty and paid a small fine. Sadly or comically, depending on one's point of view, in a little over two years since winning election on the 1869 radical Republican ticket, Anschicks, who was one of Geiger's allies in the January election debacle, had been arraigned on counts of "retailing liquor without license," "falsely personating an officer," "aggravated assault and battery," and "assault with intent to kill," as well as on two counts of "forgery." The district attorney dropped the charges of impersonating an officer and assault and battery, and Anschicks won acquittals in two separate jury trials on the forgery counts, one of which was held on the Fourth of July—a day studiously unobserved by the overwhelming majority of whites still grieving over the demise of the Confederacy. Although Anschicks subsequently faced far more serious charges, by the beginning of 1872 he was already well on his way to becoming a lawbreaker without equal among all who ever held the office of clerk of the District Court of Robertson County.[33]

In late spring of 1872, slightly over a year after his acquittal on murder charges, Brown, with Hamman's encouragement, filed a petition with the probate court to be reinstated as administrator of Sam's estate—an action that, if successful, would have resulted in Prendergast's removal. In June the court refused Brown's request and dismissed his case from the docket. At this time legal actions involving Azeline, Sam's estate, and the ownership of the Brazos River plantation were quickly multiplying. Precisely seven months after filing Hall's lawsuit, Hamman breathed life back

32. *The State of Texas vs. Assaline Hearne,* Case No. 832, "perjury," [February Term, 1872], Book "K," p. 438, MDC, Robertson County, Texas; and March 5, 1873, Book "L," p. 244, and July 2, 1873, Book "L," p. 373, MDC, Robertson County, Texas.

33. *The State of Texas vs. Conrad Anschicks,* Case No. 834, "carrying pistol," [February Term, 1872], Book "K," p. 438, and Case No. 622, "retailing liquor without license," April 22, 1870, Book "J [452–922]," p. 900, and Case No. 673, "falsely personating an officer," February 13, 1871, Book "K," p. 241, and Case No. 674, "aggravated assault and battery," February 13, 1871, Book "K," 241, and Case No. 695, "assault with intent to kill," February 20, 1871, Book "K," p. 56, and Case No. 714 and Case No. 717, November 2 & 4, 1871, Book "K," pp. 350 & 352, and Case No. 834, "carrying pistol," [June Term, 1871], Book "K," pp. 438, 508, MDC, Robertson County, Texas.

into the Erhard case. Azeline must have been weary and anxious over the parade of constables riding onto her property and serving her with court summonses, including writs and amended motions spewing out of Hall's lawsuit, her perjury indictment, and a renewal of the Erhard case once again challenging the title to the plantation. Although Hamman knew his resuscitated case had no merit, his record of success regarding suits over conflicting titles had not always been contingent on having the facts and the law on his side.[34]

By now Hamman had abandoned his contempt for politics acquired in the wake of congressional passage of the First Reconstruction Act. Initially refusing to register to vote because he wanted to be judged as "immortal in the majesty of an unconquered [Confederate] patriotism," he made peace with the newly elected local radical Republicans. He even joined Anschicks and Fidella Hall as a founding member of the Calvert Bridge Company, chartered by the Republican-dominated state legislature in the summer of 1870. At the same time the Fifth Circuit Court of the United States admitted him as attorney and counselor. In the following year, at a Robertson County Democratic rally, he was chosen as a delegate to the party's state convention, in which he was elected as its vice president. With his voter registration receipt signed by an ex-slave, Hamman voted for the first time since the end of the war in the October 1871 election in his hometown of Calvert.[35]

Hamman Renews the Claims of the Reynolds Heirs

Hamman, it will be recalled, held a contractual financial interest in the outcome of cases involving conflicting land claims originated by the heirs of Allen Reynolds. To renew the case against Azeline for ownership of her plantation, which he had lost on appeal to the state supreme court, he now petitioned to make Azeline and Prendergast defendants in the long-

34. "Petition of Benjamin Brown," [June Term, 1872], June 4, 1872, vol. "V," p. 57, PM, CCO, Robertson County, Texas; and "Supplement Petition," filed for record August 26, 1872, *Eliza Cornelia Willett (Reynolds) vs. Charles Lewis, et al.*, Case No. 662, folder #3, ODC, Robertson County, Texas.

35. Ada Margaret Smith, "The Life and Times of William Harrison Hamman" (M.A. thesis, University of Texas, 1952), pp. 109, 112, 126–27; "William H. Hamman's Speech—Prepared when a candidate for the Senate of Texas 1865," [undated] (quotation), box 2, folder 27, and Voter Registration Certificate (William H. Hamman) [stamped as having "voted in Oct. 1871"], September 15, 1871, box 2, folder 28, and "Commissions, Speeches, Letters, etc.," [copy], p. 82, box AR29, William Harrison Hamman Papers, WRC-RU, Houston, Texas.

standing case of *Eliza Cornelia Willett (Reynolds) vs. Charles Lewis.* The original Willett case had been filed before the war against Charles Lewis, Rasche Hearne, Sam Hearne, Ebb Hearne, Alley Hearne, and sixteen others, including Dred Dawson Jr. and William Cundiff. Hamman dropped Eliza Willett as a plaintiff and added Cayton Erhard and others, including Thomas C. Woodlief, who had managed the Reynolds estate for many years into the 1850s, when he finally closed it out. The gist of Hamman's strategy was to circumvent Sam's virtually unassailable adverse possession under color of title.[36]

Hamman was far too knowledgeable not to have known that his resumption of the Willett case against Azeline was hopelessly defective. Moreover, the lawsuit could be used by Prendergast to further denigrate and disparage Sam's estate. If the entire plantation might be lost in litigation at any moment, then Prendergast, by posturing as a temporary trustee of a potentially bankrupt estate, would have an excuse for making only token efforts to file required reports from year to year, refusing to pay off any of the estate's debts, and continuing his collaboration with Watts to defraud the estate of its income. Moreover, until final disposition of the Willett case, he could bill the estate for legal fees in defending the title of the 903 acres while all along knowing his likelihood of inevitably prevailing against the Reynolds heirs was excellent, if not a foregone conclusion.

In a petition in the Willett case filed in the summer of 1872, Hamman set the annual value of rents on the plantation at $4,000. Prendergast and Watts had to have known that fair rental value would have brought in close to $3,000 a year (500 or 600 cultivated acres times from $5 to $6 per acre); thus all the estate's outstanding debts—a sum at Sam's death amounting to no more than $5,000, including interest and administrative expenses—could easily have been paid off after a couple of years. A few things at this juncture were clear: managing the estate for Azeline's benefit was among the least of Prendergast's concerns. Other than callously asserting to her that the law itself owed her nothing, he never explained to her what her rights were as the sole legatee and beneficiary of Sam's estate. Prendergast, although obligated to carry out the stipulations created

36. "Supplement Petition," filed for record August 26, 1872, *Eliza Cornelia Willett (Reynolds) vs. Charles Lewis, et al.,* Case No. 662, folder #3, ODC, Robertson County, Texas; and *Cayton Erhard et al. vs. Asseline Hearne et al.,* [No number in original], Supreme Court of Texas, 47 Tex. 469; 1877 Tex. LEXIS 97, Decided June 22, 1877.

by Sam's will, relied upon Azeline's lack of knowledge of the workings of the probate court to preclude her from understanding the functions of an administrator of a decedent's estate.[37]

Political Acrimony and Democratic Party Factionalism in 1872

When, for the first time in twelve years, Texans voted in November of 1872 in a U.S. presidential election, Democratic Party factionalism made its debut in Robertson County. Spawned by the new departure movement, which gave lip service to upholding the Thirteenth, Fourteenth, and Fifteenth Amendments to the U.S. Constitution and culminated in endorsing the principles of the Cincinnati Liberal Republican platform, a controversial group of splinter Democrats called "Independents" shaped the outcomes of a few local races. Because of the machinations of the Independents, including most prominently Dr. Hammond, radical Republican Frank Hall won election as sheriff, and Rasche Hearne, running as a "straight-out" or anti–Horace Greeley Democrat, was defeated for a seat in the state legislature.[38]

Political endorsements of Rasche Hearne's candidacy touted him as one who "succeeded in doing well for himself without gathering from the poor and helpless"—a tribute that masked his life as a slaveholder who had dared, in Abraham Lincoln's words, "to ask a just God's assistance in wringing [his] bread from the sweat of other men's faces." As if to make obvious that the moral character of wealthy white planters bore no relation to their treatment of blacks, Rasche, who was eulogized as unequaled in his "robust integrity," printed his name on Ulysses S. Grant and Henry Wilson Republican ballots for distribution at the polls. More blatantly dishonest was his outright attempt to bribe black voters. Rasche's nephew William Hearne approached ex-slave Ned Butler, who was a former Davis-

37. "Supplemental Petition," filed August 26, 1872, *Eliza Cornelia Willett (Reynolds) vs. Charles Lewis, et al.*, Case No. 662, folder #3, ODC, Robertson County, Texas; "Application of F. M. Hall to require return & etc.," filed February 3, 1875, Re: Estate of Samuel R. Hearne, Docket #134, PF, CCO, Robertson County, Texas; and "Second amended original petition and first supplemental petition," filed February 18, 1884, *Asaline Hearne vs. H. D. Prendergast*, Case No. 3069, ODC, Robertson County, Texas.

38. Albert V. House, "Republicans and Democrats Search for New Identities, 1870–1890," *Review of Politics* 31(October 1969): 466–76; Moneyhon, *Republicanism in Reconstruction Texas*, pp. 176–77; *The Texas Free Press* (Hearne), October 30, 1872, p. 2, in box 1, Cavitt Family Papers, THC-TAMU, College Station, Texas; and *The Central Texan* (Calvert), "Central Texan, Extra," November 12, 1872, p. 1.

appointed county voter registrar, and took him to a room where he was left alone with Rasche. After many expressions of kindhearted feelings for Butler, Rasche yielded to an unidentified friend, who entered the room on cue. The friend offered Butler "the title to a house and plot of ground" on Rasche's plantation if Butler would "use his influence" to secure Rasche's election. Such tactics fortified Rasche's boast that he "could and would control four to five hundred Republican votes of his neighborhood." But Rasche, now allegedly "the wealthiest man and leading planter" in the Brazos Bottoms, fell short of his prediction.[39]

The "straight-out" Democrats reacted with disgust and anger toward the Independents, who comprised what they termed "the Hammond-Salter party." By openly running "fairly and squarely with the [N]egroes," Confederate veteran Charles P. Salter defeated Rasche for state representative. According to his detractors, Salter owed his election to the "vile [radical Republican] crew at Calvert." A week prior to the election, a local Hearne newspaper had proclaimed more than just its support for Rasche Hearne. It issued a warning to the "Hammond-Salter clique": "[T]he memory of these things will not pass away with the election . . . nor will retribution fail to be visited on the heads of those who secure the election of [Frank] Hall should it be done." Many decades would pass before Salter, Hammond, and other homegrown traitors to their own white race in 1872 were completely forgiven by the magnanimity of selective memory in accounts written by later-day biographers and historians.[40]

Azeline Becomes a Familiar Figure at the District Court

In 1872 Prendergast started paying annual state and county taxes on the Brazos River plantation. According to custom, he undervaluated it to the

39. Volney Cavitt quoted in the *Texas Free Press* (Hearne), October 30, 1872 (first quotation), in box 1, Cavitt Family Papers, THC-TAMU, College Station, Texas; Abraham Lincoln, "Second Inaugural Address, March 4, 1865" (second quotation), [Inscription], Lincoln Memorial, Washington, D.C.; Hearne, *Brief History and Genealogy of the Hearne Family,* p. 638 (third quotation); "Grant and Wilson Republican Ticket" and "A Card. [Attempt of H. R. Hearne to Bribe Colored Voters]," November 1, 1872 (fourth and fifth quotations), and Horatio R. Hearne quoted by "A Citizen," in "Facts for the People. The Legislative Canvass," October 30, 1872 (sixth quotation), in box 2, folder 29, William Harrison Hamman Papers, WRC-RU, Houston, Texas; and Dr. Horace Bishop quoted in McCarver and McCarver, *Hearne on the Brazos,* p. 86 (seventh quotation).

40. "A Card From Capt. C. P. Salter" [To the Voters of the 18th Senatorial district], November 1, 1872, in box 2, folder 29, William Harrison Hamman Papers, WRC-RU, Houston, Texas; *The Texas Free Press* (Hearne), October 30, 1872, p. 2 (quotations), in box 1,

county tax assessor by a little more than half of its market value by listing its worth as $9,000. Although he paid the back taxes for 1868, 1869, and 1870, he made certain to protect his own interests by tendering the taxes for the latter two years as the owner of the south half, which he claimed exclusively for himself. Subsequently, Watts, describing himself as the plantation's agent, paid the 1871 taxes on the south half. Proceeding on the theory that Azeline's conveyance to Frank Hall was invalid, Prendergast or Watts paid on time the 1871 taxes on 450 acres for her in her name only. As expected, Sheriff Hall, to improve his claim on the plantation, also paid taxes after 1870 for the entire 903 acres. Hall otherwise paid no taxes beyond those on his ownership of a few horses.[41]

In February 1873 Azeline was back in the courtroom of the Robertson County District Court in Calvert, where she witnessed firsthand the ineffectiveness of Prendergast in arguing a case on her behalf before a jury. Hamman, it will be recalled, had petitioned to make Prendergast, as Sam's administrator, a defendant in the Willett case. Hamman also petitioned to add Azeline as a defendant because Sam had willed all his estate to his son, who died subsequently intestate, leaving her as his only inheritor. Hamman noted that there was no administration of Sam's son's estate, nor was there "any need for one"—a legally dubious assertion, but there was no need for Prendergast to challenge it. Scalawag Judge John B. Rector, a Yale College graduate and Confederate army veteran who had replaced Judge Thurmond, ruled that the case would proceed against both Azeline and Prendergast. The racial composition of the jury cannot be fully determined, because of omitted names in the underenumerated federal manuscript census, but at least one or two blacks probably served as jurors.[42]

Transcripts of the trial do not exist, but Hamman, trying to stop the

---

Cavitt Family Papers, THC-TAMU, College Station, Texas; and Baker, *A History of Robertson County,* passim.

41. "Annual Account," filed February 17, 1873, and recorded April 11, 1876, Re: Estate of Samuel R. Hearne, Docket #134, PF, CCO, Robertson County, Texas; "Statement of Facts," folder #2, *Eliza Cornelia Willett (Reynolds) vs. Charles Lewis, et al.,* Case No. 662, ODC, Robertson County, Texas; Robertson County Tax Rolls, Tax Rolls for 1870, 1871, 1872, and 1873, Microfilm Reel #1198–01, TSL-AD.

42. *Eliza Cornelia Willett (Reynolds) vs. Charles Lewis, et al.,* Case No. 662, February 18, 1873, Book "L," pp. 190–92 (quotation), MDC, Robertson County, Texas; and "Rector, John B.," *TNHT,* 5: 482. After passage in 1876 by the Democratic-controlled legislature of legislation placing selection of jurors in the hands of officials appointed by district judges and requiring all jurors to be able to read and write, the chances of excluding blacks greatly increased.

statute of limitations from running immediately upon Sam's possession of the land in 1853, argued a complex, but legally inconsequential, scenario of how, by coming of age and by marriage, his clients had preserved their rights to sue Sam's legal heirs. Hamman offered in evidence two lawsuits brought against the prior owners, Dred Dawson Sr. and his son Britton Dawson, to prove that there was a temporary break in Britton Dawson's possession of the land before the completed three years of Sam's adverse possession of it. But in point of fact, adverse possession of the Dawsons barred both lawsuits, and thus the elder titles of Hamman's clients could not possibly prevent the statute of limitations from commencing instantly upon Sam's possession of the land. For these reasons, during his lifetime Sam had refused to settle with the Reynolds heirs. In short, the 1857 Cundiff and 1858 Willett lawsuits had not been filed against him within the window of three years after a cause of action had accrued to these plaintiffs, or, for that matter, to anyone else claiming to possess superior title to his Brazos River plantation.[43]

Then as now, the law itself might be certain, but the outcome of any litigation is never certain. Prendergast failed to disassemble for the jurors Hamman's specious arguments. With both the law and facts on his and Azeline's side, the jury awarded the plaintiffs "an undivided one half interest" in her 903 acres of land. Who owned the other half-interest in the land was not stated in the summarization of the judgment. But who possibly could have owned it? Certainly not Azeline, Aycock, Prendergast, or Frank Hall. If Hamman's theory of the case were correct, it would have followed that Sam held an inferior or invalid title during the time he lived on the Brazos River plantation. His sale, conveyance, or bequeathal of the land to anyone would have been of no value. Within two weeks of the jury's verdict, Judge Rector granted Prendergast his motion for a new trial. The petition cannot be found in courthouse files. The district court minutes simply state that the facts were legally sufficient to grant it.[44]

The stillbirth of justice in the first trial of the revived Willett case took

---

See: Donald G. Nieman, "Black Political Power and Criminal Justice: Washington County, Texas, 1868–1884," *Journal of Southern History* 55, no. 3 (August 1989): 400.

43. *Cayton Erhard et al. vs. Asseline Hearne et al.*, [No number in original], Supreme Court of Texas (quotations), 47 Tex. 469; 1877 Tex. LEXIS 97, Decided 1877.

44. *Eliza Cornelia Willett (Reynolds) vs. Charles Lewis, et al.*, Case No. 662, February 18, 1873, Book "L," pp. 190–92 (quotation on p. 192), and March 1, 1873, Book "L," p. 229, MDC, Robertson County, Texas.

place amidst a flurry of pleadings in the case of *F. M. Hall vs. Assaline Hearne*—a lawsuit that also pitted attorneys Hamman and Prendergast against each other. The day after the adverse verdict in the Willett case, Azeline gave her answers to interrogatories in the discovery phase of preparation for the forthcoming trial. She recalled the early days of January 1870, when Frank Hall, clutching a paper in his hand, had visited her house. Prendergast's depositions seemed designed, for the most part, to gather information on a freedman named Charles Williams. For someone who ultimately was deemed to know little or nothing, there was a great deal of effort to locate Williams and depose him, presumably because he had been present with Jim Wade, who witnessed Azeline's acknowledgment on the leasing agreement between her and Hall. Williams had been a sharecropper on Azeline's plantation but had left the area months before her alleged conveyance of it to Hall. He also had an awful reputation for telling the truth and, when finally located, was in jail in Grimes County for stealing horses. With the exception of his ill-fated interest in Williams, Prendergast's discovery efforts on behalf of Azeline were minimal.[45]

Presumably because Prendergast knew that Reverend Sloan had left the area or died, no questions were issued to him. Yet some attempt at providing evidence to establish his misconduct, incompetence, or senility would have been expected. Prendergast's lack of zeal on behalf of Azeline was probably due to the overwhelming strength of Hall's case. The list of documents that formed the basis of Hall's claim for ownership of the Brazos River plantation completed a chain of title from Sam Hearne to Frank Hall. Included were Sam's original will, Azeline's power of attorney to Sloan, the deed from Sloan to Hall, the tenancy agreement between Azeline and Hall, and a receipt by Sloan for part of the purchase price. In order for Prendergast to prevail, he had to demonstrate this chain of title to be defective. Realizing that the case was lost, Prendergast concentrated on bettering his own position as recipient of the south half of the 903 acres. He petitioned the court to dismiss Hall's lawsuit and signed it, not just as Azeline's attorney and as administrator of Sam's estate, but also

45. "Answers [to Interrogatories] of Assaline Hearne," recorded by Wyndham Kemp, February 19, 1873, and [Interrogatories to Munroe Coule (?) and John J. Whitesides], January 30, 1873, and [Interrogatories to J. L. Wilson, et al.], February 14, 1873, and [Answers of J. L. Wilson], February 22, 1873, and [Interrogatories to John W. Bergin, et al.], February 28, 1873, and "Answers [to Interrogatories] of Ophelia Holiday," February 19, 1873, and "Answers [to Interrogatories] of Jane Bentley," February 19, 1873, and "Answers [to Interrogatories] by Nelda Allen," February 19, 1873, *F. M. Hall vs. Assaline Hearne,* Case No. 1639, ODC, Robertson County, Texas.

"for himself" individually. Hamman, however, had not sued Prendergast in any role other than administrator. Simply stated, Prendergast was trying to slip himself into the case as a defendant via the back door.[46]

Hamman filed an objection arguing that the court limit Prendergast to his role as administrator and prohibit him from making himself a defendant by his own motions. To make this point more explicit, Hamman insisted that if Prendergast "had any rights" to the land in controversy "he must assert them by way of intervention." In other words, the court should require Prendergast to file a separate petition providing the justification for his request to be added as a defendant. Judge Rector ended this legal quibbling by allowing Prendergast to remain in the case individually via his own motion, but Hamman, through these procedures discovered the full measure of his courtroom adversary.[47]

By the summer of 1873, Azeline was back in the courtroom of the district court for retrial of the Willett case. Once again she listened to Hamman reiterate how his clients, by their coming of age and by marriage and because of an apparent break in the title of the previous owners of Sam Hearne's plantation, had salvaged their rights to sue for recovery of their land. She also witnessed Prendergast make a better defense than his previous uninspired one, resulting in a hung jury, which was ultimately discharged by Judge Rector. Eight months passed before another jury heard the case. The delay was due to an outbreak of yellow fever, which caused a cessation of all business activity in Calvert from September to November and cancellation of the fall term of the district court. By December the advent of colder weather ended the dreadful pandemic.[48]

The December gubernatorial contest witnessed implementation of legislative changes to the state election laws. Voting was henceforth allowed at all county precincts and was limited to one day. And for the first time since 1866, Texas voters went to the polls free of the presence of either federal troops or state policemen. Governor Davis failed to carry Robert-

46. "Notice of filing of doc[ument]s," February 16, 1872, and [Motion to quash service of a writ of sequestration], February 5, 1872 (quotation), *F. M. Hall vs. Assaline Hearne,* Case No. 1639, ODC, Robertson County, Texas.

47. [Objection to H. D. Prendergast's efforts to make himself a party to the lawsuit], filed March 11, 1873 (quotations), *F. M. Hall vs. Assaline Hearne,* Case No. 1639, ODC, Robertson County, Texas.

48. *Eliza Cornelia Willett (Reynolds) vs. Charles Lewis, et al.*, Case No. 662, June 9, 1873, Book "L," p. 310, and February 11, 1874, Book "L," p. 447, and [Adjournment of the district court by Sheriff F. M. Hall], October 4, 1873, Book "L," p. 424, MDC, Robertson County, Texas; and Baker, *A History of Robertson County,* pp. 512–15.

son County by 162 votes out of slightly over 2,100 ballots cast—a turnout not extensively lowered by the yellow fever epidemic. By a decisive statewide margin Davis lost his bid for reelection to redeemer Democratic candidate Richard Coke. When Davis refused to vacate his office on the basis of a legal technicality upheld by the Texas Supreme Court, he set off a political controversy that threatened bloodshed between armed partisans and ended only after President Grant refused in January 1874 to intervene with federal troops on Davis's behalf. Knowing that Governor Coke's administration would do nothing to curtail any violence or intimidation aimed at destabilizing black voting strength at thousands of county precinct polling stations, Texas Republicans found themselves isolated and vulnerable. Unbeknownst to the celebrants who fired a 102-gun salute at the state capitol in Austin to welcome the inauguration of Governor Coke, Democrats would control the Texas state government for the next 105 years.[49]

The Modern-day Southern Half of the Bryan City Cemetery

In the wake of Coke's inauguration, Nish Burkhalter, wishing to sell his worthless ownership rights to Azeline's twenty-three-acre tract of land in Hall's Town, appeared in the downtown Bryan business office of carpetbagger Charles Franklin ("Frank") Moore, a Union army veteran recently defeated on the radical Republican ticket for reelection as clerk of the Brazos County District Court. As a successful businessman, Frank Moore owned many valuable parcels of city real estate and was half-owner of a cottonseed oil factory—one of the most valuable pieces of property in the county. He held charter memberships in the local Horticulture Society and Agricultural and Mechanical Association and had strong connections to the city's African American leaders and influential Jewish merchant community.[50]

Frank Moore easily could have done the right thing, namely, reiterated

49. Moneyhon, *Republicanism in Reconstruction Texas,* pp. 183–96, and table 7 on p. 223; and Randolph B. Campbell, *Gone to Texas: A History of the Lone Star State* (New York: Oxford University Press, 2003), pp. 281–85.

50. Galveston *Daily News,* January 13, 1883, p. 3; Fort Worth *Daily Gazette,* January 13, 1883, p. 1; *Daily State Journal* (Austin), February 1, 1871, p. 2; and Brenham *Daily Banner,* May 23, 1877, p. 1. Sureties on Frank Moore's bond as the county's military-appointed tax assessor and collector in 1869 included Isaac Kahn, Morris Lasker, H. Regensberger, Joseph Sonnenberg, Charles Jacobs, C. M. Pearl, and Isaac Schmeidler. See: Brazos County, Texas, Commissioners Minutes, June 1, 1869, Book "A," p. 247.

to Burkhalter why his deed to the land in Bryan's black subdivision was worthless and advised him to return to Azeline the still-unrecorded deed to her from William Hall, which was part of the consideration she received four years earlier from Frank Hall for selling him her Brazos River plantation. Instead, Moore chose to remove the imperfections in the title by a fraudulent sleight of hand that he knew would not be apparent to untrained eyes. Moore first filed for record the deeds that were in Burkhalter's possession, including the original Hall deed to Azeline, along with the deeds from Azeline to Burkhalter and from Mary Moore and her husband (no relation to Frank Moore) to Burkhalter. Then Moore drafted a deed from himself to Burkhalter, conveying to him half of a city block in north Bryan in consideration allegedly for $300. Moore then drafted another deed from Burkhalter to himself for Azeline's twenty-three acres, now correctly located in "S.F. Austin No. 10" and described as the tract of land sold by W. J. Bryan to William Hall, then conveyed by Hall to Azeline, and by her through her agent Sloan to Mary Moore, and then by the Moores to Burkhalter—"all of which," Frank Moore wrote in this last deed, "will appear of Record" in the Brazos County courthouse files.[51]

In brief, Frank Moore had made a trade with Burkhalter, swapping what both knew was a worthless title to the twenty-three acres for a valid title to part of a Bryan city block of comparable worth. Burkhalter must have been pleased, because Frank Moore became saddled with the defective title. Moore, in turn, sold his interest in the twenty-three acres, which he valued at $442.50, to the Bryan Real Estate and Building Association—an ambitious enterprise to hold, buy, and sell property that he and six others had established three years earlier with an impressive initial investment of $50,000. Amusingly, Moore made, at least on paper, $142.50 on his transaction with Burkhalter. Far more captivatingly, especially to modern-day residents of Bryan, was what ultimately became of the twenty-three acres owned by Azeline. Frank Moore successfully laundered the title to the land, which became the southern half of the Bryan City Cemetery.[52]

51. Warranty deed from C. F. Moore to D. D. Burkhalter, dated January 30, 1874, filed for record on January 1, 1876, and recorded on January 5, 1876, Book "Q," p. 126, and Deed from D. D. Burkhalter to C. F. Moore, dated January 30, 1874 (quotations), and filed for record on March 9, 1874, Book "O," p. 328, RD, CCO, Brazos County, Texas.

52. Warranty deed from C. F. Moore to Bryan Real Estate and Building Association, March 13, 1874, and filed for record on April 14, 1876, and recorded on April 15, 1876, Book "O," p. 367, RD, CCO, Brazos County, Texas.

Resolution of the Hall Case in the Robertson County District Court

In February 1874 Azeline, unaware of having been divested of her land in Brazos County, traveled to Calvert for the third and final trial of the Willett case. She watched again as Hamman and Prendergast presented their arguments to a jury of twelve men. This time, however, the verdict rendered was in her and Prendergast's favor. With the facts and the law clearly on their side and correct questions having been posed to the jury by the judge, the case should have come to an end. Hamman, however, appealed the verdict to the Texas Supreme Court. Not until 1877—a full nineteen years after Willett had commenced her lawsuit against Sam Hearne—did the high court sustain the district court's ruling in favor of Azeline and Prendergast. Moreover, during the appeal Prendergast, by claiming possible bankruptcy if the Erhard clients won a reversal, continued to refuse to pay the estate's debts or give Azeline any share of the estate's profits or assets.[53]

In June 1874 Azeline again returned to Calvert for the Hall trial, in which both the evidence and the law would be stacked against her. On the stand she disavowed making any conveyance to Hall—a denial that the jury did not believe. The jury's findings were straightforward: Prendergast was granted ownership of the south half of the plantation, and Sheriff Hall was awarded ownership of "the balance of the land," or the north half. The jury also found that an administration was currently pending on Sam Hearne's estate and the land in controversy comprised part of the estate's assets, which were being lawfully administered by Prendergast. Based on the jury's verdicts, the court ordered that Prendergast would retain possession of the entire 903 acres for the purposes of administrating Sam's estate in accordance of the terms of Sam's will. In effect, Prendergast would continue to have control of the entire plantation until all litigation connected to its ownership, the debts of the estate, and all other matters related to it, were ultimately settled. By the jury's verdict, Prendergast, who lost the case, paradoxically bettered his own position.[54]

Prendergast's 1869 agreement with Azeline, in which he took owner-

53. "Petition for Writ of Error," filed September 21, 1874, folder 3, *Eliza Cornelia Willett (Reynolds) vs. Charles Lewis, et al.,* Case No. 662, ODC, Robertson County, Texas; and *Cayton Erhard et al. vs. Asseline Hearne et al.,* [No number in original], Supreme Court of Texas, 47 Tex. 469; 1877 Tex. Lexus 97, Decided June 22, 1877.

54. *F. M. Hall vs. Assaline Hearne,* Case No. 1639, June 20, 1874, Book "M," pp. 74, 85 and 91–92 (quotation), MDC, Robertson County, Texas.

ship of the south half of the Brazos River plantation in exchange for his legal fees for handling the appeal of the default judgment in the first Erhard case, had called for a deed to be executed on his demand. But at the time of Hall's lawsuit, no deed had been executed or recorded. Nor would Azeline have readily again touched any pen to any papers. But after the jury's verdict in the Hall case, no deed was required. The jury had awarded the south half of the plantation to Prendergast. His title to the land now rested securely on a district court judgment.

After Prendergast's motion for a new trial was denied, he gave notice of his decision to appeal the judgment in favor of Hall to the Texas Supreme Court, where a reversal of the award to Hall of the north half of the plantation would be unlikely, if not impossible, to obtain. If one assumes that the Hall judgment would be irreversible on appeal, then the only remaining clouds lingering over Prendergast and Hall's claims to the 903 acres would be the approaching retrial of the Aycock case and the Texas Supreme Court's pending disposition of the Willett (now renamed the Erhard) case. And what, under these presumed circumstances, was Azeline's stake in the outcome of the litigation? Her only small advantage would be to withdraw her appeal of the Hall verdict at an extremely low compromise price.[55]

The proceedings of the Hall trial suggest that Azeline never fully realized the legal implications of her actions. Because of the misplaced trust she had placed in Sloan, she participated in a perilous series of activities when dealing with property deeds and powers of attorney. Presumably, in 1873 and 1874 the barrage of litigation and lawsuits, the stream of summonses and motions duly served on her, and the criminal perjury charge to which she was subjected increased her familiarity with a judicial system that no prior experience in her life had prepared her to understand. Yet years later, when she clearly saw herself as a legal protagonist in an extraordinary lawsuit that she had initiated against her own attorney, she continued to demonstrate a woeful lack of knowledge of key legal issues in which she had been involved, for example, by stating under oath that she "never was indicted for perjury" in any case that she knew about.[56]

After the jury's disposition in the Hall case, Prendergast jokingly in-

55. *F. M. Hall vs. Assaline Hearne,* Case No. 1639, July 11, 1874, Book "M," p. 173, MDC, Robertson County, Texas.

56. "Inter[rogatories] propounded by [Plaintiff]," filed August 15, 1882 (quotation), [Answers of Azeline Hearne transcribed by F. H. Bailey, Notary Public], *Asaline Hearne vs. H. D. Prendergast,* Case No. 3069, ODC, Robertson County, Texas.

formed Judge Rector about Azeline's reaction to the adverse verdict. Prendergast told him that she had said, "Well lawyer, I gave you one half of my place to defend me in the other half and you gain your half and lose my half. It seems mighty queer to me, lawyer." That Prendergast would divulge such an insightful statement by a disgruntled client was unusual, but to tell it to the trial judge, who might possibly be ordered by the Texas Supreme Court to retry the case, was astonishing. The key to understanding Prendergast's behavior lay in his inability to comprehend that this incident could be perceived as a breach of client confidentiality. Seven years later he would have to defend in court not only this inappropriate disclosure to Judge Rector but many subsequent actions that he undertook to defraud Sam's estate and take advantage of Azeline while posturing as her legal and financial advocate. But in the summer of 1874, Prendergast could not have remotely foreseen that his client would sue him.[57]

57. "Depositions of John B. Rector In Answer to Interrogatories," June 17, 1882, and filed June 19, 1882, *Asaline Hearne vs. H. D. Prendergast,* Case No. 3069, ODC, Robertson County, Texas.

Chapter 7

Endeavoring to Wrong, Cheat, and Defraud Her

> [The] plaintiff is a poor, ignorant, and unlearned [N]egress, decrepit with age, in feeble health and greatly needing the property withheld from her.
>
> —William H. Hamman, *Assaline Hearne vs. H. D. Prendergast*

In the fall of 1874, three months after the rendering of the judgment against Azeline Hearne in the Hall case, fifty male citizens of the Empire of China appeared in the Robertson County District Court. The Chinese immigrants, who were formerly railroad workers, declared that they were over twenty-one years of age and had continuously lived and worked in California and Texas for more than five years. Republican-appointed Judge John Rector, upon hearing them swear to bear true faith and allegiance to the United States, granted them citizenship despite their ineligibility under federal law. Present were the county's leading Republican officeholders: District Clerk Conrad Anschicks, Sheriff Frank Hall, and District Attorney Isaac Ellison. Anschicks was under separate criminal indictments for swindling and for the rape of an under-ten black girl whom he had employed in his grocery store; Hall faced charges of embezzlement due to his neglect as sheriff to collect the county school tax; and Ellison was responsible for prosecuting the cases against both of them. Enormous attention centered on Anschicks, who with the help of Judge Rector got his rape case transferred to the district court from the Calvert Police Court, where a jury had wanted to "punish him *capitally*." As for the Chinese Texans, they subsequently registered to vote just in time for the off-year congressional elections.[1]

Democratic victories in the November balloting statewide were all but guaranteed. Republicans could no longer rely on help from Austin to rein in intimidation of black voters. Nevertheless, the Republican vote in Robertson County, although prevailing only in the Calvert precinct and falling over five hundred votes shy of carrying the county, was comparatively respectable. In addition, and helping to boast voter turnout, in a countywide referendum Calvert survived a strong challenge from Englewood (located south of Owensville) to become the new county seat. The close outcome caused some disappointed white residents from the interior and eastern side of the county to level charges that "the Negroes and scalawags who voted in Hearne and Calvert stole the election." A subsequent public investigation found their charges to be unsubstantiated.[2]

After the 1874 congressional elections, Democratic governor Richard Coke grumbled about "unscrupulous tricksters and demagogues," namely, scalawags and carpetbaggers, who continued to govern many East Texas counties by hoodwinking "unenlightened black voters." In spite of Governor Coke's disgust with blacks enjoying equal privileges with whites "at the ballot box and in the jury box," the freedmen in Robertson County, as in many other heavily black-populated counties in the lower Brazos River Valley, continued to play a role in the calculus of local partisan political outcomes for the next twenty years.[3]

1. Naturalization of Ah Cong [and forty-nine others from the Empire of China], [October Term, 1874], Book "M," pp. 241–42, and *The State of Texas vs. Conrad Anschicks,* Case No. 880, "Swindling," February 24, 1874, Book "M," pp. 3–4, and *The State of Texas vs. Conrad Anschicks,* Case No. 1136, "Rape," June 12, 1874, Book "M," p. 71, MDC, Robertson County, Texas; Luella Gettys, *The Law of Citizenship in the United States* (Chicago: The University of Chicago Press, 1934), pp. 62–69; *The State of Texas vs. F. M. Hall,* Case No. 1264, "Embezzlement," Criminal Court, [December Term, 1875], notation by William H. Hamman in "Memoranda" notebook, box 1, folder 5, and "Petition to the State Senate & House of Representatives from Citizens of Robertson County," [undated] (quotation), box 2, folder 30, William Harrison Hamman Papers, WRC-RU, Houston, Texas; and Norman L. McCarver and Norman L. McCarver Jr., *Hearne on the Brazos* (San Antonio: Century Press of Texas, 1958), p. 57.

2. Manuscript Election Returns for 1874, Folder for Robertson County, box 2–12/580, Secretary of State Records, RG 307, TSL-AD; J. W. Baker, *A History of Robertson County, Texas* (Waco, Tex.: Printed by Texian Press, 1970), p. 363 (quotation); and [Entries on contested election involving relocation of the county seat], vol. 2, Calvert, Texas, [May 1873–March 1876], June 2, 1875, pp. 235–36, CCM-PM, Robertson County, Texas.

3. Richard Coke, "Message from the Governor" [handwritten], p. 4, March 16, 1874 (quotations), box 96, folder 50, Governors' Papers: Coke, RG 301, TSL-AD.

Hall's Complaints against Prendergast

In early February 1875 William Hamman, on behalf of Sheriff Hall, filed a series of complaints in the probate court against Harvey Prendergast in his capacity as the executor of Sam Hearne's estate. Although Prendergast had been the estate's administrator since 1871, he had not yet paid off any of its outstanding debts—a situation that meant that original estate debts, when finally retired, would include a decade of interest charges. In addition, he had filed neither a complete inventory of the estate's property nor his required yearly reports outlining his doings and transactions. He neglected to list or pay taxes on the tracts of land that Sam had purchased in the antebellum period in Young and Limestone Counties—lands, estimated by Hamman to be worth over $2,000. Nor had he rented out the Brazos River plantation for the full amount of money that could be obtained for it. The yearly rents and profits should have been, in Hamman's words, "worth $3,000.00." Yet after five years of his administration, Prendergast claimed to have only "some $300.00 received for rents" on hand—a circumstance, according to Hamman, that proved that Prendergast had colluded with Buck Watts and other "so-called tenants" for the purpose of defrauding the estate to the injury of Sheriff Hall, who had a sizable interest in the management of the north half of the plantation, and to the disadvantage of Azeline, the estate's sole beneficiary.[4]

As if the allegations of mismanagement and negligence were not serious enough, Hamman listed other irregularities surrounding Prendergast's administration. First, the earlier problem with the bond posted for the executorship remained: the sole surety was Watts, and he was financially unable to pay the bond's amount. Second, when Prendergast made improvements on the plantation, he had made them disproportionately on the south half, in which he had set up title in himself. Not only had Prendergast failed to inform the probate court of his actions, but he never explained his financial transactions and comings and goings to Azeline, for whom he handled the Aycock and Erhard cases and served in a fiduciary capacity as the administrator of her late master's estate. Hamman asked the probate court to order Prendergast to submit his required reports with explanations as to why he never filed them. Finally, Hamman demanded that a judicial inquiry should be made into his complaints, especially his allegation regarding the matter of rents.[5]

4. "Application of F. M. Hall to require returns, etc." filed on February 3, 1875 (quotations), Re: Estate of Samuel R. Hearne, Docket #134, PF, CCO, Robertson County, Texas.

5. Ibid.

Hamman made no mention, but was fully aware, of another notable event that had occurred in the previous year during the course of Prendergast's administration. Watts, acting as the plantation's agent or manager, had filed a lawsuit against Azeline around the same time as the trial in the Hall case. Watts's case was awaiting resolution on the district court docket when Hamman filed his grievances against Prendergast. The circumstances that led to Watts's suit are not known, but Azeline apparently owed Watts "about $1,200.00 for supplies" that he had furnished her. Prendergast, in his capacity as Azeline's attorney, had stood aloof when the court served her with a summons. She predictably failed to respond. Because the exact dollar amount of damages was in dispute, Watts got a court order empanelling a jury to assess the monetary award owed him. In July 1875 a jury accordingly awarded him $937.15 with interest at 8 percent per year. Azeline's debt to Watts appeared four years later in Prendergast's reports as a liability of Sam's estate—an unpaid debt that by then had increased by accumulated interest to $1,270.[6]

In response to Hamman's grievances, Prendergast disputed all the complaints lodged against him *except* the charge that he had neglected to file annual reports specifying the estate's financial condition. Otherwise, he denied mismanaging the Brazos River plantation or conspiring with its tenants or with Watts to cheat the estate. He repeated previous exculpatory arguments that, when he initially took charge, the estate's property was in such a state of utter disrepair that he could rent out only a fraction of the land, and, more unfortunately, the title itself to the plantation was still in litigation—meaning that the ownership of the estate's core asset hinged on uncertain legal grounds. Prendergast admitted having rented to the plantation's tenants seven houses at from $80 to $100 each, but inexplicably added that this income had been "deducted from rents." A clarification came much later: he had collected no rents in 1874 due to the estate's indebtedness to the tenants for their work on building a new cotton "Gin Stand and Press," predictably, on his south half of the plantation.[7]

6. Reference to *W. W. Watts vs. Asaline Hearne,* Case No. 2063, in "Memoranda" notebook in William Harrison Hamman Papers, box 1, folder 5, WRC-RU, Houston, Texas; "Cross interrogatories propounded to Assaline Hearne, Plaintiff," [January Term, 1882] (quotation), *Asaline Hearne vs. H. D. Prendergast,* Case No. 3069, ODC, Robertson County, Texas; *W. W. Watts vs. Asaline Hearne,* Case No. 2063, June 12, 1874, Book "M," p. 66, October 16, 1874, Book "M," p. 208, and July 1, 1875, Book "O," p. 56, MDC, Robertson County, Texas; and [Evidence of claims and some accounting of the S. R. Hearne estate], in *Asaline Hearne vs. H. D. Prendergast,* Case No. 3069, ODC, Robertson County, Texas.

7. "Answer of H. D. Prendergast, Adm'r, to Motion of F. M. Hall," filed on March 26, 1875

In spite of Prendergast's failure to provide detailed refutations of Hamman's allegations, the probate court ignored Hamman's complaints, except insofar as the court insisted that Prendergast post a new bond for his administration in the sum of $22,000, or $2,000 more than his original bond. The court subsequently ordered Prendergast to make his annual report as required by law. He complied with both requirements, albeit not until the fall of 1875, at which time he added Brazos Bottom planter John Drennan as a surety on the new bond. In 1869 Drennan had signed as a surety upon Azeline's $75,000 bond for a writ of error to the Texas Supreme Court in the first Cayton Erhard case. In the postwar period Drennan had greatly increased his assets in cotton land and business property, and he was one of the first Robertson County planters to sign sharecropping contracts with Chinese laborers.[8]

In 1875 Watts still did not own enough unencumbered property to equal the total value of the bonds upon which he had signed earlier for Prendergast's actions as Azeline's attorney and Sam's administrator. Watts was hardly embarrassed by being financially unaccountable for the amounts, because by the mid-1870s he was on track to becoming one of the wealthiest cotton planters in Robertson County. Shortly after the Hall judgment, he had offered Azeline $200 a year for the rest of her life in exchange for all her interest in the Brazos River plantation. She refused. By the end of the decade, he owned in the midst of Azeline's neighborhood a prison farm, known as Watts's Convict Prison, where between thirty and forty exclusively black convicts cut down trees for a sawmill when not cultivating cotton and other crops. His prison farm, along with White's and Wilson's nearby, constituted a cruel exploitation of state penitentiary prisoners, whose rehabilitation and welfare were lost in the pursuit of private profit. By the turn of the century, Watts produced roughly two thousand bales of cotton each year on about three thousand acres of Brazos bottomland, and he became extolled, along with the Hearnes, Lewises, Whites, Wilsons, Westbrooks, Carrs, and Astins, as having "made the Brazos bottom a rival of the Valley of the Nile."[9]

(first quotation), Re: Estate of Samuel R. Hearne, Docket #134, PF, CCO, Robertson County, Texas; and "Report of H. D. Prendergast," February 28, 1878 (second quotation), vol. "Z," p. 457, PM, CCO, Robertson County, Texas.

8. "In succession of S. R. Hearne, Dec'd," [November Term, 1875], vol. "W," pp. 78–79, PM, CCO, Robertson County, Texas; Baker, *A History of Robertson County*, pp. 475 and 483; and Harvey D. Prendergast to Thomas H. Norton, "Exhibit A," [undated and unmarked], frames 0628–0632, Microfilm Reel #39, COCADT, RG 393, M1188, NA (1981).

9. "Cross interrogatories propounded to Assaline Hearne, Plaintiff," [January Term, 1882],

The combined presence of large numbers of convict laborers and smatterings of Chinese sharecroppers in the Hearne Bottoms transformed Azeline's neighborhood and provided fascinating stories for generations, including the legendary 1877 escape of seventeen black convicts from Charles Lewis's plantation. Charles's brother-in-law, Rasche Hearne, employed Chinese workers as servants in his two-story, cedar manor house, as well as contracting with many of them as farm workers on his plantation lands. Questioned about his "large experience" with "Freedmen, Convicts, and Chinamen" as renters, sharecroppers, and laborers, Rasche declared that convict labor was an unequivocal "failure"—a surprising admission from one who throughout the 1870s contracted for convicts at fifty cents per day and built special barracks for them, while the state clothed and fed them and paid the salaries of the prison guards. According to Rasche, "Chinamen" as workers were far "preferable" to "freedmen and convicts." By 1880 over half the entire number of Chinese immigrants residing in Texas lived in Robertson County.[10]

The Deveraux and Aycock Trials

In June 1875 Azeline, with Prendergast serving as her attorney, was back in the Robertson County District Court testifying in two of the earliest lawsuits ever filed against her. By now she was a common sight in the makeshift courtroom in the upper story of the Littlefield building. (No courthouse was ever built in Calvert during the time the city was the county seat.) The emotional strain of having to respond publicly in often confusing circumstances to an array of white men had to have taken its toll on her by now. The cases, which were tried consecutively, transported her

---

"3rd [interrogatory]," *Asaline Hearne vs. H. D. Prendergast,* Case No. 3069, ODC, Robertson County, Texas; *The 1880 Robertson County, Texas, Census* [containing 467 pages (census images) in Enumeration Districts 139 through 148], www.rootsweb.ancestry.com/~usgenweb/tx/robertson/census/1880/147–18.gif and 147–19.gif (accessed July 10, 2008); Manford Eugene Jones, "A History of Cotton Culture along the Middle Brazos River" (M.A. thesis, University of New Mexico, 1939), p. 23; Elmer Grady Marshall, "The History of Brazos County, Texas" (M.A. thesis, University of Texas, 1937), p. 155; and Ivory Freeman Carson, "Early Development of Robertson County" (M.A. thesis, North Texas State College, 1954), p. 133 (quotation).

10. "Dictation from H. B. [*sic*] Hearne," Hearne, Texas, undated [1887], (quotations), Call Number P-091, Hubert Howe Bancroft Collection, University of California at Berkeley, Berkeley, California; and Marilyn Dell Brady, *The Asian Texans* (College Station: Texas A&M University Press, 2004), p. 12.

back in time to the painful period surrounding Sam's death. The initial case had lingered on the docket since the spring of 1867, when John Deveraux filed one of the first of many civil lawsuits against Sam's legal representatives. During the war and prior to Sam's death, the circumstances in the case had led to a grand jury criminal indictment against him for "horse stealing."[11]

A member of Ben Brown's posse, for unknown reasons, shot and killed Deveraux a few months after he had filed his civil lawsuit against Sam's estate. Before his body "was fairly cold," the former slaveholder, who had owned Deveraux's slave mistress and her children by him, obtained temporary letters of administration from the district court judge. Deveraux, however, had never rewritten his 1864 last will and testament, in which he named S. R. Perry as his executor with instructions to transport his illicit slave concubine and their three children out of Confederate Texas. Perry filed Deveraux's wartime will for record in early 1868 and successfully petitioned the court to have himself appointed as the estate's administrator. For the next seven years, Perry, who promptly made himself a plaintiff in Deveraux's lawsuit against Sam, diligently persevered in trying to recover civil damages from Sam's estate.[12]

Whatever testimony Azeline gave on the witness stand in defense of Sam's wartime behavior in breaking his agreement with Deveraux failed to impress the jury. It returned a verdict for Perry as administrator of Deveraux's estate for damages of $500 and tacked on interest due from January 1, 1866, making the total award $881.66. Although the court ordered Prendergast to pay the amount in the due course of his administration, he delayed paying it, just as he had sidestepped other creditors with finalized court judgments: by pleading that at any moment the title

11. *S. R. Perry, Adm[inist]r[ator] of J. S. B. Deveraux, vs. S. R. Hearne,* Case No. 905, [Spring Term, 1867], Book "J [452–922]," p. 598, and *The State of Texas vs. Samuel R. Hearne,* Case No. 443, [Fall Term, 1864], Book "J [452–922]," pp. 507 (quotation) and 540, and [Spring Term, 1867], Book "J [452–922]," p. 575, MDC, Robertson County, Texas; and Baker, *A History of Robertson County,* p. 518.

12. William H. Farner to Charles Griffin, July 9, 1867 (quotation), "Subassistant Commissioner Records filed under 'Sterling, Texas,'" BRFAL, [unmicrofilmed], RG 105, NA; "Will of John S. Deveraux," dated May 28, 1864, and filed January 3, 1868, "In the Matter of the Estate of John S. B. Deveraux," Docket #50, PF, CCO, Robertson County, Texas; *S. R. Perry, Adm[inist]r[ator] of J. S. B. Deveraux, vs. S. R. Hearne,* Case No. 905, [June Term, 1875], June 15, 1875, Book "O," pp. 4–5, and [Spring Term, 1868], April 8, 1868, Book "J [452–922]," p. 655, MDC, Robertson County, Texas; and *The State of Texas vs. John R. Harlan,* Case No. 494, April 23, 1868, and October 20, 1868, Book "J [452–922]," pp. 713 and 754–55, MDC, Robertson County, Texas.

to the entire plantation could be rendered invalid and concomitant damages would bankrupt Sam's estate. The Deveraux judgment is noteworthy because it placed the last few years of Sam's life in an uncharacteristically bad light. There was no logical reason for Sam, one of the wealthiest planters in the county in the 1860s, to have exposed himself to needless legal difficulties over a horse.[13]

Azeline's inability to clarify what occurred and thus absolve Sam suggests that he might have been, as his brothers and cousins later alleged, mentally impaired due to heavy drinking. Freedmen's Bureau agent Joshua Randall, who filed many reports about the probating of Sam's will, never refuted the rumors about Sam's drinking. Sam's purchases on credit at Greenwood Brown's store totaling $123 on three seemingly random occasions in 1863 and 1864 reveal large purchases of alcohol: over 60 percent of the value of the items that Sam bought was comprised of bottles of whiskey and brandy. Finally, it is noteworthy that Randall never filed reports advocating special consideration for Azeline but rather showed considerable sympathy for complaints lodged by Rasche Hearne. Had Randall accepted Rasche's interpretation of Sam and Azeline's story? Randall, it will be recalled, documented for Rasche, not Azeline or the handful of Robertson County white Republicans, the abnormalities in the bureau's administration of Sam's estate.[14]

After the conclusion of the Deveraux case, the trial of the case of *Thomas P. Aycock vs. Asaline Hearne* entirely consumed the next two days. After a history of unexplained removals in 1868 and 1871 of default judgments against Azeline, Aycock finally obtained his day in court. Although Aycock was now residing in California, where he was hoping to regain his failing health, his ownership of one-half of the total value of Sam's estate was at stake pending the outcome of this case. The trial recounted how and why the Freedmen's Bureau took over control of the administration of Sam's estate in July 1867 and suspended any jurisdiction by the

13. *S. R. Perry, Adm[inist]r[ator] of J .S. B. Deveraux, vs. S. R. Hearne,* Case No. 905, [June Term, 1875], June 15, 1875, Book "O," pp. 4–5, and July 3, 1875, Book "O," pp. 64–65, MDC, Robertson County, Texas.

14. Joshua L. Randall to Joel T. Kirkman, June 8, 1867, "Subassistant Commissioner Records filed under 'Sterling, Texas,'" BRFAL, [unmicrofilmed], RG 105, NA; Notation of William H. Farner on "Brown's Store. Robertson County, Texas [account of] Mr. S. R. Hearne Bo[ugh]t of Greenwood Brown," [undated], Re: Estate of Samuel R. Hearne, Docket #134, PF, CCO, Robertson County, Texas; and [Evidence of claims and some accounting of the S. R. Hearne estate], in *Asaline Hearne vs. H. D. Prendergast,* Case No. 3069, ODC, Robertson County, Texas.

civil courts over matters regarding it. Although the case file has been lost or misplaced, summary remarks in the district court minutes provide an outline of the argument made by the lawyer who represented Aycock.[15]

Prendergast, acting as Azeline's lawyer, acknowledged that his client and her son had conveyed to Aycock shortly after Sam's death one-half of their interest in Sam's estate in exchange for Aycock's legal services in sustaining Sam's will against all other claimants. But, according to Prendergast, Aycock's endeavors on their behalf had come to naught: only the intervention of the U.S. Army and the Freedmen's Bureau had prevented Sam's will from being overturned. In response, Aycock's lawyer maintained that his client had upheld his part of the contract by having prepared for trial to defend the will in the civil courts, but Azeline surreptitiously had a military commission appointed and got the case tried in a special military court. While the jury might have been captivated by details of the operations of the Freedmen's Bureau eight years earlier, it returned a verdict in favor of Azeline. When the court overruled a motion for a new trial, Aycock's lawyer appealed the case to the Texas Supreme Court, where it lingered for another seven years.[16]

Resignations of District Clerk Anschicks and Sheriff Hall

At the time of the Deveraux and Aycock trials in June and July 1875, respectively, District Clerk Anschicks and Sheriff Hall resigned their offices. After standing trial for rape on three separate occasions and spending much time in and out of jail, Anschicks was subsequently convicted in 1881 in a fourth trial held through a change in venue in neighboring Milam County. He was denied a new trial and sentenced to seven years in the

15. *Thomas P. Aycock vs. Asaline Hearne,* Case No. 1113, June 18, 1875, Book "O," p. 7, MDC, Robertson County, Texas; J. L. Walker and C. P. Lumpkin, *History of the Waco Baptist Association of Texas* (Waco, Tex.: Byrne-Hill Printing House, 1897), pp. 224–26, and Alfred L. Brigance to Charles Griffin, August 30, 1867, frames 105–6, Microfilm Reel #10, and Joshua L. Randall to J. P. Richardson, November 4, 1867, frames 348–49, Microfilm Reel #14, BRFAL, RG 105, M821, NA (1973).

16. *Thomas P. Aycock vs. Asaline Hearne,* Case No. 1113, February 20, 1871, Book "K," pp. 57–58, MDC, Robertson County, Texas; Reference to *Thomas P. Aycock vs. Asaline Hearne,* Case No. 1113, [May Term, 1876], Robertson County District Court, in "Memoranda" notebook in William Harrison Hamman Papers, box 1, folder 5, WRC-RU, Houston, Texas; [Evidence of claims and some accounting of the S. R. Hearne estate], in *Asaline Hearne vs. H. D. Prendergast,* Case No. 3069, ODC, Robertson County, Texas; Dallas *Weekly Herald,* December 14, 1882, p. 7.

state penitentiary. His first trial in the Calvert Police Court had resulted in his receiving the death sentence; his second trial, a twenty-year prison sentence; and third trial, five years. His wife subsequently divorced him, won custody of their children, and continued running the family's landmark dry goods and grocery store in Calvert. Unlike the drawn-out legal predicaments of Anschicks, Sheriff Hall's indictment for embezzlement of tax monies ended in the fall of 1875, when he consented to a judgment against him for $16,122.66.[17]

Sheriff Hall's failure to collect the school tax and pay it over to the state treasury originated with Judge Rector's 1871 decision granting injunctive relief to a challenge to the Republican-imposed levy that financed an innovative statewide public school system for both whites and blacks. By procuring legal injunctions against the tax, the Democrats had hoped to capitalize politically by demolishing the public schools and the unpopular taxes supporting them. In general, Texas taxpayers paid their assessments in counties where Democratic politicians had not incited resistance to the tax or where local officials had threatened forced sales of land owned by property holders refusing to pay. Because Texas tax rates during Reconstruction were hardly excessive when compared to northern states, the underlying political motivation had been the Democratic belief that the Edmund J. Davis government was illegitimate because it had been imposed by federal intervention, based on the votes of former slaves, and controlled largely by scalawags. As early as 1871 Sheriff Hall, along with many other Texas scalawags who resided in competitive election districts, had become a bit drained of their extreme Republicanism.[18]

Before Sheriff Hall entered into the consent judgment, he and his wife

17. *The State of Texas vs. Conrad Anschicks,* Case No. 1136, "Rape," June 12, 1874, Book "M," p. 71, and June 3, 1876, Book "O," p. 334, and *The State of Texas vs. Conrad Anschicks,* Case No. 880, "Swindling," March 20, 1875, Book "M," p. 469, and [Anschicks's resignation as clerk of the district court], June 8, 1875, Book "O," p. 1, and *Dora Anschicks vs. Conrad Anschicks,* Case No. 3193, June 18, 1883, Book "Q," p. 396, and *The State of Texas vs. F. M. Hall,* Case No. 2195, "Embezzlement," [Consent Judgment], October 29, 1875, Book "O," pp. 250–52, MDC, Robertson County, Texas; Dallas *Weekly Herald,* June 19, 1875, p. 4, and November 10, 1881, p. 4; and *Texas State Gazetteer and Business Directory, 1884–5,* Microfilm Reel #146 ([Chicago, Ill.]: R. L. Polk & Co. n.d.), p. 198.

18. Edmund J. Davis to John B. Rector, February 15, 1872, and March 1, 1872, "Official Letter Book, November 15, 1871–May 20, 1872," pp. 341–43, folder 90, Governors' Papers: Davis, RG 301, TSL-AD; "Treasurer's Report," [March Term, 1876], pp. 1–2, [March 1876 to September 1879], CCM, Robertson County, Texas; and Carl H. Moneyhon, "Public Education and Texas Reconstruction Politics, 1871–1874," *Southwestern Historical Quarterly* 92 (January 1989): 406–8.

conveyed all their rights to the old Sam Hearne plantation to the sureties, including Ben Brown and Benjamin Hammond, on Hall's sheriff bond. These conveyances partially reimbursed them for payments they had made as Hall's bondsmen of liabilities totaling about $42,000. In early March 1876, when Frank Hall died of bad health at the age of twenty-seven, he was mourned not only by virtually all Robertson County blacks but by many notable Independent Democrats as well.[19]

In 1876 the Republicans and Independents still controlled, albeit precariously, local politics, holding on to the offices of sheriff, county clerk, and county judge. But evidence of sharply divided partisan beliefs and considerable political maneuvering was exposed in the 1876 county election results: Rutherford B. Hayes defeated Samuel J. Tilden by a one-vote majority; Governor Coke overcame his Republican challenger by 176 votes; and a pro-Republican 100-vote margin rejected the new Texas constitution, which easily passed statewide. Democrats, not content to have dismantled the Republican state police force, the state militia, and the public schools, replaced the Republican-drafted 1869 constitution with one that severely truncated executive authority and circumscribed legislative power to the extent that even the most trivial state government action required constitutional amendments. The redeemer Democratic document, which was designed to put an end to Reconstruction, was adopted by men who took pride in their Confederate past, advocated principles discredited by the bloodshed of the Civil War, and were convinced of their racial superiority over the descendants of black Africans.[20]

Prendergast Sues Azeline

Along the Brazos River the cotton industry was still flourishing in 1876, but Robertson County's extraordinary growth had markedly slowed. Cal-

19. *The State of Texas vs. F. M. Hall,* Case No. 2195, October 29, 1875, Book "O," pp. 250–52, MDC, Robertson County, Texas; "Answers of the witness Ben Brown," [Depositions of B. F. Hammond and Ben Brown], June 22, 1882, *Asaline Hearne vs. H. D. Prendergast,* Case No. 3069, ODC, Robertson County, Texas; "Order of County Court Bonds," November 19, 1874, pp. 301–5, RCC, CCO, Robertson County, Texas; and Ernest Emory Bailey, comp. and ed., *Texas Historical and Biographical Record: With a Genealogical Study of Historical Family Records* (Austin: By the Author, 1900), pp. 310–13.

20. Letter from Thomas J. McHugh to W. Q. Wyser, [undated], quoted in Baker, *A History of Robertson County,* pp. 517–18; Manuscript Election Returns for 1876, Folder for Robertson County, box 2–12/585, Secretary of State Records, RG 307, TSL-AD; and Richard R. Moore, "Reconstruction," in Ben Procter and Archie P. McDonald, *The Texas Heritage* (St. Louis, Mo.: Forum Press, 1980) p. 103.

vert, according to Republican county clerk Thomas J. McHugh, bore "a resemblance to the prosperous days of 1870–71" only on Saturdays "when the Brazos [Bottoms] fairly vomits out Freedmen." Yet, with the exception of the usual quota of delinquent taxpayers, the county's finances were in good condition, all county offices were "carpeted and fixed comfortable," and the county finally had its badly needed new jail—"a little beauty" unrivaled by any other in the state. In addition, local politics was on the verge of becoming unpredictable due to the new National Greenback Labor Party's exploitation of growing agrarian unrest. Under the leadership of Robertson County's own William Hamman, the Greenbackers would soon replace the Republicans as the second largest political party in Texas. But before the first local Greenback club was organized, Prendergast sued Azeline, his own client.[21]

Prendergast was in the process of handling the appeal of the Hall case to the Texas Supreme Court. He was Azeline's appellate lawyer and was also the administrator of the estate in which she was the sole heir under Sam Hearne's will. Yet, without bothering to withdraw as her counsel and as Sam's executor, he sued her—an action that must have caught the attention of more than a few at the district court building. Although the case file is missing or misplaced, the docket sheet has survived. It states that Prendergast's suit was based on a written agreement with Azeline for a specific amount of money. The district court duly issued her a summons, and she predictably failed either to answer it or appear in court. A default judgment in favor of Prendergast was thus issued in late June 1876 for $672. If someone tried to explain the suit to Azeline, the details she received about this judgment against her would have been thoroughly bewildering.[22]

Years later Hamman stated that Prendergast's lawsuit against Azeline was for legal services that he rendered her in the Hall case. Prendergast's July 1869 agreement, giving him the south half of the plantation in return for nothing more than his setting aside the default judgment by a writ of error, had not covered his further handling of the case on appeal. Yet his own interests were as much at stake as Azeline's, because the Texas Supreme Court might question the particular part of the district court verdict awarding him the south half of the Brazos River plantation. If the high court upheld the decision in its entirety, which was far more likely,

21. Letter from Thomas J. McHugh to W. Q. Wyser, [undated] (quotations), quoted in Baker, *A History of Robertson County,* pp. 517–18; and "Greenback Party," *TNHT,* 3: 317–18.

22. *H. D. Prendergast vs. Asaline Hearne,* Case No. 2544, June 28, 1876, Book "O," pp. 383–84, MDC, Robertson County, Texas.

then Prendergast's subsequent judgment lien of $672 would have been secondary and inferior to Frank Hall's ownership of the north half. But a chance remained that the judgment for Hall might be overturned, thus restoring Azeline to ownership of the north half. In this event, Prendergast's monetary judgment would give him a lien encumbering her half of the plantation and forcing anyone adverse to his claim to deal with him as a judgment creditor. To further his goal, he asked the district court for an execution for the $672. Although the sheriff reported that Azeline had no property or anything of value on which he could levy, Prendergast had nevertheless successfully perfected his default judgment against her. The upshot was that if Azeline's appeal were successful, Prendergast would be positioned to sell the north half to satisfy his monetary judgment and could, in effect, without providing any adequate consideration, legally swindle the land away from her.[23]

During the following year, 1877, the Texas Supreme Court disposed of the second Erhard case by affirming the judgment in the Robertson County District Court in favor of Azeline. The high court ruled, to nobody's surprise, that exemption from lawsuits allowed by the statute of limitations was a valid defense of Sam Hearne's title to the Brazos River plantation, despite the fact that, between the time of the partition of Dred Dawson's estate in 1845 and Sam's arrival in 1853, there was no actual possession of the 903 acres by Dred's son or by someone holding under him. Hamman's lengthy, but groundless, legal challenges on behalf of himself and the heirs of Allen C. Reynolds to Sam's title thus came to an end. The high court's decision should have silenced Prendergast's constant laments that if Azeline were to lose the case, then Sam's estate would be "entirely insolvent." Prendergast had justified his decisions to delay paying the estate's debts while the case was on appeal, because not only were the 903 acres the principal asset of the estate but the money demands on it alone, for $10,000 in damages and rents since 1858, would far exceed the total of all yet unpaid estate debts.[24]

23. "Civil Bill of Costs," December 22, 1876, *H. D. Prendergast vs. Asaline Hearne,* Case No. 2544, contained in *Asaline Hearne vs. H. D. Prendergast,* Case No. 3069, [Special file], and "Asaline Hearne, complaining of Harvey D. Prendergast," [by Hamman & Adams], [Pleadings file, January Term, 1882], *Asaline Hearne vs. H. D. Prendergast,* Case No. 3069, ODC, Robertson County, Texas.

24. *Cayton Erhard et al. vs. Asseline Hearne et al.,* [No number in original (Case No. 662)], Supreme Court of Texas, 47 Tex. 469; 1877 Tex. LEXIS 97, June 22, 1877, Decided; and "Answer of Adm[inistrato]r to Motion of W[illia]m M. Rice," [October Term, 1875], November 8, 1875 (quotation), vol. "W," p. 77, PM, CCO, Robertson County, Texas.

Prendergast Purchases the Hall Judgment for Henry Lee Lewis

After the resolution of the second Erhard case, the only remaining obstacles to clarification of ownership of the Brazos River plantation were embodied in two virtually irreversible judgments still on appeal to the Texas Supreme Court: Aycock's appeal of his case against Azeline and her appeal of the Hall judgment. If the lower court decisions were upheld, then the assignees of Hall and his wife would own the north half of the plantation and Prendergast's unencumbered ownership of the south half would be affirmed. In early January 1878, when the time arrived to prepare for planting new crops, Watts, who had been managing the plantation since 1871, expressed his desire to sever his connection with Prendergast and Azeline. Watts had purchased, presumably at a sizable discount, the largest and still unpaid claim against Sam's estate, the 1872 court judgment for $1,289.06 obtained by George H. Dunn, one of the creditors to whom Sam owed money at his death. Watts had also unsuccessfully tried to buy out all Azeline's interest in the plantation, but upon learning that Prendergast was planning to purchase the Hall judgment for Charles Lewis's son, Henry Lee, Watts wrote Prendergast an ultimatum insisting that Sam's estate be closed up. He made his demand as blunt as possible: "*I want what little I have if any interest out of it & shall demand it.*"[25]

Having worked closely with Prendergast for years, Watts had to suspect that the scheme to make Henry Lee Lewis the owner of the north half of the plantation would constitute the most sophisticated shenanigans ever perpetrated in the long-drawn-out defrauding of Azeline of her lawful inheritance. Once Lewis owned the Hall judgment, Prendergast, without Azeline's knowledge or approval, would dismiss the Hall appeal. Most likely due to Prendergast and Lewis's persuasive powers, Watts abandoned his demands to get the estate closed and himself extricated from managing the plantation. A few years later he regretted not having stood by his January 1878 ultimatum. When Azeline brought forth her far-reaching accusations of wrongdoing against Prendergast and Lewis in a lawsuit filed in the district court, Watts experienced fears for his own potential

25. *George Dunn vs. H. D. Prendergast, Adm'r S. R. Hearne dec'd,* Case No.1582, October 10, 1872, Book "L," p. 53, MDC, Robertson County, Texas; W. W. Watts to H. D. Prendergast, January 7, 1878 (quotation), [Probate Claims and Accountings File], and "Interrogatories propounded to Sam Bell," [Witnessed by A. M. Rushin, Clerk of the County Court of Robertson County], June 17, 1882, and filed for record June 19, 1882, [Interrogatories File], *Asaline Hearne vs. H. D. Prendergast,* Case No. 3069, ODC, Robertson County, Texas.

liability as a party to the alleged fraudulent activities and as a surety on Prendergast's bond as administrator of Sam's estate.[26]

As a young child with his parents, H. L. Lewis had made the 1852 trip from Louisiana to Texas. When the Civil War broke out, he was almost fifteen years of age. He spent most of the war years attending school in England, and after graduating from Norwich University and traveling extensively throughout Europe, he returned home to Robertson County. When the extension of the H&TC Railroad approached Hearne, he became a dry goods and grocery store owner in the bustling new town and soon came to be a staunch anti-Reconstruction Democrat. In one instance in the fall of 1871, while at the head of a mob, he took point-blank aim with "a sixteen shooting rifle" at the town's Republican mayor. He was married the following year, continued in the banking business until 1875, and when his health started to fail became extensively involved in cotton farming. During this period he defended the use of convict labor in the Brazos Bottoms and financed the digging of some of the county's first artesian wells. At the end of the decade, he purchased the Hall judgment with Prendergast's assistance, but his precise reasons for wanting to acquire the north half of the old Sam Hearne place remain mysterious. All that is known is that H. L. Lewis took possession of the land in the spring of 1880 after the dismissal of the Hall appeal. Then in the fall, when his father died, he took over the management of the extensive family plantation lands.[27]

The Lewis family's interest in the Brazos River plantation might have been related to an unpleasant falling-out in the autumn of 1867 between Mary Ellen Hearne, the widow of Lum Hearne, on the one hand, and Rasche Hearne, on the other. The old pioneer Louisiana Hearne and Lewis tribe fractured along the bloodlines of the Miles Hearnes and the Ransom

26. "Asaline Hearne, complaining of Harvey D. Prendergast," [by Hamman & Adams], December 22, 1881, [Pleadings File, January Term, 1882], *Asaline Hearne vs. H. D. Prendergast,* Case No. 3069, ODC, Robertson County, Texas; and "Petition of W. W. Watts asking to be discharged from administrator's bonds," filed on June 22, 1882, Re: Estate of Samuel R. Hearne, Docket #134, PF, CCO, Robertson County, Texas.

27. L. E. Daniell, comp., *Personnel of the Texas State Government* (Austin, Tex.: Smith, Hicks & Jones, State Printers, 1889), pp. 289–90; Galveston *Daily News,* July 8, 1869, p. 1, and October 23, 1880, p. 1; Charles F. Putnam to Edmund J. Davis, November 4, 1871 (quotations), box 301–77, folder 220, Governors' Papers: Davis, TSL-AD; McCarver and McCarver, *Hearne on the Brazos,* p. 9; and "Second Amended Original Petition and First Supplemental Petition," [Hamman and Adams], filed February 18, 1884, [Pleadings File], *Asaline Hearne vs. H. D. Prendergast,* Case No. 3069, ODC, Robertson County, Texas.

Hearnes, putting Rasche, along with his sister Adeline and his nephews, William Hearne and H. L. Lewis, in an uneasy coexistence with Mary Ellen Hearne and her four sons, Charles, Selby, John, and Millard Filmore. The disproportionate involvement by Rasche and the Lewis family in matters touching on Sam's old plantation suggests that Azeline might have had a special connection with the Miles group. In a wealthy former slaveholding extended family in which cousins had married cousins, the conversations recorded in court depositions between H. L. Lewis and Azeline reveal an uncommon familiarity. They do not, however, establish that they shared one of the family's Louisiana secrets, which Mary Ellen threatened to expose during her anger at Rasche after Lum's death.[28]

Alternatively, H. L. Lewis might have simply wanted to plant cotton on additional bottomland purchasable at a discounted price with the help of Prendergast, who often had handled his family's legal matters. Yet again, Lewis might have been motivated by a straightforward dislike of Hamman, who had the largest law practice in central Texas due in large part to his success in tenaciously litigating conflicting claims over land titles in the Brazos Bottoms. Not only had Hamman brought lawsuits against the Lewis family to contest titles to its plantation lands, but he had been ruthless since the end of the war, as Prendergast expressed it, "in trying to get the old Sam Hearne place." Yet by 1878 there existed yet another possible reason for the Lewis family to despise Hamman: he dramatically abandoned the Democratic Party.[29]

Greenbackers and Exodusters

Hamman had been a longtime Democratic political leader, serving as a member of the county committee and as a state convention delegate since the early 1870s. He became preoccupied, however, with national monetary reform, and when the Texas Democrats at their 1878 state convention

28. "Statement of Samuel B. Killough," Re: Estate of C. C. Hearne, Docket #37-B, PF, CCO, Robertson County, Texas; *Horatio R. Hearne vs. Mary Ellen Hearne, Ex[ecu]t[or],* Case No. 1312, filed January 8, 1868, Re: Estate of C. C. Hearne, Docket #37-B, PF, CCO, Robertson County, Texas; and *Horatio R. Hearne vs. Mary Ellen Hearne, Ex[ecu]t[or],* Case No. 1312, [Spring Term, 1870], April 18, 1870, Book "J [452–922]," p. 881, MDC, Robertson County, Texas.

29. "Cross Interrogatories propounded to Assaline Hearne, Plaintiff," [signed by H. D & F. H. Prendergast, Att[orne]ys for Def[endan]ts], certified as a true copy on August 15, 1882, Question 16 (quotation), [Witnessed by F. H. Bailey, Notary Public], November 16, 1882, and filed for record November 20, 1882, [Interrogatories File], *Asaline Hearne vs. H. D. Prendergast,* Case No. 3069, ODC, Robertson County, Texas.

rejected his minority platform report making federally controlled greenback dollars full legal tender for all debts, including U.S. treasury obligations, he had walked out of the convention. Hamman then accepted the nomination for governor by the Greenback Party, whose platform resonated with dissident agrarian and inflationist Democrats but also appealed to those annoyed with the convict labor law, importation of Chinese laborers, and dismantlement of the tax-supported public school system. The regular Republicans made no nominations for state offices, but a dissenting faction fielded a straight Republican ticket. Although the Democrats easily won the statewide elections, Hamman polled a respectable 23 percent of the ballots cast for governor.[30]

Hamman's candidacy scrambled Robertson County political affiliations. The Greenback platform attracted many white tenant farmers plagued by debts and low farm prices, and it split black voters over the issue of fusion with the Greenbackers. An altercation leading to fisticuffs at a political rally between black leaders Harriel Geiger, a pugnacious and ambitious Hearne blacksmith, and Richard Allen, a Houston building contractor running for lieutenant governor on the straight Republican ticket, exposed the rift in the ranks of the county's Republicans. Geiger had followed Hamman into the Greenback Party, as did longtime influential scalawag Republican leader Fidella Hall. With "brotherly love existing between the greens and the blacks," in the sardonic words of a pro-Democratic newspaper, the Robertson County Greenbackers successfully elected Fidella Hall to the county judgeship and Hal Geiger to the state legislature. In the governor's race, Hamman carried Robertson County by a comfortable margin. After once confidently predicting that the African race would be "doomed" if given the ballot, Hamman had pandered to audiences of blacks for their votes. In addition, Hamman successfully defended Geiger after his arrest and indictment for striking Allen.[31]

In the wake of the counterrevolution of redeemer Democrats against the accomplishments of the southern Republican governments, thousands

30. Ada Margaret Smith, "The Life and Times of William Harrison Hamman" (M.A. thesis, University of Texas, 1952), pp. 136–37; and Alwyn Barr, *Reconstruction to Reform: Texas Politics, 1876–1906* (Dallas, Tex.: Southern Methodist University Press, 2000; reprint ed., 1971), pp. 44–53.

31. Galveston *Daily News,* October 9, 13, November 5, 15, 1878; Brenham *Weekly Banner,* October 9 (first quotation) and 11, 1878; Manuscript Election Returns for 1878, Folder for Robertson County, box 2-12/589, Secretary of State Records, RG 307, TSL-AD; "Geiger, Harriel G.," *TNHT,* 3: 122; and Smith, "The Life and Times of William Harrison Hamman," p. 102 (second quotation).

of blacks despaired of ever achieving political justice, economic prosperity, and freedom from violence. By the end of the 1870s, many left Texas, Louisiana, and other southern states for Kansas. During the winter of 1879–80 the so-called Kansas fever broke out along the entire line of the H&TC Railroad, including Robertson and Brazos Counties. After blacks from Hearne dispatched five men on an exploratory trip and their report upon their return was optimistic, hundreds of their racial counterparts left Robertson County. Their dramatic departure constituted the short-lived but legendary "Exoduster" movement. Often led by ministers, the migration took a toll on the congregations of many churches. A black communicant in Calvert, when over half of the members in his congregation departed, complained that "[t]he exodus has nearly ruined us here." The search by Robertson County blacks for a fresh start in Kansas ironically coincided with Rasche Hearne's fabled trips to North Carolina, where he and his agents enticed black workers to come to Texas. Desiring to escape conditions differing "from the old bondage in little beyond the name," many accepted contracts to work on the Hearne and Lewis families' Brazos Bottoms plantations.[32]

Azeline Sues Prendergast

At some point in early 1881—over fourteen years after the death of the father of her children, nearly twelve years after her conveyance to Prendergast of the south half of her plantation in exchange for his legal services, eleven years after her sale of its entirety to Frank Hall for $2,000 and a tract of land in Bryan's Freedman Town, ten years after the appointment by the probate court of Prendergast as administrator of Sam's estate, seven years after the district court's rendition of the Hall judgment, and a year after the dismissal of its appeal to the Texas Supreme Court—Azeline decided to sue Prendergast, her attorney. Then as now, members of the legal profession were notoriously unwilling to sue their fellow lawyers, especially a member of the same local bar association or someone they saw regularly in court. Having difficulty finding a local attorney to

32. Letter by W. L. Molloy from Bryan, Texas, November 26, 1879, in *Southwestern Christian Advocate,* December 4, 1879, p. 2 (first quotation); Galveston *Daily News,* July 5, 1879, p. 2; Robert G. Athearn, *In Search of Canaan : Black Migration to Kansas, 1879–80* (Lawrence: Regents Press of Kansas, 1978), p. 197; McCarver and McCarver, *Hearne on the Brazos,* p. 60 (second quotation); Letter by A. M. Gregory from Calvert, Texas, April 20, 1880, in *Southwestern Christian Advocate,* May 20, 1880, p. 2 (third quotation); and New York *Times,* September 23, 1879 (fourth quotation).

represent her, she turned to her neighbor and Hamman's father-in-law, George Worthy Laudermilk, for advice. He recommended that she hire acting county judge Thomas J. Simmons.[33]

Since the fall of 1879 a district court order had installed Simmons to replace Fidella Hall, whom the court had removed for trying to fill a vacant office on the commissioners' court with a fellow Greenbacker rather than with another appointee properly commissioned by Democratic governor Oran M. Roberts. By the beginning of 1881, when Azeline was shopping for a lawyer, Geiger, Hamman, Hall, and the Robertson County Greenbackers had lost their control over local politics to a coalition of Republicans and Independent (or "anti-Bourbon") Democrats, who subsequently formed the nucleus of a strong Texas Independent movement. Hamman, who again in 1880 had unsuccessfully campaigned for the governorship, failed to carry even his home county. In addition, Geiger was defeated for reelection to the state legislature.[34]

After Azeline interviewed Simmons, she decided he was too young and told Laudermilk that she wanted "an older man." Yet there is evidence that Simmons, who delayed getting back to her, had already decided not to represent her. She then informed Laudermilk that she wanted his son-in-law to be her lawyer. Laudermilk set up an appointment at his store on the public road near her house for Hamman to meet with her. Azeline, of course, needed no introduction to Hamman. She had observed him at first hand as the opposing attorney in a host of lawsuits involving her for over a decade. In early April 1881, Azeline employed Hamman, her old legal nemesis and a twice-defeated Greenback candidate for the Texas governorship, to sue Prendergast. In what would be her last legal battle, she selected to represent her one of the state's most successful and capable attorneys and, as developments unfolded, one who would serve with

33. Untitled Instrument, [Contract between Azeline Hearne and William H. Hamman], dated April 2, 1881, and filed for record June 6, 1881, Book "7," pp. 448–49, Microfilm Reel #963292, RD, CCO, Robertson County, Texas; Joe G. Bax, "A Summation of the Proceedings of the Probate and District Courts of Robertson County Relative to Asaline Hearne," [typescript manuscript in possession of the author, June 5, 2000], p. 20; and "Depositions of Asaline Hearne and G. W. Laudermilk," [Interrogatories propounded to George W. Laudermilk], November 16, 1882, and filed November 20, 1882, *Asaline Hearne vs. H. D. Prendergast,* Case No. 3069, ODC, Robertson County, Texas.

34. *The State of Texas: Ex. Rel. D. W. White, et al. vs. P. W. Hall, Co. Judge of Robertson County,* Case No. 2855, October 27, 1879, Book "P," p. 629, and June 19, 1880, Book "Q," pp. 51–52, MDC, Robertson County, Texas; Galveston *Daily News,* June 8, 1880, p. 1, and November 5, 1880, p. 1; and Barr, *Reconstruction to Reform,* p. 63 (quotation).

undivided loyalty as her defender, advocate, and friend. She would need someone who was all these things and more.[35]

Azeline, revoking any previous authority that she might have given to Prendergast or Watts, retained Hamman to maintain her rights to the ownership of the Brazos River plantation and to all the revenues accruing to it. In exchange for his legal services, she signed the most unadulterated of contingency contracts—agreements dependent on the highly doubtful possibility of an attorney's success in taking legal action for his client. On no other basis could Hamman have taken her case, given the time and effort required preparing for negotiations or a trial. The plantation at issue was described as the 903 acres lying between the land owned on the north by Hamman and his father-in-law Laudermilk and "the Barziza plantation" on the south, and between the Brazos River on the west and the public road on the east. For his services Azeline granted Hamman all the land except a hundred acres—the same quantity that Sam in his will had guaranteed to her if their son failed to provide adequately for her.[36]

On Azeline's behalf in late November 1881, Hamman fired an initial salvo at Prendergast in the Robertson County Probate Court. His petition echoed many of the ineffective charges that he had made in 1875 while representing Sheriff Hall's interests. Hamman claimed that Prendergast, as administrator of Sam's estate, had misapplied for the past two years the annual rents and profits amounting to about $2,000 a year, had failed to file any of his required annual exhibits or statements of the conditions of the estate, and had demonstrated no reason for any further administration of it. He asked for a court order removing Prendergast as administrator. Although subsequently cited by the court to file his required reports, Prendergast put off doing so until the following spring of 1882, which in turn prompted Hamman's rehash of the same charges in yet another unsuccessful petition to have Prendergast removed and the estate closed. But by now these minor skirmishes dragging along without resolution in the

35. "Depositions of Asaline Hearne and G. W. Laudermilk," [Interrogatories propounded to George W. Laudermilk], November 16, 1882 (quotation), and filed November 20, 1882, *Asaline Hearne vs. H. D. Prendergast,* Case No. 3069, ODC, Robertson County, Texas; Untitled Instrument, [Contract between Azeline Hearne and William H. Hamman], dated April 2, 1881, and filed for record June 6, 1881, Book "7," pp. 448–49, Microfilm Reel #963292, RD, CCO, Robertson County, Texas; and Bax, "A Summation," p. 20.

36. Untitled Instrument, [Contract between Azeline Hearne and William H. Hamman], dated April 2, 1881 (quotation), and filed for record June 6, 1881, Book "7," pp. 448–49, Microfilm Reel #963292, RD, CCO, Robertson County, Texas.

probate court had been eclipsed by far more explosive developments in the district court.[37]

Three days before Christmas Day 1881, Hamman dropped the equivalent of a bombshell on Prendergast. He filed a lawsuit against him on Azeline's behalf that consisted of twelve handwritten pages, which he had to write out three times in order to provide copies for himself, the defendant Prendergast, and the Robertson County District Court. His petition was both complex and surprising, and even by today's standards has been judged as a "credible work product" that "has survived the test of time." It mingled multiple claims, including attorney malpractice, fraud, keeping property from its rightful owner, breach of fiduciary duty, and failure to render legally required accountings, as well as trespass to try title. In writing it Hamman could not rely on "boiler plate" language in legal form books that was then, and still is, usually counted on to contain the wording for most any cause of legal action. Nor could he rely upon reading previous court decisions in which he might locate some idea of what a judge would desire to hear, because at the time Hamman drafted his petition, there was no reported Texas case law covering attorney misconduct or malpractice. Nor were there any statutes dealing with the unprofessional conduct of lawyers written by the U.S. Congress or any state legislature.[38]

Even if Hamman's lawsuit had not been so extraordinary, it provided a succinct chronology of Azeline's life, from shortly after her emancipation down to 1881. His original petition and the answers it elicited from Prendergast, along with additional sworn affidavits and depositions made by herself, her neighbors, and others who had impinged on her affairs, laid bare a tale of the legal entanglements she had endured for well over a decade. Hamman began by reviewing the substance of Sam's will, summarizing how Azeline became the owner of 903 acres of bottomland along the Brazos River, discussing Ben Brown and Prendergast's administration of Sam's estate, and recapitulating how it and Azeline had become mired

37. "Complaint for removal of administrator," [William H. Hamman and Francis M. Adams], filed for record November 25, 1881, and "Motion to remove Administrator & close the estate," [William H. Hamman], filed for record May 27, 1882, Re: Estate of Samuel R. Hearne, Docket #134, ODC, Robertson County, Texas.

38. Bax, "A Summation," p. 21 (quotations); and "Asaline Hearne, complaining of Harvey D. Prendergast," [by Hamman & Adams], December 22, 1881, [Pleadings File, January Term, 1882], *Asaline Hearne vs. H. D. Prendergast,* Case No. 3069, ODC, Robertson County, Texas.

in litigation over Sam's unpaid debts. At this point he demonstrated how the debts—totaling $4,762.26 with accrued interest—could have been fully paid off in just over three years if the plantation had been "prudently and economically managed."[39]

At this juncture in his lawsuit, Hamman pointed out that by 1870 Azeline and Prendergast had an important preexisting relationship. In order to compensate him, as her attorney, to set aside the default judgment against her in the previous year for the title to the Brazos River plantation, she had executed a document giving him the south half of the plantation. For purposes of her accusations against Prendergast, Hamman thus alleged that, from 1870 forward, Prendergast, as Azeline's attorney and as administrator of Sam's estate, had acted in a "fiduciary capacity." The legal business he contracted to perform for her and the money and property he handled for her ought never to have been for his own gain but rather for her sole benefit. In other words, Prendergast had for over a decade systematically violated his legal relationship with Azeline—an association that should have entailed confidence and trust, on the one hand, and a high degree of good faith, on the other.[40]

By today's standards any attempt at summarizing the reports and annual accounts filed with the probate court by Prendergast would fail to accomplish anything useful. The first of his reports was not filed until early in 1878, and Azeline's lawsuit against him prompted the last ones for 1880, 1881, and 1882, which were prepared by H. L. Lewis, who at least attempted to follow normal accounting procedures. Lewis, uneasy with his handwritten ledger-sheet reports, indicated to Prendergast on the bottom page of the first one, "[D]on't present the a/c to the Court in my handwriting." Lewis also wanted Prendergast to obtain a good accountant to review them before transliterating them. Ignoring both suggestions, Prendergast submitted them, still in Lewis's handwriting, to the district court. All of the reports were miserable imitations of what they should have been. Had they been prepared correctly, they would have shown a beginning

39. Bax, "A Summation," pp. 21–22; and "Asaline Hearne, complaining of Harvey D. Prendergast," [by Hamman & Adams], December 22, 1881 (quotation), [Pleadings File, January Term, 1882], *Asaline Hearne vs. H. D. Prendergast,* Case No. 3069, ODC, Robertson County, Texas.

40. Bax, "A Summation," p. 23 (quotation); and "Asaline Hearne, complaining of Harvey D. Prendergast," [by Hamman & Adams], December 22, 1881, [Probate Claims and Accountings File], in *Asaline Hearne vs. H. D. Prendergast,* Case No. 3069, ODC, Robertson County, Texas.

balance for each year and an ending balance for the previous year, with revenues itemized and added to the current balance, with expenditures similarly listed and deducted after court approval. The year-end balances should have described what was on hand and could have been in the form of cash, gold, cotton bales, or promissory notes, among others.[41]

According to Hamman's analysis of the reports, since 1870 Prendergast should have amassed in rent for the Brazos River plantation and sale of stock in the H&TC Railroad a total of $17,500. Hamman averred that the estate's debts should have long been paid off and, as a consequence, there was no current justification for an administrator—an assumption that conveniently ignored Sam's documented belief that neither his son nor Azeline could manage the wide-ranging affairs of the plantation without substantial and long-term assistance. But Azeline was a fifty-six-year-old adult and the sole heir of Sam's estate. To question the need for an administration to last over a full fifteen years after a decedent's death was hardly unreasonable. Hamman moved on to discuss the current situation of his client.[42]

Azeline, according to Hamman, had no means of support other than the items of property described in the financial reports. Since Prendergast had been administrator, she had been in a "destitute and helpless condition." He had never given her any money nor explained to her any of his actions as executor. Hamman drew a sharp contrast between Prendergast and Azeline. The former was "a man of intelligence," a businessman, and "a practicing lawyer of more than twenty years experience," but the latter was "a poor, ignorant, and unlearned [N]egress, decrepit with age, in feeble health and greatly needing the property withheld from her." The manor house, in which Azeline had lived for twenty-eight years, was in dire need of repair. She had little food and clothing to alleviate her considerable suffering. These conditions, according to Hamman, were products of a deliberate disregard by Prendergast of her welfare in violation of his fiduciary obligation. Although Prendergast had pretended throughout

41. Bax, "A Summation," p. 64; vol. "W," pp. 376–91, PM, CCO, Robertson County, Texas; and "Recapitulation: Estate, S. R. Hearne In a/c with H. D. Prendergast, Adm'r, 1880, 1881, and 1882," prepared by H. L. Lewis, [undated] (quotation), [Probate Claims and Accountings File], in *Asaline Hearne vs. H. D. Prendergast,* Case No. 3069, ODC, Robertson County, Texas.

42. Bax, "A Summation," p. 23; and "Asaline Hearne, complaining of Harvey D. Prendergast," [by Hamman & Adams], December 22, 1881, [Probate Claims and Accountings File], in *Asaline Hearne vs. H. D. Prendergast,* Case No. 3069, ODC, Robertson County, Texas.

his relationship with her to be her friend, counsel, and legal advisor, his behavior was in point of fact designed to defraud her and appropriate her property for himself.[43]

Hamman then moved on to discuss the Hall case, in which Azeline had retained Prendergast to defend her. From Hamman's unique perspective of having served as the opposing counsel in this case, he was able to assert facts that made Prendergast appear greedy and self-centered. Prendergast had not been content to act in the single capacity as Azeline's attorney. He had answered Hall's suit not just as her lawyer and the administrator of Sam's estate but also on his own behalf, as owner of the south half of the plantation pursuant to her 1869 conveyance as compensation for his legal services. Hamman detailed the inordinate attention Prendergast gave to his own interests. He had used estate money to improve the value of the plantation, but the improvements had not been equitably divided. On his south half he had paid out about $3,000 to build a new cotton gin and press, and several houses, but on the north half he had spent less than $400.[44]

If Hamman's original complaint failed up to this point to grab the attention of the court, the next few paragraphs certainly did. After Azeline lost the Hall case, Prendergast handled its appeal to the Texas Supreme Court, but while acting as her appellate lawyer, he had sued her, in Hamman's words, for a "pretended" amount of $500—a sum Azeline allegedly owed him for his legal services rendered in the Hall case. Prendergast had not withdrawn as her attorney while suing her. Instead, by "taking advantage of her ignorance" and "abusing the confidence she placed in him as her attorney, friend, and adviser," he obtained a default judgment against her for the money in the district court. His actual intention was to levy upon, and have the sheriff sell the north half of, the plantation to satisfy his judgment, thereby swindling her of the land by appropriating it to himself. With estate money collected by him, Prendergast then had purchased the Hall judgment from its owners for H. L. Lewis. The former position of Hall on appeal thus fell to the ownership of Lewis, Prendergast's collabo-

43. "Asaline Hearne, complaining of Harvey D. Prendergast," [by Hamman & Adams], December 22, 1881 (quotations), [Probate Claims and Accountings File], in *Asaline Hearne vs. H. D. Prendergast,* Case No. 3069, ODC, Robertson County, Texas.

44. *F. M. Hall vs. Assaline Hearne,* Case No.1639, [1872], ODC, Robertson County, Texas; "Asaline Hearne, complaining of Harvey D. Prendergast," [by Hamman & Adams], December 22, 1881 (quotations), [Probate Claims and Accountings File], in *Asaline Hearne vs. H. D. Prendergast,* Case No. 3069, ODC, Robertson County, Texas.

rator and friend. In order to place the north half securely in Lewis's hands, Prendergast, without Azeline's knowledge and consent, "corruptly and treacherously" dismissed her appeal—an action that all but destroyed her chances to regain title and possession. Prendergast's manipulations were exceptionally sophisticated. Although Hamman undoubtedly explained them to Azeline, she probably did not fully understand them.[45]

Having brought the chronology of Azeline's legal affairs up to date, Hamman concluded his petition with a series of specific requests: (1) the district court issue an injunction preventing the sheriff from selling the north half or, for that matter, selling any other property belonging to Azeline or in which she had any legal or equitable interest; (2) Prendergast be removed as administrator and the administration of Sam's estate be closed; (3) Prendergast make available a complete and proper accounting from 1870 up to the present time, and, accordingly, a judgment against him be issued for whatever money remained over and above the estate's indebtedness and the reasonable and necessary costs entailed during his administration of it; (4) the court declare that the acquisition of the Hall judgment was "bought in trust" for Azeline, meaning that its purchase had been only for her benefit; (5) Azeline's 1869 conveyance of the south half of the plantation to Prendergast be set aside and, if not, that she at least be reimbursed $3,000 for the improvements made to the south half; and (6) the default judgment that Prendergast obtained against Azeline for his legal fees in the Hall case be declared "fraudulent" and thus nullified.[46]

One can only imagine Prendergast's reaction at being served with the notice to answer Hamman's petition. Hopefully, he had finished his lunch before reading it. A formidable lawsuit written by one of the most accomplished attorneys in the state was now lodged against him. It had to have raised the highest level of his concern, even for an experienced lawyer such as himself. It was no ordinary lawsuit. Sixteen years after her emancipation, an illiterate and uneducated freedwoman was litigating in a Texas district courtroom with her well-to-do and well-known white attorney. Prendergast's reputation would be at stake. Battling for acceptance by a jury or

45. *H. D. Prendergast vs. Asaline Hearne,* Case No. 2544, Book "O," p. 383, MDC, Robertson County, Texas; Bax, "A Summation," pp. 25–27; and "Asaline Hearne, complaining of Harvey D. Prendergast," [by Hamman & Adams], December 22, 1881 (quotations), [Probate Claims and Accountings File], in *Asaline Hearne vs. H. D. Prendergast,* Case No. 3069, ODC, Robertson County, Texas.

46. "Asaline Hearne, complaining of Harvey D. Prendergast," [by Hamman & Adams], December 22, 1881 (quotations), [Probate Claims and Accountings File], in *Asaline Hearne vs. H. D. Prendergast,* Case No. 3069, ODC, Robertson County, Texas.

a judge would be contested stories of his relationship with Azeline. In early January 1882, Prendergast produced a nine-page response in his characteristically illegible handwriting that began by asserting various defenses.[47]

Prendergast, shopping for a more sympathetic forum, argued that the district court lacked the authority to try the case. Because he was the administrator of Sam's estate, the Robertson County Probate Court, he claimed, had exclusive jurisdiction. His next defense was that Azeline was improperly joining "different courses of action": a suit against him both as administrator for money and as an individual to set aside different judgments. Hamman probably skipped hastily over these conventional rejoinders, but the next one unquestionably caught his attention. Prendergast argued that Azeline's petition showed "on its face" that she had "no interest whatsoever" in the Brazos River plantation or in its proceeds or rents. In other words, Prendergast was admitting, if everything claimed in her petition was accurate, that his administration of Sam's estate had resulted in removing her as the plantation's owner. But if Azeline owned nothing, then what possible rationale existed for any continuance of Prendergast's administration when there was nothing to administer?[48]

Prendergast raised two final defenses, which Hamman anticipated: all Azeline's claims were barred by the statute of limitations; and no wrongdoing by him alleged in her petition could be proven beyond a preponderance of the evidence. The former constituted an excellent argument, because the legally mandated time period within which her claims could be brought had expired. The latter was a general demurrer, which put all issues in controversy and maintained that the evidence that Azeline had produced was insufficient in point of law to make out her case. But Texas courts were courts both of law and of equity, and Hamman hoped that the court would be guided not just by narrow formulated bodies of law, but by ethical concerns for basic fairness and justice that ideally ought to control interactions among all individuals. For this reason Hamman's petition had stressed Prendergast's neglect of his fiduciary responsibilities as her attorney and as the administrator of Sam's estate, of which Azeline was the sole beneficiary under Sam's will.[49]

47. [Response of H. D. Prendergast], filed January 6, 1882, [Pleadings File], *Asaline Hearne vs. H. D. Prendergast,* Case No. 3069, ODC, Robertson County, Texas.

48. [Response of H. D. Prendergast], filed January 6, 1882 (quotations), [Pleadings File], *Asaline Hearne vs. H. D. Prendergast,* Case No. 3069, ODC, Robertson County, Texas; and Bax, "A Summation," pp. 27–28.

49. [Response of H. D. Prendergast], filed January 6, 1882, [Pleadings File], *Asaline Hearne*

After listing his affirmative defenses, Prendergast's response became disorganized. He embarked upon a host of self-serving statements that, although containing nothing that needed to be pled, constituted a marvelous mirror reflecting his true thoughts and feelings. Yet it cannot be ruled out that he deliberately included them in order to place prejudicial facts before the jury, assuming that during trial the judge would so permit. What was obviously apparent was that Hamman's allegations of fraud and fiduciary misconduct annoyed him. Prendergast might have briefly considered filing a countersuit against Hamman for fraudulently colluding with Brown in 1869 to secure unfairly a default judgment against Azeline for the entire Brazos River plantation. But Hamman and Brown's high jinks had rebounded to Prendergast's benefit as Azeline's attorney, and thus any tale of these previous shenanigans was best avoided. Prendergast thus chose another line of attack.[50]

Prendergast demanded that the court examine the appropriateness of Hamman being allowed to represent Azeline. Hamman, Prendergast pointed out, had been the counsel who obtained the Hall judgment, which had awarded his client ownership and possession of the north half of the plantation. And now, as Azeline's lawyer, Hamman was alleging this judgment was obtained by fraud and should be set aside. Yet this criticism of Hamman was unusual, because conflicts of interest, now as then, were as a rule asserted by clients and not by opposing counsel. The Hall case had been settled in 1874. Frank Hall had died two years later, and Prendergast had purchased the judgment as agent for H. L. Lewis. Prendergast did not specify any obligations that Hamman might still owe to Hall or his estate. Nor could he have done so. What irritated Prendergast was that Hamman's familiarity with the facts in the Hall case would now work to Azeline's advantage.[51]

Prendergast claimed that he had dealt with Azeline "in the utmost good faith and liberality." He had furnished her with "a house to live in for

vs. H. D. Prendergast, Case No. 3069, ODC, Robertson County, Texas; "Asaline Hearne, complaining of Harvey D. Prendergast," [by Hamman & Adams], December 22, 1881, [Probate Claims and Accountings File], in *Asaline Hearne vs. H. D. Prendergast,* Case No. 3069, ODC, Robertson County, Texas; and Bax, "A Summation," pp. 28–29.

50. [Response of H. D. Prendergast], filed January 6, 1882, [Pleadings File], *Asaline Hearne vs. H. D. Prendergast,* Case No. 3069, ODC, Robertson County, Texas.

51. [Response of H. D. Prendergast], filed January 6, 1882, [Pleadings File], *Asaline Hearne vs. H. D. Prendergast,* Case No. 3069, ODC, Robertson County, Texas; and Bax, "A Summation," p. 29.

more than ten years worth five dollars a month"—an allegation that implied once Azeline conveyed the south half of the plantation to him she had no right to live in the old log cabin manor house. He and Watts had provided her "with money and provisions for many years amounting to more than $1,200.00." Prendergast had spent "several hundred dollars" defending her in civil and criminal suits brought against her, and he and Watts had levied on her land only after the district court rendered its judgment in the Hall case and she refused "to secure them in future advances [to her] by a lien on the land or a part of it." He had paid out of his own pocket "more than $200.00" to post the appeal bond against the Hall judgment to the Texas Supreme Court, and in other cases, specifically, the Erhard and Aycock cases, he had represented her "without one dollar as compensation." Prendergast naturally did not mention that his own interest in the south half of the Brazos River plantation had been at stake in these cases. From 1869 to the present, he claimed, he had "stood by" her "as her friend and att[orne]y" and had "to the best of his ability defended what he believed to be her rights."[52]

While appealing the Hall case, Prendergast stated that at his own expense he had consulted with "many able and learned lawyers," and the consensus of outside counsel was that the Hall judgment was not reversible on appeal. He accordingly advised Azeline to compromise the case by obtaining for herself "a competency and a home for her life." At this point much discussion followed regarding the so-called compromise, which entailed Prendergast and H. L. Lewis's purchase of the Hall judgment. Hamman, it will be recalled, had made the dealings surrounding this purchase one of the centerpieces of Prendergast's grotesque behavior as Azeline's attorney. As Prendergast rationalized it, Lewis had agreed, "after much trouble and negotiation," to pay Azeline "$120.00 per year as an annuity during her life and to furnish her a house." Moreover, Lewis's offer was written out, signed by him, and explained to her many times—actions that all occurred before the dismissal of the Hall appeal. According to Prendergast, she had supposedly "consented" to this agreement, even though her signature on any such offer was never brought into evidence.[53]

52. [Response of H. D. Prendergast], filed January 6, 1882 (quotations), [Pleadings File], *Asaline Hearne vs. H. D. Prendergast,* Case No. 3069, ODC, Robertson County, Texas; and Bax, "A Summation," pp. 29–30.

53. [Response of H. D. Prendergast], filed January 6, 1882 (quotations), [Pleadings File], *Asaline Hearne vs. H. D. Prendergast,* Case No. 3069, ODC, Robertson County, Texas; and H. L. Lewis to Assaline Hearne, [March (?), (1880?)], [unsigned and undated agreement], filed February 20, 1884, in "Special File," *Asaline Hearne vs. H. D. Prendergast,* Case No. 3069, ODC, Robertson County, Texas.

Prendergast alleged that out of the proceeds of Sam's estate he paid Azeline "$800.00 in gold," but he did not specify when he gave her the money. Nor did he explain his failure to file his annual accountings, which would have exhibited this conveyance. Rather, he reiterated his timeworn excuse for not performing his required duties: until "the last year or two" the entire estate, if sold, would not have liquidated its outstanding debts. While containing a backhanded admission that the estate perhaps currently had a sufficient amount of cash on hand to pay off its debts, his reasoning was based on the slim to nonexistent possibility of losing on appeal either the Aycock or second Erhard case. Prendergast claimed that when the estate's creditors pestered him to sell off assets, he refused because he "was under a moral if not legal obligation to protect [Azeline]." Naturally, he failed to identify precisely what assets he would have sold, given the detail that, before he became the estate's executor, Azeline had conveyed away to him and Hall the entire Brazos River plantation.[54]

After reading Prendergast's response, Hamman, in a supplemental petition filed in early February 1882, decided to join H. L. Lewis as a defendant to the suit. Hamman alleged that Lewis, knowing Prendergast was the administrator of Sam's estate and counsel to Azeline, "did collude, confederate, and combine" with Prendergast to divest Azeline of her legal inheritance. According to Hamman, Prendergast, who already claimed the south half of the plantation, put Lewis in possession of the north half by purchasing the Hall judgment and then dismissing Azeline's appeal to the Texas Supreme Court of the verdict for Hall. Thus both Lewis and Prendergast were still "endeavoring to wrong, cheat, and defraud her" out of the property that they were withholding from her.[55]

Hamman's adding Lewis as a defendant sparked two notable developments. First, Watts, fearing Hamman might prevail on his allegations regarding the conspiratorial dealings of Prendergast and Lewis, petitioned the probate court to be relieved as a surety on Prendergast's bond. Watts, no doubt, was pleased when the court granted his request and discharged him from all liability for the future acts of Prendergast as administrator of Sam's estate. Secondly, Lewis and Prendergast, also anticipating that Hamman might triumph, drew up an agreement stating that: (1) they were "equal owners of the S. R. Hearne farm of 903 acres in the Brazos Bot-

54. [Response of H. D. Prendergast], filed January 6, 1882 (quotations), [Pleadings File], *Asaline Hearne vs. H. D. Prendergast,* Case No. 3069, ODC, Robertson County, Texas.

55. "First Supplemental Petition," [Hamman and Adams], filed February 7, 1882 (quotations), [Pleadings File], *Asaline Hearne vs. H. D. Prendergast,* Case No. 3069, ODC, Robertson County, Texas.

tom"; (2) if Azeline recovered the north half or any part of it, then Prendergast would share half the losses out of his ownership of the south half; and (3) if the entire north half were lost, then Lewis would be the joint owner of the south half with Prendergast. Finally, the agreement stated both men were "equally interested in profits and losses until they are ready to divide or sell the place."[56]

In the summer of 1883, Prendergast's formal response to Lewis's addition as a defendant repeated material already pled, although this time devoid of unnecessary self-serving inanities. In February 1884 Hamman again amended Azeline's petitions. By this time, through the discovery process and perhaps a bit of outside investigation, Hamman had put together a better picture of the financial situation of Sam's estate. He estimated the current market value of the Brazos River plantation at $20 per acre, or just over $18,000, but ignored the value of Sam's tracts of land in Limestone and Young Counties. Hamman alleged that annual rentals should easily have averaged $2,000. Therefore, from the time of his appointment as administrator in 1871 to Azeline's filing suit against him in 1881, Prendergast should have collected $20,000. Purportedly, Sam's shares of railroad stock had been sold for $1,000, raising money assets to $21,000. Subtracting Sam's debts, which amounted to less than $5,000 at his death, combined with subsequent legitimate administrative expenses, Prendergast should have cleared all unpaid obligations and realized around $13,000 remaining on hand, had he properly managed the estate. Yet, according to Prendergast's accountings, Azeline received no money.[57]

Hamman then returned to the crucial issue of Prendergast's breach of his fiduciary duties to Azeline. Prendergast's explanation of the so-called compromise settlement was adverse to her interest in the best of circumstances. Any communication between H. L. Lewis and Prendergast concerning the title to the north half of the plantation was, while the Hall case was on appeal, a violation of Prendergast's obligations to Azeline as both her attorney and administrator of Sam's estate. But Prendergast told Lewis everything relative to Azeline's title to the plantation—confidential

56. Petition of W. W. Watts, July 24, 1882, Book "W," p. 391, PM, CCO, Robertson County, Texas; and "H. D. Prendergast and H. L. Lewis Agreement," dated December 1, 1883 (quotations), [Special File], *Asaline Hearne vs. H. D. Prendergast,* Case No. 3069, ODC, Robertson County, Texas.

57. "Demurrer & Exceptions of Def[endan]ts," [H. D. Prendergast], filed June 14, 1883, and "Second Amended Original Petition and First Supplemental Petition," [Hamman and Adams], filed February 18, 1884, [Pleadings File], *Asaline Hearne vs. H. D. Prendergast,* Case No. 3069, ODC, Robertson County, Texas; and Bax, "A Summation," pp. 31–32.

information that Prendergast acquired as administrator and as her attorney, that Lewis could not have acquired in any other way, and that Prendergast had no right to tell him or others, or to use, except for Azeline's benefit. Not only did Prendergast admit that he had made the arrangements to have the Hall judgment purchased from the legal representatives of the deceased Frank Hall, but discovery disclosed that the total cost to Lewis in buying the Hall judgment was a mere $800—an incredible bargain for a parcel of property valued at $9,000.[58]

Unless the assignees of Hall's interest in the plantation had known with certainty that Azeline would dismiss the Hall appeal and had been aware of liens or encumbrances adhering to its north half, they could not have accurately calculated the value of their claims to the land's title—circumstances that Prendergast used to his and Lewis's advantage in negotiating the price for buying out their rights. Hamman's complaint was not that the purchase of the Hall judgment on appeal was an unacceptable way of disposing of the adverse claim and additional litigation but rather that the judgment should have been purchased on Azeline's behalf. It had never occurred to Prendergast to help her buy the judgment by lending her money secured by a lien on the land. Had he, or even Lewis, done so, Hamman would have had no objection, and a central part of Azeline's lawsuit would have evaporated. The remainder of Hamman's final amended pleadings brought the estimate of damages owed to Azeline up to date by claiming that Prendergast now held additional money, namely, $6,000 in rental money received during the last four years for the north half of the plantation and $2,500 from the sale of estate property. Neither of these items had been properly accounted for by Prendergast, because he was still remiss in rendering his annual accounts. At this point Azeline's pleadings, as drafted by Hamman, were ready for trial. Hamman's battle plan was obvious, but Prendergast filed a short rejoinder to Hamman's last effort.[59]

Still stung by Hamman's accusations of professional misconduct, Prendergast complained that Hamman's behavior in the Hall case was "*contrary to . . . the rules of law controlling the duty of an attorney to his*

58. "Second Amended Original Petition and First Supplemental Petition," [Hamman and Adams], filed February 18, 1884, [Pleadings File], *Asaline Hearne vs. H. D. Prendergast,* Case No. 3069, ODC, Robertson County, Texas.

59. Bax, "A Summation," p. 33, n. 29; "Second Amended Original Petition and First Supplemental Petition," [Hamman and Adams], filed February 18, 1884 (quotation), and "Def[endan]ts Exceptions," [H. D. Prendergast], dated February 19, 1884, and filed February 20, 1884, [Pleadings File], *Asaline Hearne vs. H. D. Prendergast,* Case No. 3069, ODC, Robertson County, Texas.

client to the court and to the public and destructive of the dignity and respect for that profession which its eminent members have always zealously maintained and upheld." Prendergast's description of attorney misconduct amounted to a reiteration of his earlier accusation: that Hamman could not ethically be allowed to label as "a fraud and a wrong" the dismissal of a writ of error to the Texas Supreme Court that constituted a favorable resolution of a case he handled for a previous client who had successfully sued his current client. Accordingly, Prendergast asked the court to refuse to allow Hamman to represent Azeline. The court declined Prendergast's request.[60]

Did Prendergast's conduct as Azeline's attorney meet, at the very least, the same standards he outlined for Hamman? The conspiratorial measures taken by Prendergast and Lewis as detailed by Hamman were an example of the most prejudicial action to a client's interest that could possibly be imagined. Confidentiality, then as now, was the most fundamental and incontestable concept recognized by both attorneys and their clients. Prendergast deliberately exposed to Lewis the details of Azeline's legal affairs in order to allow him to devise a strategy to obtain $9,000 of prime cotton land for $800 in acquired claims. Azeline never consented to this scheme, nor had Lewis and Prendergast bothered to disclose it to her. Her interests were ignored. Prendergast purchased the Hall judgment on behalf of Lewis, not on behalf of Azeline, and after Prendergast dismissed the Hall appeal, any chance of her continued ownership of the north half of the Brazos River plantation had all but vanished.[61]

By February 1884 all the preliminaries to litigating were over, and the battle lines in Azeline's lawsuit against Prendergast and Lewis were firmly drawn. In the previous year both Hamman and Prendergast had signed an agreement allowing the entire matter to be tried before W. D. Wood as a special judge, because the current district court judge, William E. Collard, was legally disqualified for having served at one time as a court-appointed appraiser of Sam's estate. The complicated discovery phase of the lawsuit had lasted almost three years and had been forcefully pursued. Many individuals, including many African Texans, filed sworn answers to questions asked of them by Prendergast and Hamman. Their statements, preserved

60. "Def[endan]ts Exceptions," [H. D. Prendergast], dated February 19, 1884, and filed February 20, 1884 (quotations), [Pleadings File], *Asaline Hearne vs. H. D. Prendergast,* Case No. 3069, ODC, Robertson County, Texas.

61. Bax, "A Summation," pp. 34 and 76.

in the records of the Robertson County courthouse for over a hundred years, form an amazing glimpse into the last years of the life of a Texas freedwoman who, for a brief moment after the Civil War, had been one of the wealthiest ex-slaves in the former Confederacy.[62]

62. "Agreement to try before special judge," [signed by W. H. Hamman and H. D. Prendergast], dated June 14, 1883, and filed the same day, [Pleadings File], *Asaline Hearne vs. H. D. Prendergast,* Case No. 3069, ODC, Robertson County, Texas.

Chapter 8

The Old House Hasn't Killed You Yet

> He [Prendergast] never gave me a mouthful of provisions or a rag of clothing. He told me the law would not allow him to give me anything, that the place was in debt. I have cried to him for money or something to eat without getting it.
>
> —AZELINE HEARNE, "INTERROGATORIES TO ASSALINE HEARNE AND W. G. LAUDERMILK," *Assaline Hearne vs. H. D. Prendergast*

THE WORLD SURROUNDING A litigant's life is always more fascinating than the written allegations made by attorneys in prosecution or defense of a lawsuit. Over twenty persons filed sworn depositions to questions propounded by counsel in Azeline Hearne's lawsuit against Harvey Prendergast and H. L. Lewis. Not everyone subpoenaed to answer interrogatories replied, but the discovery phase of the suit demonstrated not only its complexity but also the extent to which it took on a life of its own. Moreover, one glaring peculiarity stood out: Azeline filed sworn answers to questions asked by her own lawyer, William Hamman. Attorneys seldom depose their own witnesses, because they know what their testimony will be and strive to avoid revealing it to the opposing counsel. There must have been a reason for Hamman to make an exception for Azeline, who was now universally referred to as "Puss"—a nickname not unique to her. She shared it with other black women who were among her contemporaries.[1]

Hamman deposed Azeline because he believed that she might not live long enough to appear at trial. At fifty-seven years of age at the time of her deposition, she was in poor physical condition. Her health during the last ten years had been, in her own words, "very bad." On many days she was barely able to hold her head up while working. She complained of "ailing all the time" and sometimes of being "sick in bed" for extended periods. A freedman living near her house on the neighboring Barziza place testified that she called her sickness "phptysis." Another neighbor used the same term in describing her health: "[Azeline] has been in very bad health . . . and is not able to do a days washing, and frequently has phthysic so bad she is not able to do anything at all." Phthisis was also called "pulmonary tuberculosis" and more vaguely considered to be any "wasting of the body" due to an atrophic disease.[2]

Azeline testified she had known Prendergast for about ten years, which would have been no earlier than the summer of 1869, when she had retained him to set aside the default judgment in favor of the first set of Erhard plaintiffs. She had known H. L. Lewis for fifteen years, suggesting that her recollection of him began when he returned after the war from his schooling in England. She had lived in Robertson County in the same house on "the Sam Hearne place" for nearly thirty years—a statement con-

1. "Deposition of Jasper Miles," [Witnessed by F. H. Bailey, Notary Public], November 16, 1882, and filed for record November 20, 1882 (quotation), [Interrogatories File], *Asaline Hearne vs. H. D. Prendergast,* Case No. 3069, ODC, Robertson County, Texas; and Ruthe Winegarten, Janet G. Humphrey, and Frieda Werden, *Black Texas Women: 150 Years of Trial and Triumph* (Austin: University of Texas Press, 1995), p. 276. When and why Azeline's nickname became transmogrified from "Press" to "Puss" is unclear. One contemporary meaning of "puss" expressed genuine affection for a woman, and another was associated with the game "puss-in-the-corner," which was popular among children. See: *Webster's New Twentieth Century Dictionary of the English Language,* unabridged 2nd ed. (n.p.: William Collins Publishers, Inc., 1980), p. 1466.

2. "Depositions of Asaline Hearne and G. W. Laudermilk," November 16, 1882 (first, second, and third quotations), and filed for record November 20, 1882, and "Deposition of Wash Lockett," November 16, 1882, and filed for record November 20, 1882 (fourth quotation), and "Deposition of Mary Miles," November 16, 1882, and filed for record November 20, 1882 (fifth quotation), [Witnessed by F. H. Bailey, Notary Public], [Interrogatories File], *Asaline Hearne vs. H. D. Prendergast,* Case No. 3069, ODC, Robertson County, Texas; and *American Pocket Medical Dictionary,* 15th ed. revised (Philadelphia: W. B. Sander's Company, 1934), p. 658 (sixth and seventh quotations).

sistent with her arrival during slavery in 1853, following the large Hearne family migration the previous year. She had lived briefly after emancipation in Galveston with, in her words, "the son of Samuel R. Hearne and myself." She was with her son on the island at the time of his death from yellow fever. For roughly "half the time" of the last ten years, she had "been about from house to house at work for something to live on." When away from her house, she had "sewed, washed dishes and cooked for black people for something to eat."[3]

Hamman's written questions to her focused on the Hall lawsuit. Sheriff Frank Hall had sued her for ownership of the entire Brazos River plantation, but a jury awarded him only the north half after confirming Prendergast as owner of the south half. Azeline admitted that Prendergast had been her attorney in the case but asserted that he had never talked to her about it, its appeal, or "what was best to do." She learned about the dismissal of her appeal of the Hall judgment only when "Gen[eral] Hamman" informed her of it. Prendergast had never discussed the possibility of her purchasing the Hall claim for her own benefit. Nor had she at any time allowed him to buy the claim for himself, for Lewis, or for anyone else. In short, she proclaimed, "He never told me whether the suit was going on or not and *never told me anything at all about it no way.*" Hamman's questions at least established that Azeline had been completely uninformed about the greater part of the Hall case, including its appeal and dismissal, and the acquisition of the title to the north half of the plantation by Lewis.[4]

The Compromise Agreement

In regard to her having accepted money or verbally agreeing to any compromise for any interest she had in the plantation, Azeline testified that neither Prendergast nor Lewis, in her words, "ever paid me a dollar for the land I live on." Prendergast, during his entire tenure as administrator of Sam's estate, had contributed "eleven dollars in all" to her support, welfare, and sustenance. He never sent a doctor to see her nor brought her any medicine, food, or supplies. He never made any repairs to her house.

3. "Depositions of Asaline Hearne and G. W. Laudermilk" (quotations), [Witnessed by F. H. Bailey, Notary Public], November 16, 1882, and filed for record November 20, 1882, [Interrogatories File], *Asaline Hearne vs. H. D. Prendergast,* Case No. 3069, ODC, Robertson County, Texas.

4. Ibid.

He had explained to her only that "the law would not allow him" to give her any money because the estate "was in debt."[5]

But after Azeline filed a lawsuit against Prendergast, he brought her "a paper" to sign and informed her that upon her signing it he would give her ten dollars a month for as long as she lived. In addition, he promised to build "a little house" on the plantation for her to live in. She refused to sign the paper, mainly because, as she explained, "he was so anxious" for her to sign it—a circumstance that caused her to suspect that "there was something wrong about it." Prendergast never told her the paper was a compromise agreement by which she would have given up to Lewis all her rights and interest in the plantation. Prendergast told her only, in her words, "it would make a sure thing on my being provided with a house." Buck Watts, Lewis, and others also urged her to sign, but she always had refused. Other than asking her to sign the paper and mentioning the ten dollars per month and the new house, Prendergast limited his visits to telling her "howdy," and saying: "Well, the old house hasn't killed you yet, and you ain't dead yet." He "always said the same thing over every time he came," including that she "better take his offer."[6]

Asked to elaborate on her interactions with Prendergast and any favors, gifts, or cash he might have given her, she replied that sometimes when she saw him he asked her to come to his house in Calvert because "his wife was without a cook." Azeline admitted to accepting many of these offers. Prendergast purchased the train tickets for her to and from Hearne and Calvert, and she stayed at times two weeks and sometimes longer at his house, where she worked at different chores: "I would cook, clean up house, set the table, wash dishes and do *just as I would if I was hired*." When she desired to return home, Prendergast's wife usually gave her "a calico dress" on the days when she left.[7]

Hamman's questions for Azeline turned to the condition of the original cedar "log house," built when she and Sam had arrived in the Brazos Bottoms. The old manor house was now "in very bad condition" and "propped up with eight or nine poles." Part of the roof had recently collapsed. For the last ten or twelve years, the house had been "growing in worse order every year" and "never had any repairing done to it but once"—a renovation performed for her by Watts, who had a new roof put on it about two

5. Ibid.
6. Ibid.
7. Ibid.

years after Sam Hearne died. She frequently relayed to Prendergast details of its dilapidated condition, but he told her "all he could do" was build her a new one and give her ten dollars a month for the rest of her life if she signed "the paper." This paper, or compromise agreement, received considerable attention in the interrogatories to the many witnesses either subpoenaed or asked to submit sworn affidavits to the court.[8]

The original compromise agreement, drafted two months before the dismissal of the Hall appeal, appears in the case file. Dated March 1880, with a blank left for filling in the precise day, it was handwritten by Prendergast and signed by Lewis but significantly *not signed* by Azeline. In it Lewis stated that he had purchased the claims of the heirs of Frank Hall, along with the claims of "Ben Brown and others holding a mortgage or bond in trust" on Hall's interest in the Brazos River plantation. It also stated that Azeline appealed the Hall judgment to the Texas Supreme Court for not only her own benefit but also for "the benefit of [her] creditors as well." The mutual consideration making a binding contract between Lewis and Azeline then followed: in exchange for her dismissing the Hall appeal and relinquishing "*any rights she may have in and to [the Sam Hearne] place,*" he promised to pay her "the sum of ten dollars per month during her natural life." This version of the contract did not include a promise to provide her with a new house and was contingent upon the Texas Supreme Court sustaining the judgment in her favor in the Aycock case. By the end of 1882, when Aycock's appeal was finally dismissed, and thus no longer posed a threat to Lewis securing an unencumbered title to the north half of the plantation, future compromise offers incorporated a pledge to build Azeline a new house in either the town of Hearne or on the plantation. The gist of Prendergast and Lewis's long-standing settlement offer was common knowledge throughout Azeline's neighborhood.[9]

Many of Azeline's friends or acquaintances tried to convince her to conclude a deal with Prendergast. She adamantly refused, telling them she "did not want to hear anything that Prendergast had to say." After she retained Hamman and filed suit, Prendergast and Lewis persistently sought her belated consent to a dismissal of the Hall appeal. Their behavior con-

8. Ibid.

9. "H. L. Lewis to Assaline Hearne," [signed by H. L. Lewis], dated March 1880 and filed for record February 20, 1884 (quotations), [Special File], and "Cross Interrogatories propounded to Assaline Hearne and G. W. Laudermilk," [by H. D. Prendergast], filed for record August 15, 1882, [Interrogatories File], *Asaline Hearne vs. H. D. Prendergast,* Case No. 3069, ODC, Robertson County, Texas; and Dallas *Weekly Herald,* December 14, 1882, p. 7.

tradicted their claims that she had consented to the unsigned March agreement. They naturally tried to conceal from Hamman their entreaties to Azeline because their intention was to destroy the most important element of her lawsuit against them. On two instances during the spring of 1882, Lewis had raised the issue of the compromise agreement with her. The first took place at her home, where he offered her $120 dollars a year and a new house on the plantation for as long as she lived. She refused and he left. The second occurred at the nearby residence of Jasper Miles, an elderly and illiterate, albeit extremely influential, local black leader who, during his enslavement in Louisiana, had known both Azeline as Sam's slave concubine and Lewis as a newborn baby. At Miles's grocery store on Rasche Hearne's plantation, Lewis again asked Azeline to sign the paper. In her words, "I told him no, that I had not made any trade, that he had done all the talking and I had done the listening." At this point, in front of Miles, Lewis "pulled out some money" and said to her, "[H]ere is a hundred dollars and I will fetch you the other tomorrow if you will sign that paper, enough to make up five hundred dollars." Azeline declined the money. Miles and other witnesses for the most part substantiated her account of these two meetings and provided additional details about them.[10]

Sam Bell had accompanied Lewis during his first visit with Azeline at her home and answered questions as a witness for Prendergast and Lewis. According to Bell, who had been traveling by chance at the time with Lewis on the public road, Azeline said she "had been wanting to see [Lewis] for some time, that she was actually suffering for something to eat." To which Lewis replied, "Well, Puss . . . you know the trade we made. I was to give you a Hundred & Twenty ($120.00) Dollars a year; and I paid you the 1st payment ($10.00) & sent you the 2nd payment which you refused to take." To which she replied: "You sent it by a [N]egro, and I was afraid there was some trick in it." Somewhat annoyed, Lewis responded by telling her that she had put him "to a good deal of trouble and expense," because he had bought up other claims that he never would have purchased had he not "made the trade" with her; to which Azeline replied, "Why, what claims?" Lewis answered that he had bought the "Hall claim and the Buck Watts claim," whereupon Azeline said: "I did not know that you

10. "Depositions of Asaline Hearne and G. W. Laudermilk" (quotations), [Witnessed by F. H. Bailey, Notary Public], November 16, 1882, and filed for record November 20, 1882, [Interrogatories File], and "Deposition of Jasper Miles," [Witnessed by F. H. Bailey, Notary Public], November 16, 1882, and filed for record November 20, 1882, [Interrogatories File], *Asaline Hearne vs. H. D. Prendergast*, Case No. 3069, ODC, Robertson County, Texas.

had bought any claims, I thought you were the agent of Mr. Prendergast." Most likely neither Azeline nor Hamman knew until Bell's deposition that Lewis had purchased, presumably at a discount, Watts's claims against the estate, which included the Dunn claim along with Watts's 1875 judgment against her. In regard to the compromise agreement, Azeline genuinely, albeit incorrectly, believed Lewis was acting for Prendergast, and not vice versa. The initial ten dollars had been given to her by Prendergast, who apparently failed to make clear that the money was from Lewis—a circumstance leading Azeline to include it in the $11 total given her by Prendergast. Moreover, it was Prendergast, not Lewis, who had placed the second payment in a sealed envelope and given it to a freedman to take to her.[11]

In regard to the meeting at his store, Miles testified that Lewis greeted Azeline with a question: "Puss, you didn't come to town to sign the contract, why was it you didn't come?" She replied, "What contract?" Once again, Lewis was referring to the compromise agreement. After he reiterated his terms, Azeline replied that she had never agreed to anything. Miles then recounted Lewis's offer to give her $500—$100 immediately for signing and the balance on the next day. Her initial response was a dramatic silence. In Miles's words, "Puss Hearne did not look around or make any answer; but began talking about her sufferings" and how it was only "by the goodness of the black people that she had anything to live on at all." Lewis then declared that he had given her some meat and molasses in direct response to her whining to him about how she was starving: "Puss, you oughtn't to blame me as I have furnished you some things and money, and would have given you more but you refused it and also refused to sign the contract." Azeline responded, "I don't blame you, as much as I do the balance of the party"—a reference, of course, to Prendergast.[12]

On the following day, Prendergast tried to make, as recalled by Miles,

11. "Interrogatories propounded to Sam Bell" (quotations), [Witnessed by A. M. Rushin, Clerk of the County Court of Robertson County], June 17, 1882, and filed for record June 19, 1882, and "Depositions of Asaline Hearne and G. W. Laudermilk," [Witnessed by F. H. Bailey, Notary Public], November 16, 1882, and filed for record November 20, 1882, and "Deposition of Press [John] Henderson," [Witnessed by F. H. Bailey, Notary Public], November 16, 1882, and filed for record November 20, 1882, [Interrogatories File], *Asaline Hearne vs. H. D. Prendergast,* Case No. 3069, ODC, Robertson County, Texas; and *W. W. Watts vs. Asaline Hearne,* Case No. 2063, July 1, 1875, Book "O," p. 56, MDC, Robertson County, Texas.

12. "Deposition of Jasper Miles" (quotations), [Witnessed by F. H. Bailey, Notary Public], November 16, 1882, and filed for record November 20, 1882, [Interrogatories File], *Asaline Hearne vs. H. D. Prendergast,* Case No. 3069, ODC, Robertson County, Texas.

"one last effort to save something" for Azeline out of Sam Hearne's estate. Accompanied by John H. Stewart, a local schoolteacher who later served as the fourth former slave elected to represent Robertson County in the Texas legislature, Prendergast hoped to convince her to sign the compromise agreement. Walking up alone from Miles's store to his family's cabin, Prendergast went searching in vain for Azeline. According to Miles, Prendergast said upon returning that he "could not find Puss, that he could not catch up with her, that she was an ignorant creature and would not stop to listen to anything for her own good." Turning to Stewart, Prendergast judiciously added, again according to Miles, "he had met with several white women that was [*sic*] just as ignorant." Prendergast then launched into a long and informative discussion about the financial circumstances surrounding "the Sam Hearne place" and the lawsuit brought by Azeline against himself and Lewis.[13]

Prendergast explained that what help—"and it wasn't a great deal"—he had given Azeline, he had given her not for any rights she possessed "but merely to help her along." He had come by merely to let her know "what was working against her in Austin," that he "wasn't trying to beat her out of the land," and that he had no interest himself in these matters other than that he would be willing to give her $600 to sign the compromise agreement for both her and Lewis's benefit. At this point, if Miles's recollection was correct, the inducement money had just increased by $100. Prendergast then added that he also "would clear her of the nine hundred dollar judgment and that was *as far as he would go*." In effect, he was now willing to forego collecting his own judgment against her for his legal fees in handling the Hall appeal, but at the same time he ominously hinted that there were other judgments for which she would be liable that were not his responsibility as the administrator of Sam's estate. He capped off his explanation of his disinterested generosity with a self-serving assertion that "he would not throw away his reputation by fooling the old lady out of any of her rights." Perhaps this statement revealed the degree

13. "Cross Interrogatories to Jasper Miles," [(H. D.) Prendergast & (F. H.) Prendergast], June 14, 1882, Question #2 (first quotation), and "Deposition of Jasper Miles" (second, third, and fourth quotations), [Witnessed by F. H. Bailey, Notary Public], November 16, 1882, and filed for record November 20, 1882, [Interrogatories File], *Asaline Hearne vs. H. D. Prendergast,* Case No. 3069, ODC, Robertson County, Texas; and Barry A. Crouch, "Hesitant Recognition: Texas Black Politicians, 1865–1900," *East Texas Historical Journal* 31, no.1 (1993): 56.

to which Hamman's allegations against him had upset his moral sensibilities, but it more likely indicated that Prendergast knew that his behavior was now under intense scrutiny.[14]

Sensing that the tone of his conversation with Miles needed to be changed, Prendergast decided to threaten Azeline. If she put him through "the trouble of defending the suit," then his benevolence to her would disappear, there would be no other chance for such a favorable compromise, and even if she won the suit he would immediately "put a nine hundred dollar judgment on the place." To leave no doubt about what would happen to her if she won the case, Prendergast reiterated that he "*would slap his judgment in the next day*," and it would be followed by many similar judgments against her "amounting up to between four and five thousand dollars." Prendergast argued that Azeline would never be able to pay these debts, would lose her one hundred acres, and would wind up with nothing.[15]

Hamman interpreted the events at Miles's store as evidence of Prendergast's mean-spirited tactics corroborating his selfish designs. Prendergast, according to Hamman, had acquired his default judgment against Azeline during the course of Hall's litigation in order to cloud the title to the plantation and force anyone adverse to his claim on its south half to deal with him as a judgment creditor. He secured and then perfected his judgment while serving both as her attorney and administrator of Sam's estate—an act that constituted a breach of his professional responsibilities to her. At the very least, Prendergast would have been able to pay himself any fees owed to him out of funds received or rent money collected by the estate. He never told Azeline that there was still a large amount of equity and potential rental income in a plantation valued, if Hamman's figures were correct, at $18,000, even encumbered by debts with accumulated interest totaling as high as $5,000. Nor had he ever mentioned to her

14. "Deposition of Jasper Miles" (first, second, third, fifth, and sixth quotations), [Witnessed by F. H. Bailey, Notary Public], November 16, 1882, and filed for record November 20, 1882, and "Deposition of Austin Miles" (fourth quotation), [Witnessed by F. H. Bailey, Notary Public], November 16, 1882, and filed for record November 20, 1882 [Interrogatories File], *Asaline Hearne vs. H. D. Prendergast,* Case No. 3069, ODC, Robertson County, Texas; and Joe G. Bax, "A Summation of the Proceedings of the Probate and District Courts of Robertson County Relative to Asaline Hearne," [typescript manuscript in possession of the author: typescript, June 5, 2000], p. 40.

15. "Deposition of Jasper Miles" (quotations), [Witnessed by F. H. Bailey, Notary Public], November 16, 1882, and filed for record November 20, 1882, [Interrogatories File], *Asaline Hearne vs. H. D. Prendergast,* Case No. 3069, ODC, Robertson County, Texas.

the lands in Limestone and Young Counties that were part of her rightful inheritance.[16]

According to Miles's testimony, after the abortive follow-up meeting at his store, Azeline confessed to him that she had "hid out from Prendergast." She also stated that she would not under any terms sign a contract with Prendergast or Lewis, and she declared that "rather than they should have the place she would give Gen[eral] Hamman her whole interest to defend her rights." Miles, along with Stewart, advised her to accept the compromise agreement. It was in her best financial and material interests to do so, especially given the alternative of gaining title to one hundred acres of the plantation with no guarantee of protection from further lawsuits. Yet on some level both Miles and Stewart must have known that her decision was irrevocable and shaped by an overriding consideration: she preferred to die free from the humiliation of having allowed Prendergast one last opportunity to swindle her out of the entirety of her inheritance. Her final trial would be in the court of public opinion in the Brazos Bottoms black community. Miles and Stewart had to respect the choice she had made: her resolution to sue her lawyer and H. L. Lewis would expose the gap between justice and the law in Robertson County.[17]

Jasper Miles and his wife Mary offered further details describing Azeline's life during the previous four or five years. Mary stated that Azeline had stayed at their house "one to two weeks out of every month" and had visited other places "in the same way." Azeline was always "very bare for clothes." When she stayed with them, she had always taken off what little clothing she had and put on Mary's clothes, as Mary explained, "so as to appear decent when at my house." Jasper stated that Azeline was "very close and economical in her habits." Neither of them had seen her "with a cent." She repeatedly told them that she "didn't have a nickel" and "did not get anything off of the [Sam Hearne plantation]." She frequently asked them for medicine, which they provided her at no charge when able. She never had money to see a doctor; nor could they recall when she had ever seen one. Jasper testified that Watts had often supported her during the past decade while he supervised the cultivation of the plantation, but Azeline had told him that, although Watts had given her more than any other white man, he "did not furnish much at that." More recently, within

16. Bax, "A Summation," p. 40.

17. "Deposition of Jasper Miles" (quotations), [Witnessed by F. H. Bailey, Notary Public], November 16, 1882, and filed for record November 20, 1882, [Interrogatories File], *Asaline Hearne vs. H. D. Prendergast,* Case No. 3069, ODC, Robertson County, Texas.

the past two or three years, Jasper had "furnished her a great deal" from "his own table" and John Henderson had also provided her "a great deal in the same time." Another freedman showing considerable generosity to her was Wash Lockett, who periodically bought her small amounts of flour and meat, which he charged to his account at Laudermilk's store. Azeline never reimbursed Henderson or Lockett, and Jasper and Mary never received any money from her for what they gave her "except she helped about the house."[18]

When Azeline hired Hamman to represent her, he took charge of caring for her health and assisted her in many ways in which others had been unable or unwilling to do. Hamman paid for all the medicine she obtained at his father-in-law's store. He was the first in over a decade to hire a physician to attend to her. In one revealing letter written by Lewis to Prendergast, which unexplainably found its way into the case file, Lewis bragged about how he chased off "a [N]egro" whom Hamman had employed to "dig a well for old Puss." In Lewis's words, "I scared him nearly to death—I'll bet he [Hamman] don't get another one to try it." Yet a new or revamped well in Azeline's backyard on the south half of the plantation, which was then owned by Prendergast, could only have enhanced the land's value at Hamman's expense. Moreover, Lewis had recently sunk artesian wells on his extensive family lands and enjoyed fresh and pure water flowing at rates of twenty gallons per hour. One can only wonder what possible reason Lewis had in mind to justify his callous behavior toward Azeline and the well digger.[19]

Prendergast's Misconduct toward Azeline

Through his interrogatories to other witnesses, Hamman exposed the details of the controversial purchase of the Hall judgment. Before Frank Hall

18. "Deposition of Jasper Miles" (fifth, seventh, ninth, tenth, eleventh, twelfth, and thirteenth quotations), [Witnessed by F. H. Bailey, Notary Public], November 16, 1882, and filed for record November 20, 1882, and "Deposition of Mary Miles" (first, second, third, fourth, sixth, and eighth quotations), [Witnessed by F. H. Bailey, Notary Public], November 16, 1882, and filed for record November 20, 1882, and "Deposition of Wash Lockett," [Witnessed by F. H. Bailey, Notary Public], November 16, 1882, and filed for record November 20, 1882, [Interrogatories File], *Asaline Hearne vs. H. D. Prendergast,* Case No. 3069, ODC, Robertson County, Texas.

19. "Deposition of G. W. Laudermilk" February 16, 1884, [Witnessed by F. H. Bailey, Notary Public], [Interrogatories File], and H. L. Lewis to H. D. Prendergast, May 9, 1884 (quotations), [Special File], *Asaline Hearne vs. H. D. Prendergast,* Case No. 3069, ODC, Robertson County, Texas; and Dallas *Herald,* November 17, 1881, p. 3.

died, he had conveyed away any interest and title that he had to the Brazos River plantation to the signers on his sheriff's bond. Because of his defalcation caused by his failure to collect the state school tax, he owed money to all who had signed his bond. Ben Brown purchased the share of the Hall claim owned by Benjamin Hammond, along with claims belonging to the other sureties, and then in the summer of 1879 sold all his rights, in turn, to Lewis for $600 in cash. Brown swore under oath, "[Prendergast] paid me the money out of his own pocket but stated at the time that the purchase was for Henry Lewis." At this juncture, Lewis merely needed to clear the interests of Hall's former wife and her new husband. They sold out the following year to Prendergast, who once again stated he was acting on behalf of Lewis. The bottom line was that, in exchange for $800 in claims, Lewis received the north half of the Brazos River plantation once Prendergast dismissed the Hall appeal.[20]

Although Prendergast must have told Brown and Hall's former wife about the liabilities clinging to the Brazos River plantation, including the monetary judgments against Sam's estate, none of Hall's deposed sureties mentioned having knowledge of factors that might have driven down the value of their claims. Of some interest, however, were their answers to a cross-interrogatory designed to probe Watts's possible involvement in purchasing the Hall judgment. Brown and Hammond testified in June 1882 that they could not recall ever having been approached by Watts to buy their claims to Frank Hall's rights to the plantation. A month later Watts successfully petitioned the Robertson County Probate Court to be relieved as a surety on Prendergast's bond as administrator of Sam's estate. Watts had to have been upset upon learning that Prendergast had tried to drag him into the negotiations to purchase the Hall judgment. Watts's petition also occurred, perhaps not by accident, during the same week that the probate court issued a summons for Prendergast to appear and explain why he should not be removed from the administration of Sam's estate as asked for in Azeline's complaint.[21]

20. *The State of Texas vs. F. M. Hall, B. F. Hammond, Ben Brown, et al.,* Case No. 2195, October 30, 1875, Book "O," pp. 250–52, MDC, Robertson County, Texas; "Depositions of B. F. Hammond and Ben Brown" (quotations), June 22, 1882, and filed the same day, [Witnessed by A. M. Rushin, Clerk of the County Court of Robertson County], and "Deposition of W. Crawford Allen," February 2, 1884, and filed for record February 14, 1884, [Witnessed by Henry E. Shelley, Notary Public], [Interrogatories File], and *Asaline Hearne vs. H. D. Prendergast,* Case No. 3069, ODC, Robertson County, Texas.

21. "Cross Interrogatories propounded to B. Brown & Dr. B. F. Hammond," [By H. D. Prendergast], filed June 14,1882, Question #3, and "Depositions of B. F. Hammond and Ben

Through the discovery phase of the district court lawsuit, Hamman sought to document Prendergast's breach of confidentiality to Azeline. He subpoenaed the trial judge in the Hall case, John Rector, to testify—an act that was as highly unusual then as it would be today. Rector, engaged in private law practice in Austin at the time, sat for a deposition in the summer of 1882. After the ruling against Azeline in the Hall case, over which he had presided in the Robertson County District Court, Prendergast had told him "as a joke" the disgruntled statements Azeline expressed about his handling of her case. She found it strange that she had given him half her land to defend her but somehow managed to lose her half while keeping his. Prendergast, while "laughing" during the retelling of Azeline's words of bewilderment, also revealed that, as her attorney, he had been unable to secure her ownership of the north half of the plantation because, without consulting him, she had foolishly conveyed away the entire plantation with a deed. Prendergast was referring to his employment in 1869 to set aside the default judgment against her attained by the first set of Erhard plaintiffs and to her execution in early 1870 of a deed to Frank Hall via the Reverend Richard Sloan.[22]

The posttrial conversation between Prendergast and Judge Rector established that Prendergast had portrayed his own client as a confused and ignorant woman whose testimony could not be trusted—a characterization that prejudiced the possible outcome of her appeal and subjected her to suspicions of false swearing. A central question of fact in the Hall case had been whether Azeline made a legal conveyance to Hall. In spite of the possibility that the Texas Supreme Court might exercise its option to remand the case to Rector for retrial, Prendergast let slip that she had essentially lied under oath about the transfer to Hall and that she had been disillusioned over his performance as her attorney. The chances would have been slim that during a retrial Rector would have forgotten such state-

---

Brown," June 22, 1882, and filed for record on the same day, [Witnessed by A. M. Rushin, Clerk of the County Court of Robertson County], [Interrogatories File], *Asaline Hearne vs. H. D. Prendergast,* Case No. 3069, ODC, Robertson County, Texas; "Petition of W. W. Watts asking to be discharged from administrator's bonds," filed on June 22, 1882, and "Citation to H. D. Prendergast, adm[inistrato]r," July 10, 1882, and executed on July 12, 1882, Re: Estate of Samuel R. Hearne, Docket #134, PF, CCO, Robertson County, Texas; and Petition of W. W. Watts, July 24, 1882, Book "W," p. 391, PM, CCO, Robertson County, Texas.

22. "Depositions of John B. Rector" (quotations), June 17, 1882, and filed for record June 19, 1882, [Witnessed by Henry E. Shelley, Notary Public], [Interrogatories File], *Asaline Hearne vs. H. D. Prendergast,* Case No. 3069, ODC, Robertson County, Texas.

ments made to him by Azeline's own lawyer. Fortunately for Prendergast, not only were there no reported Texas cases regarding attorney malpractice or irresponsibility, but also the establishment of the State Bar Association of Texas, with one of its prime purposes to enforce a "Code of Professional Responsibility," was decades away. One hundred years later Prendergast's disbarment would have been all but certain, but in his day issues of attorney misconduct were, for the most part, undefined and addressed only when they surfaced before the court in direct connection with a trial. Little, if any, consideration existed for the possibility that violations of professional ethics might occur outside the courtroom.[23]

Rector testified that Prendergast had defended Azeline in the Hall case "as well as it could be done." Although an unenthusiastic endorsement of Prendergast's legal talents, Rector's statement was a reasonable comment on the course of this trial, in which Azeline had already greatly injured her own cause. In other cases against her tried in his court in which Prendergast served as her attorney, namely, the Aycock and Erhard cases, Rector claimed that Prendergast had "defended the causes with energy and skill" in circumstances in which "the interests involved were large." In order to win, the lawyers on both sides had, according to Rector, "exerted themselves strenuously." Rector thus admitted that, *at least in the courtroom,* there was nothing he knew that would indicate that Prendergast had failed to do his duty in representing Azeline.[24]

Impeaching Hamman and Azeline's Reputations

Prendergast's efforts at discovery or interrogatories to witnesses were designed, first, to muddy Hamman with insinuations of attorney misconduct, and second, to establish that Azeline's reputation for truth and veracity was unreliable. Such tactics were odd at best, if not completely off the mark, because Hamman's alleged misconduct was largely irrelevant to Prendergast and Lewis's defense. The judicial climate of the times, as previously noted, limited the issue of his opposing counsel's conduct to actions in the courtroom. Moreover, Prendergast knew his initial petitions to have Hamman removed as Azeline's attorney, due to behavior "destructive of

23. Bax, "A Summation," pp. 69–70 (quotation) and 77; and *Burrow vs. Arce,* Case No. 98–0184, Supreme Court of Texas, 997 S.W.2d 229; 1999 Tex. LEXIS 86; 42 Tex. Sup. J. 932, Decided July 1, 1999.

24. "Depositions of John B. Rector" (quotations), June 17, 1882, and filed for record June 19, 1882," [Witnessed by Henry E. Shelley, Notary Public], [Interrogatories File], *Asaline Hearne vs. H. D. Prendergast,* Case No. 3069, ODC, Robertson County, Texas.

the dignity and respect" of the legal profession, had been summarily rejected by the court. In regard to his attempt to prove that Azeline's sworn testimony was untrustworthy, no one testified that she had agreed to dismiss the Hall appeal other than the defendants, Prendergast and Lewis, who could not even produce a properly signed contract.[25]

By questioning Hamman's motives for his prolonged interest in her plantation, Prendergast wanted Azeline to acknowledge that Hamman had "been trying to get the old Sam Hearne place ever since the war" and he now held her claims "to all of it but 100 acres." She responded by maintaining that she knew nothing about his desire to acquire the land, but it was true that she had "deeded Gen. Hamman all but one-hundred acres to bring this suit" and "to protect [herself] in the one-hundred acres against Mr. Prendergast and Mr. Lewis." Wanting Azeline also to admit that in 1869 Hamman had arrogantly taken possession of the plantation, Prendergast asked: "Did he ride over the place and take control and did he look like he thought the place belonged to him?" To which Azeline replied, "He did." Prendergast then asked her whether she had at that time hired him as her attorney to get the place back from Hamman—a task that Prendergast wanted her to admit he successfully performed for her. Azeline responded affirmatively, that she had hired him, in her words, "to bring a suit to get the place back for me, but I never have derived any benefit from the place."[26]

Prendergast's queries, designed to sully his opposing counsel, went off track when he asked Hamman's father-in-law if it had been difficult to rent out land in his neighborhood during the last six or seven years. Because Hamman owned a farm previously possessed by his wife's family and located next to Azeline's residence, the question was designed to corroborate that the small amount of rents collected over the years by Pren-

25. "Def[endan]ts Exceptions," [H. D. Prendergast], dated February 19, 1884, and filed February 20, 1884 (quotation), [Pleadings File], *Asaline Hearne vs. H. D. Prendergast,* Case No. 3069, ODC, Robertson County, Texas.

26. "Cross Interrogatories propounded to Assaline Hearne, Plaintiff," [signed by H. D. & F. H. Prendergast, Att[orne]ys for Def[endan]ts], certified as a true copy on August 15, 1882, Questions 1, 2, 15, and 16 (first, second, and fifth quotations), and "Depositions of Asaline Hearne and G. W. Laudermilk" (third, fourth, sixth, and seventh quotations), [Witnessed by F. H. Bailey, Notary Public], November 16, 1882, and filed for record November 20, 1882, [Interrogatories File], *Asaline Hearne vs. H. D. Prendergast,* Case No. 3069, ODC, Robertson County, Texas; and Untitled Instrument, [Contract between Azeline Hearne and William H. Hamman], dated April 2, 1881, and filed for record June 6, 1881, Book "7," pp. 448–49, Microfilm Reel #963292, RD, CCO, Robertson County, Texas.

dergast as administrator of Sam's estate had been in line with prevailing market rental prices. Laudermilk replied that he had "not had any difficulty in this respect whatsoever" and did "not know of the trouble of others in this respect." Prendergast pressed on: "[D]oes he [Hamman] rent it out or work [N]egroes on it? [H]as he made [the farm] profitable for the last 6 or 7 years?" Laudermilk replied that Hamman had rented out the land and hired freedmen as laborers. He did not believe that Hamman had made it profitable for the period in question, but he did not know the particulars of his son-in-law's business, or for that matter, that of any of his neighbors. This line of inquiry was meaningless, because the former Laudermilk farm, as Prendergast knew, was an insignificant holding among the seven-thousand-plus acres of land Hamman possessed in Robertson County, not to mention tracts of land and many oil and gas leases he owned in other East Texas counties.[27]

Prendergast wasted considerably more time and energy trying to discredit Azeline. He asked Hammond, Brown, and Laudermilk whether her "reputation for truth and veracity" was "good or bad." Hammond, who during slavery had fathered, but never acknowledged, four children with one of his slaves, was "unable to answer," apparently because he had not seen Azeline in many years. Brown, however, did not equivocate: "I know the reputation of Assaline Hearne in her community in which she resides for truth and veracity, and such reputation is bad. . . . I would not believe her on oath." But Laudermilk, who had lived continuously as her immediate neighbor since the early years of the war, stated that he did not know "anyone of her color" who had a better reputation and never heard her reputation "discussed as bad." Moreover, whenever she had talked to him or talked to others in his presence, she had been, as far as he knew, completely truthful.[28]

27. "Cross Interrogatories propounded to Assaline Hearne, Plaintiff," [signed by H. D. & F. H. Prendergast, Att[orne]ys for Def[endan]ts], certified as a true copy on August 15, 1882, Questions 32 and 33 (third quotation), and "Depositions of Asaline Hearne and G. W. Laudermilk" (first and second quotations), [Witnessed by F. H. Bailey, Notary Public], November 16, 1882, and filed for record November 20, 1882, [Interrogatories File], *Asaline Hearne vs. H. D. Prendergast,* Case No. 3069, ODC, Robertson County, Texas; and Robertson County Tax Rolls, 1882–1891, Tax Rolls for 1884, p. 59, Microfilm Reel #1198–02, TSL-AD.

28. "Cross Interrogatories propounded to B. Brown & Dr. B. F. Hammond," [H. D. Prendergast], filed for record June 14, 1882, Questions 6 and 7 (first and second quotations), and "Cross Interrogatories by Defendants" [(H. D.) Prendergast and (F. H.) Prendergast], filed July 7, 1883, Questions 1–10, and "Depositions of B. F. Hammond and Ben Brown" (third and fourth quotations), [Witnessed by A. M. Rushin, Clerk of the County Court of Robertson

The responses of black witnesses who were queried about Azeline's reputation for telling the truth proved entertaining as well as informative. Prendergast asked them to state specifically the names of persons whom they could identify as having worse reputations for veracity than Azeline. Henry Hutchins, John Wallace, Wash Lockett, Soloman Baker, and Ephraim Davis testified that they knew "lots of people" or "a great many" or "many a one" who had worse reputations, but they did not wish to reveal their names. In Baker's words, "I don't want to name anybody as I might make enemies by it." And Davis added, "[I]f I was to name them it might bring up a row again." However, M. P. Freeman, a schoolteacher and the only black witness able to write his name on his deposition, and Jasper Miles took seriously their task to name individuals with worse reputations, singling out a half-dozen individuals for this dubious attribute. All the freedmen questioned stated that Azeline's reputation was good, and a few, including Freeman and Davis, claimed they did not know anyone with a better reputation. Interestingly, not a single one of them knew she had been charged with perjury or impeached on the stand as a witness. Moreover, most had never previously considered the queries put to them by Prendergast, whether they or her neighbors had regarded her as always truthful, once thought she had not been truthful, or recalled when she first started to be truthful.[29]

Special Judge W. D. Wood's Ruling

By agreement of counsel, on February 20, 1884, Azeline's lawsuit at last trudged its way to trial before Judge W. D. Wood, who had been appointed as a "special judge" to try the case. The disqualified regular judge, William E. Collard, was once a court-appointed appraiser of Sam's estate. Although Judge Wood gave Hamman the right to file various eleventh-hour trial amendments, all of Hamman's hard work proved to be in vain.

County], June 22, 1882, and filed the same day, and "Deposition of G. W. Laudermilk" (fifth and sixth quotations), February 16, 1884, [Witnessed by F. H. Bailey, Notary Public], February 16, 1884, and filed for record February 18, 1884, [Interrogatories File], *Asaline Hearne vs. H. D. Prendergast,* Case No. 3069, ODC, Robertson County, Texas; and e-mail entitled "Re: Lucy Hammond" from Bill Norton of Austin, Texas, to the author, dated Friday, October 13, 2006.

29. "Depositions of M. P. Freeman, Soloman Baker, Wash Lockett, Ephraim Davis, Henry Hutchins, John Wallace, and Jasper Miles" (quotations), [Witnessed by F. H. Bailey, Notary Public], February 16, 1884, and filed for record February 18, 1884, [Interrogatories File], *Asaline Hearne vs. H. D. Prendergast,* Case No. 3069, ODC, Robertson County, Texas.

When Wood sustained Prendergast's demurrer and exceptions, the facts were never reached. The court ruled in favor of Prendergast and Lewis *as a matter of law*. The statute of limitations defense trumped all ethical requests to rectify the injustices perpetrated against Azeline. Wood ordered Prendergast and Lewis to go free, and the case was stricken from the district court docket. Hamman immediately gave notice of Azeline's intention to appeal the ruling against her, but in this case he was not committed to handling the appeal. His contract with Azeline had been merely to bring suit on her behalf. Moreover, he knew that a reversal would be highly unlikely because the appeal would by necessity hinge entirely on whether Judge Wood's ruling was merely an erroneous interpretation of the law.[30]

In the middle of March 1884, Azeline appeared before a notary public and swore under oath that she could not pay the cost of her appeal to the Texas Supreme Court. The law provided that, in cases where indigent appellants were unable to pay costs or post required bonds, they could prosecute their appeals by making proof of their financial condition before the county judge or the court that tried the case. Proof could be in the form of an affidavit. The law did not require that the affidavit be made in front of the county judge but did clearly specify that if the affidavit was made before some other official, then the county judge had to certify the adequacy of the evidence of indigence. In Azeline's case, the trial court could not provide the required certification because it had adjourned several days before she executed her affidavit. She thus needed, but neglected, to have her affidavit certified by the county judge. Hamman's law partner, Francis M. Adams, was apparently the one who botched Azeline's appeal. Nevertheless, she was proceeding to her third and final visit to the highest court in Texas, which in itself was an amazing odyssey, considering she had been an enslaved woman nineteen years earlier.[31]

On May 22, 1884, the Texas Supreme Court disposed of the case. The opinion was written by Chief Justice Asa Hoxie Willie, who in 1867 had been removed from the state's high court by federal military officials as an impediment to Reconstruction. In actuality, Justice Willie's hands were tied. Although Azeline's affidavit was in proper form and correctly sworn to by her before a notary public, it *had not been certified by the county*

30. *Asaline Hearne vs. H. D. Prendergast,* Case No. 3069, Book "Q," p. 384, February 20, 1884, MDC, Robertson County, Texas.

31. *Asaline Hearne vs. H. D. Prendergast,* Case No. 5219, Supreme Court of Texas, 61 Tex. 627; 1884 Tex. LEXIS 161, May 22, 1884, Opinion Delivered.

judge. As Willie explained, the law granted "the privilege of litigating in [the Texas Supreme Court] without securing the officers of court payment for their services rendered in the cause—a privilege to be enjoyed under certain circumstances, and in a manner expressly provided by the statute, and its provisions in these respects must be substantially pursued." Azeline had not complied with the letter of the law. Her appeal was dismissed. The case had finally come to an end.[32]

32. Opinion of Asa Hoxie Willie quoted in ibid.; and "Willie, Asa Hoxey," *TNHT,* 6: 995.

Chapter 9

Divested by the Courts

Asaline Hearne has no interest in the administration of the property of S. R. Hearne.

—H. D. Prendergast quoted in "Consent of Adm[inistrato]r to Dismissal," filed September 17, 1884

For all practical purposes, Azeline Hearne's case against Harvey Prendergast and H. L. Lewis had only a threadbare chance of life after Judge W. D. Wood made his ruling against her in the Robertson County District Court. Because there was nothing more to file, such as evidentiary materials or further discovery, the only life remaining in the case had been confined to the appeal. In a strange twist, however, someone placed a few personal letters in the district court records that one would never expect to find in any litigation file. Two letters written by Lewis to Prendergast postdated the verdict handed down by Judge Wood. No county official acknowledged or signed them. Because the letters were prejudicial to Prendergast and Lewis, it was as though someone wanted to expose the disparity between what they had alleged in their pleadings and reports to the district and probate courts, on one hand, and what they had said to each other in their private and confidential correspondence, on the other.

The Tracts of Land in Young and Limestone Counties

During the course of Azeline's lawsuit against Prendergast, she had continued to file complaints against him as the administrator of Sam Hearne's estate. At one point Prendergast pleaded his inability to respond until many of the papers, "now absent from the [probate] court" due to their use in the district court case, were located. Otherwise, all of his responses were predictable: Azeline, he argued, had no interest in the estate's administration, even though she was its only heir and beneficiary, because she had "been divested by the courts of all interest in the S. R. Hearne farm." Yet Prendergast knew the estate held assets other than the Brazos River plantation. As he further explained, "There is no other property whatsoever belonging to [the estate] *except two tracts of wild land about 1000 acres in Young and Limestone Counties.*" Because he had offered to turn these unimproved lands over to Azeline, she had "no grounds" for any grievance. Repeating his well-worn litany of problems, Prendergast stated that he had "protected the estate" for many years and "through much litigation," always incurring "extra expenses" for refusing to sell off all the estate's assets and continuously dealing with "dilapidated conditions" and many "other obligations" that had required his attention.[1]

In May 1882, in the midst of the discovery phase of Azeline's suit, Champe Carter Jr., the former Freedmen's Bureau agent who had strung up freedmen by their thumbs, filed a petition in the probate court requesting Prendergast write a deed to him for all the interest the estate had in these lands. His petition referenced a February 1873 contract giving him the right to buy these tracts of land. But unexplainably, Prendergast never asked the probate court's approval to make a contract for their sale. If Hamman's figures were correct, the market value of the two tracts was around $2,000. Although the probate court decreed that whatever interest the estate had in these lands be transferred to Carter, Prendergast deliberately ignored the order.[2]

At roughly the same time in March 1884, when Azeline made her ill-fated appeal to the Texas Supreme Court of Judge Wood's ruling, Prendergast explained to the Robertson County Probate Court his refusal to convey to Carter the lands in Young and Limestone Counties. After reiterating that Azeline's divestiture of all her interests in the Brazos River plantation had been once again acknowledged in a district court ruling recently handed down against her, he pointed out that the estate still owed "approximately $2,000.00 in debt to creditors." And, complicating mat-

1. "Report of Adm[inistrato]r," [H. R. Prendergast], filed December 21, 1883 (quotations), Re: Estate of Samuel R. Hearne, Docket #134, PF, CCO, Robertson County, Texas.

2. "Petition of Champe Carter Jr.," filed for record May 18, 1882, and recorded May 22, 1882, vol. "W," pp. 376–77, PM, CCO, Robertson County, Texas.

ters, "much of the rents" had been spent on "necessary improvements" without which "the estate" could not be rented out. To sell off assets to pay debts would, according to Prendergast, "result to an injury to Assaline Hearne." In other words, all money received from selling the unimproved lands would have to be used to pay off the estate's debts, thus leaving Azeline with nothing, whereas all income, rents, and profits from the Brazos River plantation were earmarked for its owners, Prendergast and Lewis. Prendergast concluded by asking the probate court for permission to use the rents from the Brazos River plantation to pay the estate's debts and thus avoid selling "the wild lands." The court concurred, rescinding its earlier order to convey the lands to Carter.[3]

Azeline's lands in Young and Limestone Counties, the only remaining assets in the estate's holdings she retained, were destined to be sold to pay off the estate's debts. Two of the letters that mysteriously wound up in the district court case file establish that Lewis demanded the sale of these two tracts of land. Just prior to the Texas Supreme Court's dismissal on a technicality of Azeline's appeal, Lewis told Prendergast, who was now living in Austin, that he "had better write out a full release of old Puss to the land in [Young] and Limestone Counties." Lewis claimed that "she had sent for him the other day" and said that she "will sign the paper." He set the consideration at $200 in cash and the estate's payment of the Deveraux judgment for about $700, or just less than half the market value of the lands. In July 1884 Lewis informed Prendergast that all but fifty-seven acres of the land in Limestone County had been sold for back taxes, and "some attention" should be given to the individual who only last year had bid on the remaining acres. "Try," Lewis implored Prendergast, "to find a purchaser for both tracts." Not only had Prendergast never paid the local taxes on the lands, but he and Lewis never considered avoiding the unnecessary sale of Azeline's assets as a higher priority to protecting their own pecuniary interests in the estate. It was also apparent that Prendergast had abrogated most of his responsibilities to Lewis, who was now paying most attention to the duties of administrating Sam's estate.[4]

Once Lewis purchased the Hall judgment, he had begun managing the

3. "Report of Adm[inistrato]r to Hon[orable] John E. Crawford, County Judge," [H. R. Prendergast] (quotations), filed during March Term, 1884, Re: Estate of Samuel R. Hearne, Docket #134, PF, CCO, Robertson County, Texas.

4. Henry Lee Lewis to Harvey D. Prendergast, May 9, 1884 (first, second, and third quotations), and July 10, 1884 (fourth and fifth quotations), [Special File], *Asaline Hearne vs. H. D. Prendergast,* Case No. 3069, ODC, Robertson County, Texas.

day-by-day affairs of both halves of the Brazos River plantation. When Lewis submitted to Prendergast his substandard attempts at an accounting for the years 1880, 1881, and 1882, he included a warning to get a "good accountant to make this out once again as yours." He also involved his widowed mother, Adeline Lewis, who owned a gristmill and cotton gin, in the operations of the plantation. In 1883 she rented one hundred acres at four dollars an acre on her son's north half. This family arrangement continued in subsequent years because a public rental would have garnered a higher payment of up to at least a dollar more per acre. The following year, if Lewis can be believed, the plantation had "*the finest crop on it that it has ever had*." In November 1885 his mother decided to "to take the place"—a probable reference to both the north and south halves—at a reduced three dollars per acre for the following year. Lewis's hand-sketched diagram of the plantation showed his plans to replace the old fencing surrounding over five hundred acres of improved land—a task that had, according to Prendergast, always previously proven to be financially impossible. By this time, however, the administration of Sam's estate had been terminated.[5]

In the middle of September 1884, almost four months after the Texas Supreme Court's dismissal of Azeline's appeal and nearly eighteen years after Sam's death, Prendergast's administration finally came to an end. With virtually nothing left to administer, and thus with no more assets to mismanage or misappropriate, Prendergast filed a petition to have his administration terminated. He stated for the final time his catchphrase that Azeline "has no interest in the administration of the property of S. R. Hearne." As a consequence, the interests of all involved dictated his agreeing to the long-standing requests of Hamman that the administration be terminated. Prendergast never filed a final accounting, as required by the probate court. Although he submitted to the court Lewis's attempts at an accounting for the years 1881 through 1883, the information was never

5. "Estate, S. R. Hearne, dec'd In a/c with H. D. Prendergast, Administrator, 1880, 1881, and 1882" (first quotation), November 18, 1883, and [Contract] Adeline M. Lewis, per H. L. Lewis, Agent, and H. D. Prendergast, Administrator, December 7, 1882, and ["Rough sketch"], in Henry Lee Lewis to Harvey D. Prendergast, January 29, 1885, and Henry Lee Lewis to Harvey D. Prendergast, July 10, 1884 (second quotation), [Special File], and Henry Lee Lewis to Harvey D. Prendergast, November 7, 1885 (third quotation), [Probate Claims and Accounting File], *Asaline Hearne vs. H. D. Prendergast,* Case No. 3069, ODC, Robertson County, Texas; and *Texas State Gazetteer and Business Directory, 1892,* p. 679, Microfilm Reel #149, Evans Library, Texas A&M University, College Station, Texas.

transcribed into proper form and written into the official record. To whom and at what prices the lands in Young and Limestone Counties were sold were not reported. Presumably at this point, nobody cared or was in a position to do anything about it.[6]

In the month following the termination of Sam's estate, Grover Cleveland and the Democrats captured the White House for the first time since the Civil War. In Robertson County, James G. Blaine squeaked by Cleveland by an extremely narrow margin. Popular incumbent Democratic congressman John H. Reagan prevailed by a mere eighty-six votes against his practically unknown Republican challenger. In the gubernatorial contest, with Greenback and Republican candidates also in the field, Democratic governor John Ireland received a plurality of the ballots cast. Among similarly divided opposition, John Stewart, the black leader and schoolteacher who had tried to convince Azeline to accept Lewis's compromise agreement, triumphed in the race for state representative. In Azeline's heavily black second precinct, which included the town of Hearne, Ebenezer Hearne's son William won election to the county commissioners' court. A dozen years earlier William had cut his political teeth as an intimidator of black Republican voters in a highly contested commissioners' court election. Since then he had adjusted to the new political realities by drifting into the fragile Texas Independent movement via the Greenback Party.[7]

Robertson County's stalwart Democrats were ecstatic over Cleveland's election. They shared his "sympathy toward the South" and hoped any chances for a revival of the so-called horrors of Congressional Reconstruction were now at last quashed. Yet many Democrats in the agrarian wing of their party and those opposed to civil service reform hardly adored the new president-elect. Among the Democrats, who wanted to build permanent solidarity in their party's ranks upon the principle of white supremacy, were many who dreaded confronting divisive nonracial issues looming on the horizon, such as statewide prohibition of alcoholic beverages and a host of concerns associated with the use of the state's public lands. In terms of its direct impact, Cleveland's victory over Blaine signaled a shift in federal

6. "Consent of Adm[inistrato]r to Dismissal," filed for record September 17, 1884 (quotation), Re: Estate of Samuel R. Hearne, Docket #134, PF, CCO, Robertson County, Texas.

7. Manuscript Election Returns for 1884, Folder for Robertson County, box 2–12/615, and Manuscript Election Returns for 1872, Folder for Robertson County, Affidavits of William McKinney, January 15, 1872, Charles Jefferson, January 13, 1872, and Thomas J. Powell, January 15, 1872, box 2–12/572, Secretary of State Records, RG 307, TSL-AD.

patronage, causing Republicans and Independents to lose their sixteen-year control over post office masterships—a matter of no trivial importance, especially in Calvert and Hearne, the county's two largest towns.[8]

John Randolph Hearne

In early February 1885, Prendergast learned from Lewis an astonishing development regarding the Brazos River plantation. Beverly W. Beckham, a wealthy Brazos bottomland planter, had encountered John Randolph Hearne, the son of Lum Hearne, "down at Franklin" in the courthouse "nosing around" the public records. Beckham told Lewis that John was "going to bring suit as one of the heirs of S. R. Hearne for the Plantation." One can only guess what response this news elicited from Prendergast, because no further correspondence between him and Lewis, or for that matter with anyone else, has survived or been uncovered. At first blush the prospect of dealing with another lawsuit over the plantation's ownership and title must have caused him considerable anguish, especially given the volatile outcome of a possible jury trial. This time around, the plaintiff would be the son of Sam's well-known brother, for whom the town of Hearne was named. On further reflection, however, knowing that the statute of limitations for filing such a lawsuit had long passed must have been of considerable comfort. John would face a virtually insurmountable legal barrier to winning his case, and no responsible attorney would advise him otherwise.[9]

John Hearne had been seven years old at the outbreak of the Civil War. He later attended college in Virginia, and in 1876 he moved from Hearne to Palestine, located about eighty miles to the northeast. By then the International & Great Northern Railroad connected both towns and accelerated their growth as railroad junctions. By early 1885, when John was snooping through the records at the Franklin courthouse, he was a successful Palestine druggist and banker who, like Lewis, owned large inherited family land claims in Robertson County. Although it is difficult to detect the reason why John threatened to sue Prendergast and Lewis over

8. Alwyn Barr, *Reconstruction to Reform: Texas Politics, 1876–1906* (Dallas, Tex.: Southern Methodist University Press, 2000, reprint ed., 1971), pp. 62–76 (quotations on pp. 67 and 76); and Gregg Cantrell, *Kenneth and John B. Rayner and the Limits of Southern Dissent* (Urbana: University of Illinois Press, 1993), p. 192.

9. Henry Lee Lewis to Harvey D. Prendergast, January 29, 1885 (quotations), [Special File], *Asaline Hearne vs. H. D. Prendergast,* Case No. 3069, ODC, Robertson County, Texas.

title to his deceased uncle's Brazos River plantation, the best guess is that the split in the extended Hearne family prompted by his father's death and subsequent intramural litigation over debts and land titles explains part of John's dislike of Lewis.[10]

The remarkable economic collaboration among the migrating Louisiana cohort of the Hearne family clan had disintegrated in the fall of 1867, when Rasche Hearne offended Mary Ellen Hearne immediately after she received news of her husband Lum's death. Because the pioneer generation's leaders were usually remote vendors of lands purchased or inherited by the subsequent generation, friendly lawsuits among the latter to clear up complexities surrounding their numerous land titles were quite common. But the lawsuits in the late 1870s and early 1880s over property or land involving H. L. Lewis on one side, and John Hearne, John's uncle Wash Hearne, and John's bankrupt brother Selby on the other, were adversarial. They exacerbated the division between the Miles Hearnes and Ransom Hearnes. Comprising the former side were most prominently Adeline Lewis, her children, her brother Rasche Hearne, and her childless sister Rhoda Lee Cox, or "Aunt Rhoda," as her relatives called her.[11]

Aunt Rhoda once owned over a hundred slaves in antebellum Louisiana, and her memories of her relatives allegedly exceeded that of anyone else. While living with her sister Adeline in the city of Hearne at the turn of the century, she furnished many details about her side of the family to the compiler of the Hearne family genealogy. Her penned words of admiration were frequently excerpted verbatim in the 754-page family history published in 1907. But Aunt Rhoda reported only token information about the lives of the Ransom Hearnes, with whom her closest relatives were inextricably linked by endogamy and history. She had avoided altogether so much as acknowledging Sam Hearne's existence. In regard to Lum's son John Hearne, she noted only that he lived in Palestine, Texas,

10. Pauline Buck Hoxes, *A Centennial History of Anderson County, Texas* (San Antonio, Tex.: The Naylor Company, 1936), pp. 305–7; and Norman L. McCarver and Norman L. McCarver Jr., *Hearne on the Brazos* (San Antonio: Century Press of Texas, 1958), p. 16.

11. *Horatio R. Hearne vs. Mary Ellen Hearne, Ex[ecu]t[or],* Case No. 1312, April 18, 1870, Book "J [452–922]," p. 881, and *Charles Lewis and H. L. Lewis vs. S. W. Hearne,* Case No. 2703, May 18, 1877, Book "P," p. 96, MDC, Robertson County, Texas; "Original Petition," [Hamman and Adams], June 13, 1882, and filed for record June 14, 1882, in *John R. Hearne vs. Henry L. Lewis,* Case No. 3110, and "Petition," [Hamman and Adams], undated and filed for record March 4, 1874, in *G. W. Hearne vs. Charles Lewis,* Case No. 2077, ODC, Robertson County, Texas.

and neglected to mention he was by then president of the Patton-Worsham Drug Company, an enormously successful pharmaceutical wholesaler.[12]

John Hearne was bluffing when he told Beckham about filing a lawsuit to recover the Brazos River plantation. Nor did he have Azeline's well-being in mind. John's remarks, however, had caused Lewis to make a special trip to see Azeline. In Lewis's words, "I went to see Puss and proffered to assist her to go after the children of her deceased sister." Her sister's family was presumably still living in Bryan's Hall's Town or Freedman Town in neighboring Brazos County. In response to Lewis's offer, Azeline "seemed very thoughtful and said that as soon as the weather settled she would let me know when she wanted to go." Lewis then gave her his word to "advance her the $50.00"—an ambivalent promise of a gift or a loan, and more money than needed to purchase a round-trip train ticket from Hearne to Bryan. Although most likely a gift, the money might have been part of the consideration for her signing releases to the tracts of land in Young and Limestone Counties. More important, Lewis learned that John Hearne had not been in contact with her, because he mentioned no corroborating details of John's litigious intentions. These minor matters did not constitute the most significant information to be gleaned from Lewis's January 29th epistle to Prendergast. His letter is the last known reference indicating that Azeline was still alive.[13]

The Deaths of Harvey Prendergast, William Hamman, and H. L. Lewis

Apart from managing his family's extensive plantation lands, including the Brazos River plantation, Lewis traveled extensively, taking trips to Mexico as well as serving as vice president of the 1884 and 1885 Cotton Expeditions in Vicksburg and New Orleans, respectively. In 1888 he followed in the footsteps of his father, Charles Lewis, and ran as a candidate for the state legislature. The convict labor issue dominated the campaign. With state prisoners serving as inexpensive substitutes for local farm workers, the payrolls of the Brazos Bottoms plantations went into the coffers

12. William T. Hearne, *Brief History and Genealogy of the Hearne Family: From A.D. 1066, when they went from Normandy with William the Conqueror over to England, down to 1680. [sic] when William Hearne the London Merchant came to America, and on down to A.D. 1907* (Independence, Mo.: Press of Examiner Printing Company, 1907), pp. 640, 646, and 650–52; and Hoxes, *A Centennial History of Anderson County,* p. 306.

13. Henry Lee Lewis to Harvey D. Prendergast, January 29, 1885 (quotations), [Special File], *Asaline Hearne vs. H. D. Prendergast,* Case No. 3069, ODC, Robertson County, Texas.

of the state government rather than the hands of local businessmen. When the merchants in the city of Hearne petitioned Governor Ireland to end the use of convict labor in the Brazos Bottoms, Lewis countered with his legendary campaign slogan "More and Cheaper Convicts." He won election as a Democrat to the Texas House of Representatives, where he authored labor legislation designed to reinforce planters' control over their hired hands by discouraging anyone from inducing them to break their contracts after they had received any wages in advance. Lewis failed, however, to lower the price of convict labor. His votes on convict-lease issues were offset by ex-slave Alexander Asberry, a Republican from Calvert who also won election in 1888 as a state representative from Robertson County.[14]

Prendergast did not live long enough to see Lewis take his seat in the state legislature. He died in the fall of 1886 in Austin, where for the last six years he had been trying many cases, many of them on behalf of railroad companies, before the Texas Supreme Court or the old Commission of Appeals. He was nonetheless considered a resident of Robertson County. He was fifty-two years of age at his death and died intestate, even though he was a lawyer with seven children, some of whom were minors. His extensive real estate holdings made his probate proceeding complex. His probate file occupied five folders and exceeded in its bulk of papers any other nineteenth-century file among the extant Robertson County courthouse records. Thomas Simmons, the county judge who had appeared too young to Azeline to handle her lawsuit, administered Prendergast's estate. With the probate court's approval in May 1889, Simmons sold Prendergast's interest in the plantation to Lewis at a discounted price of $12 per acre, or $5,500 cash—an amount considerably under market value, since this consideration was just $1,000 more than Simmons declared the 451.5 acres to be worth to the tax assessor-collector. Because he had control over Prendergast's legal papers and correspondence, Simmons most likely was the individual who placed Lewis's letters—still in their original envelopes, with canceled stamps postdating Judge Wood's verdict against Azeline—in the district court files.[15]

14. L. E. Daniell, comp., *Personnel of the Texas State Government* (Austin, Tex.: Smith, Hicks & Jones, State Printers, 1889), pp. 289–90; Henry Lee Lewis to Harvey D. Prendergast, July 10, 1884, [Special File], *Asaline Hearne vs. H. D. Prendergast,* Case No. 3069, ODC, Robertson County, Texas; J. W. Baker, *A History of Robertson County, Texas* (Waco, Tex.: Printed by Texian Press, 1970), p. 275 (quotation); McCarver and McCarver, *Hearne on the Brazos,* p. 13; and Merline Pitre, *Through Many Dangers, Toils, and Snares: The Black Leadership of Texas, 1868–1900* (Austin, Tex.: Eakin Press, 1985), p. 74.

15. Re: Estate of H. D. Prendergast, Docket #553, PF, CCO, Robertson County, Texas;

In 1890, almost a year after Lewis acquired ownership of the entire Brazos River plantation, Hamman, at sixty years of age, was assassinated. In the late 1880s he had become one of the chief financial backers of the Cherokee Land and Iron Company, located just outside of the town of Rusk in East Texas. Hoping to mine and process iron ore, the company developed an entire new community named New Birmingham. By 1890 the town was connected by two railroads, possessed graded streets, and boasted one of the largest hotels in the state. At the moment when the foundry, town, and its investors seemed on the verge of fabulous success, a local grocery store merchant filed charges of slander against Hamman. The lawsuit, in which Hamman defended himself, was unpleasant. On July 14th the merchant stepped out of his store into the street and fired two shotgun blasts at close range at Hamman, killing him instantly. His body was taken back to Calvert, where his funeral was the largest ever witnessed in Robertson County. Hamman died not knowing that within three years the Cherokee Land and Iron Company would fail and New Birmingham would eventually become a ghost town. Also unknown to Hamman, who, like Prendergast, died intestate, was the extent of the enormous wealth he bequeathed to his children due to their inheritance of his many East Texas oil leases.[16]

Five years later, in the spring of 1895, Lewis, a forty-nine-year-old widower with five minor children, breathed his last breath. His large fortune in "real estate, stock, and bonds, together with a heavy life insurance" was left in the hands of three administrators, one of whom was Prendergast's son, Finis M. Prendergast. His two daughters inherited what was then often referred to as "the Puss Hearne place." The older received the north half, the younger the south half. The older daughter also inherited her father's "elegant and commodious residence" in the town of Hearne, not far from the house of her grandmother, Adeline Lewis. After the death of her brother Rasche Hearne the following year, Adeline was one of only two living survivors of the pioneering Louisiana generation of Hearnes and

---

and [Confirmation of the sale of the north half of the 903 acres to H. L. Lewis], in RE: Estate of H. D. Prendergast, Book "J," p. 178, Microfilm Reel #964219, PM, CCO, Robertson County, Texas.

16. "New Birmingham, Texas," *TNHT,* 4: 295–96; Ada Margaret Smith, "The Life and Times of William Harrison Hamman" (M.A. thesis, University of Texas, 1952), pp. 199–201; and Ed Kilman writing for the Houston *Post* in 1943 in "Commissions, Speeches, Letters, etc.," vol. 2, p.115, box AR29, William Harrison Hamman Papers, CAH-UT, Austin, Texas.

Lewises. The other was Nancy K. Hearne, the wife of Sam's brother Selby. Of the hundreds of adult slaves, including Azeline, whom the Hearnes and Lewises brought with them in the early 1850s, nothing is known of those still living at the end of the century.[17]

Circumstances Surrounding the Death of Azeline Hearne

A mere hint, but hardly conclusive proof, that Azeline was alive during the early 1890s is contained in a host of deeds written for Hamman's widow, Ella Virginia Hamman, to convey away her interest in her deceased father's lands in the Brazos Bottoms. In March 1890 George Laudermilk died, just four months before the murder of his son-in-law in New Birmingham. The deeds drafted in 1892 describe one of the land's boundaries as "the [northeast] corner of the Puss Hearne place at a stake set in the Hearne & Mumford Prairie Road." Had the author of the description of the land used the convention of stating "the *old* Puss Hearne place" to signify the demise or permanent departure of a landowner, then the deeds would most certainly have postdated Azeline's death or exodus from Robertson County. But the author did not do so—a fact leaving open the possibility that Azeline might still have been alive during the early 1890s.[18]

Had Azeline survived Hamman's death in 1890, she would have been sixty-five years of age and would have continued for the remainder of her life to be a tenant at will of the relatives of the Lewis family. Were she still residing in her dilapidated house—which unless repaired would have by then decayed to virtual rubble—she most likely would have been wandering from cabin to cabin in the Brazos Bottoms seeking work, food, and shelter from her cherished network of black friends and acquaintances. If she died on the Brazos River plantation or in the bottomlands, which was extremely likely, then her neighbors and companions would surely have buried her next to Sam. Yet there is no record or collective memory of when she died or where she was buried.

17. Hearne, *Brief History and Genealogy of the Hearne Family,* pp. 623–53 (first and third quotations on p. 646); and Deed from Ella V. Hamman to Jimmie I. Larkin, April 23, 1892 (second quotation), filed for record June 30, 1892, vol. 27, p. 74, Microfilm Reel #1477505, RD, CCO, Robertson County, Texas.

18. Deed from Ella V. Hamman to Jimmie I. Larkin, April 23, 1892 (quotation), and filed for record June 30, 1892, vol. 27, p. 74, Microfilm Reel #1477505, RD, CCO, Robertson County, Texas. See also copies of related deeds in box 12, folder 1, William Harrison Hamman Papers, WRC-RU, Houston, Texas.

Over a century later, on the site at the southeastern corner of the antebellum plantation where the old Sam Hearne manor house faced the Hearne-to-Mumford public road (present-day F.M. 50), a dirt road perpendicularly entered the property and, with acres of cotton growing to the north and west, made a left turn around an old log and barbed wire fence surrounding a neglected and overgrown area. Juxtaposed against the mowed lawns surrounding a couple of small modern houses built after the Second World War, the fenced-off spot remained an anomalous area that was probably the location of many burial sites, including the unmarked graves belonging to Sam and Azeline Hearne.

By the turn of the twenty-first century, all recollections of Azeline, along with the story of how she was cheated out of her sizable inheritance, were lost to history. The only words distantly touching on her life were spoken in the summer of 1999 by Norman McCarver Jr., an exceptionally knowledgeable Robertson County historian. His exact words were, "One of the Hearne brothers was crazy and he caused his relatives a lot of trouble." Questions regarding additional details about the specific identity of the alleged irrational brother, who had to have been Sam, were met with McCarver's admission of lack of further knowledge of the matter.[19]

Tracking down Azeline's sister's relatives has thus far proven to be an impossible task. Two black women with the surname Hearne and with close spelling variations of her first name are buried near each another in one of the oldest sections of Greater Riverside Cemetery. This part of the city of Hearne's large black graveyard contains few visible grave markers, and many of them are unreadable, having deteriorated with the passage of time. Commercially cut stones in this section are extremely rare; the professionally made marker on the grave of "Azeleaner Hearne" is thus an anomaly. The dates inscribed under her name reveal that she lived from 1865 to 1912. The 1910 census lists her as "Asalena Hearne" at the matching age of forty-four, and married to Jessie Hearne. She had given birth to fourteen children. Behind her grave to the right is a smaller and less conspicuous unadorned white marker with the name badly eroded,

19. Interview with Norman L. McCarver Jr. in Hearne, Texas, August 16, 1999. For many years the Collette family owned the part of the old Samuel R. Hearne plantation, where the original manor house was built in the early 1850s. The entire 903 acres, worth millions of dollars at the turn of the twenty-first century—a market value that includes the land's gas wells and water rights—has been in the possession of farmers and landowners of Italian-American descent since the middle of the twentieth century.

but a directory lists it as "Azalene Hearne," who was born in 1908 and died in 1973. At the turn of the twenty-first century, there was no collective remembrance of these two apparently related souls, but their names remain a testimony to memories of Azeline by subsequent generations of descendants of slaves owned by the Hearne and Lewis families.[20]

20. Tombstone of Azeleaner Hearne (b. Mar. 25, 1865–d. Mar. 20, 1912) in Greater Riverside Cemetery (first quotation), [Location: 30 51 42.5 N/96 35 53.5 W], Hearne, Texas; Bureau of the Census, *Thirteenth Census of the United States, 1910—Population,* Microfilm Reel #1585, Texas, Robertson County, Precinct #2, Enumeration District 106, May 3, 1910, Sheet #19, p. 19B (second quotation), T624, NA (1912–1914); and Verna Corn Floyd and Vernelle Corn, *Cemeteries in Robertson County, Texas* (n.p.: D. Armstrong Co., Inc., 1980), p. 192 (third quotation). The directory compiled by Floyd and Corn erroneously records Azeleaner's name as "Azele Anne" and lists the dates of her birth and death incorrectly as "5/23/1865–5/20/1912" (see: ibid.).

Conclusion

I went down to the polls and took my six-shooter. I stayed there until the polls closed. Not a [N]egro voted.

—O. D. Cannon quoted in Cantrell, *Kenneth and John B. Rayner*

Radical Republicans in the northern states at the end of the Civil War understood that enfranchisement, land, and education had to be secured for southern blacks before there could ever be hope for, in Massachusetts senator Charles Sumner's words, "a new order of things." Sumner's convictions reflected the dreams and aspirations of virtually all former slaves in the ex-Confederate South. If he and others of like mind were correct, then during the summer of 1867 in Galveston, ex-slaves Doctor Samuel Jones Hearne and his mother Azeline Hearne, in the words of later-day historian W. E. B. Du Bois, "stood a brief moment in the sun." Dock was enrolled in a school operated by the Freedmen's Bureau; he owned one of the finest cotton plantations in the American South; and having turned twenty-one years of age, he qualified to register to vote. Dock's father Samuel R. Hearne would have been pleased if he had lived to witness these revolutionary events. One can only imagine Sam's reaction had he been able to observe the promising, although also short-lived, ensuing years when the Republican-controlled Texas Supreme Court ruled that the Fourteenth Amendment abrogated the state law against interracial marriages.[1]

1. Charles Sumner quoted in *The Right Way* (Boston, Mass.), October 20, 1866; W. E. Burghardt Du Bois, *Black Reconstruction: An Essay toward a History of the Part Which Black*

Unfortunately, Dock and Azeline's summer interlude on the Texas Gulf Coast was the last tranquil and secure existence they ever enjoyed. That winter Dock died in the dreadful yellow fever epidemic, and a little over a year later a frivolous lawsuit to contest Azeline's title to the Brazos River plantation circumvented the U.S. Army's ban on litigating matters concerning Sam's estate. Freedmen's Bureau special agent Oscar F. Hunsaker, who had taken Dock and Azeline out of the Brazos Bottoms soon after the U.S. Congress took control of the process of Reconstruction, had predicted that unless Dock was represented by a capable attorney he would lose his entire inheritance. Hunsaker was correct, although subsequent events demonstrated that it would have taken more than just a good lawyer to prevent Azeline, who was Dock's sole inheritor under his father's will, from receiving anything other than counterfeit justice.[2]

The noble attempt after the Civil War to build a biracial democracy upon the ruins of slavery did not fail because of misguided notions in the minds of carpetbaggers, scalawags, and former slaves, who comprised the southern Republican Party constituencies. Nor was the period of emancipation and Republican Party dominance devoid of lasting accomplishments, but the hope of achieving genuine legal equality and economic justice was unattainable, not just for Azeline but also for all freedom's first generation and subsequent generations of African Texans as well. The elimination of prejudice against their race fell beyond the range of possibility. After years of slavery most Anglo Texans believed that God had made the descendants of black Africans an inherently inferior people and only through an illegitimate effort could earthly authorities artificially elevate them to full equality with the Caucasian race.

Even during the brief years of Republican Party control of the Texas state government, when the laws were modernized to be theoretically colorblind, intractable problems in the judicial system remained, such as how to

Folk Played in the Attempt to Reconstruct Democracy in America, 1860–1880 (New York: Russell & Russell, 1935), p. 30 (quotation); and Peter Wallenstein, *Tell the Court I Love My Wife: Race, Marriage, and Law—An American History* (New York: Palgrave Macmillan, 2002), pp. 81–93. For the relationship of the evolution of interracial marriage laws in the post–Civil War Deep South, including Texas, with the crystallization of Jim Crow segregation laws by the turn of the twentieth century, see Peter Wallenstein, "Reconstruction, Segregation, and Miscegenation: Interracial Marriage and the Law in the Lower South, 1865–1900," *American Nineteenth Century History* 6, no. 1 (March 2005): 57–76.

2. Oscar F. Hunsaker to Joel T. Kirkman, July 31, 1867, frame 343, Microfilm Reel #14, COCADT, RG 393, M1188, NA (1981).

eradicate unjust practices and create a mechanism to guarantee fairness. Because the North ultimately lacked the will to indemnify the freedmen with long-term protection from predatory lawyers, landowners, businessmen, swindlers, and Klansmen by using military-secured political institutions, it was not surprising that the civil courts presided over wholesale violations of Sam's stipulations in his last will and testament. What was remarkable, however, was that it took a full sixteen years to divest Azeline of her inheritance.

Upon the death of her son in 1868, Azeline had become the sole legatee of Sam's estate at a time when ex-slaves were commonly referred to as Mr. or Mrs. So-and-so's "freedman" or "freedwoman." But no control exercised by whites rendered Azeline anyone's "freedwoman"—a circumstance that in and by itself made her a target of vigilante gangs of "white brotherhoods" in the immediate postwar years. Exacerbating matters was her ownership of a magnificent antebellum cotton plantation, which ostensibly gave her unparalleled economic freedom. Most whites viewed freedwomen enjoying a life of extraordinary independent means as impossible, if not completely preposterous. Her wealth made her an obvious target for elites, who were far better equipped than roughs and rowdies to use the legal system to defraud her for years and eventually in 1884 to completely strip her of her interest in Sam's estate.[3]

An argument could be made that Azeline stood a better chance of achieving a semblance of justice and fair play in Robertson County than she would have in almost any other county in the state. Until the enactment in the early twentieth century of a state poll tax as a prerequisite for voting and the establishment of the white-only Democratic primary, Robertson County blacks courageously tried to influence local and state government at the ballot box. Their power to shape politics lasted almost thirty years, from 1868 until 1897. An entire generation either voted the straight Republican ticket or allied itself with groups of dissident whites who challenged Democratic rule. Coalitions with white voters in the 1870s and 1880s included Independents, Greenbackers, and Prohibitionists, and culminated in the 1890s with the volatile Populist crusade, which threatened to give Texas blacks a renewed toehold in the electoral balance of power at the state level of government. In addition, with the exceptions of attorney William H. Hamman and planter Henry Lee Lewis, major players in Azeline's life after her enslavement were Texas antisecessionists,

3. Entry on p. 122 (quotations), [February Term, 1867], CCM-PM, Robertson County, Texas.

transplanted northerners, and reluctant Confederates or men who, after the war, supported, collaborated with, or curried favor with the federal army, the Freedmen's Bureau, and Republican officeholders.

Although prewar unionism was a prime source of postwar Republicanism, in Robertson County it failed to lead to a predictable range of postwar partisanships or motivations. Sam Hearne's white relatives had been unwavering supporters of Sam Houston in the late antebellum period, but they became steadfast anti-Reconstruction Democrats during the immediate postwar period. Antisecessionist Ben Brown, who after the war served briefly as a gunman for the Freedmen's Bureau, maintained the labor stability desired by large Brazos Bottoms planters by waging vigilante reprisals on white brotherhood and Ku Klux Klan violence against blacks. But he was later imprisoned on murder charges by the U.S. Army. More in line with what might be expected were the careers of half-brothers Fidella and Frank Hall, who were members of a prominent unionist slaveholding family. They became influential scalawag Republican officeholders dedicated to implementing the franchise for the freedpeople and protecting them from white hostility. Attorney Harvey Prendergast, who at the war's end seemed satisfied that division had not prevailed and eagerly looked forward to resuming his legal practice, enjoyed early on the confidence of local Republican leaders and officials. Although Azeline herself ranked Prendergast as a villain higher than any other individual in her gloomy Dickensian tale of legal troubles and tribulations, the search for clear-cut heroes is discouraging.

New England carpetbagger Joshua L. Randall stands out as the top candidate for praise in dealing with the constant injustices perpetrated during the immediate postwar years against the newly freed slaves. He became the first Freedmen's Bureau agent in the county to win the trust of the overwhelming bulk of them. From April 1867 until January 1869, under dangerous circumstances, Captain Randall, as one student of Randall's career has noted, did "a magnificent job . . . certainly the best he could do." At one point Randall detailed how the understaffed bureau's goal of securing justice for Dock and Azeline had been compromised by the "corruption and malfeasance" of its subordinate officials. Yet he documented the bureau's shortcomings for anti-Reconstructionist Rasche Hearne, not for Azeline—a testament due less to any racial bias of his own than to his inability to craft postwar affairs just as he pleased. Any shred of hope for justice for Azeline would have required, at the very least, a prolonged presence of federal officers like him in Robertson County. After Randall closed up the Freedmen's Bureau office, the subsequent legal injustices that divested Azeline from her lawful inheritance made the bureau's financial mismanagement of Sam's estate in 1867 and 1868 appear by comparison a golden age for Azeline's hopes for judicial fairness.[4]

After the departure of the Freedmen's Bureau and federal troops, and without the sustained effort of local civil authorities to assure an honest administration of the law, Azeline was destined to sink into a judicial morass, where the odds of her receiving justice were virtually nil—a situation that characterized not only Robertson County but most of the ex-Confederate South once the federal government surrendered the authority it had possessed during Congressional Reconstruction. The unique circumstances of millions of newly freed slaves hoping for evenhanded and impartial treatment could have been secured by nothing short of long-term outside intervention. The overwhelmingly poor, landless, and uneducated beneficiaries of the equal protection clause of the Fourteenth Amendment were at a disadvantage, economically and socially, in avoiding all but the most dependent of relationships. Thrown into a market-driven society in which they were presumed to be incapable of sharing in the market's rewards, the best possible compromise seemed to be to give them no more than the opportunity to come and go as they pleased and reap the benefit of their own labor. Most whites viewed the entrepreneurial, legal, and property rights of former slaves as favors or special privileges and not matters guaranteed by either law or common sense.

Yet men with opposing views regarding the status of blacks in the postwar period were in firm control of the Robertson County government when the most egregious and far-reaching legal wrongs occurred to Azeline. It will never be known why local Republican officeholders permitted Hamman's baseless lawsuit to circumvent the Freedmen's Bureau's ban on litigating matters involving Sam's estate and win a fraudulently obtained default judgment for Cayton Erhard and other Reynolds heirs for the title to Azeline's Brazos River plantation. Any of the Republican-appointed officials, including most notably the clerk of the district court, the district attorney, or the district court judge, could have prevented it. Perhaps they chose to ignore her betrayal by former bureau agent Ben Brown,

4. Andrew J. Torget, "Carpetbagger on the Brazos: The Texas Freedmen's Bureau in Robertson County," *Agora: An Online Undergraduate Journal of the Humanities* 1, no. 2 (Winter 2000): 12 (first quotation); and [Unsigned Letter to Brevet Major General Joseph J. Reynolds], February 11, 1868 (second quotation), frames 0715–0721, Microfilm Reel #39, COCADT, RG 393, M1188, NA (1981).

whose posse assured their own safety and protection. Maybe they shared Brown's low opinion of Azeline, which stemmed from an acceptance of the Lewis and Hearne families' story regarding her relationship with Sam. Like many other Republican scalawags and carpetbaggers, they came to their positions with racially prejudiced notions of their own. Their reluctance to sustain her claims to an amount of wealth far greater than what they themselves possessed would have been more understandable if they believed that Azeline, as Sam's slave mistress, had been a seductive and manipulative "Jezebel" responsible for his miscegenation, alcoholism, and embarrassing last will and testament. Given their overriding problem of stemming pervasive white depredations and cruelties against the freedpeople, the judicial marginalization of Azeline might not have troubled them at all.[5]

The most complex character in Azeline's story was Hamman. In the late 1860s and 1870s, he was an anti-Reconstruction Democrat and one of her chief antagonists. By the 1880s, however, he evolved into her most capable advocate and foremost supporter. By then he was, admittedly, unraveling injustices caused in large part by his earlier legal shenanigans and wrongdoing. Yet to his credit Hamman progressed from a bitter ex-Confederate soldier possessing coldhearted notions about blacks to an anti-Democratic politician energetically campaigning for black votes as a two-time Greenback candidate for the Texas governorship. Until Azeline hired him to be her lawyer, she was never advised of the true condition of her inherited estate, nor of her rights as its beneficiary, and had remained ignorant of the implications of the legal papers and conveyances that either she signed or her agents executed in her name. But for Hamman's enterprising lawsuit on her behalf against Prendergast and H. L. Lewis, the story of how she was defrauded by rapacious attorneys, bungling judges, and unresponsive or incompetent officials would not have been preserved in the files of the Robertson County courthouse records.

Among the other dramatis personae were individuals who performed individual brave acts or extraordinary services on Azeline's behalf but failed to follow up, and thus inevitably let her down. For example, but for Dr. Jeremiah Collins heroically filing Sam Hearne's last will and testament for record with the probate court, his wealthy brothers and cousins would never have been required to deal with his estate through the court system

5. For a discussion of "Jezebel" and "Mammy" stereotypes, see Deborah Gray White, *Ar'n't I a Woman? Female Slaves in the Plantation South* (rev. ed., New York: W. W. Norton & Company, 1999), chap. 1, pp. 27–61.

and his final wishes would have stayed buried with him. Yet Dr. Collins refused to accept Sam's request to be appointed administrator of his estate. If Hunsaker, acting on the authority of the U.S. Army, had not commanded Robertson County officials to suspend all litigation involving Sam's estate, then jury nullification in any trial contesting the validity of Sam's will would have been assured during the immediate postwar years. Yet Hunsaker, acting as Dock's attorney, never took the proper steps to settle Sam's estate, or to open an administration on Dock's considerable inherited estate, or to defend Azeline's new position as Dock's sole heir.

The Reverend Richard Sloan was a kindhearted and elderly preacher who became a carpetbagger Republican appointee to the Brazos County Commissioners' Court, but he permanently injured Azeline's interests through his ineffectiveness and senility. After Sloan's mishandling of her affairs, no one other than Prendergast could be found to take over the unfinished administration of Sam's estate from the discredited and incarcerated Brown. The probate court's approval of Prendergast exposed the limited number of persons who were either competent, able to find sureties to qualify, or willing to take on the responsibilities of Sam's executor. Azeline subsequently became nothing more than a bothersome obstacle in the way of Prendergast and his accomplices' prolonged fraud. Plantation manager Buck Watts, who was one of her so-called tenants and thus benefited financially throughout the 1870s from his collusion with Prendergast, reached a point in the late 1870s when he could no longer participate in the perennial fleecing of her and Sam's estate. By then, however, Azeline fully understood the extent to which Prendergast had managed the estate to the exclusion of her interests.

Azeline's most determined and daring act was triggered by Prendergast's complicity with the Lewis family to divest her of every last penny in Sam's estate. Against a backdrop of deteriorating race relations—ranging from shortchanging of sharecroppers to trumped-up debt peonage, and from working black convicts to their deaths on prison farms to tossing black women refusing to leave the "ladies coach" from slowly moving departing trains—Azeline sued Prendergast, her own lawyer and fiduciary, rather than allow him to buy out at a discount whatever remaining rights she had left to the Brazos River plantation. In doing so, she turned her back on compensation from Lewis that would have placed her in a far more secure financial position than most southern black women could have ever hoped to enjoy. Respected local black leaders advised her to accept Prendergast and Lewis's offers, which gradually increased in the value tendered as the trial date approached. But she refused. By taking a principled stand and challenging the long-standing vulnerability faced by black women in a patently white racist patriarchal society, Azeline won the enduring admiration of her network of friends and neighbors in the Brazos Bottoms.[6]

Although the existence of a viable local political opposition to the Democrats might have given Azeline a greater chance at achieving justice than someplace where restoration of white supremacy rapidly occurred (in 1874, with Richard Coke's accession to the governorship), nothing could immunize Robertson County from the hardening racial oppression and pervasive cruelty against blacks that characterized East Texas throughout the second half of the nineteenth century. Had Azeline lived into the late 1880s, she would have known every detail of the infamous killing of ex-slave Harriel Geiger, whom voters had twice sent to the Texas House of Representatives, first as a Greenbacker in 1878 and then as a Republican in a special election in 1881.

While in Austin, Geiger had obtained a license to practice law. Despite overcoming years of no education, uncompensated labor, and blindness in one eye, his refusal to kowtow to informal white rules for acceptable black behavior, combined with his success as a blacksmith, politician, and lawyer, resulted only in infuriating the vast majority of whites. Back home in Robertson County in 1886, while defending prostitutes against charges of vagrancy, he made a supposedly disrespectful remark to O. D. Cannon, a prominent Hearne attorney. In retaliation, Cannon "calmly raised his revolver and put five bullets into Geiger." His failure to imprint his supposed inferiority into his mind was etched into his body by bullets. At Cannon's trial whites on the jury ignored the law and the facts and set him free. Jury trials subsequently acquitted him of charges of murdering two other men. In 1899 he killed a fourth man and received a sentence of life in prison in the state penitentiary. By then, however, Cannon had made his name synonymous with, in the words of turn-of-the-century white supremacists, "the end of Negro rule in Robertson County."[7]

6. Merline Pitre, *Through Many Dangers, Toils, and Snares: The Black Leadership of Texas, 1868–1900* (Austin, Tex.: Eakin Press, 1985), pp. 130–51, and 225, n. 33 (quotation).

7. Pitre, *Though Many Dangers,* p. 58; Gregg Cantrell, *Kenneth and John B. Rayner and the Limits of Southern Dissent* (Urbana: University of Illinois Press, 1993), p. 239 (first quotation); Dallas *Morning News,* May 19, 1886, p. 3; and Scott Field quoted in Richard Denny Parker, *Historical Recollections of Robertson County, Texas, with Biographical & Genealogical Notes on the Pioneers & Their Families* (Salado, Tex.: Anson Jones Press, 1955), p. 49 (second quotation).

The termination of black officeholding, and thus what contemporaries of the period referred to as the "end to reconstruction," occurred during the presidential election of 1896—one of the most acrimonious elections ever in Texas political history. Facing likely defeat of their ticket in a fair and free election, Robertson County Democrats realized that only "severe measures" would "assure the election of white people to office." According to popular legend, Cannon, then serving as the Democratic county judge and having just been acquitted of taking payoffs from lawyers to dismiss cases, orchestrated the "concerted effort" throughout the county that "restored white supremacy." At the courthouse in Franklin, forty men with Winchester rifles allegedly turned away all but Democratic voters. At another rural precinct, "a masked man" stole the ballot box and the voting returns from the presiding election official. And at yet another precinct, the Democratic candidates for sheriff and for tax collector, "one with a gun and the other with a club," kept blacks from voting. Blacks from the Hearne Bottoms, who had fallen into line behind a brass band moving toward the city of Hearne to vote, were met at the Little Brazos Bridge by an armed and mounted group of Democrats, who dispersed the blacks and tossed their musical instruments into the river. When they finally arrived in Hearne, "a great number of pistol shots were fired in front of the polls." Yet by midafternoon, word got to Judge Cannon that despite the countywide voter fraud and intimidation, the outcome still hung in the balance. Cannon himself later recalled: "I went down to the polls and took my six-shooter. I stayed there until the polls closed. Not a [N]egro voted."[8]

Had Cannon's boast that he had personally "stood off a thousand blacks" been true, there would have been no need to defraud ex-slave Alexander Asberry of his election to a second term in the Texas House of Representatives. When Asberry, running on the Populist-Republican fusion ticket, learned that he had been deliberately "counted out," he threatened to contest the election. The hot-tempered Cannon tracked Asberry down in a Franklin saloon and shot him in the arm. Legend arose that the wounded Asberry took off running so fast for Calvert that even blood-

8. Pitre, *Through Many Dangers,* p. 150; Norman L. McCarver and Norman L. McCarver Jr., *Hearne on the Brazos* (San Antonio: Century Press of Texas, 1958), p. 27 (first, fourth, and fifth quotations); Lawrence Ward St. Clair, "History of Robertson County, Texas" (M.A. thesis, University of Texas, 1931), p. 154 (second and third quotations); Parker, *Historical Recollections of Robertson County,* pp. 48–49; and Cantrell, *Kenneth and John B. Rayner,* p. 240 (sixth, seventh, eighth, and ninth quotations).

hounds playfully turned loose on him never caught up with him. When another black candidate, Jesse S. Smith, easily won election in the Calvert precinct to a seat on the county commissioners' court, he declined to face Judge Cannon at the scheduled administering of his oath of office. It was Smith's only option, because Democrats brandishing rifles to discourage him from taking office awaited his arrival at the courthouse. Embellishments of these events incorrectly hold that after 1896 Robertson County blacks "remained away from the polls." Although blacks continued until 1904 to vote in substantial numbers, albeit at separate presidential ballot boxes, their influence in shaping the outcome of any state, district, or county election had been eliminated. In the early twentieth century, the triple impact of physical violence and intimidation, poll taxes, and white-only primaries disfranchised, immobilized, and dishonored them for a subsequent sixty years.[9]

In spite of the legends of Cannon's deadly transgressions, his malicious deeds alone did not typify the unsteady and slow manner in which Reconstruction in Robertson County inextricably ground to a halt and was ultimately eradicated. The undermining of attempts to assure basic justice to former slaves began in the summer of 1865, when they were assembled by federal soldiers moving from plantation to plantation through the Brazos bottomlands and told of their emancipation. Between that moment and the turn of the century, a combination of old habits, racist doctrines, economic coercion, and extraordinary cruelty persistently thwarted the national interest to transform southern society. The conventional forces even penetrated the two key groups, the Freedmen's Bureau and the Republican Party, that were in the vanguard of promoting change. Far too much of what had been before the war existed after it—a situation that generated the collapse of radical Reconstruction in the state at large, but especially in Robertson County. An enduring antebellum social and economic system that had been untouched by the direct path of the war and augmented by a postwar prosperity sparked by the arrival of the railroad, supplied the forces of reaction and racism with means to cope with

9. Cantrell, *Kenneth and John B. Rayner,* p. 240 (first quotation); and J. W. Baker, *A History of Robertson County, Texas* (Waco, Tex.: Printed by Texian Press, 1970), pp. 164 (second quotation) and 165 (third quotation). Asberry was one of the last of forty-two black Reconstruction-era legislators. The very last one was Robert L. Smith of Colorado County, who in 1897 gave an emotional speech in support of a resolution against lynching. See: "African Americans and Politics," *TNHT,* 1: 51–55.

and stand firm against the revolutionary changes that radical Republicans sought to impose.[10]

The nature of the paralyzing cultural inertia in Robertson County that so effectively established a postemancipation regime of white domination and black subordination was evidenced a century later, when misconceptions of what actually occurred during the era were still deeply entrenched in the community's historical psyche. Interpretations of Robertson County history written prior to the civil rights movement of the 1960s and 1970s by local residents, reared on long-held convictions about the causes of the Civil War and legends of carpetbagger misrule, lasted way beyond the segregationist and discriminatory structures that redeemer mythology established. At the turn of the twenty-first century, the majority of the luncheon clientele at Hearne's landmark Dixie Café, decked out with unfurled Confederate battle flags, agreed that one of the most important historical truths about "The War Between the States" was that its underlying cause was not to sustain slavery: "The South[erners] fought to protect their rights and to be free to decide things for themselves." A historical marker in Calvert's Virginia Field Park enshrined an accepted belief in the unprovoked punishment of "Southern sympathizers" by occupying federal troops. An oft-quoted local history fed a related myth that during Reconstruction the "Ku Klux Klan" was "the only way a white southerner could combat the dictatorial measures of Radical Republican government and the swarm of politicians who came south"—a contention that staffers at the *Hearne Democrat* newspaper office accepted as an indisputable, albeit regrettable, truth.[11]

One hundred forty years after the Civil War, and more than forty years

10. The contention that, in Texas, the antebellum social structure and infrastructure was only shaken but not destroyed by the Civil War and thus afterward made opposition to change greater than elsewhere in the ex-Confederate states is presented in Carl H. Moneyhon, *Texas after the Civil War: The Struggle of Reconstruction* (College Station: Texas A&M University Press, 2004).

11. [Lunchtime conversations between the author and anonymous patrons], Dixie Café, 708 South Market Street, Hearne, Texas, August 16, 1999 (first and second quotations); Interview with Gracia Thibodeaux in the office of the *Hearne Democrat,* 120 West Third Street, Hearne, Texas, June 3, 1999; "Virginia Field Park" (third quotation), [Official Texas Historical Marker (est. 1969)] located facing East Burnett Street between Pin Oak and Maple Streets, Calvert, Texas; and McCarver and McCarver, *Hearne on the Brazos,* p. 25 (fourth and fifth quotations). The Virginia Field Park marker reads: "Was Site during Reconstruction, 1868–1873, of 'Sky Parlor' (Room Built on Pole, as a Tree House) to Serve as Prison for Southern Sympathizers." Although after the war a small contingent of U.S. soldiers encamped in the park, the jail room built off the ground on poles was located in Bryan, not in Calvert. See: Glenna Four-

removed from the days of Jim Crow, the overwhelming majority of white residents in Robertson County consisted of men and women as polite, generous, and compassionate as any on earth, but the staying power among them of long-discredited falsehoods and myths about the Civil War and Reconstruction and the extraordinary level of denial that a belief in them required were unpardonable, given the unspeakable inhumanity of the slave system and the heartbreaking amount of violence and injustice perpetrated upon generations of blacks after their emancipation. Yet by choice and by necessity, Robertson County, given its multiethnic population, was slowly atoning for its nefarious past. Closure to a long-standing racial insensitivity made regional news in 2002, when "Mojo," an otherwise nameless young black man whose mummified corpse served for eighty years as a freakish display for poker and domino games in a back room of a Calvert funeral parlor, was, fittingly on Juneteenth, laid to rest with a proper burial. Nevertheless, at the time of Mojo's funeral, no grand recognition had been made regarding how profoundly a system of inhuman racial and chattel slavery saturated the soil of Robertson County and that enduring problems of racial acrimony, cultural division, and economic disparity inevitably flowed from this great sin.[12]

Freedmen and freedwomen undeniably made their own history, but they did not make it under conditions chosen by themselves. Their choices were limited. Azeline's attempt to secure justice occurred in the context of the unwavering determination by whites to curtail basic property rights of blacks as well as to emasculate their political and civil rights. Subsequent decades of moral and physical courage on the part of Robertson County blacks were required for them to win recognition of their fundamental constitutional rights in the courtrooms of their local government. It was a tragedy that such a state of affairs existed not only in Robertson County but also throughout most of the ex-Confederate South. It was also regrettable that the story of Azeline's life and her place in local African American history were lost, pilfered, and betrayed for over a century by later-day writers who mingled folklore with bigotry to distort what occurred during Reconstruction.

The tribulations of Robertson County blacks after the Civil War, in-

---

man Brundidge, *Brazos County History: Rich Past—Bright Future* (Bryan, Tex.: Family History Foundation, 1986), p. 29.

12. "Calvert to Join, Say Bye to Mojo," *The Eagle* (Bryan–College Station), June 19, 2002, p. 1 and 6; and *The Daily Texan* (Austin), June 20, 2002.

cluding the stories of those killed outright, beaten, or raped and those broken in spirit by decades of imposed peonage, legal and economic injustices, and daily humiliations, deserve to be told honestly and forthrightly—a task that entails the story of the complicity of many pillars of the community in sustaining the brutality and indignities that for generations devastated and demolished the property, bodies, and minds of African Texans. If the mockeries of justice and agonizing hardships brought about by years of omnipresent and unyielding persecution and oppression are left unacknowledged, then the ability to see racism in the future will remain obstructed and whites will continue to scapegoat blacks by blaming them for crime, welfare abuses, and other social problems. If the violation of a people and their history is the worst crime of all, then the next worse transgression is not to remember. Robertson County forgot about Azeline Hearne, but the real calamity would be if she and others like her who struggled bravely, yet suffered terribly, on their long walk to freedom were forgotten a second time.

Appendix

Timeline of Major Legal Events

1866

November 28th Dr. Collins deposits S.R.H.'s will in the Robertson County Probate Court but takes no further action.

November 30th George Washington Hearne and Horatio R. Hearne apply to be appointed coadministrators of S.R.H.'s estate *pro tem.*

December 18th J. W. Cunningham applies to be appointed administrator of S.R.H.'s estate *with the will annexed.*

1867

January 11th Cunningham is appointed administrator of S.R.H.'s estate *with the will annexed.*

February 23rd Lorenzo Hearne is appointed administrator of S.R.H.'s estate, *pendente lite.*

July 15th The Freedmen's Bureau prohibits any further action in the civil courts in regard to issues involved in settling the S.R.H. estate and takes over its administration.

1868

June 18th Ben Brown is appointed as administrator of S.R.H.'s estate, *with the will annexed.*

Shortly after October 15th Default judgment entered against A.H. in Aycock's lawsuit against her to recover his attorney's fees is stricken from the district court record.

1869

Early January Captain Randall shuts down the Freedmen's Bureau office in Robertson County.

April 16th A default judgment for Cayton Erhard and other Reynolds heirs against A.H. for the title to the Brazos River plantation is fraudulently obtained in the Robertson County District Court.

Shortly after June 25th Ben Brown is arrested by military authorities for the murder of Dr. Maxwell.

July 22nd A.H. signs a contingency-fee agreement with Harvey Prendergast to set aside the April 16th default judgment against her in the Erhard case.

September 27th A.H. grants a power of attorney to Reverend Richard Sloan.

October 8th A.H. revokes any previous power of attorney granted to Ben Brown, signs a second power of attorney to Sloan, and hires the law firm of Hollingsworth and Broaddus to recover the rents owed to her by Israel S. Campbell and Jim Wade.

October 15th Hollingsworth and Broaddus file a petition to military authorities requesting their assistance to help A.H. recover the rents owed her by Campbell and Wade.

October 18th Prendergast files for record his July 22nd agreement with A.H. that allows him to be in immediate possession of the southern half of her plantation and own the current rents accruing to it.

Mid-October The U.S. Supreme Court rejects Ben Brown's petition for a writ of habeas corpus and for release from imprisonment by military authorities.

October 22nd & 23rd Hamman posts bonds that hoodwink military authorities into allowing him to take control of the crops on A.H.'s plantation.

November 10th–11th The army reverses its position on Hamman's bonds and executes the original distress warrant requested on October 15th by Hollingsworth and Broaddus.

November 30th–December 3rd The four-day balloting in the 1869 gubernatorial election results in the gubernatorial victory of radical Republican Edmund J. Davis.

1870

January 4th Acting as A.H.'s attorney, Sloan conveys her entire plantation to Frank Hall for about $1,200, some goods out of his store, and some land adjacent to Bryan's "Freedman Town." Title to the land is conveyed to A.H. by Hall's brother, W. N. Hall.

January 6th Deed from A.H. to Frank Hall is recorded in Robertson County. A.H. signs an additional agreement acknowledging him as the owner of the Brazos River plantation and herself as a tenant at will.

January 9th A.H.'s revocation of power of attorney to Ben Brown and her second power of attorney to Sloan are filed for record in Robertson County.

January 25th A.H. revokes her power of attorney to Sloan.

February 4th A.H.'s January 25th revocation of her power of attorney to Sloan is filed for record in Robertson County.

March 14th The Texas Supreme Court rules in favor of A.H. in its reversal of the district court's ruling in the Cayton Erhard case.

March 24th Civil officers of Brazos County request military authorities to remove Sloan as county commissioner for malfeasance in office.

March 30th A.H.'s first power of attorney to Sloan is filed for record in Brazos County.

July 15th Acting without A.H.'s authorization, Sloan sells her land adjacent to Bryan's "Freedman Town" to Mary Moore.

1871

February 28th Prendergast applies to be administrator *de bonis non* of S.R.H.'s estate and subsequently makes Buck Watts the manager of the Brazos River plantation.

March 14th The worthless deed from A.H. to Mary Moore is filed for record in Brazos County.

April 12th Sloan fraudulently sells A.H.'s land adjacent to Bryan's "Freedman Town" to a another buyer named Burkhalter.

June 30th Mary Moore and her husband sell their worthless claim to A.H.'s land in Bryan's "Freedman Town" to Burkhalter.

1872

January 26th Frank Hall sues A.H., Prendergast, and Watts, alleging that the control of the Brazos River plantation by the latter two is designed to convert the income produced by it to their own use.

June 4th Petition of Ben Brown to replace Prendergast as administrator of S.R.H.'s estate is denied.

August 26th Hamman revives his case against A.H. on behalf of the Reynolds heirs.

1873

March 3rd Hamman objects to Prendergast's trying to make himself a party to the Hall suit in a different role than as administrator of S.R.H.'s estate.

July 2nd Perjury charges against A.H. stemming from contradictory answers to interrogatories in the Hall case are dropped by the district attorney.

1874

January 26th The following deeds involving A.H.'s land adjacent to Bryan's "Freedman Town" are filed for record in Brazos County: from W. H. Hall to A.H. and from Mary Moore and her husband to Burkhalter.

January 30th Burkhalter sells his worthless claim to A.H.'s land in Bryan's "Freedman Town" to C. F. Moore.

March 9th The deed from Burkhalter to C. F. Moore is filed for record in Brazos County.

March 13th C. F. Moore sells his worthless claim to A.H.'s land in Bryan's "Freedman Town" to Bryan Real Estate and Building Association.

June 20th Jury verdicts in the Hall case give Prendergast ownership of the south half and Hall ownership of the north half of the Brazos River plantation. The court orders Prendergast to retain possession of the entire plantation for the purposes of administrating S.R.H.'s estate.

September 21st Hamman appeals the verdict for A.H. in the second Erhard case to the Texas Supreme Court.

1875

June 18th Aycock loses his case in the district court against A.H. to recover his attorney's fees.

July 1st Watts sues A.H. for $937 to recover money that he allegedly lent to her.

1876

April 14th Deed from C. F. Moore to Bryan Real Estate and Building Association is filed for record in Brazos County. C. F. Moore's successful laundering of the title to A.H.'s land adjacent to Bryan's "Freedman Town" is completed.

June 28th Prendergast is awarded a default judgment against A.H. for $672.

December 22nd Prendergast obtains execution on his judgment against A.H. for $672.

1877

June 22nd Texas Supreme Court rules in favor of A.H. in the second Erhard case, which Hamman brought against her on behalf of the Reynolds heirs.

1878

January 7th Watts makes a demand to Prendergast to close the administration on S.R.H.'s estate.

1879

Fall and Winter Hundreds of Robertson County blacks leave for Kansas in the "Exoduster" movement and H. L. Lewis buys the claim of Hall currently on appeal to the Texas Supreme Court.

1880

March H. L. Lewis offers to pay A.H. $10 a month for the rest of her life in exchange for her relinquishing all her claims to the Brazos River plantation.

May Prendergast dismisses the Hall appeal.

1881

April 2nd A.H. hires Hamman to maintain her rights to the title and interest in the Brazos River plantation and to all the revenues adhering to it.

December 22nd A.H. sues Prendergast merging multiple claims, including attorney malpractice, fraud, keeping property from its rightful owner, breach of fiduciary duty, failure to render legally required accountings, as well as trespass to try title.

1882

February 7th Hamman joins H. L. Lewis as a defendant to A.H.'s suit against Prendergast.

May 18th Champe Carter files application to have land owned by S.R.H. in Limestone and Young Counties deeded to him.

June 22nd Watts petitions to be relieved as a surety on Prendergast's bond as administrator of S.R.H.'s estate.

November 16th A.H. gives a sworn deposition in her case against Prendergast.

December 9th The commission of appeals of the Texas Supreme Court upholds the verdict for A.H. in the Aycock case.

1883

June 14th Hamman and Prendergast agree to have A.H.'s suit against Prendergast and H. L. Lewis tried before Judge W. D. Wood.

December 1st Agreement is made between Prendergast and H. L. Lewis to the effect that if any part of the Brazos River plantation is lost to A.H. then they agree on how to equally share the loss.

1884

February 20th Judge W. D. Wood renders a verdict for Prendergast and H. L. Lewis. A.H. gives notice of her appeal to the Texas Supreme Court.

March 14th A.H. appears before a notary public and swears she cannot pay the cost of her appeal.

May 9th Letter from H. L. Lewis to Prendergast suggests they get a full release from A.H. to the lands in Limestone and Young Counties.

May 22nd A.H.'s appeal to the Texas Supreme Court is dismissed on a technicality and her lawsuit against Prendergast comes to an end.

1885

January 29th Letter from H. L. Lewis to Prendergast reports John R. Hearne's threat to bring suit to reclaim the Brazos River plantation.

1889

March 6th H. L. Lewis buys the south half of the Brazos River plantation from Prendergast's estate. H. L. Lewis becomes its sole owner.

Bibliography

PRIMARY MATERIALS

Manuscript Collections

Federal Documents

Washington, D.C.

• The National Archives

Bureau of the Census. *Population Schedules of the Seventh Census of the United States, 1850*. M432 (1963).

Bureau of the Census. *Eighth Census of the United States, 1860*. Agricultural Census, Production of Agriculture, "Schedule 4" M653 (1967).

Bureau of the Census. *Population Schedules of the Eighth Census of the United States, 1860*. M653 (1967).

Bureau of the Census. *Population Schedules of the Ninth Census of the United States, 1870*. M593 (1965).

Bureau of the Census. *The 1880 Robertson County, Texas, Census* [containing 467 pages (census images) in Enumeration Districts 139 through 148]. www.rootsweb.com/~usgenweb/tx/robertson/census/1880/0000read.htm (accessed Jan. 10, 2004).

Bureau of the Census. *Thirteenth Census of the United States, 1910—Population*. T624 (1912–1914).

Records of the Adjutant General's Office, 1780s–1917. Case Files of Applications from Former Confederates for Presidential Pardons ("Amnesty Papers")

1865–1867. Group I: Pardon Applications Submitted by Persons From the South. Record Group 94. M1003 (1977).

Records of the Bureau of Refugees, Freedmen, and Abandoned Lands. Records of the Assistant Commissioner for the State of Texas, Bureau of Refugees, Freedmen, and Abandoned Lands, 1865–1869. Record Group 105. M821 (1973).

Records of the Bureau of Refugees, Freedmen, and Abandoned Lands. Records of the Assistant Commissioner for the State of Texas, Bureau of Refugees, Freedmen, and Abandoned Lands, 1865–1869. "Subassistant Commissioner Records filed under 'Sterling, Texas.'" [Unmicrofilmed]. Record Group 105.

Records of the Bureau of Refugees, Freedmen, and Abandoned Lands. Records of the Superintendent of Education for the State of Texas, 1865–1870. Record Group 105. M822 (1973).

Records of the U.S. Army Continental Commands, 1821–1920. Correspondence of the Office of Civil Affairs of the District of Texas, the 5th Military District, and the Department of Texas, 1867–1870. Record Group 393. M1188 (1981).

War Department. *Index to Compiled Service Records of Confederate Soldiers Who Served in Organizations from the State of Texas.* Record Group 109. M227 (1955).

Texas State Papers

Austin, Texas

• Texas State Library, Archives Division

"Brief for the appellant filed by Ballinger, Jack, and Mott," March 9, 1870. *Asaline Hearne vs. Cayton Erhard and others.* Case file M-5761. Texas Supreme Court Records. RG 201.

County Real and Personal Tax Rolls. [Microfilm]. Records of the Comptroller of Public Accounts. Ad Valorem Tax Division.

Governors' Papers and Records, Record Group 301

Richard Coke
Edmund J. Davis
Andrew Jackson Hamilton
Elisha M. Pease

Manuscript Election Returns. Secretary of State Records. RG 307.

Registers of Elected and Appointed State and County Officials, 1860–1885. Secretary of State Records. RG 307.

Texas Confederate Military Service Records. [Microform]. Compiled from muster rolls in the Texas State Archives, 1999.

Voter Registration Lists, 1867–1869. [Microfilm].

Brazos, Robertson and Galveston County Records

Bryan, Texas

• County Commissioners Court

Commissioners Minutes, Book "A."

• County Clerk's Office.

Record of Deeds, Books "H," "I," "K," "L," "M," "N," "O," and "Q."

Vital Statistics. *Marriage Records,* Book "B."

• Office of the District Clerk

District Court Record Books. *Civil Minutes of the District Court,* Books "C" and "E."

Franklin, Texas

• County Commissioners Court

Commissioners Court Minutes, October 1, 1842–June 1, 1871, May Term 1873–. 14 vols. (BC, D1, C, 2, 3, A–I).

Commissioners Court Minutes/Police Minutes, November 16, 1863–June 1, 1871, 1 volume.

• County Clerk's Office

Deeds-Transcribed 1838–1901. [Books "M," "N," "P," "Q," and "V" and Books "7" and "27"]

General Index to Deeds (Reverse), 1838-1901 [Book "L&M"]

General Index to Probate Minutes, 1838–1928. 2 volumes.

Index to Probate Cases No. 198 [April 30, 1838–September 1, 1939].

Official Bond Record. 1838–1842, January 28, 1850–June 1, 1870, December 6, 1876–July 12, 1887, November 14, 1900–. 6 volumes [1, two unlabeled, C–E].

Probate File, 1838–1897. [Case papers filed in probate cases in county court].

Probate Minutes, 1838–1909. 36 vols. [A, C–M, O, Q–T, V, W, I, J, M, 1–14].

Records of the County Court, Book "B."

Robertson County Tax Rolls, 1838–1910.

Transcript Synopsis of A–P Records Relating to Robertson County "Families" 1838–[?]. [Microfilm Reel # 964224].

• Office of the District Clerk

Civil [and Criminal] Cases Disposed Of. June 26, 1843–. [Papers filed in civil cases instituted originally and by appeal in district court].

Dora Anschicks vs. Conrad Anschicks, Case No. 3193

Thomas P. Aycock vs. Asaline Hearne, Case No. 1113

William H. Cundiff vs. Dred Dawson , et al., Case No. 594

Britton Dawson vs. William C. Duffield & Wife, Case No. 346

P. C. Dechard vs. Assaline Dechard, Case No. 2027

George Dunn vs. H. D. Prendergast, Adm'r S. R. Hearne dec'd, Case No. 1582

F. M. Hall vs. Assaline Hearne, Case No. 1639

A. L. Hearne, et al. vs. J. W. Cunningham, Administrator, Case No. 978

Asaline Hearne vs. H. D. Prendergast, Case No. 3069

G. W. Hearne vs. Charles Lewis, Case No. 2077

Horatio R. Hearne vs. Mary Ellen Hearne, Ex[ecu]t[or], Case No. 1312

John R. Hearne vs. Henry L. Lewis, Case No. 3110

S. P. Hollingsworth and A. S. Broaddus vs. Asaline Hearne, Case No. 1402

John E. Houghton vs. John S. Moore, Case No. 1860

Charles Lewis and H. L. Lewis vs. S. W. Hearne, Case No. 2703

B. Nichols & Co. vs. S. R. Hearne, Case No. 930

S. R. Perry, Adm[inist]r[ator] of J. S. B. Deveraux, vs. S. R. Hearne, Case No. 905

H. D. Prendergast vs. Asaline Hearne, Case No. 2544

The Heirs of Allen Reynolds vs. Britton Dawson, Case No. 180

William M. Rice vs. Samuel R. Hearne, Case No. 971 and [renumbered] Case No. 791

Jonathan Smith vs. J. W. Griffin and S. R. Hearne, Case No. 854

The State of Texas vs. Conrad Anschicks, Cases Nos. 622, 834, 673, 674, 695, 714, 717, 880, 834, and 1136

The State of Texas vs. Ben Brown and B. F. Hammond, Case No. 661

The State of Texas vs. M. Conley [sic], Case No. 659

The State of Texas vs. B. Cooksey, Case No. 471

The State of Texas vs. F. M. Hall, Case No. 1264

The State of Texas vs. F. M. Hall, B. F. Hammond, Ben Brown, et al., Case No. 2195

The State of Texas vs. James G. Halloway, Case No. 521

The State of Texas vs. John R. Harlan, Case No. 494

The State of Texas vs. Assaline Hearne, Case No. 832

The State of Texas vs. Columbus [sic] C. Hearne, Case No. 236

The State of Texas vs. Samuel R. Hearne, Case No. 443
The State of Texas vs. Telephus A. Johnson, Cases Nos. 213, 215, 234, and 401
The State of Texas vs. Hiram Nixon, Case No. 470
The State of Texas: Ex. Rel. D. W. White, et al. vs. P. W. Hall, Co. Judge of Robertson County, Case No. 2855
The State of Texas vs. Marks Wilson, Cases Nos. 617, 624, 625, 626, 627, 628, 642, 643, 644, 645, 646, 647, 648, 649, 651, 757
W. W. Watts vs. Asaline Hearne, Case No. 2063
Eliza Cornelia Willett (Reynolds) vs. Charles Lewis, et al., Case No. 662

Minutes of the District Court. June 24, 1844–September 29, 1859. 4 volumes (D, 1 unlabeled, A, H). October 1, 1838–. 20 volumes (1 unlabeled, C, 1 unlabeled, I–U, W–Z). October 23, 1843–Spring Term 1880, 10 volumes.

Galveston, Texas
• Galveston Health Department.
"Interment Record, 1866–1881." [Microfilm]. Rosenberg Library.

Personal Papers

Arlington, Texas
• The University of Texas at Arlington Libraries, Special Collections Division.
George Antonio Nixon Collection, 1799–1917

Austin, Texas
• Center for American History, The University of Texas at Austin
Josephus Cavitt Papers
Benjamin H. Epperson Papers
James Madison Hall Papers
William H. Hamman Papers
James W. Throckmorton Papers and Letter Book

Berkeley, California
• Hubert Howe Bancroft Collection, University of California at Berkeley
Dictation from H. B. [*sic*] Hearne

College Station, Texas
• Texas History Collection, Cushing Memorial Library, Texas A&M University
Cavitt Family Papers
Ruth M. Hull Papers

Houston, Texas
• Woodson Research Center, Fondren Library, Rice University
William Harrison Hamman Papers

Tucson, Arizona
• Bloom Southwest Jewish Archives, The University of Arizona Library
The Max Wesendorff file

Newspapers

Brenham *Banner,* 1871
Brenham *Daily Banner,* 1877
Bryan *Daily Eagle,* 1925–1926
Bryan *Weekly Eagle,* 1904, 1931
Calvert *Picayune,* 1912
The Central Texan (Calvert), 1872
Daily State Journal (Austin), 1871–1872
The Daily Texan (Austin), 2002
Dallas *Herald,* 1858–1861, 1865, 1867–1870
Dallas *Morning News,* 1886, 1930
Dallas *Weekly Herald,* 1875, 1881–1882
The Eagle (Bryan–College Station), 2002
Flake's Daily Bulletin (Galveston), 1866, 1869
Fort Worth *Daily Gazette,* 1883
The Free Man's Press (Austin), 1868
Galveston *Daily News,* 1866–1869, 1872, 1878, 1879, 1880, 1883
Galveston *Tri-Weekly News,* 1870
Galveston *Weekly News,* 1860, 1861, 1870, 1875
Houston *Daily Times,* 1869
Houston *Post,* 1893, 1943
Houston *Union,* 1869–1870
Iowa State Daily Register, 1866
New Orleans *Advocate,* 1867–1868
New York *Times,* 1869, 1879
The Northern Standard (Clarksville), 1860
Nueces Valley (Corpus Christi), 1871
The Right Way (Boston, Massachusetts), 1866
San Antonio *Express,* 1869
The Southern Intelligencer (Austin), 1860

Southwestern Christian Advocate, 1879-1880
The Texas Free Press (Hearne), 1872
Tri-Weekly State Gazette (Austin), 1869
The Weekly Free Man's Press (Galveston), 1868
Weekly State Gazette (Austin), 1865–1866

Government Publications

Texas, State of. Constitutional Convention. *Journal of the Texas State Convention, Assembled at Austin, February 7, 1866, Adjourned April 2, 1866.* Austin, Texas: Southern Intelligencer Office, 1866.

Texas, State of. Legislature. *Journal of the House of Representatives. Eighth Legislature.* Austin: Printed by John Marshall & Co., State Printers, 1860.

Texas, State of. Legislature. *Journal of the House of Representatives of the State of Texas: Extra Session of the Eighth Legislature* [Journal of Adjourned Secession]. Austin: Published by John Marshall, State Printers, 1861.

Texas, State of. Legislature. *Texas Senate Journal: Eleventh Legislature.* Austin: Printed at the Office of the State Gazette, 1866.

U.S. Army. Fifth Military District. State of Texas. General Order No. 19. *Tabular Statement, Showing the Number of Votes Cast in Each County For and Against the Constitution, and for State Officers. Tabular Statement, Showing Number Votes Cast in Each County for Members of Congress. Tabular Statement, Showing the Votes Cast in Each District for Senators and Representatives. Statement, Showing Vote by Counties for Clerks of District Courts, Sheriffs, and Justices of the Peace.* Austin: February 1, 1870, pp. 1–46.

U.S. Army. Fifth Military District. State of Texas. General Order No. 73. *Tabular Statement Of Voters (white and colored) Registered in Texas at Registration in 1867, and at Revision of the Lists in 1867–'68–'69; showing also the number (white and colored) Stricken Off the Lists. Tabular Statement Of Votes (white and colored) cast at Election held in the State of Texas, under the authority of the Reconstruction Acts of Congress.* Austin: April 16, 1870, pp. 1–9.

U.S. Census Office. *The Seventh Census of the United States: 1850.* Washington, D.C.: Government Printing Office, 1853.

U.S. Department of Interior. Patent Office. *Annual Report of the Commissioner of Patents for the Year 1869.* United States Patents #89, 144 (April 20th), #95, 338 (September 28th), and #97, 083 (November 23rd), 41st Cong., 2nd sess., 1869. H. Ex. Doc. 102 vol. 1. Serial 1420.

U.S. Secretary of State. *United States Statutes at Large: Compiled, Edited, and Indexed by Authority of Congress under the Direction of the Secretary of State.* 18 vols. Washington, D.C.: U.S. G.P.O., 1937.

U.S. War Department. *Index to Compiled Service Records of Confederate Soldiers Who Served in Organizations from the State of Texas* [microform] (1955). [Microcopy No. 227].

Published Collections of Letters and Documents

"African American Baptist Annual Reports, 1865–1900." "Texas." B2001–25. [Microfilm]. N.p.: Scholarly Resources, Inc., n.d.

John Bell vs. C. C. Hearne, et al. Louisiana Supreme Court. 10 Louisiana Ann. 515; 1855 La. LEXIS 277. Decided 1855.

Burrow vs. Arce, Case No. 98–0184. Supreme Court of Texas. 997 S.W.2d 229; 1999 Tex. LEXIS 86; 42 Tex. Sup. J. 932. Decided July 1, 1999.

Cannon's Administrator vs. Vaughan, Supreme Court of Texas, 12 Tex. 399; 1854 Tex. LEXIS, Decided 1854.

Cayton Erhard et al. vs. Asseline Hearne et al. [No number in original]. Supreme Court of Texas. 47 Tex. 469; 1877 Tex. LEXIS 97. Decided June 22, 1877.

Collie-Cooper, Mary, comp. *Brazos County Texas 1870 Census.* Typescript: Bryan, Texas: Collie-Cooper Enterprises, 1987. Evans Library, Texas A&M University, College Station, Texas.

Collie-Cooper, Mary, comp. *Robertson County Texas 1860 Census.* Typescript: July 4, 1985, Evans Library, Texas A&M University, College Station, Texas.

Ex parte Yerger. Supreme Court of the United States, 75 U.S. 85; 19 L. Ed. 332, U.S. LEXIS 1085; 8 Wall. 85. Decided October 25, 1869.

Gammel, Hans Peter Nielson, comp. *The Laws of Texas, 1822–1897.* 10 vols. Austin, Texas: The Gammel Book Company, 1898.

Hary, Ruth J., and Janis J. Hunt, comp. *Abstract Book 1863–1866 Brazos County Tax Assessor-Collector, Brazos County, Texas.* Typescript: undated. The Carnegie Center of Brazos Valley History. Bryan, Texas.

Asaline Hearne vs. C. Erhard and others. [No number in original (Case No. 3221)]. Supreme Court of Texas. 33 Tex. 60; 1870 Tex. LEXIS 87. Decided March 1870.

Asaline Hearne vs. H. D. Prendergast. Case No. 5219. Supreme Court of Texas. 61 Tex. 627; 1884 Tex. LEXIS 161. Decided May 22, 1884.

John R. Hearne vs. Solomon L. Gillett. Case No. 4898. Supreme Court of Texas. 62 Tex. 23; 1884 Tex. LEXIS 182. Decided June 10, 1884.

Texas Almanac for 1867. Galveston, Tex.: Richardson & Co., 1867.

Texas State Gazetteer and Business Directory, 1884, 1885, 1892. [Microfilm]. Evans Library, Texas A&M University, College Station, Texas.

Betsy Webster vs. T. J. Heard. [No number in original]. Supreme Court of Texas. 32 Tex. 685; 1870 Tex. LEXIS 60. Decided 1870.

A. P. Wooldridge, assignee, vs. George Roller. Supreme Court of Texas. 52 Tex. 447; 1880 Tex. LEXIS 13. Decided January 29, 1880.

Autobiographies, Family Histories, Memoirs, and Diaries

Chaffin, William L. *A Biographical History of Robert Randall and His Descendants, 1608–1909.* New York: The Grafton Press, 1909.

Hearne, William T. *Brief History and Genealogy of the Hearne Family: From A.D. 1066, when they went from Normandy with William the Conqueror over to England, down to 1680. [sic] when William Hearne the London Merchant came to America, and on down to A.D. 1907.* Independence, Mo.: Press of Examiner Printing Company, 1907.

Jacobs, Harriet A. *Incidents in the Life of a Slave Girl.* Ed. Nellie Y. McKay and Frances Smith Foster. New York: W. W. Norton & Company, 2001.

Myers, Joseph Allen. "Life of Joseph Allen Myers: Written in the Month of November 1927." Typescript, taken from a ledger with the handwritten text of Joseph Allen Myers, by William Allen Myers, November 20, 2001. Bryan Public Library, Bryan, Texas.

Rawick, George P., ed. *The American Slave: A Composite Autobiography.* Westport, Conn.: Greenwood Press, 1972–1979.

Books, Articles, Lectures, and Pamphlets by Contemporaries

Brown, John Henry. *Indian Wars and Pioneers of Texas.* Austin, Tex.: n.p., n.d., reprint ed., 1988.

Helper, Hinton Rowan. *The Impending Crisis of the South: How to Meet It.* New York: A. B. Burdick, 1859.

Olmsted, Frederick Law. *The Cotton Kingdom: A Traveller's Observations on Cotton and Slavery in the American Slave States.* Ed. Arthur M. Schlesinger Sr. New York: Modern Library College Editions, 1984.

Reagan, John H. *Memoirs, with Special Reference to Secession and the Civil War.* Ed. Walter Flavius McCaleb. New York: Neale Pub. Co., 1906.

Terrell, Alexander W. "The Negro." [Undated manuscript (1908?)], pp. 1–24. Center for American History, The University of Texas at Austin, Austin, Texas.

Walker, J. L., and C. P. Lumpkin. *History of the Waco Baptist Association of Texas.* Waco, Tex.: Byrne-Hill Printing House, 1897.

Interviews and E-mail Correspondence

E-mail "Re: Lucy Hammond" from Bill Norton of Austin, Texas, to the author, dated Friday, October 13, 2006.

Interview with Norman L. McCarver Jr., Hearne, Texas, August 18, 1999.

Interview with John H. Miles Jr., Hearne, Texas, December 4, 1999.

Interview with Gracia Thibodeaux, Office of the *Hearne Democrat,* 120 West Third Street, Hearne, Texas, June 5, 1999.

Lunchtime conversations between the author and anonymous patrons. Dixie Café, 708 South Market Street, Hearne, Texas, August 16, 1999.

SECONDARY MATERIALS

Reference Works

American Pocket Medical Dictionary. 15th ed., revised. Philadelphia: W. B. Sander's Company, 1934.

Bailey, Ernest Emory, comp. and ed. *Texas Historical and Biographical Record: With a Genealogical Study of Historical Family Records.* Austin: By the Author, 1900.

Black, Henry Campbell. *Black's Law Dictionary.* 4th ed. St. Paul, Minn.: West Publishing Co., 1951.

Brice, Donaly E., and John C. Barron. *An Index to the 1867 Voters' Registration of Texas.* CD-ROM #1354, Bowie, Md.: Heritage Books, Inc., 2000.

Burnham, W. Dean. *Presidential Ballots: 1836–1892.* Baltimore: The Johns Hopkins Press, 1955.

Daniell, L. E., comp. *Personnel of the Texas State Government.* Austin, Tex.: Smith, Hicks & Jones, State Printers, 1889.

Floyd, Verna Corn, and Vernelle Corn. *Cemeteries in Robertson County County, Texas.* N.p.: D. Armstrong Co., Inc., 1980.

Hewett, Janet B., ed. *The Roster of Confederate Soldiers, 1861–1865.* 16 vols. Wilmington, N.C.: Broadfoot Publishing Co., 1995.

Robinson, Edgar Eugene. *The Presidential Vote, 1896–1932.* Stanford, Calif.: Stanford University Press, 1934.

Sanborn Fire Insurance Maps. Bryan, Texas. July 1896 and June 1912. Teaneck, N.J.: Chadwyck-Healey, 1990. Microfilm ed.

Speer, William S., and J. H. Brown. *The Encyclopedia of the New West.* Marshall, Tex.: The United States Biographical Publishing Company, 1881.

Texas Historical Records Survey. Inventory of the County Archives of Texas. *No. 198. Robertson County [Franklin].* Robertson County, Texas: March 1941.

Texas State-wide Records Project. *Index to Probate Cases of Texas. No. 198, Robertson County, April 30, 1838–September 1, 1939.* San Antonio, Tex.: State-wide Records Indexing and Inventory Program, 1941.

Tyler, Ron, Douglas E. Barnett, Roy R. Barkley, Penelope C. Anderson, and Mark F. Odintz, eds. *The New Handbook of Texas.* 6 vols. Austin: The Texas State Historical Association, 1996.

Webster's New Twentieth Century Dictionary of the English Language. Unabridged 2nd ed. N.p.: William Collins Publishers, Inc., 1980.

Unpublished Doctoral Dissertations and Other Manuscripts

Bailey, Lelia. "The Life and Public Career of O. M. Roberts, 1815–1883." Ph.D. diss., University of Texas, 1932.

Bax, Joe G. "A Summation of the Proceedings of the Probate and District Courts of Robertson County Relative to Asaline Hearne." [Typescript manuscript in possession of the author, June 5, 2000].

Carson, Ivory Freeman. "Early Development of Robertson County." M.A. thesis, North Texas State College, 1954.

Freeman, Lynn Anne McCallum. "Miscegenation and Slavery: A Problem in American Historiography." M.A. thesis, Queen's University, 1991.

Gray, Ronald N. "Edmund J. Davis: Radical Republican and Reconstruction Governor of Texas." Ph.D. diss., Texas Tech University, 1976.

Jones, Manford Eugene. "A History of Cotton Culture along the Middle Brazos River." M.A. thesis, University of New Mexico, 1939.

Keener, Charles Virgil. "Racial Turmoil in Texas, 1865–1874." M.S. thesis, North Texas State University, 1971.

Marshall, Elmer Grady. "The History of Brazos County, Texas." M.A. thesis, University of Texas at Austin, 1937.

Scott, Paul R. "The Democrats and Their Opposition: A Statistical Analysis of Texas Elections, 1852–1861." Typescript. Texas History Collection. Texas A&M University Archives, College Station, Texas.

Smith, Ada Margaret. "The Life and Times of William Harrison Hamman." M.A. thesis, University of Texas, 1952.

St. Clair, Lawrence Ward. "History of Robertson County, Texas. M.A. thesis, University of Texas, 1931.

Williams, Rhea Hughston. "History of Education in Robertson County." M.A. thesis, Southern Methodist University, 1937.

Internet Web Sites

American Life Histories: Manuscripts from the Federal Writers' Project, 1936–1940. http://memory.loc.gov/ammem/wpaintro/wpahome.html (accessed July, 6 2008).

Ancestry.com. *1850 and 1860 United States Federal Census* [online database]. Provo, Utah: The Generations Network, Inc., 2005 and 2004.

Confederate Indigent Families Index. Texas State Library. www.tsl.state.tx.us/arc/cif/index.html (accessed July 8, 2008).

Dred Scott, Plaintiff in Error, vs. John F. A. Sandford, quoted in "Dred Scott Case: The Supreme Court Decision." www.pbs.org/wgbh/aia/part4/4h2933.html (accessed June 10, 2003).

"Ebenezer Hearne Cemetery." Robertson County TXGenWeb Site. www.rootsweb.com/~txrober2/EBENEZER HEARNECEMETERY.html (accessed June 20, 2006).

French *prénom* "Azéline." www.prenoms.com/echerche/prenom.php/fiche/azeline (accessed Jan. 21, 2003).

In the Matter of Benjamin Brown, et al. Petition (File Date: October 8, 1869), 11 pp., Term Year: 1869. *U.S. Supreme Court Records and Briefs, 1832–1978.* Thomson Gale, Texas A&M University, College Station, http://galenet.galegroup.com/servlet/SCRB?uid=0&srchtp=a&ste=14&rcn=DW111215861 (accessed April 3, 2007).

The Inflation Calculator. www.westegg.com/inflation (accessed Feb. 15, 2003).

Johnson, Telemachus Louis Augustus Albertus. "Off the Beaten Path in Waco, Texas." www.barbaramartin.com/offbeatenpath.html, copyright 2003 by Barbara Martin (accessed May 30, 2005).

"Pedigree Chart Download GEDCOM," [Thomas and Sally Hearne]. www.Family Search.com/af/pedigree_chart.asp?recid=43811593 (last updated March 22, 1999, Intellectual Reserve, Inc., 1999; accessed Oct. 26, 2002).

Historical Markers and Monuments

Abraham Lincoln, "Second Inaugural Address, March 4, 1865." [Inscription]. Lincoln Memorial, Washington, D.C.

"El Camino Real (1972)." [Official Texas Historical Marker]. Located one mile east off Highway 6 at Benchley on the Old San Antonio Road, Robertson County, Texas.

"Virginia Field Park (1969)." [Official Texas Historical Marker]. Located facing East Burnett Street between Pin Oak and Maple Streets, Calvert, Texas.

Books

Athearn, Robert G. *In Search of Canaan: Black Migration to Kansas, 1879–80.* Lawrence: Regents Press of Kansas, 1978.

Baker, J. W. *A History of Robertson County, Texas.* Waco, Tex.: Printed by Texian Press, 1970.

Barr, Alwyn. *Black Texans: A History of Negroes in Texas, 1528–1971.* Austin, Tex.: Jenkins Publishing Company, 1973.

———. *Reconstruction to Reform: Texas Politics, 1876–1906.* Dallas, Tex.: Southern Methodist University Press, 2000, reprint ed., 1971.

Baum, Dale. *The Shattering of Texas Unionism: Politics in the Lone Star State during the Civil War Era.* Baton Rouge: Louisiana State University Press, 1998.

Brady, Marilyn Dell. *The Asian Texans.* College Station: Texas A&M University Press, 2004.

Brundidge, Glenna Fourman. *Brazos County History: Rich Past—Bright Future.* Bryan, Tex.: Family History Foundation, 1986.

Buenger, Walter L. *Secession and the Union in Texas.* Austin: University of Texas Press, 1984.

Calvert, Robert A., Arnoldo De León, and Gregg Cantrell. *The History of Texas.* 3rd ed. Wheeling, Ill.: Harlan Davidson, Inc., 2002.

Campbell, Randolph B. *An Empire for Slavery: The Peculiar Institution in Texas, 1821–1865.* Baton Rouge: Louisiana State University Press, 1989.

———. *Gone to Texas: A History of the Lone Star State.* New York: Oxford University Press, 2003.

———. *A Southern Community in Crisis: Harrison County, Texas, 1850–1880.* Austin: Texas State Historical Association, 1983.

Cantrell, Gregg. *Kenneth and John B. Rayner and the Limits of Southern Dissent.* Urbana: University of Illinois Press, 1993.

Cash, Wilbur J. *The Mind of the South.* New York: Alfred A. Knopf, 1941.

Crouch, Barry A. *The Freedmen's Bureau and Black Texans.* Austin: University of Texas Press, 1992.

Du Bois, W. E. Burghardt. *Black Reconstruction: An Essay toward a History of the Part Which Black Folk Played in the Attempt to Reconstruct Democracy in America, 1860–1880.* New York: Russell & Russell, 1935.

Foner, Eric. *Reconstruction: America's Unfinished Revolution, 1863–1877.* New York: Harper & Row, 1988.

Friend, Llerena B. *Sam Houston: The Great Designer.* Austin: University of Texas Press, 1954, paperback ed., 1979.

Genovese, Eugene D. *Roll, Jordan, Roll: The World the Slaves Made.* New York: Pantheon Books, 1974.

Gettys, Luella. *The Law of Citizenship in the United States.* Chicago: The University of Chicago Press, 1934.

Gould, Lewis L. *Alexander Watkins Terrell: Civil War Soldier, Texas Lawmaker, American Diplomat.* Austin: University of Texas Press, 2004.

Hoxes, Pauline Buck. *A Centennial History of Anderson County, Texas.* San Antonio, Tex.: The Naylor Company, 1936.

Jordan, Winthrop D. *White Over Black: American Attitudes Toward the Negro, 1550–1812.* Chapel Hill: University of North Carolina Press, 1968.

Lowe, Richard G., and Randolph B. Campbell. *Planters and Plain Folk: Agriculture in Antebellum Texas.* Dallas, Tex.: Southern Methodist University Press, 1987.

Marten, James. *Texas Divided: Loyalty and Dissent in the Lone Star State, 1856–1874.* Lexington: University of Kentucky Press, 1990.

McCarver, Norman L., and Norman L. McCarver Jr. *Hearne on the Brazos.* San Antonio: Century Press of Texas, 1958.

McComb, David G. *Galveston: A History.* Austin: University of Texas Press, 1986.

Moneyhon, Carl H. *Republicanism in Reconstruction Texas.* Austin: University of Texas Press, 1980.

———. *Texas after the Civil War: The Struggle of Reconstruction.* College Station: Texas A&M University Press, 2004.

O'Brien, Michael. *Conjectures of Order: Intellectual Life and the American South, 1810–1860.* Chapel Hill: University of North Carolina Press, 2004.

Parker, Richard Denny. *Historical Recollections of Robertson County, Texas, with Biographical & Genealogical Notes on the Pioneers & Their Families.* Salado, Tex.: Anson Jones Press, 1955.

Parsons, Chuck, and Marianne E. Hall Little. *Captain L. H. McNelly—Texas Ranger: The Life and Times of a Fighting Man.* Austin, Tex.: State House Press, 2001.

Pitre, Merline. *Through Many Dangers, Toils, and Snares: The Black Leadership of Texas, 1868–1900.* Austin, Tex.: Eakin Press, 1985.

Procter, Ben, and Archie P. McDonald. *The Texas Heritage.* St. Louis, Mo.: Forum Press, 1980.

Ramsdell, Charles William. *Reconstruction in Texas.* Austin: University of Texas Press, 1910; reprint 1970.

Richardson, Rupert N., Ernest Wallace, and Adrian Anderson. *Texas: The Lone Star State.* 5th ed. Englewood Cliffs, N.J.: Prentice Hall, 1988.

Richter, William L. *Overreached on All Sides: The Freedmen's Bureau Admin-*

istrators in Texas, 1865–1868. College Station: Texas A&M University Press, 1991.

Simpson, Harold B. *Hood's Texas Brigade: A Compendium*. Hillsboro, Tex.: Hill Jr. College Press, 1977.

Smallwood, James M. *Time of Hope, Time of Despair: Black Texans during Reconstruction*. Port Washington, N.Y.: Kennikat Press, 1981.

Thorpe, Earle E. *Eros and Freedom in Southern Life and Thought*. Durham, N.C.: Seeman Printery, 1967.

Wallace, Ernest. *Texas in Turmoil, 1849–1875*. Austin, Tex.: Steck-Vaughn Co., 1965.

Wallenstein, Peter. *Tell the Court I Love My Wife: Race, Marriage, and Law—An American History*. New York: Palgrave Macmillan, 2002.

Weinstein, Allen, Frank Otto Gatell, and David Sarasohn, eds. *American Negro Slavery: A Modern Reader*. 3rd ed. New York: Oxford University Press, 1979.

White, Deborah Gray. *Ar'n't I a Woman? Female Slaves in the Plantation South*. Rev. ed. New York: W. W. Norton & Company, 1999.

Williamson, Joel. *New People: Miscegenation and Mulattoes in the United States*. New York: Free Press, 1980.

——. *A Rage for Order: Black/White Relations in the American South since Emancipation*. New York: Oxford University Press, 1986.

Winegarten, Ruthe, Janet G. Humphrey, and Frieda Werden. *Black Texas Women: 150 Years of Trial and Triumph*. Austin: University of Texas Press, 1995.

Wooster, Ralph A. *Lone Star Generals in Gray*. Austin, Tex.: Eakin Press, 2000.

——. *Texas and Texans in the Civil War*. Austin, Tex.: Eakin Press, 1995.

Wyatt-Brown, Bertram. *Southern Honor: Ethics and Behavior in the Old South*. New York: Oxford University Press, 1982.

Articles

Baum, Dale. "Chicanery and Intimidation in the 1869 Texas Gubernatorial Race." *Southwestern Historical Quarterly* 97, no. 1 (1993): 37–54.

Campbell, Randolph B. "Fighting for the Confederacy: The White Male Population of Harrison County in the Civil War." *Southwestern Historical Quarterly* 104 (July 2000): 23–39.

Cantrell, Gregg. "Racial Violence and Reconstruction Politics in Texas, 1867–1868." *Southwestern Historical Quarterly* 93, no. 3 (1990): 333–55.

Crouch, Barry A. "'All the Vile Passions': The Texas Black Codes of 1866." *Southwestern Historical Quarterly* 97, no. 1 (1993): 13–34.

———. "Hesitant Recognition: Texas Black Politicians, 1865–1900." *East Texas Historical Journal* 31, no. 1 (1993): 41–58.

———. "A Spirit of Lawlessness: White Violence, Texas Blacks, 1865–1868." *Journal of Social History* 18 (Winter 1984): 217–32.

Delaney, Robert. "Matamoros, Port for Texas during the Civil War." *Southwestern Historical Quarterly* 58 (April 1955): 473–87.

Hodes, Martha. "The Mercurial Nature and Abiding Power of Race: A Transitional Family Story." *American Historical Review* 108, no. 1 (February 2003): 84–118.

House, Albert V. "Republicans and Democrats Search for New Identities, 1870–1890." *Review of Politics* 31 (October 1969): 466–76.

Macy, Katherine Young. "Notes on the History of Iowa Newspapers, 1836–1870." *University of Iowa Extension Bulletin,* July 1, 1927; Bulletin No. 175, pp. 85–89.

McBride, Lawrence W., and Frederick D. Drake. "Abraham Lincoln and the Rule of Law," *National Council for History Education, Inc.: Ideas, Notes, and News about History Education* 14, no. 9 (May 2002): 7.

Moneyhon, Carl H. "Public Education and Texas Reconstruction Politics, 1871–1874." *Southwestern Historical Quarterly* 92 (January 1989): 392–416.

Nieman, Donald G. "Black Political Power and Criminal Justice: Washington County, Texas, 1868–1884." *Journal of Southern History* 55, no. 3 (August 1989): 391–420.

Nolan, Libbie. "The Great Civil War: Opposite Sides." *Landmark* [The Waukesha County (Wisconsin) Historical Society] 26 (Spring 1983): 24.

Postell, Leona. "Father and Son, Confederate and Federal Soldiers." *Landmark* [The Waukesha County (Wisconsin) Historical Society] 13 (Summer 1970): 4.

Smallwood, James M. "When the Klan Rode: White Terror in Reconstruction Texas." *Journal of the West* 25 (October 1986): 4–13.

Torget, Andrew J. "Carpetbagger on the Brazos: The Texas Freedmen's Bureau in Robertson County." *Agora: An Online Undergraduate Journal of the Humanities* 1, no. 2 (Winter 2000): 1–14.

Wallenstein, Peter. "Reconstruction, Segregation, and Miscegenation: Interracial Marriage and the Law in the Lower South, 1865–1900." *American Nineteenth Century History* 6, no. 1 (March 2005): 57–76.

White, William W. "The Texas Slave Insurrection of 1860." *Southwestern Historical Quarterly* 52, no. 3 (January 1949): 259–85.

Index

AH in index refers to Azeline Hearne, SH to Sam Hearne.